LittleBIGPlanet

FOREWORD

First of all, on behalf of everyone at Media Molecule, I'd like to thank you for buying our game. We really enjoy making games so it's rather super that folks like you allow us to make a living from it. In return, we'd like you to discover how fun it can be to make games for us all to play! We've spent a lot of time scratching our heads to work out how to unleash your playful creativity without distracting you with tedious technical details. I hope you're as happy with the result as we are.

There are many ways that you might want to play our game. In some senses, *LittleBigPlanet* is more than a game but that sounds tediously philosophical. You might try thinking of it as a big toy box. That conjures up a broader image of play that includes both games and creativity. It's a part of how we learn stuff as children but it's also part of how we express ourselves as adults. This expression can come from the clothes you wear all the way to the levels you make. Expression could be simply the levels you choose to play and the experiences you share with other people. Expression could be making a *LittleBigPlanet* statue of your cat and sending a picture of it to your mum. We hope that *LittleBigPlanet* will give you a place to express yourself, however you choose to do it.

The guide you are about to read will show you all sorts of tricks to help you Play, Create and Share. I'd like you to treat the Create aspect in a similar way as the Play aspect. It should be fun and experimental. With this in mind, the most important thing to learn is where the 'undo' button is. Once you know how to undo, and have prodded the button a few times to convince yourself that it really does work, all creative inhibitions should be merrily thrown out the window. If you aren't entirely certain of what something does, don't be afraid to just try it out! If you aren't happy with the result, press the undo button. If only everything in life was so convenient.

I hope by now that you have a sense of what *LittleBigPlanet* is all about (and if you aren't, then the following pages should leave you in little doubt). We're not only presenting you with a finished game, but with the tools and the support to make entirely new experiences. *LittleBigPlanet* will evolve, and it's up to you, the community, to help us decide what the next evolutionary steps are. We'll be backing you up every step of the way! But for now, we've spent a long time making this game and are a little tired. So we'd appreciate it very much if you could get stuck into *LittleBigPlanet* and make some groovy stuff for us to play with.

We can't wait to see what you come up with!

David Smith, Co-lead designer of *LittleBigPlanet*

BASICS 4
STORY MODE

CREATING A LEVEL

Basics

Welcome to *LittleBigPlanet*
The Basics

Welcome to LittleBigPlanet—a world of infinite possibilities, where imagination becomes reality and the powers of creation are firmly in your hands. As you prepare to meet the Creator Curators and explore their wondrous realms, you can use this guide as a constant companion to help you build your own unique levels, explore all of LittleBigPlanet's nooks and crannies, or enjoy the fun puzzles and places built by other players. The possibilities are truly endless!

MEET YOUR SACK PERSON

It's time to meet your sack person. Awww bless, isn't it cute? You'll get to know this lovable little sack-star soon enough, but in the meantime—the residents of *LittleBigPlanet* need your help! Many characters and their creations have gone mysteriously missing, and nobody knows why. It's a good thing you've arrived just in time. Your help is required in unraveling this worrying conundrum and catching the sneaky culprit red-handed.

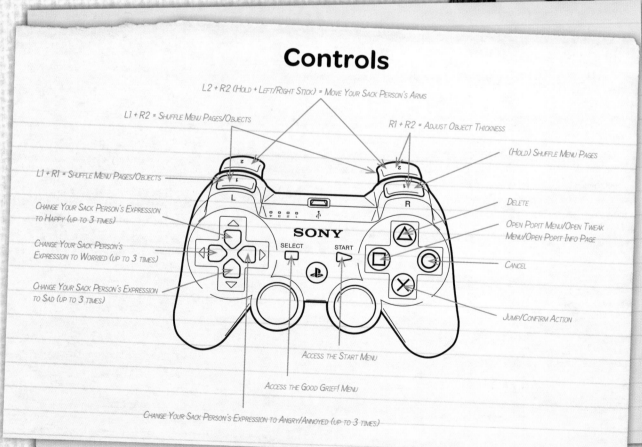

Controls

L2 + R2 (HOLD + LEFT/RIGHT STICK) = MOVE YOUR SACK PERSON'S ARMS

L1 + R2 = SHUFFLE MENU PAGES/OBJECTS

R1 + R2 = ADJUST OBJECT THICKNESS

(HOLD) SHUFFLE MENU PAGES

L1 + R1 = SHUFFLE MENU PAGES/OBJECTS

CHANGE YOUR SACK PERSON'S EXPRESSION TO HAPPY (UP TO 3 TIMES)

CHANGE YOUR SACK PERSON'S EXPRESSION TO WORRIED (UP TO 3 TIMES)

CHANGE YOUR SACK PERSON'S EXPRESSION TO SAD (UP TO 3 TIMES)

DELETE

OPEN POPIT MENU/OPEN TWEAK MENU/OPEN POPIT INFO PAGE

CANCEL

JUMP/CONFIRM ACTION

ACCESS THE START MENU

ACCESS THE GOOD GRIEF! MENU

CHANGE YOUR SACK PERSON'S EXPRESSION TO ANGRY/ANNOYED (UP TO 3 TIMES)

Using Menu Screens

Press ↑, ↓, ←, or → to highlight an option, and press ✕ to confirm. To return to the previous menu screen, press ◉.

Using Your Pod

Your *POD* is a cross between your bedroom and your garden shed—in other words, it's the place to chill out! It may be empty when you enter it for the first time, but as you explore *LittleBigPlanet* further, you'll pick up lots of keepsakes and decorations to help brighten things up.

The Wireless Controller in your POD is your very own computer, inventory, and access device. Stand in front of it and press ◉ to start navigating *LittleBigPlanet*.

Story Mode

Make your way across the *LittleBigPlanet* globe to discover the weird and wonderful worlds of the Creator Curators. Use the left stick to navigate between the Creator Curators, and press ✕ to make a selection.

The first area your sack person will visit is *The Gardens*. This idyllic setting is the perfect place to learn the tricks and skills required to successfully explore the inventive landscapes of *LittleBigPlanet*.

You'll soon learn that the *King of The Gardens* is just one of the legendary Creator Curators responsible for tending the creations on *LittleBigPlanet*. When you've proven your worth to the King of The Gardens, it's time to travel to new lands and learn more skills.

Start Menu

Press **START** during gameplay and the Start Menu will be displayed. Choose *Return to POD* or *Restart Level*, or select any of the following options:

Videos and Voice-overs

Having trouble with *LittleBigPlanet* or your latest masterpiece? Don't get flustered: check out a wide selection of helpful tutorial videos—there are plenty to find on your travels!

Settings

Alter the *LittleBigPlanet Display Settings* and *Audio Settings*.

About This Level

Learn more details about the level you're exploring: who created it, the sights to see, and what you can expect to do there.

CONTROLLING YOUR SACK PERSON

Move the left stick ← or → to run to the left or the right. Move the left stick ↑ to move into the background or ↓ to move into the foreground.

Press ✕ to jump. Tap it lightly to perform a smaller jump, or hold it for a longer, more athletic leap. Press and hold **R1** to grab hold of objects. You can only grab on to soft objects.

Tilt the Wireless Controller to shake your sack person's head. Press **L3** and tilt the Wireless Controller to wiggle your sack person's hips. Use the directional buttons to change expression: press ↑ for happy, ↓ for sad, ← for worried, and → for annoyed. Continue pressing a directional button to increase the expression (up to three times).

To move your sack person's arms around, press and hold **L2** and use the left stick, or press and hold **R2** and use the right stick.

THE POPIT MENU

The *Popit* Menu is the most important tool you'll come across in the world of *LittleBigPlanet*. Press ◉ and it literally "pops" into the air above your sack person's head. Think of the Popit Menu as an interactive lasso that's capable of amazing things; it contains almost all of the creative options at your disposal. You'll learn all of its ins and outs, modes, and options as you go, but the basics follow.

Customizing Your Sack Person

Press ◉ to open the Popit Menu. Highlight and select the *Customize Character* icon and use the left stick to peruse the available options. Press **L1** or **R1** to shuffle between pages. Press ✕ to try an item on and press ✕ again to take it off.

Retry

Occasionally, even the most skilled players get stuck. It's nothing to get upset about! If there really is no way out, press ◉ to open the Popit Menu, select the *Retry* icon and press and hold ✕ for a few seconds. It's not pretty, but your sack person will spring back good as new!

Stickers and Decorations

There are many Stickers and Decorations to collect on your journey through *LittleBigPlanet's* Story Mode. Press ⊙ to open the Popit Menu, then highlight and select the *Stickers & Decorations* icon to take a look at your prized treasures.

Even better than finding new Stickers and Decorations is actually using them. Press ⊗ to select an item, then use the left stick to move it around the environment. Move the right stick ⬅ or ➡ to rotate a Sticker or

Decoration, and move the right stick ⬆ or ⬇ to change its size. Once happy, press ⊗ to stamp the chosen embellishment into place. Press ⊙ to return to the Popit Menu.

To remove a Sticker or Decoration, open the Popit Menu, choose the Stickers & Decorations icon, and select the *Stickers & Decorations Edit Tool*. Use the left stick to move the Edit Tool over the desired item, which will emit a glow. Press ⊗ to lift the item into the air, and press ⊙ to delete it and exit the Popit Menu.

Using the PLAYSTATION®Eye Camera

If a PLAYSTATION®Eye camera is connected to the PLAYSTATION®3 system and you have collected some PLAYSTATION®Eye Stickers, you can create some personalized pictures.

Point the PLAYSTATION®Eye at the desired subject, open the Popit Menu, choose the Stickers & Decorations icon, and select the PLAYSTATION®Eye *Camera* page.

Select a Sticker shape and move it around the scenery: when it's in the right place, press ⊗ to capture your image and stamp it into position. Don't take pictures of anything rude, though!

GETTING STARTED ONLINE

Discover the wonder of *LittleBigPlanet* with other players—otherwise known as *Happy Gadders*—from all over the world via PlayStation®Network. It's a brilliant way to make some new sack-buddies!

To meet new friends online and gain access to *MyMoon* and the *InfoMoon*, you'll need to complete the first three levels in 'The Gardens'. When looking at the *Info Pages* of any level, choose *Play Online* to join up with anyone currently playing that level in *LittleBigPlanet*. Remember that you can choose to *join* or *invite* your friends or other Happy Gadders when viewing their Info Page.

Playing Together Online

When exploring *LittleBigPlanet* online with friends or anyone else, please bear in mind a few simple pointers:

- The first person to enter a level automatically becomes the host and, between levels, their personalized POD becomes the group's lobby.

- If the host chooses to go somewhere—be it from the POD to a level or from a level to the POD—all other players automatically follow.

- Players invited to join the group will not become hosts.

- If anyone leaves the group, all players will be asked if they would like to follow that particular player.

- You can see who you are following in the Player Management Screen. This can be accessed by pressing **START** and selecting *Manage Players*.

Oh Behave

Playing online and mixing with the *LittleBigPlanet* community comes with certain responsibilities. It's one LittleBig happy family—and that means that we all need to respect each other's feelings. So, as tempting as it is, please refrain from being rude! No swearing, no rude drawings, and nothing that would offend your granny.

Good Grief! Menu

The *Good Grief!* Menu is the place to report any offensive content uploaded by other players online. We all want to keep *LittleBigPlanet* as clean and respectable as possible, so please let Sony Computer Entertainment America know if you discover any questionable content. Simply press **SELECT** at any time and the Good Grief! Menu will be displayed, through which a grief report can be submitted directly.

Quick Play

Want to explore a new level with other online players straight away? No problem! Choose *Quick Play* and you'll be whisked away to a random new level where other Happy Gadders are already having fun.

Checking Out Other Levels and Their Creators

Jump into *LittleBigPlanet* with the online community, and check out the creations that other members have been publishing. Have a look at *Recent* levels that have been published, or *Search* for something more specific.

Online Start Menu

There are a few additional options that become available within the Start Menu once you are online:

Manage Players

When exploring *LittleBigPlanet* with other players online, use the *Manage Players* option to mute certain players or, if you are the host, remove them from the current level.

Friends

See if anyone you know is online in *LittleBigPlanet* and manage your existing list of online friends.

LBP Messages

Have you received anything from another Happy Gadder? Check *LBP Messages* to see if they have sent you an *Object Plan* to use within *Create* mode.

MY MOON

My Moon is the place where creativity flourishes and can be accessed via your POD space station.

Within My Moon, select *Create* to start building a new level from scratch. To revisit previously created levels, select *Play* or *Create*. To share a creation with the *LittleBigPlanet* online community, select *Publish*. We've got a very detailed Creating section, which can be found elsewhere in this guide, but to get you up and running, some basics are provided below.

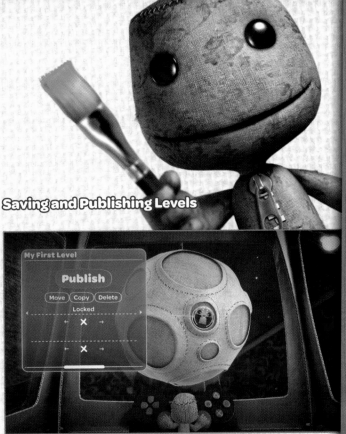

In Create mode, select the item or tool you want to use via the Popit Menu, then use the left stick to navigate around, and press ✕ to select an area to create within. If you're creating a brand new level and the idea of a blank canvas is too scary, feel free to select a template to work from. When working on your creations, bear the following handy hints in mind:

- There is a nifty jetpack available for those hard-to-reach areas. Press the directional button to put it on or take it off.

- Use the right stick to zoom in and out to give yourself a better view of what you are creating.

- In Create mode, there is a useful thermometer on the left-hand side of the screen that indicates how much more you can cram into your creation.

- You can make life easier by changing the view to display a special *Grid*. Press **START** to access the Grid and select *View* to alter your *Popit Settings*.

- To try out your creation, press **START** and select *Change to Play Mode*. To return to Create mode, press **START** and select *Change to Create Mode*.

- For help from a handy tutorial, just press **START** and select the *Videos* option.

- To return to your POD at any time, press **START** and select *Return to POD*.

If You Build It First, You Must Play

To access My Moon, you must complete the first three levels of The Gardens.

Saving and Publishing Levels

To save a level you've created in My Moon, press [START] and choose *Save*. If you choose *Leave Level* at any point, you will get the chance to *save* your progress before returning to the POD. To share a new level with the rest of the *LittleBigPlanet* online Happy Gadders, follow these simple steps:

1. From the POD, access My Moon and select a level to publish.

2. At the top of each page is the name of each level. Highlight the name and press the S button to access the virtual keyboard and rename your level.

3. Add a small description of your level for the benefit of other online players. Press L1 or R1 to access the Set Description page and press ✕ to access the virtual keyboard.

4. From the Publish page, choose one of the following options for a new level: Copy, Move, Delete, Set Icon or Lock. The Set Icon option allows a badge of your choice to represent your creation online. The Lock option prevents other players from copying your ideas.

5. Highlight Publish and press ✕ to share your creation with other Happy Gadders.

THE FUN BEGINS NOW

You've now been armed with the basic information needed to venture out into the wonderfully whimsical world of *LittleBigPlanet*. The following pages promise to walk you through its realms, helping you collect each and every Sticker, Decoration, Object, Material, and all of the other building blocks you'll need to then create your own levels. Make sure you also take the time to follow our dedicated Creating section, which will have you building your own magnificent masterpieces soon enough. However, the thing you need to do most of all—have fun!

THE KING

The Gardens

The Gardens are your first stop in the world of LittleBigPlanet. Presided over by the stately Curator Creators—the King and her royal highness, the Queen—this English utopia is filled with overgrown foliage, royal steeds, rickety watermills, and even a state-of-the-art skateboard which you can, and will, ride to victory.

During your travels across these lush lands, you'll encounter some helpful creatures and make some new friends, like the omni-present (and somewhat fragile) Dumpty. However, The Gardens have a dark side. When night falls, you may find yourself having to escape from a haunted castle high atop a hill. You're not afraid of things that go bump in the night, are you?

Story: Chapter 1

The Gardens

First Steps

It's time to start exploring LittleBigPlanet! Your first stop—the King's Garden. Once you have set your first cushy foot on the ground, start heading to the right to meet His Majesty. According to the stately King, he and his wife (the Queen) created these lovely gardens and everything in them. With a happy nod of his head, he sends you on your way. Kick off the adventure by heading down the path!

Level Complete Gifts

✓	Costume
	Big Kiss
	Bunny Ears

Collected All Gifts

✓	Stickers
	The Gardens Concept

✓	Objects
	The Gardens Concept with Frame

Aced Level Gifts

✓	Costume
	Pirate Hook
	Pirate Eye Patch

COLLECTORS TAKE HEED

NOT EVERY PRIZE BUBBLE CAN BE FOUND SIMPLY BY COMPLETING THE STORY MODE. THERE ARE HUNDREDS TO BE GATHERED BY PLAYING THROUGH THE TUTORIALS AS WELL!

LEARN TO RUN AND JUMP!

A King's Welcome!

SHUT IT DOWN!

SEE THAT LIGHT POST YOU JUST PASSED BY? THIS IS CALLED THE CLOSE-LEVEL POST, AND IT'S NOT HERE JUST FOR DECORATION. IN ADDITION TO SPRUCING UP THE ENVIRONMENT, THE CLOSE-LEVEL POST CAN HELP ELIMINATE ALL KINDS OF CONFUSION. ONCE YOU PASS THIS POST, NO ADDITIONAL PLAYERS ARE ALLOWED TO ENTER THE LEVEL. YOU WOULDN'T WANT SOME LATE ARRIVING SACKPERSON DROPPING IN HALFWAY THROUGH AND CONFUSING EVERYONE ELSE, WOULD YOU? AS SOON AS IT'S BEEN CROSSED OVER, THE SIGN ATOP THE POST HAS A RED "X" STRUCK THROUGH IT, INDICATING THAT THE LEVEL IS NOW OFFICIALLY CLOSED TO OUTSIDERS.

Dumpty Sat on the Wall

Check out Dumpty just a few skips down the path, sitting on a wall. This happy, egg-shaped fellow wants to see your running and jumping skills. Why not give it a go? Run up the ramp and hop across the gaps.

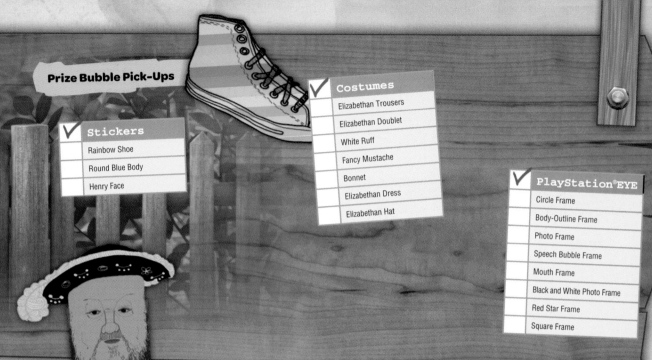

Prize Bubble Pick-Ups

✔ Stickers

	Rainbow Shoe
	Round Blue Body
	Henry Face

✔ Costumes

	Elizabethan Trousers
	Elizabethan Doublet
	White Ruff
	Fancy Mustache
	Bonnet
	Elizabethan Dress
	Elizabethan Hat

✔ PlayStation®EYE

	Circle Frame
	Body-Outline Frame
	Photo Frame
	Speech Bubble Frame
	Mouth Frame
	Black and White Photo Frame
	Red Star Frame
	Square Frame

THE KING

A Hop and a Jump

This is something everyone should know. Press ⊗ to jump! To get more air time, hold down ⊗ for a longer period of time.

You also can jump between different planes in the level (back, middle, and front). If you stand on the front or middle plane and in front of an object or ledge that is low enough to jump onto, pressing ⊗ causes you to hop up to the next level. To jump back down, press down on the left stick and tap ⊗.

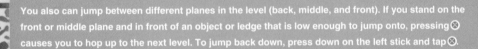

Dumpty

Rainbow Shoe Switch Trigger

DUMPTY HAD A GREAT FALL

Normally, pushing someone as helpful as Dumpty off a ledge wouldn't be a very nice thing to do. However, Dumpty doesn't mind. Hop up onto the wall and give him a nice shove, won't you? When the good-natured chap falls over, he breaks in two, spilling out his lovely Score Bubbles. Grab them all as quickly as possible, and then leave him to pick up the pieces.

BUBBLES WORTH THE TROUBLES

SCORE BUBBLES CAN BE FOUND BOTH IN PLAIN SIGHT AND IN NOT-SO-OBVIOUS HIDDEN AREAS ALL THROUGHOUT EACH STORY LEVEL. COLLECTING THEM GIVES YOU POINTS! IF YOU CAN MANAGE TO COLLECT FIVE OR MORE IN QUICK SUCCESSION (WITHIN A SECOND OR TWO OF EACH OTHER), YOU EARN A SCORE MULTIPLIER. YOU CAN CONTINUE TO EXPAND THE MULTIPLIER WITH EVERY SUCCESSIVE BATCH OF FIVE SCORE BUBBLES YOU COLLECT. DON'T TAKE TOO LONG IN BETWEEN BUBBLES, OR THE MULTIPLIER RESETS.

ONE SMALL SCORE BUBBLE IS WORTH 10 POINTS, WHILE LARGE SCORE BUBBLES ARE WORTH 50 POINTS (AND OFTEN HOLD PRIZES, TO BOOT).

Hop onto the wall at the top of the ramp and then drop to the floor below. A second set of ramps and gaps spread just a bit farther apart should give you a good jumping exercise. Remember to hold down ⊗ to make it across those gaps.

WHAT'S IT ALL A-BOOT?

SEE THAT HANGING CARDBOARD CUTOUT OF A SHOE DANGLING OVER THE TOP OF THE WALL? THAT IS A STICKER SWITCH USED IN A STICKER PUZZLE. WHILE YOU CAN'T INTERACT WITH IT YET, YOU WILL BE ABLE TO ONCE YOU ACQUIRE A SPECIAL STICKER AND THEN RUN THROUGH THE LEVEL ON A SECOND PLAYTHROUGH. REMEMBER THIS SPOT FOR LATER!

RACE FOR THE ACE!

To complete the level 100% and earn all Gifts, you may have to give it another go. Once the level is beaten, play through again as you would normally, but take a moment to stop at the top of this wall. Now that you have the required Rainbow Shoe Sticker, it should make more sense.

Select the Rainbow Shoe from the Stickers Page of your Popit Menu and slap it on the Sticker Switch. This lowers a Start Gate just beyond the right of the wall. Hop down and step on the gate to start a race!

Once the gate opens, you have 120 seconds to race through the level to the finish line. The good news is that every time you collect a Score Bubble, the countdown timer in the top right corner temporarily stops. The even better news is that the hanging bird suspended over the collapsing bridge is ready and waiting for you to leap and grab onto, then swing safely across. When you get to it, leap and hold **R1** to grab the bird, and then use your momentum to swing across before releasing and safely landing on the other side. The finish line is not too far off from here (just before the Queen). As long as you make it before the 120 seconds are up, you'll receive an extra 1,200 points!

Dumpty's Triumphant Return

See? We told you Dumpty would be all right. There he is, sitting atop a pedestal of mushrooms. Go about collecting the Score Bubbles hanging around in a quick, consecutive fashion, trying to grab at least five at a  time before the multiplier resets. Don't forget to see what Dumpty has to offer inside his egg-shaped body. This time, doing so requires a pull instead of a push.

SOMETHING TO GRAB ON TO

IF YOU HAVEN'T ALREADY TRIED TO DO SO, THIS IS THE PERFECT OPPORTUNITY TO HAVE A GO AT GRABBING AND HOLDING ON TO OBJECTS. THIS HANDY OPTION ALLOWS YOU TO HOLD ON TO SPONGY ITEMS AND OBJECTS IN LITTLEBIGPLANET FOR DEAR LIFE. TO DO SO, WALK UP TO DUMPTY AND PRESS AND HOLD R1. ONCE YOU HAVE A NICE GRIP, YOU CAN USE THE LEFT STICK TO PUSH OR PULL THE OBJECT. GO AHEAD; GIVE IT A TRY! TO RELEASE DUMPTY, SIMPLY LET GO.

Traverse the hilly hillside, collecting the Score Bubbles along the way. Remember, in order to drop from one plane to another, press down on the left stick and tap ⊗. On the other side, quickly hop over the flowery speed bumps and follow the arrow up the ramp.

Collapsing Bridge

THE KING

Prize Bubbles x7

Watermill

Watermill... of Death!!!

That skull and crossbones sign is not posted just to scare you. The water below is deadly, as it's got a layer of Horrible Gas floating around it. One touch of this gaseous lethal material sends you sailing back to the previous Checkpoint. Carefully hop onto a gap in the watermill and ride it until you are at the top, then hop over each panel in order to collect the Score Bubbles as they pass by.

Dumpty's Bounty of Prizes

Dumpty's still got some tricks up his curly sleeves. Check out and collect the large Prize Bubbles to his left for a handful of costume items that, once popped, are added to your Popit Menu. You get: **Fancy Mustache**, **Elizabethan Dress**, **Elizabethan Doublet**, **Bonnet**, **Elizabethan Hat**, **Elizabethan Trousers**, and **White Ruff Costume** items.

KEEP YOUR EYES ON THE PRIZE

NOT ALL BUBBLES ARE CREATED EQUALLY IN LITTLEBIGPLANET. THESE LARGE PRIZE BUBBLES CONTAIN FUN NEW COSTUMES THAT YOU CAN USE TO CUSTOMIZE YOUR OUTFIT. FOR MORE INFORMATION ON CUSTOMIZING, MAKE SURE YOU HEAD OVER TO THE INTRODUCTION CHAPTER AT THE FRONT OF THIS BOOK.

A SECOND, THIRD, AND FOURTH CHANCE

AS AN ASTUTE RESIDENT OF LITTLEBIGPLANET, YOU MUST HAVE NOTICED THESE ROUND OBJECTS—OTHERWISE KNOWN AS CHECKPOINTS—STRATEGICALLY PLACED THROUGHOUT EACH LEVEL. IF YOU PASS BY ONE, IT ACTIVATES AND LIGHTS UP. ONCE A CHECKPOINT IS ACTIVATED, IF YOU HAPPEN TO SHUFFLE OFF THIS MORTAL COIL (OR, IN MORE SIMPLE TERMS, PERISH), IT REAPPEARS FROM INSIDE THE CHECKPOINT. HOWEVER, THESE CHECKPOINTS ARE NOT UNENDING OR UNLIMITED. IN MOST CASES, IF YOU CONTINUE TO PERISH FOUR SUCCESSIVE TIMES BEFORE FINDING A NEW CHECKPOINT TO ACTIVATE, THEN YOU MUST RESTART THE LEVEL ANEW OR RETURN TO THE POD.

A Helping Hand

Go ahead and push Dumpty again, knocking him off his pedestal. If you push instead of pull, he should remain intact when he falls, allowing you to use him as a steppingstone to

get up to the Score Bubbles atop the ledge to his right. Just be sure to break him apart and collect the Score Bubbles inside before continuing on.

First Steps

15

Pop Goes the Sackperson!

Occasionally, you are going to get stuck, such as on your attempts to cross this bridge. That green-colored slat at the end is not here for a nice decorative touch. Once you attempt to cross, the whole thing collapses, sending you deep down into an impenetrable pit. The only way out is to, quite literally, "Pop" yourself. Pull up the Popit Menu, make sure you have the "Retry" icon selected, then press and hold ✕. It's not a pretty sight, but almost instantly, you appear at the last activated Checkpoint.

BIRD ON A WIRE TO ACE THE LEVEL

You may have noticed that once you Popped yourself at the bottom of the pit and reappeared at the Checkpoint, a hanging bird showed up, suspended above the pit. In order to "Ace" the level and earn the coveted prizes, you have to make it through without perishing. It's tough—but not impossible!— to do on the first playthrough. However, this can easily be achieved the second time through during the Race mentioned in an earlier secret.

Prize Bubbles x3

Round Blue Body Switch Trigger

Rainbow Shoe (Switch Triggers x2))

Beavers

Prize Bubbles x8

Her Highness Requests Your Aid

Up ahead is the Queen, and she's quite a lovely lady, indeed. Make sure to curtsy or bow appropriately, and then do as she wishes; she is royalty, you know.

The Queen requests that you fancy up the card character just beyond the tutorial window to her left. Grab the three Prize Bubbles laid out at her feet to collect the Stickers inside, and then get ready to do some serious decorating. The Stickers acquired are the **Rainbow Shoe**, the **Henry Face**, and the **Round Blue Body**.

STICKERS!

STICKERS CAN BE USED TO DECORATE ITEMS AND OBJECTS, AS WELL AS FOR SOLVING STICKER PUZZLES. TO USE A STICKER, PULL UP THE POPIT MENU AND SELECT THE STICKER ICON. USE THE LEFT STICK OR DIRECTIONAL BUTTONS TO HIGHLIGHT A STICKER, AND THEN PRESS ⊗ TO CHOOSE IT. ONCE YOU'VE SELECTED A STICKER, USE THE LEFT STICK TO MOVE IT TO THE DESIRED LOCATION AND THE RIGHT STICK TO ROTATE IT BY PRESSING LEFT AND RIGHT, AS WELL AS ZOOM IT IN/OUT BY PRESSING FORWARD AND BACK. LASTLY, YOU CAN FLIP THE STICKER BY PRESSING DOWN **R3**. TO SLAP A STICKER IN PLACE, PRESS ⊗.

Let's try our hand at decorating, shall we? Open your Popit Menu and Select the Sticker Icon. Next, choose the "Round Blue Body," move it over the corresponding cardboard piece, and press ⊗ to slap it in place. Easy! But the shoes are a bit more challenging. Go back to the Sticker Icon from the Popit Menu and choose a "Rainbow Shoe." The first one is already facing the right direction, so just maneuver it over the piece and press ⊗. To place the Sticker on the right foot, first press down on **R3** to flip it, and then put it in its place.

Once all three Stickers have been placed on the appropriate Sticker Switches, the figure begins to move to the right. Exit out of the Popit Menu and follow him up the ramp. Up top, the dangling, decorated cardboard King Henry lowers a drawbridge, allowing you to continue with the adventure.

The Queen waits for you just past the ramp. For your due bravery and decorating diligence, she has bestowed upon you eight PLAYSTATION®Eye Frames inside this bunch of Prize Bubbles. If you're lucky enough to have a PLAYSTATION®Eye, then you can have lots of fun with these items. Hop on the red button to receive a cool tutorial on how to use 'em! There are eight frames: **Black And White Photo Frame**, **Body-Outline Frame**, **Circle Frame**, **Mouth Frame**, **Photo Frame**, **Red Star Frame**, **Speech Bubble Frame**, and **Square Frame**.

THE PLAYSTATION®EYE'S HAVE IT!

IF YOU HAVE A PLAYSTATION®EYE CAMERA PLUGGED INTO YOUR SYSTEM, THEN YOU CAN USE IT TO PLACE YOUR VERY OWN PICTURES AND DESIGNS INTO YOUR STICKERS—IT'S TRUE. JUST ACCESS THE POPIT MENU AND HEAD OVER TO THE PLAYSTATION®EYE CAMERA PAGE (FROM THE STICKERS AND DECORATIONS PAGES) AND SELECT A FRAME THAT SUITS YOUR TASTES. FOR MORE INFORMATION ON HOW TO USE THE PLAYSTATION®EYE CAMERA, CHECK OUT THE INTRODUCING CHAPTER AT THE FRONT OF THIS BOOK.

Beavers Bearing Gifts!

Look at the opposite end of the drawbridge to notice two sets of peering eyes. These eyes are attached to a couple of twittering beavers who are generously about to shower

you with a bevy of Score Bubbles. For maximum multiplier points, keep moving before the bubbles appear, and head down to the bottom of the ramp. Hang out for a moment or two at the bottom, then turn around and run back up. By this time, all the Score Bubbles have collected on the ground, making for one quick collection and giving you a 4X multiplier.

Fit for a King

It looks like this is the end of the road—literally. To finish the level, stand in front of the scoreboard and see how well you did. If you followed this walkthrough to a T, then you should have collected all 18 items and are

rewarded with a few extra goodies. However, you're not quite done yet! If you want to Ace the level, you are going to have to play through it again without dying—this includes not using the Retry action.

Story: Chapter 2

The Gardens

Get a Grip

It's time to delve deeper into The Gardens, and learn some exciting and fun new things while there. Our friend the King is here to give your sackperson a quick lesson on the finer mechanics of grabbing.

✓	Materials
	Dark Green Wood
	Grass
	Green Check Denim
	Green Floral Fabric
	Grey Tweed
	Orange Floral Fabric

✓	Tools
	Sticker & Decoration Edit Tool

Level Complete Gifts

✓	Costume
	Happy Eyes
	Pink Cat Nose

Collected All Gifts

✓	Stickers
	The Fairy Tale Concept

✓	Objects
	The Fairy Tale Concept with Frame

Aced Level Gifts

✓	Costume
	Pirate Shorts
	Pirate Waistcoat

KEBABS

IF IT'S SOFT AND SPONGY, YOU CAN GRAB IT

THE KING REVEALS THAT YOU CAN GRAB ON TO CERTAIN MATERIALS. AS LONG AS THESE ITEMS/MATERIALS HAVE A SPONGY CONSISTENCY, YOU CAN GRAB, HANG ON, PUSH, PULL, SWING, ETC. GO AHEAD AND TRY IT OUT! USE THE SMALL, SQUARE-SHAPED SPONGE TO THE KING'S RIGHT BY APPROACHING IT AND PRESSING/HOLDING R1 TO GRAB ON.

Grab the sponge block and push it forward until it rests against the wooden wall to the right. The wall is otherwise too tall to climb over, but using the sponge as a stepping stone to hop onto does the trick!

LEARN TO GRAB THINGS

Something to Grab on to

The Gardens continue to delight with their many secrets and surprises. Now that you've taken your first steps and made friends with the stately King, her royal highness the Queen, and their faithful and ever breakable subject, Dumpty, are you ready to see what else they have in store for you?

Prize Bubble Pick-Ups

✓ Stickers

- Black Crown Outline
- Blue Monkey
- Castle Sketch Window
- English Rose
- Golf Club Bottom
- Grass Rough Doodle
- Green Castle Banner
- Leaf Doodle
- Moody Cloud
- Noughts & Crosses

POSTCARDS

✓ Stickers

- Orange Flowers
- Red Flowers
- Red Mushroom
- Sun Doodle
- Tea Pot
- Tudor House
- Tudor View
- Victorian Man Sketch
- Wooden Steed

✓ Objects

- Blue Moon
- Cheering Crowd
- Curly Cloud
- Fancy Cloud
- Gold Tea Cup
- Hovel
- Large Wooden Steed
- Loose Cloud
- Mushroom Block
- Oak Tree
- Round Cloud
- Seesaw
- Small Flag
- Small Wooden Steed

✓ Objects

- Smart Hovel
- Snail Shell
- Soccer Ball
- Tall Tree
- Tower
- Twisty Cloud

✓ Decorations

- Donkey Tail
- Eye Spring
- Orange Flower
- Pink Flower
- Purple Flower

THE KING

- Yellow Star Switch Trigger
- Prize Bubbles x3 (Triggered by Switch)
- Prize Bubbles x5 (Triggered by Switch)
- Tea Pot Switch Trigger
- Wooden Steed
- Prize Bubbles x1
- Prize Bubbles x1
- Yellow Star Switch Trigger

ROUSTABOUT ON THE ROOFTOPS

See those two Prize Bubbles perched on the rooftops?
You can scale up there to grab them by using the
large **R1** block on the other side of the wall. To
do so, hop onto the **R1** block from atop the wall. If
you miss the jump, you can use the smaller, green,
floral fabric-decorated block to get on top of the R1
block. Drag it over so it is sitting in front of the
larger block, then jump from that one to the next.
Now, from atop the **R1** block, just leap over to the
rooftop to the left and grab the two Prize Bubbles;
they hold the **Tudor House** and **Tudor View Stickers**.

STAR STRUCK #1

See that star-shaped cardboard cutout up above
the rooftops? It has a Sticker Switch! You should
remember them from the previous level. When you
place the correct Sticker on the switch, you are
showered with prizes! But wait, you don't have a
star-shaped Sticker in your Popit Menu, do you?
Don't fret. The Yellow Star Sticker you're looking
for is at the end of the next level. Return here
once it's in your possession, place it on the
corresponding Sticker
to reveal a set of
three Prize Bubbles.
They contain the **Smart
Hovel**, **Tower**, and **Hovel
Objects**.

To scale the next wall, grab and push the **R1** block so that it's against the wall. Then position the small, green, floral fabric-decorated block so that you can use it to get onto the top of the **R1** block. Now you can hop over the wall!

The spongy ramp on the other side can help your sackperson get over the next obstacle. Grab and drag it to the wall to the right, then run up it until your weight causes it to topple over (or jump and grab its top from the other side), changing the direction of the ramp so it leads up to the top of the wall. Run up and hop over to grab the Prize Bubble on the other side!

Tea for Two?

This Prize Bubble holds the **Tea Pot Sticker**, which also happens to be another Sticker Switch Trigger. This Sticker, when placed on that similarly shaped object dangling above, can make magical things happen. Go ahead and slap the Sticker on that tea pot-shaped cardboard cutout hanging above to see what happens next.

Well, what do you know? Two more Prize Bubbles are revealed. These hold the **Noughts & Crosses** and **Golf Club Bottom Stickers**.

STAR STRUCK #2

If you guessed that there is a second Switch Trigger in the shape of a star hovering right above your head, well, you are right! Make sure to return to this area and slap the Yellow Star onto the hanging cardboard cutout. The result—the hanging mobile it's attached to raises, lowering three more Object and Material-containing Prize Bubbles in the process. You get the **Soccer Ball Object**, the **Grey Tweed Material**, and the **Gold Tea Cup Object**.

Need for Steed

The wooden steed up ahead can give you a fun and quick ride. To get it going, grab its soft spongy material at either end, then push/pull it toward the top of the sloped hill. Be sure to hop on before it begins to gain too much momentum and roll down the hill, or you might miss out on a wild ride!

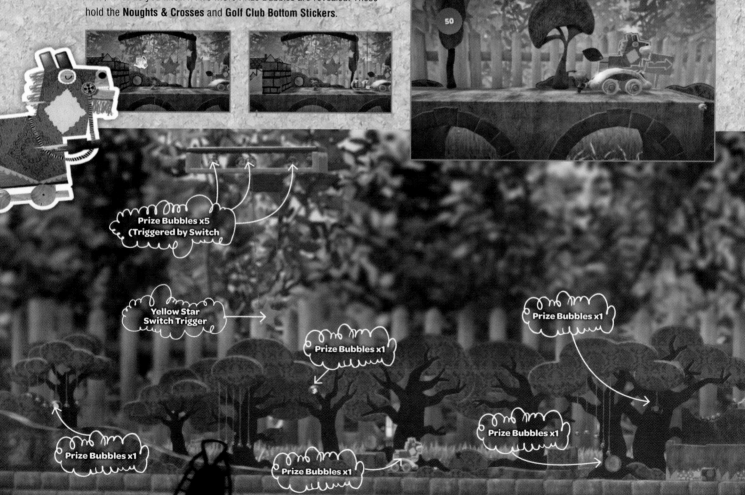

Prize Bubbles x5
(Triggered by Switch)

Yellow Star
Switch Trigger

Prize Bubbles x1

Prize Bubbles x1

Prize Bubbles x1

Prize Bubbles x1

Prize Bubbles x1

Saddle Up!

Once you hop onto the steed, make sure you are positioned to be at the very topmost portion of the steed's curved platform. From this site, you should be high enough to grab the slew of hanging Score and Prize Bubbles as the steed speeds down the hill. The prize for doing so is the **Leaf Doodle Sticker**.

TREATS IN THE TREETOPS – PART 1

Pay attention to the low-hanging treetop that you can hop onto while riding the steed down the hill. Getting up to such dizzying heights leads to a hidden Sticker nestled in the round, bushy leaves.

To get up to the treetops, ride the steed down the first slope until it hits a brief landing. As soon as it does (and before it resumes its downward descent for the remainder of the hill), take a leap of faith to the right toward the tree ledge. Once on the treetops, hop up and around to the right until you locate the Sticker, then just drop down on top of it to grab it. You get the **Victorian Man Sketch Sticker** inside this Prize Bubble for your troubles. Missing the jump unfortunately requires you to restart the level, as the steed becomes wedged in place at the bottom of the hill.

SHOOTING STAR #3

There's also a Yellow Star Sticker Puzzle up here. The star-shaped cutout is hanging right above the treetop. Once you have the Yellow Star Sticker, return here and slap it on the Sticker Switch for five more Prize Bubbles! You get the **Large Snail Shell Object**, the **Blue Moon Object**, the **Darkest Brown Wood Object**, the **Tall Tree Object**, and the **Dark Green Wood Material**.

The second steed in this next area offers a bit of advice. For a little more "oomph" when grabbing/dragging an item or object, press ✕ repeatedly. Try it out to get the steed over the hump!

DON'T GET LEFT BEHIND!

You weren't going to forget that Prize Bubble hidden behind where the steed was resting, were you? Before moving on, make sure you retrace your steps to find it nestled against the small wall, hosting a **Wooden Steed Sticker inside**.

Take the High Road

Down in this next area, you come to what looks like a dead end. However, with a little elbow grease and some good old-fashioned effort, you can get onto the platform above. Take a moment, though, to rummage for a hidden Prize Bubble before moving on.

HIDDEN GOODIES

The tree with the Checkpoint is hiding a Prize Bubble behind its trunk! Walk over to the left edge of its roots and press up on the left stick to hop to the back plane. From here, you can walk behind the tree trunk and grab the hidden goodie—the **Sun Doodle Sticker**.

Grab and move the small, green, floral fabric-decorated block all the way to the right until it is against the far wall. Once in place, hop onto it and then up to the curved portion of the platform, grabbing the Score Bubbles in the process.

Once up top, grab and move the next steed all the way to the left until it drops into place inside the small grooves. From here, you probably want to continue onward and upward, but before you do, take a grand leap off the steed toward the dangling Prize Bubble to gain the **English Rose Sticker**.

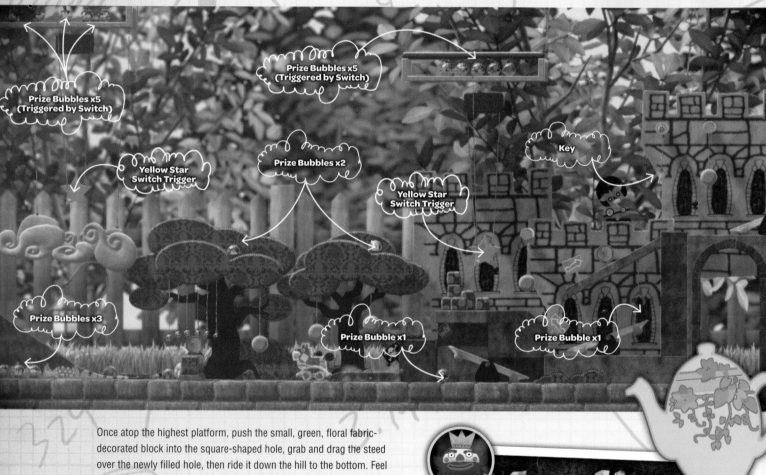

Prize Bubbles x5
(Triggered by Switch)

Prize Bubbles x5
(Triggered by Switch)

Prize Bubbles x5
(Triggered by Switch)

Yellow Star
Switch Trigger

Prize Bubbles x2

Key

Yellow Star
Switch Trigger

Prize Bubbles x3

Prize Bubble x1

Prize Bubble x1

Once atop the highest platform, push the small, green, floral fabric-decorated block into the square-shaped hole, grab and drag the steed over the newly filled hole, then ride it down the hill to the bottom. Feel free to let out a "whoopee" if you feel like it.

Don't forget to grab the three Prize Bubbles to the left before continuing. They hold the **Orange Flowers**, **Grass Rough Doodle**, and **Red Flowers Stickers**. How lovely!

The Old Hang and Swing

The helpful steed in this next section of the level offers up some advice about hanging and swinging. In order to move on AND traverse the Horrible Gas-filled water, you must swing from one hanging sponge ball to the next.

THE MECHANICS OF SWINGING

SWINGING IS A LOT OF FUN, EVEN FOR THOSE WHO PREFER TO KEEP BOTH FEET PLANTED FIRMLY ON THE GROUND. TO SWING, FIRST FIND AN OBJECT THAT YOUR SACKPERSON CAN SWING ON. NEXT, JUMP UP AND PRESS AND HOLD R1 TO GRAB THE OBJECT, AND THEN USE THE LEFT STICK TO GAIN MOMENTUM BY PRESSING THE DIRECTION YOU WANT TO SWING. TO LET GO, RELEASE R1, BUT BE SURE TO PRESS AND HOLD IT AGAIN IF YOU ARE SWINGING ACROSS A SET OF CONSECUTIVE OBJECTS OR ITEMS.

Swing from one sponge ball to the next until you are back on solid ground. Drop down into the small chamber below and grab the Prize Bubble down here. It holds the **Blue Monkey Sticker**.

Getting out of the chamber requires a bit of inertia and physics. Hop onto the seesaw so that the left portion is in the downward position under your weight, then quickly run up its length and jump over to the platform before the opposite end drops.

The Reachable Unreachable Sticker

You might have already tried to grab that Prize Bubble hovering just out of your reach above the next seesaw. It's not impossible to get; however, it may take a few attempts. Here's the easiest way to do so: run to the left of the seesaw to lower that side all the way down, then quickly run to the top and jump as high as you can go. Alternatively, grab one of the small, green, floral fabric-decorated block above and drag it down onto the seesaw. Position it at the opposite end, and then jump off of it to reach the bubble. Either way, one or two tries, and the **Castle Sketch Window Sticker** is yours!

Use the seesaw to get up to the platform to the left. Continue on by swinging over the gap using the hanging sponge ball. However, there's some good secret stuff to grab first!

STAR STRUCK #4

That's right—your eyes are not deceiving you. There is a fourth Star Sticker Puzzle hanging above this platform. When you've got that Yellow Star Sticker from the next level, return here and use it to reveal five more Prize Bubbles. These contain the **Small Grey Flag Object**, the **Orange Floral Fabric Material**, the **Green Check Denim Material**, **Seesaw Object**, and the **Grass Material**.

TREATS IN THE TREETOPS – PART 2

There are some more Prize Bubbles to be discovered nestled amongst the treetops to the left of this platform. To reach them, hop up onto the stack of small, green, floral fabric- decorated blocks and push the top two over so they end up creating a ramp to the tree. If one falls down through the gap, don't fret; you can jump off the block and onto the treetop from this position. Up top, two more Prize Bubbles await. They hold the **Green Castle Banner Sticker** and the **Moody Cloud Sticker**.

And yes, you did see a few more star-shaped Sticker Puzzles along the way. You'll be returning here in due time. Carry on.

STAR STRUCK #5

Well, what do you know? Here's yet another Star Sticker Puzzle up above the clouds, just to the left of the treetops. Hop onto these cumulous tufts once you've acquired the Yellow Star Sticker, and use it to get the building blocks to create your own clouds. These five Prize Bubbles contain the **Curly Cloud Object**, the **Round Cloud Object**, the **Fancy Cloud Object**, **Loose Cloud Object**, and the **Twisty Cloud Object**.

Return to the platform and swing across to the next ramp. Up above, that little rambunctious tyke in the sports car has something to tell you in between giggles. Approach him to hear what he has to say.

Prize Bubbles x4 (Triggered by Decorating Steed)

The Queen

Prize Bubbles x2

Prize Bubble x1 (Behind Queen)

KEYS AND MINI-GAMES

CHALLENGE KEYS ARE QUITE USEFUL OBJECTS, DON'T YOU THINK? THE CHALLENGE KEYS FOUND IN LITTLEBIGPLANET UNLOCK MINI-GAMES. ONCE UNLOCKED, THESE NEW CHALLENGES CAN BE ACCESSED FROM THE POD. HEED THE LITTLE ONE'S ADVICE, AND BE SURE TO KEEP A LOOK OUT—SOME CHALLENGE KEYS ARE REALLY HARD TO FIND!

There is a **Challenge Key** just to the right of the tyke. Even for a full-grown sackperson such as yourself, it's still a bit too high to reach, but by using the seesaw along with the sponge ball, grabbing it is easier than it seems. Just hop on the seesaw and lower its right side, then run up to the opposite side, leap and grab the sponge, and swing over to the Challenge Key. You've just unlocked the Castle Climb Score Challenge. We'll pay (and play) it a visit shortly.

Queen of Decorations

The Queen greets you with some words of encouragement and a request. If you can manage to decorate her wooden steed's tail, you may proceed on your merry way. To help out, she bestows on you two Prize Bubbles. One contains the **Donkey Tail Decoration**, and the other the **Sticker & Decoration Edit Tool**.

DECORATION 101

PLACING DECORATIONS

IT'S TIME TO BRING OUT YOUR INNER DECORATOR. DON'T FRET—IT'S EASY! JUST OPEN POPIT AND SELECT THE STICKERS & DECORATIONS ICON. MOVE TO THE DECORATIONS PAGE AND CHOOSE A DECORATION YOU WANT TO USE AND PLACE. THAT'S RIGHT, IT'S LIKE THE STICKERS FEATURE. IN FACT, IT'S EXACTLY LIKE THE STICKERS FEATURE. YOU DO REMEMBER HOW TO PLACE STICKERS, DON'T YOU?

USING THE STICKER & DECORATION EDIT TOOL

PLACING STICKERS AND DECORATIONS IS EASY, BUT IT CAN AT TIMES BE A TRICKY BUSINESS. DON'T WORRY. AS LONG AS YOU HAVE THE HANDY STICKER & DECORATION EDIT TOOL, YOU CAN JUST AS QUICKLY LIFT AND DELETE STICKERS & DECORATIONS AS YOU PLACED THEM. TO USE THIS HANDY TOOL, ACCESS POPIT AND SELECT THE STICKER & DECORATION EDIT TOOL. IT CAN BE FOUND IN BOTH YOUR STICKERS AND DECORATIONS PAGES. ONCE IN HAND, USE THE LEFT STICK TO MOVE THE TOOL AROUND THE SCREEN AND TARGET/SELECT THE STICKER OR DECORATION YOU WANT TO EDIT. WHEN IT'S HIGHLIGHTED, YOU CAN PRESS ✕ TO PICK IT UP. ONCE IT'S BEEN PICKED UP, YOU CAN PRESS DOWN ON R3 TO FLIP IT, ✕ TO PLACE IT SOMEWHERE ELSE, OR ⬤ TO DELETE IT. HOW MARVELOUS!

Go ahead and give it a try—you know you want to! Select the Donkey Tail Decoration from the Decorations Page in the Popit Menu and place somewhere near the back of the wooden steed. For a job well done, you are rewarded with four more Prize Bubbles. These contain the **Eye Spring**, **Orange Flower**, **Purple Flower**, and **Pink Flower Decorations**.

WHAT'S BEHIND THE ROYAL THRONE?

There is a deviously placed Prize Bubble hidden behind the Queen. Make sure to hop all the way to the back plane and scoot behind her to reveal the **Black Crown Outline Sticker**.

THE KING

Prize Bubbles x5 (Triggered by Switch)

Yellow Star Switch Trigger

Prize Bubble x1

Day at the Races

Feel like a race? Hop on the wooden steed and grab hold of its spongy reigns. By holding on, the steed begins to move forward. When the starting gates open, you have 30 seconds to reach the finish line and earn an extra 300 points. Just don't let go, and enjoy the ride!

Once you reach the finish line, hop up onto the small mushroom to grab the Prize Bubble containing the **Red Mushroom Sticker**, then feel free to take a victory lap—the audience loves you, they really do. When you're ready, stand in front of the scoreboard to see how well you did!

STAR STRUCK #6

When you've got the Yellow Star Sticker from the next level, do make sure to return to this area after racing down the hill on the steed. It's right before the final jump near the finish line. There's a Star Sticker Puzzle hanging between the cheering spectators. Use that Yellow Star Sticker to drop down five more Prize Bubbles to gain the **Large Wooden Steed Object**, the **Green Floral Fabric Material**, the **Small Wooden Steed Object**, the **Mushroom Block Object**, and the **Cheering Crowd Object**.

See You Soon!

The Yellow Star Sticker Switch required to snag the rest of the Prize Bubbles in this level is found in the next—Skate to Victory. You won't achieve it until the very end of the level, but be sure to return to this Get a Grip area to grab the rest of the goodies once the Sticker has been acquired.

The Gardens

Skate to Victory

Evening has fallen upon The Gardens, but that doesn't mean it's time to rest—there are still plenty of goodies to uncover and things to discover!

Start

✓ Stickers

	Big Green Bird
	Bingo
	Blue Knight
	Blue Postcards
	Brick Wall Sketch
	Chips Logo
	Cotton Wheel
	Crazy Sign
	Fancy Swirls
	Golf Logo
	Green Castle Flag
	Green Doodle
	Green Finish
	Green Start
	Green Submarine
	King of Hearts

✓ Stickers

	King Stamp
	King's Head
	Neon Kababs
	Pixel Fish Blue
	ROFL
	Scary Ghost
	Sketch Bricks
	Start Text
	Thick Sketch Bricks
	Tudor Tower
	Vince Meat Pie
	Wheel of Fun
	Yellow Crest
	Yellow Danke
	Yellow Star

Level Complete Gifts

✓ Costume
Bunny Tail

✓ Background
The Gardens

Collected All Gifts

✓ Stickers
Very Early *LittleBigPlanet* Concept

✓ Objects
Early *LittleBigPlanet* Concept with Frame

Aced Level Gifts

✓ Costume
Pirate Hat

ANDLAKE & CO.
ONE MILE
4 1 8
156

Prize Bubble Pick-Ups

✔ Decorations

Decorations	
Cloth Leaf	
Leaf	
Pink Springy Star	

✔ Tools

Tools	
Camera Tool	

✔ Costumes

Costumes	
Funny Face Glasses	

✔ Objects

Objects	
Birdy of String	
Blue Star Light	
Cardboard Castle	
Dumpty	
Ghost on String	
Green Star Light	
Large Flag	
Mushroom Tree	
Pinwheel	

✔ Audio

Audio
"Get it Together"
"Skipping Syratki" by Kenneth Young

✔ Objects

Objects	
Red Star Light	
Rocking Glass	
Silver Fork	
Silver Knife	
Skateboard	
Water Wheel	
Windmill	
Wobbly Tree	

THE KING

Prize Bubbles x3 (Triggered by Switch)

Windmills

Prize Bubbles (Triggered by Switch)

Prize Bubble x1

Yellow Star Switch Trigger

Prize Bubbles x2

Prize Bubbles x8

Prize Bubbles x5

Yellow Star Switch Trigger

INTRODUCING RACES

No More Mr. Nice King

Right off the bat, the King lets you know that things are about to get a bit more difficult from here on out. Beyond the tranquil hills lies a scary castle filled with all sorts of ghouls, goblins, and things that go bump in the night. Up for the challenge? Of course you are.

To get going, grab ahold of the hanging bird to the right of the King, and don't let go. It lifts you up to a high ledge where a series of three windmills can be found atop precarious platforms separated by gaps filled with belching Lethal Gas. The only way across is to grab hold of the sponge balls attached to the spinning windmills, and then use their momentum to launch you over to each platform.

Skate to Victory

27

TWINKLE, TWINKLE LITTLE STAR STICKER PUZZLE

That star-shaped cardboard cutout houses another Sticker Switch. You don't have the correct Sticker at the start of the first time you play this level; however, you do snag it eventually. Once it's in your possession, be sure to return here. Slap the Yellow Star Sticker on the Sticker Switch to reveal three Prize Bubbles that are dropped into the teacups; the bubbles contain the **Beige Cotton Material**, the **Large Grey Flag Object**, and the **Red Star Light Object**.

Three o'Clock and All is Well!

Naturally, you want to collect those Score Bubbles, as well as the Sticker-filled Prize Bubbles atop the last platform. To do so, be sure to time your release as each windmill

rotates toward the 3:00 position, and press to the right and the left stick for a little extra push. The Stickers inside the Prize Bubbles include **Tudor Tower**, **Wheel of Fun**, and **ROFL**.

All Fall down

The last platform holding the Prize Bubbles collapses under your weight, sending you crashing down toward the ground. In order to grab the Prize Bubble nestled in the crook of the platform just below, press the left stick to the right as you fall to steer in that direction. For your troubles, you get the **Green Doodle Sticker**.

A fifth Prize Bubble containing the **King Stamp Sticker** awaits you at the bottom.

STAR LIGHT, STAR BRIGHT

There's also a large, rotating Sticker Puzzle down in this area. Once you have the Yellow Star Sticker in your possession, slapping it on the Sticker Switch reveals four Prize Bubbles. Collect them all to gain the **Rocking Grass**, **Blue Star Light**, **Tall Cardboard House**, and **Pinwheel Objects**.

Lethal Liquid

Follow the sign with the pointing arrow to continue up the path. Just ahead, a Prize Bubble-filled watermill provides the perfect safe transport over the lethal water. Make sure to grab all of the eight Prize Bubbles and collect the Stickers inside. You gain the **Start Text**, **Green Finish**, **Green Start Light**, **Neon Kebabs**, **Blue Postcards**, **Fancy Swirls**, **Blue Knight**, and **Green Submarine Stickers**.

On the other side of the watermill, hop up and grab the dangling bird, then ride it up to the higher ledge. Make sure to press to the right with the left stick as you ascend in order to grab the Prize Bubble with the **Chips Logo Sticker** inside.

A SHORT DETOUR

Once up top, don't leave this area without grabbing the two Prize Bubbles hanging at the cliffside to the left. Leap and grab onto the dangling bird, swing to the left to grab the first Prize Bubble, then drop off of it to grab the second. Snag them to receive the **Big Green Bird** and **Pixel Fish Blue** Stickers.

Start

Prize Bubbles x5 (Triggered by Switch)

Yellow Star Switch Trigger

Jetpack

Prize Bubble x1

Prize Bubbles x3

Prize Bubble x1

Say Cheese!

Up top, the Queen has taken a moment out of her busy royal schedule to fill you in on the finer points of the **Camera Tool**, which just happens to be sitting inside the Prize Bubble to her right.

SMILE FOR THE CAMERA

A PICTURE CAN TAKE A MAGIC MOMENT AND PRESERVE IT FOREVER. AND HERE ON LITTLEBIGPLANET, YOU'RE NEVER SHORT OF MAGIC MOMENTS TO COLLECT. THIS IS WHERE THE CAMERA TOOL COMES IN HANDY! YOU CAN USE THIS TOOL TO CREATE YOUR OWN STICKERS. TO DO SO, GO TO THE MY PICTURES PAGE IN THE STICKERS & DECORATIONS PAGES, AND YOU'LL FIND THE TAKE A PHOTO TOOL. SIMPLY SELECT IT, THEN USE THE LEFT STICK TO MOVE THE PICTURE FRAME AND THE RIGHT STICK TO ZOOM IT IN AND OUT. PRESS ⊗ TO SNAP IT, AND YOU'VE GOT A PICTURE CAPTURED IN THE FORM OF A STICKER THAT YOU CAN PLACE WHEREVER YOU LIKE!

POSTCARDS

The Jet Set

Have you been wondering how to get up to those high-hanging Score Bubbles among the treetops? Well, why not strap that jetpack to your back and hover right on up there? It looks like Dumpty is back in one piece, and he seems to be an authority on these machine-powered contraptions. To use one, just step right up and walk into it.

Skate to Victory

USING JETPACKS

FLYING YOUR VERY OWN JETPACK COULDN'T BE EASIER. JUST MOVE AROUND IN THE AIR USING THE LEFT STICK. TO GET A BIT MORE "OOMPH," HOLD DOWN ⊗. YOU CAN EVEN STILL GRAB STUFF BY PRESSING AND HOLDING DOWN R1. GO AHEAD AND GIVE IT A TRY. JUST NOTE THAT YOU CAN ONLY FLY AS FAR AS THE CHAIN THE JETPACK IS TIED UP TO (WE HAVE TO KEEP THEM CHAINED UP FOR INSURANCE REASONS–YOU UNDERSTAND). IF YOU WANT TO TAKE OFF THE JETPACK, JUST HIT ⊕.

Use the jetpack to collect the hanging Score Bubbles, then fly above the treetops to collect the Stickers and Decorations up top. You get the **King's Head** and **King of Hearts Stickers**, and the **Leaf Decoration**.

SHOOT FOR THE STARS

While you're flying high up among the treetops, (and if you've acquired that Yellow Star Sticker at the end of this level), you might as well activate the Sticker Switch found here. Use the Yellow Star to drop five Prize Bubbles: the **Silver Fork**, **Birdy on String**, **Silver Knife**, **Wobbly Tree**, and **Light Brown Wood Objects**.

It looks as if a raised drawbridge temporarily blocks your path. However, if you pick up and drop a few of the stacked sponge balls into the hanging box, their combined weight lowers the box and triggers the drawbridge to fall.

Dump Dumpty

Ah, poor Dumpty. Grab onto his upper portion while you're flying around on that jetpack and drop it to the side. There's a handful of Score Bubbles to grab inside his lower half. Go on—he won't mind.

Tower of Terror

Check just beyond the drawbridge to find the spooky castle that the King discussed earlier. Steel your nerves and dull your senses, as it's going to be one terror-filled ride. To progress, quickly dash underneath the stomping boot when it rises. Make sure you clear it before it stamps down, or you might be squashed in the process!

A KICK IN THE PANTS

Before you move past the boot, hop onto it and let it launch you up in the air. Just out of sight is a Prize Bubble containing a **Green Castle Flag Sticker**.

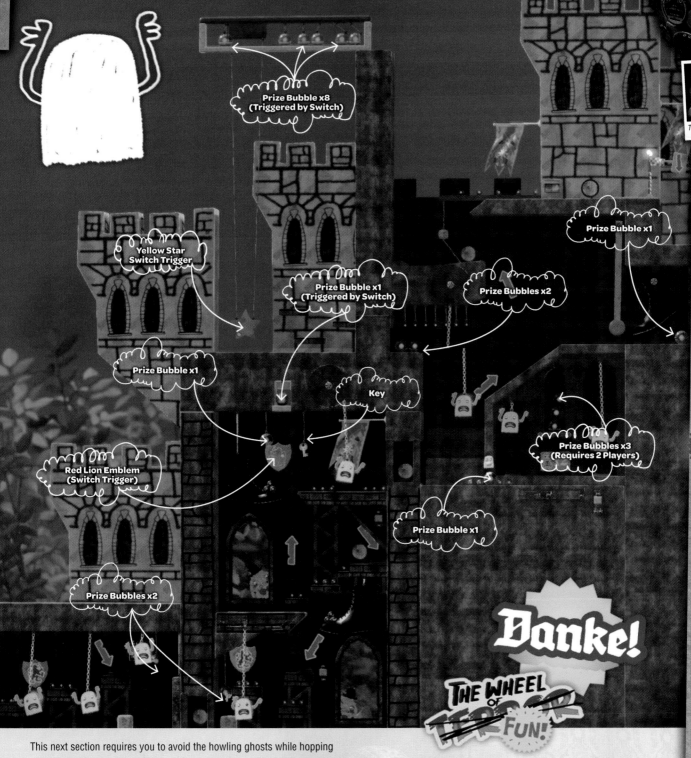

Prize Bubble x8
(Triggered by Switch)

Prize Bubble x1

Yellow Star
Switch Trigger

Prize Bubble x1
(Triggered by Switch)

Prize Bubbles x2

Key

Prize Bubble x1

Prize Bubbles x3
(Requires 2 Players)

Prize Bubble x1

Red Lion Emblem
(Switch Trigger)

Prize Bubbles x2

Danke!

THE WHEEL OF ~~TERROR~~ FUN!

This next section requires you to avoid the howling ghosts while hopping up to the switch on the top right platform. In order to do so, you must first grab the small block at the right side of the room and drag/push it all the way to the left. Be careful, though. One touch from the ghost vaporizes you instantly. Not a pretty sight.

Be patient and wait for each ghost to rise safely above your sackperson before scooting underneath. Once the block is wedged into place against the leftmost platform, wait for the first ghost to rise out of the way, then hop up onto the block and then the platform beyond.

Once you are on the platform, wait for the ghosts to lower before leaping over each to reach the switch. Stepping on the switch raises the gate to the right, allowing you to continue.

Before jumping off the highest platform with the switch, locate the Prize Bubble near the ceiling to your right. To collect the **Scary Ghost Sticker** inside, wait for the ghost to lower all the way to the ground, and then take a leap of faith.

Skate to Victory

31

Another ghost haunts the confines of this next room. Instead of floating up and down, it moves in more of a haphazard fashion. Keep an eye on it while avoiding it at all costs. To grab that **Cotton Wheel Sticker** inside the Prize Bubble just beyond the gate, drag the small block a bit to the left and then use it to reach the prize.

Wait for the ghost to rise out of your way, and then push the block to the right until it is wedged against the lowest platform. Next, use it to get up to the platform and then leap across to the next, avoiding the ghost's advances at all costs. Once it's safe to do so, leap up to the last platform and activate the switch. A large boot drops to floor, leading to safe passage to the next spooky room above.

Up here, things are relatively calm (don't mind Dumpty, he's just keeping an eye on you). The ghost above is too high to have any dangerous effect on you, so you can take a breather and hop up to the switch to the right.

Once you've activated the boot, drop down onto it and ride it up to the next portion of the room.

USE THAT BOOT FOR BOOTY

You can use the boot's momentum to launch yourself into the air and grab the two goodies hanging from the ceiling. Press ⊗ just as the boot reaches its apex, launch into the air, and grab the Prize Bubble containing the **Brick Wall Sketch**.

To grab the **Challenge Key** and unlock the Survivor Challenge, repeat the process, except this time, jump to the right a bit. Just make sure you avoid the spooky ghost as you do so.

SWITCH TO YOUR SHIELD

In addition to the Sticker and Challenge Key, there is also a Sticker Puzzle up here. Locate the puzzle and make a note of it. Once you have the required Sticker—the Red Lion Emblem—you can slap it on the Sticker Switch to reveal the **Get it Together** and **Skipping Syratki** Audio.

Double Trouble

Inside the next room, grab the Prize Bubble containing the **Sketch Brick Sticker,** and then listen to what the ghost on the wall has to say. According to the ghost, the area to the right is a co-op challenge. In order to traverse and/or activate the area, you need a friend to join in.

CO-OP CHALLENGES

WHENEVER YOU SEE A SIGN THAT SHOWS AN IMAGE OF A SACK PERSON WITH A NUMBER NEXT TO IT, THAT MEANS THE AREA, CHALLENGE, OR PUZZLE INVOLVES MORE THAN ONE PLAYER. THE NUMBER OF FRIENDS REQUIRED TO SOLVE THE PUZZLE IS ALWAYS POSTED ON THE SIGN. FOR THIS CHALLENGE, YOU NEED A TOTAL OF TWO PLAYERS (X2) TO UNLOCK THE PRIZE BUBBLES ABOVE.

If you don't have someone to play with, then continue on and pass this area by. However, if you are playing with others or someone in the room can join in, then go ahead and tackle this challenge together.

It Takes Two

To solve the Two-Player Puzzle, one player must jump on the far switch to the right while the other jumps on the closer one to the left. To make it challenging, two deadly ghosts dangle over

the switches. Wait for them to rise, and then quickly jump onto the switches at the same time. Your rewards for doing so are three Prize Bubbles containing the **Vince Meat Pie** and **Yellow Danke Stickers**, as well as a **Funny Face Glasses Costume**.

The Final Ascent

Avoid the ghost and jump up the oscillating blocks, then climb the ramp to the next area. Up here, a boot continually kicks a sponge ball attached to a stick. The key to moving on is to grab the sponge and wait for the boot to kick it. As the stick swings almost all the way upward, let go of the sponge to be flung to the next platform. However, before doing so, sneak behind the boot as it triggers to grab the **Bingo** and **Yellow Crest Stickers**.

FAR FLUNG

With the proper timing, you can reach those Score and Prize Bubbles on the far platform to the left. Grab hold of the sponge, make sure the ghost is out of the way, and then almost instantly release the moment the boot gives your sackperson a boot to the rear. The two Prize Bubbles here hold the **Thick Sketch Bricks** and **Golf Logo Stickers inside**.

In addition to the Prize Bubbles up here, there is a secret room to the left. Pass through what looks like a solid wall to enter it. In order to reveal the room's secrets, you're going to need to solve the Sticker Puzzle. Make a mental note and return here during a successive playthrough. The reward for doing so is a batch of six Prize Bubbles. You receive the **Ghost on String Object**, the **Dark Brown Wood Material**, the **Hessian Fabric Material**, the **Cardboard Castle Object**, the **Darkest Brown Wood Material**, and the **Dumpty Object**.

To exit the spooky castle, all that's left to do is grab the small block suspended by a rope, which causes a ramp leading outside to drop. Collect the Score Bubbles that come with it, and then head out for safety.

Dumpty to the Rescue!

Dumpty waits for you outside the castle with a set of wheels. In order to escape, he needs you to drag the skateboard to get it moving and then hop on for a wild ride. The moment the gates open, you have 180 seconds to get to the Finish Gate.

Get to work! Run to the front of the skateboard and grab and drag it, tapping ⊗ for a little more power. As soon as the skateboard starts to roll forward enough with enough inertia to carry it down the hill, hop on and grab hold—it's going to be a wild ride! In fact, it's pretty much a given that Dumpty could fall off somewhere along the way.

A RETURN TRIP?

Once you've hit the Finish Gate, hop off the skateboard and run back along the track—there are a variety of goodies to be found.

To start, locate the two trees not too far to the left of the Finish Gate (it's more than likely Dumpty's broken body can be found strewn about here as well). A **Challenge Key** that unlocks a Score Challenge hangs from the trees. To grab it, drag Dumpty's two pieces underneath it to create a set of platforms for you to jump off of.

Once you've acquired the Challenge Key, continue to the left to grab the goodies inside the Prize Bubbles (you'll gain the **Cloth Leaf** and **Pink Springy Star** Decorations), and then keep running underneath the ramp without stopping until you reach a dead end. Here, you find the **Crazy Sign Sticker**.

We Love the Moon!

Grab the Prize Bubbles for a bevy of Objects and Materials. You gain the **Skateboard Object**, the **Pink Floral Material**, the **Water Wheel Object**, the **Mushroom Tree Object**, the **Green Star Light Object**, the **Wooden Struts**, and the **Blank Background**.

Right next to the platform where the Queen is perched is a hanging bird holding onto a Prize Bubble. It's a strong possibility that the Sticker inside is the key to triggering all of those switches you've been noticing. Now that you have the **Yellow Star Sticker**, be sure to return to the previous level—Get a Grip—as well as replay this level to find the remaining goodies.

Meet the Creator Curators

Just up the hill, the King bids you farewell while explaining that he is one of eight Creator Curators who reside over the Story worlds in *LittleBigPlanet*. Prepare to meet seven more along your quest! And get ready to meet Zola in the next area—The Savannah!

Step on the scoreboard to see how well you did, and prepare to move on!

THE KING

Mini Levels!

The Gardens
Mini Levels!

Castle Climb Challenge

CLIMB TO THE TOP OF THE CASTLE – BEAT THE TIMER AND COLLECT POINTS!

How to Unlock: Collect the Key in Get a Grip

Hassle at the Castle

Welcome to the Castle Climb Challenge. The objective—beat the timer and get to the finish line as fast as you can for a high score. As with some of the races you've already experienced, you can temporarily pause the countdown timer while also collecting points by collecting Score Bubbles.

This is a basic race for the finish line. As with all Challenges, you need not worry about seeking out hidden Prize Bubbles, since there aren't any. To begin the race, climb the ramp and step on the pad in front of the gate. As soon as it opens, you're off! You have 120 seconds to make it from the bottom to the top of the castle, surviving the hazards and pitfalls along the way. While there is

plenty of time, you can find yourself running short of it if you start missing jumps or getting stuck at certain obstacles. When you reach the finish line, the leftover time is allotted to your score.

General Tips

Keep moving! Yes, this is stating the obvious, but there's no time for dilly-dallying now, is there? Make sure not to waste too much time trying to get that one Score Bubble you missed, as it may end up costing you more points by going back for it than if you just kept going.

If you miss a jump and find yourself back a ways, do the almost unthinkable act and either Pop yourself or find a way to perish (such as dropping onto those nasty spikes). Frequently, it's faster to reappear at a Checkpoint instead of retracing your steps.

Wait for it! Jumping or releasing at the last possible second should help you get across some of the tougher obstacles, such as the swinging sponge balls and seesaws. There are a few spots where taking it right to the edge is the only way to reach that next platform or swing.

Practice makes perfect! Yes, it's a cliché, but it's worth repeating. The more you replay and practice running through the course, the more familiar you become with it. And the more familiar you become with it, the faster and more adept you will be getting through it.

Tie Skipping

SKIP OVER THE KING'S TIE

How to Unlock: Collect the Key in Skate to Victory

Defy the Tie

Welcome to Tie Skipping! Keep jumping over the King's tie—without getting knocked off the platform. Survive and collect Score Bubbles for as long as you can before you perish.

This fun, addictive, and challenging mini-game has you jumping over the King's rotating tie as Score Bubbles drop from above. As always, each Score Bubble is worth 10 points, although they don't drop down fast enough to earn any multipliers. The real kicker is that the King's tie rotates faster and faster with each Score Bubble you pick up. If it manages to knock you off the platform, you fall to your death, and it's Game Over.

Skateboard Freefall

HOLD ON TIGHT AND RIDE THE SKATEBOARD

How to Unlock: Collect the Key in Skate to Victory

Speed Skating

Fancy a race? Grab the skateboard and pull it to get moving, and then jump on it quick! Once aboard, grab to hold on and pump ⊗ to speed up. Beat the timer and get to the finish line as fast as you can for that high score!

This Challenge is all about speed. The moment the gates open, you have 120 seconds to hop on the skateboard and ride it down the series of ramps and jumps to the finish line at the bottom. There is plenty of time to do so, but a speedier achievement results in a higher score.

THE KING

General Tips

Time is definitely of the essence in this Challenge, as your score depends on how quickly you can make it to the finish line. The most time-consuming bit is getting the skateboard moving. To maximize this time, quickly race out of the gate, and grab the back of the skateboard. From this position, start moving it toward the ramp, tapping ⊗ while pressing the left stick to the right to get it going quickly. As soon as it starts moving, hop onto the board and grab hold as it begins to move down the ramp.

While there isn't necessarily a spot on the board that makes it travel faster than another, it's important to keep tapping ⊗ when the wheels are on the ground to continually spur the board onward.

Keep it straight! Your weight affects the skateboard—especially when in the air. If the board begins to tip too far backward or forward, you can adjust its airborne arc by pressing the left stick in the opposite direction.

General Tips

This Challenge starts off easy enough, but around the twentieth Score Bubble, the tie really begins to pick up speed. Stay alert and execute short hops over the tie rather than high jumps.

Try not to move to the sides of the platform, as doing so puts you in a precarious position. Instead, stay in the center as long as you can, only touching the left stick for movement if you get pushed one way or another.

It's all about timing. There's really no "sweet spot" in terms of when to jump, as the tie just keeps getting faster and faster. As a rule, be sure to jump as the tie begins its downward rotation toward you.

ZOLA

The Savannah

It sure is hot in **The Savannah**! After conquering The Gardens you meet King Zola, the Curator Creator of this fiery realm. But not everything is swingin' around here. Zola's been having some problems with his servants lately. It appears something (or someone) is bothering his buffalo and he's placing you in charge of solving this bovine conundrum!

As you travel through these burning hot lands, you'll find out what is bugging the buffalo. But as soon as one mystery is solved another pops up! Looks like Meerkat Mum's baby boy is missing. This new case takes you through the dark underground of the Meerkat Kingdom. Who knows what you'll find down there!

The Savannah
Swinging Safari

Now that you have bid farewell to the King and his lovely garden, it's time to explore what the other Creator Curators of LittleBigPlanet have to offer. Next up is something really hot— The Savannah. This section is brought to you by the fearsome lion, Zola. Select the Swinging Safari Seal from your Pod and get ready for some fun in the sun!

✓	Costume
	Stripy Lycra
	Zebra
	Cat Eyes
	Cork Hat
	Zebra Head
	Cute Lion Ears
	Lion Mask
	Scary Fangs
	Lion's Mane
	Lion Nose
	Lion's Tail
	Zebra Tail

✓	Objects	
	Submarine Launcher	
	Large Drum	
	Giraffe & Tree	
	Jumping Ape	
	Hanging Ape	
	Wobbly Ape	
	Big Crab Claw	
	Octopus Tentacle	
	Orange Boar Fish	
	Mean Piranha	
	Giraffe & Tree & Platform	
	Banana	
	Bird Wing	

Level Complete Gifts

✓	Costume
	Pink Fashion Sunglasses
	Green Daisy

Collected All Gifts

✓	Stickers	
	The Savannah Concept	

✓	Objects	
	The Savannah Concept with Frame	

Aced Level Gifts

✓	Costume
	Ringmaster Jacket

FIND ZOLA

Land Ho!

It's quite a ways from The Gardens to The Savannah, and in this case, the quickest way from A to B is by submarine. Luckily, the King happened to have one ready for use. So in you went and now here you are, still in the submarine and about to land in Zola's territory.

Head for the big red button in the center of the submarine and give it a good stomp. When the button is activated, the submarine launches out of the water and crash-lands on shore, taking out a poor monkey bystander. Whoops…

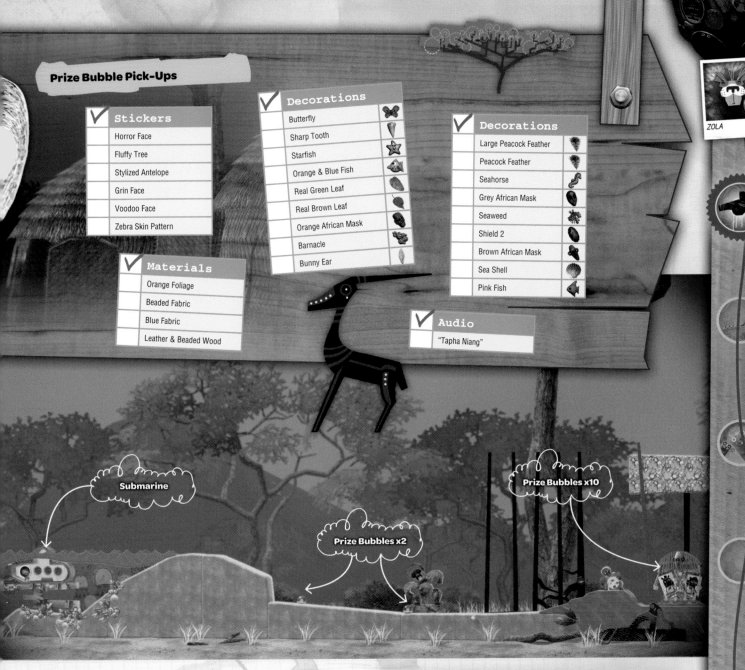

Prize Bubble Pick-Ups

✓ Stickers

Horror Face	
Fluffy Tree	
Stylized Antelope	
Grin Face	
Voodoo Face	
Zebra Skin Pattern	

✓ Decorations

Butterfly	
Sharp Tooth	
Starfish	
Orange & Blue Fish	
Real Green Leaf	
Real Brown Leaf	
Orange African Mask	
Barnacle	
Bunny Ear	

✓ Materials

Orange Foliage
Beaded Fabric
Blue Fabric
Leather & Beaded Wood

✓ Decorations

Large Peacock Feather	
Peacock Feather	
Seahorse	
Grey African Mask	
Seaweed	
Shield 2	
Brown African Mask	
Sea Shell	
Pink Fish	

✓ Audio

"Tapha Niang"

ZOLA

Submarine

Prize Bubbles x2

Prize Bubbles x10

Did I Do That?

Looks like you broke the monkey. Good thing it was only a statue! But you're not in the clear just yet. Walk up to the right to find a monkey sitting on the top of the small hill. He tells you that the broken statue was actually one of Zola's creations! You'd better head to Zola's tree palace to try to make amends.

Back It Up

To keep things interesting, the Creator Curators leave Prize Bubbles in unlikely places. Their favorite hiding spots include places you zoomed over while in or on a moving object. So anytime you happen to, say, fly over a large distance in a torpedo-like submarine, it's best to turn around and see if you happened to miss any goodies.

Before continuing on toward Zola's tree palace, backtrack a bit and collect the two Prize Bubbles you flew over in the submarine. The first bubble contains the **Seaweed Decoration** under the sub. The second one, which contains the **Submarine Launcher Object**, is located farther back.

Looking the Part

As you head past the talking monkey, you stumble across a Prize Bubble motherlode. Ten lovely Costume pieces are there for the taking: **Cat's Eyes**, **Zebra Head**, **Cute Lion Ears**, **Lion Mask**, **Scary Fangs**, **Lion's Mane**, **Zebra Costume**, **Lion's Tail**, **Zebra Tail**, and **Lion Nose**. Snag them all at once to earn a x3 score multiplier. Why not try on a few of your new costume pieces? You are in The Savannah, after all, so try on something a bit wilder.

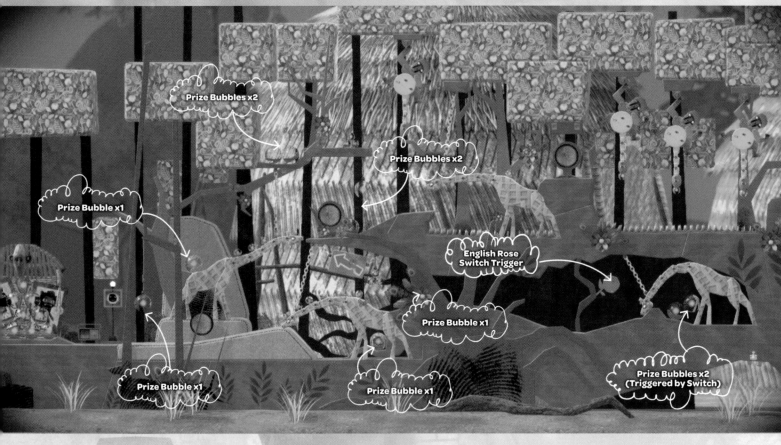

Prize Bubbles x2

Prize Bubbles x2

Prize Bubble x1

English Rose Switch Trigger

Prize Bubble x1

Prize Bubble x1

Prize Bubble x1

Prize Bubbles x2 (Triggered by Switch)

Climb aboard

When you're done dressing up, it's time to move out! Pass the Close-Level Post and collect the Prize Bubble dangling in the air; it contains the **Wobbly Ape Object**.

Just down the way, you come across more of The Savannah's wildlife. Large giraffes stand before you; their long necks, lined with Score Bubbles, sway up and down. Before making a dash for the Score Bubbles, hop down to pick up the Prize Bubble containing the **Orange & Blue Fish Decoration**. It's found near the first giraffe's legs.

Climb aboard the first giraffe as it lowers its neck to the ground. Snatch all the Score Bubbles and continue down the giraffe's back. The path continues to the right just a little bit more. Head that way for a special surprise.

WALK THIS WAY

It may not look like it's worth the trip to head down the path to the right, not when you can see lots of Score Bubbles and more giraffes to the left. But you'd be surprised! After all, this is *LittleBigPlanet*! It's always worth the trip! Take the path to the right to collect a hidden Prize Bubble. It contains the **Large Peacock Feather Decoration** and a Sticker Switch Puzzle. A Prize Bubble holding the **Giraffe & Tree Object** and a Prize Bubble containing the **Stripy Lycra Costume** are locked behind a giraffe's neck. The only way to reach them is by having the giraffe lift up its head. To do this, open your Popit and find the English Rose Sticker from The Gardens. Place the Sticker on the Sticker Switch next the giraffe, and watch its head rise.

Collect all the Prize Bubbles from the side path, then return to the first giraffe and walk out onto its neck. A second giraffe faces you and brings its neck down just as the neck you are on swings up. Jump onto the second giraffe and collect every bubble in sight, including the Prize Bubble containing the **Giraffe & Tree & Platform Object**.

Turn around and jump onto the platform to the right. Snag the Prize Bubbles that contain the **Peacock Feather Decoration** and the **Butterfly Decoration**. Make sure to activate the Checkpoint. Things are about to get a bit more dangerous.

I See Your Point

Another swaying giraffe stands ahead, and it's important you time your jump correctly. If you miss the giraffe, you fall into a pit of spikes. You don't want to get skewered, right? Hop onto the giraffe and collect all the Score Bubbles.

JUST HANGING OUT

Before going any farther, turn back to the left and wait for the giraffe's head to reach its highest point. Look! A monkey's tail is dangling down. That sneaky little monkey thought you wouldn't notice him. But it's a good thing he doubted you. That monkey is your ticket to hidden bubbles! Leap from the giraffe's head and grab onto the monkey's tail. He gives out a screech, but don't let that bother you. Use his tail to swing to the ledge on the left. Snag the bubbles there, including the two Material Prize Bubbles— **Orange Foliage** and **Beaded Fabric**—then head back to the giraffe.

Move across to the right to find more spikes—many more. To get safely across this vast pit of pointy objects, use the monkeys' tails hanging above. Their tails are made of sponge and can be used to swing across the obstacle. Just be careful when leaping from one monkey tail to the next.

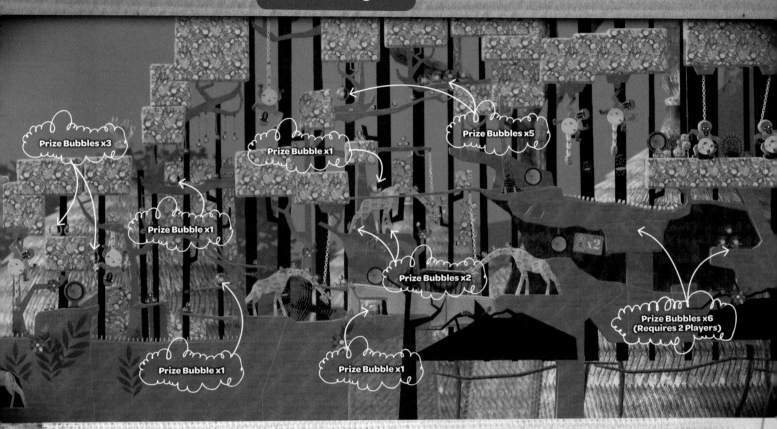

As you reach the end of the spike pit, you see another ledge. Thankfully, there is a monkey ready with a helping hand—literally! Jump up and grab his spongy hand, then swing to the bright orange ledge. Careful! It's a bit wobbly.

Jump to the next ledge, where you discover another little spring ledge overhead. This time, a Prize Bubble containing the **Grin Face Sticker** sits on the platform. But no matter how high you jump, the ledge is just out of reach. That doesn't mean you can't still collect the bubble! It just takes a bit more maneuvering.

Plan B

Lots of times, bubbles that look easy to get are actually just out of reach. But don't give up! No bubble is completely unattainable. Sometimes, you just have to think outside the box. Observe the surrounding area, and take into account that there may be alternative paths to that elusive bubble.

On a Ledge

To reach the Prize Bubble above your head, first move to the right and grab the giraffe's head as it sways down. Next, hop onto the giraffe's neck and walk down to its butt. Now you are even with the Prize Bubble! Hop onto the bubble's ledge and snag the Grin Face Sticker before turning back to the giraffe.

Walk up to the animal's back and turn around to face left. There is another ledge, and more bubbles. Leap onto the ledge and run up to the left. More and more Score Bubble are found! And what's this? The platform that formerly housed the helpful monkey is just ahead, and it holds more delicious Score Bubbles.

Now just when you thought it couldn't get any better, you see two Prize Bubbles resting on the next platform. One bubble contains the **Real Green Leaf Decoration** and the other holds the **Stylized Antelope Sticker**. There is also a Prize Bubble holding the **Hanging Ape Object** in between the two platforms. Lucky day! Collect the two on the platform first, then jump down to snag the third one. As you land on the level below, you find yourself back with the monkey and its helping hand.

Here We Go Again!

Make your way back across the spike pits and land by the giraffe.

ON A DIFFERENT PLANE

Don't grab the giraffe's head just yet; there's one more Prize Bubble to retrieve before moving ahead. To the right of the giraffe's noggin is a Prize Bubble containing the **Horror Face Sticker**, which appears to be completely trapped. But remember that earlier tip. No bubbles in *LittleBigPlanet* are completely unattainable. Move back to the farthest plane until you are behind the exposed tree roots in the background. Move to the right to sneak behind the orange fabric wall and collect the trapped Prize Bubble.

Grab the giraffe's head once more and ride up to the ledge on the right. Walk in front of the Checkpoint, and grab the head of the next giraffe. Once you can reach the large drum to the left, make the jump and collect all the Score Bubbles. You're probably tempted to leap right from the large drum to the next giraffe's head. But don't go for it. Turn back around to the right and climb over the previous giraffe until you reach the Two-Player Puzzle down the little alleyway past the giraffe's bottom.

JUST ME AND YOU AND A FEW BUBBLES

HERE IS YOUR SECOND TWO-PLAYER PUZZLE. REMEMBER, YOU CAN ONLY SOLVE THIS TYPE OF PUZZLE WITH ANOTHER SACKPERSON. SO GRAB A FRIEND AND GET TO IT! SET THE FIRST PLAYER ON THE SLIGHTLY ELEVATED BLOCK TO THE LEFT OF THE BIG RED BUTTON. THEN HAVE THE SECOND PLAYER STAND ON THE BUTTON. THIS RAISES THE BLOCK SO THAT THE FIRST PLAYER CAN JUMP ONTO THE LEDGE TO THE RIGHT AND COLLECT THE PRIZE BUBBLES THERE. ONE BUBBLE CONTAINS THE **VOODOO FACE STICKER**, ONE HOLDS THE **REAL BROWN LEAF DECORATION**, AND ONE CONTAINS THE **CORK HAT COSTUME PIECE**.

NOW HAVE THE FIRST PLAYER STEP ON THE RED BUTTON FOUND ON THE LEDGE. THIS CAUSES A TALL BLOCK TO THE LEFT TO DROP DOWN, REVEALING THREE MORE PRIZE BUBBLES. ONE BUBBLE HOLDS THE **BIG CRAB CLAW OBJECT**, ONE CONTAINS THE **ORANGE BOAR FISH OBJECT**, AND ONE HOLDS THE **MEAN PIRANHA OBJECT**.

I See More Monkeys

Get back on top of the large drum and jump onto the platform to the left. Collect the two Prize Bubbles hiding out behind the nearby giraffe. One bubble holds the **Sea Shell Decoration** and the other contains the **Bunny Ear Decoration**. Now grab the giraffe's head and ride up to the next level. Don't forget to collect all the bubbles on the giraffe, especially the Prize Bubble holding the **Large Drum Object**.

Pass the Checkpoint on the right and what do you see? More monkeys and spikes! Leap onto the first monkey's tail and swing backward. That's right, backward. When you have enough momentum, jump onto the elevated plane behind the Checkpoint. Run all the way to the left, collecting bubbles along the way. Don't stop at the upside down monkey; instead, keep running and leap to the lower level. This should award you at least a x5 point multiplier.

After gathering all the bubbles in the area, including the Prize Bubble holding the **Blue Fabric Material**, return to the upside down monkey and grab his spongy hand. As soon as you have a good grip, the monkey lurches up into the air and brings you to the bubble-ridden tree branches of The Savannah. Gather every bubble in sight and make sure to get the Prize Bubbles that contain the **Leather & Beaded Wood**, the **Banana Object**, the **Grey African Mask Decoration**, the **Brown African Mask Decoration**, and

the **Orange African Mask Decoration**. Now return to the monkeys and spikes. Swing across the sharp obstacles and land safely on the other side.

It's Not a Monkey

A row of bouncing baboons stand in your way. How do you know they are baboons and not monkeys? Well, just take a look at their fiery red bottoms! Actually, those bottoms are dangerous. If you touch them, you're toast. The fiery pits under the baboons are just as deadly.

FIRE!!!

Ouch! This blazing and charred material is hot! If you aren't careful, you can get seriously hurt. Lethal materials like this are found all throughout LittleBigPlanet, and they all have different effects on your little sack body. For the fire material, touching it once means you get singed. If you touch it a second time, you get burned to a crisp.

Zola the Magnificent

Jump across the lethal fire material, being careful not to touch the baboons' bottoms, and collect the Prize Bubble holding the **Jumping Ape Object**. Look up; you are now at the throne of Zola, the Creator Curator of The Savannah. Magnificent, isn't he?

Step up to Zola's throne and grab the **Tapha Niang Audio Object**. He greets you with a proposition. He shall forgive the destruction of his creation if you can find out what is troubling the buffalo. You want to be forgiven, don't you? You better check on the buffalo.

WHAT'S WRONG WITH THE BUFFALO?

So where are They?

First, you have to find the buffalo. Head right and grab onto the dangling monkey's hand. Swing across to the Prize Bubble containing the **Bird Wing Object**. Once you have retrieved it, don't let go! Swing back to the throne and land on the large drum. Jump down to the most forward

plane and land on another Prize Bubble resting on a tree branch. This time, the bubble holds the **Pink Fish Decoration**. Leap off the branch and make your way down to the orange floor.

HORSE IN THE SAVANNAH?

After reaching the floor, turn left and walk down the slope where you find a Sticker Puzzle. Pull up the Popit and select the Wooden Steed Sticker. Place it on the Sticker Switch, and four Prize Bubbles appear! The Prize Bubbles contain the **Shield 2 Decoration**, the **Seahorse Decoration**, the **Barnacle Decoration**, and the **Sharp Tooth Decoration**.

A Start Gate lies ahead. Once it opens, you find the disturbed buffalo stampeding underfoot. You have to get past them in order to continue, and the only way to do that is to hop down into their stampede.

STAMPEDE!

Jump down into the stampede and hop on the first buffalo. Leap from buffalo to buffalo, and collect the upcoming Prize Bubble that holds the **Starfish Decoration**. Keep buffalo jumping until you get to the upside down monkey. Grab the monkey's spongy hand to be lifted out of the stampede.

Be Lazy

Jumping from buffalo to buffalo to get past the stampede is a lot of work. So take the easy way out, and simply move to the furthest back plane and walk behind the buffalo.

Swing to the left until you can reach the nearby tree branches. Move left from branch to branch and snag all three Prize Bubbles hiding in the trees. One bubble holds the **Fluffy Tree Object**, one contains the **Zebra Skin Pattern Sticker**, and one holds the **Octopus Tentacle**. When you have all the bubbles, return to the upside down monkey and swing to the right. Land on the platform and look out onto the pit of spikes.

Swing to Victory

Use the monkeys dangling from the trees to get across the spikes and swing over the Finish Gate. Just ahead, one of Zola's monkeys tells you that they have found out what's been bothering the buffalo. But before you can check it out, you have to finish this level! Jump onto the zebra striped Scoreboard and get ready for the next great adventure!

ZOLA

The Savannah
Burning Forest

Fresh from the Swinging Safari, you have been given a new mission from Zola, The Savannah's Creator Curator. Your task is to find out what has been scaring his buffalo. If you can do this, then Zola can forgive you for the little mishap at the beginning of the previous level.

Level Complete Gifts

✓ **Costume**
Green Checked
☐ Black and Pink Dress

Collected All Gifts

✓ **Stickers**
☐ Big Cat Concept

✓ **Objects**
☐ Big Cat Concept with Frame

Aced Level Gifts

✓ **Costume**
☐ Long Mustache

WHAT'S SCARING THE BUFFALO?

It's Getting Hot in Here

As soon as you pop from the Entrance Barrel, one of Zola's monkeys gives you the latest news. The ground is on fire! If you don't want to end up as a pile of cinders, then you better watch your step. Thanks, monkey, but you already know all about fire danger from Swinging Safari.

A SECRET? ALREADY?

Before you even start out on this new level, there is already a secret to be revealed. Hop onto the rocky area behind the talking monkey and move to the left where a seesaw rests on a bed of fire. Leap from the seesaw to the safe ground just ahead to collect the **Challenge Key** and the Prize Bubble that contains the **Coco Wood Material**.

From the talking monkey, move to the right and cross the player post. Ahead is a sea of fire and molten material, with only little platforms of safe ground scattered about. Jump from platform to platform, collecting Score Bubbles along the way. Once you have reached the sixth platform, take a breather.

In order to get to the next area, use the monkey's spongy hand to swing to the rocky outcrop. Climb the steep rock steps until you reach the top Checkpoint. Don't miss any Score Bubbles along the way!

Stickers ✓

- Attitude Face
- Pigeon House
- Crazy Eyes
- Amazing Diamond

Decorations ✓

- Shield 1
- Cardboard Support
- Dangly Motif
- Tiger Nose
- Bear Nose
- Green Rope

Objects ✓

- Big Snappy Croc
- Large Red Vase
- Buffalo Emitter
- Croc King
- Wooden Buffalo
- Scary Ornament
- Feathered Spiky

Costume ✓

- Orange Stripy
- Antlers

Materials ✓

- Coco Wood
- Mahogany Wood
- Zebra Fabric

Audio ✓

- "Rock the Jungle"

ZOLA

Prize Bubble x1

Cat Head Switch Trigger

Prize Bubble x1 (Triggered by Switch)

Prize Bubble x1 (Triggered by Switch)

Prize Bubbles x3

Prize Bubble x1 Challenge Key

Running on Hot Coals

Just past the Checkpoint the magma path continues, this time with the buffalo stampede running across it. Maybe their tough hoofs can handle the heat? Catch a lift on the back of a buffalo and ride over to the left directional arrow. Jump onto the rocky platform and ignore the arrow for a bit. Instead, keep going right and gather all the Prize Bubbles found in the little cave ahead. One bubble contains the **Amazing Diamond Sticker**, one holds the **Big Snappy Croc**, and one contains the **Zebra Fabric Material**.

Return to the arrow and this time, do what it says. Jump onto the back of one of the buffalos heading left.

CAN'T YOU READ THE SIGN?

As you approach the right directional arrow, look the other way. Don't even think about going right. Going left is much cooler! When you keep going left, you come across all sorts of bubbles. Make sure not to miss the Prize Bubble containing the **Wooden Buffalo Object**. There is also a Sticker Puzzle here, but you won't be able to do it until you find the Cat Head Sticker in the next level. Once you have the sticker, the path to the locked-away Prize Bubble opens up, dropping balls of zebra fabric over the buffalo. This newly accessible Prize Bubble contains the **Buffalo Emitter Object**.

Something More Sinister

Leap onto the platform with the right directional arrow and gather the bubbles around you. Oh, what's this? You can't reach the Prize Bubble above your head? Well, if you've solved the Sticker Puzzle on the platform to the left, then you can use balls of zebra fabric hanging down to swing up to the elusive Prize Bubble containing the **Scary Ornament Object**.

Run up the bridge to the right, and listen to the update from another one of Zola's monkeys. It looks like the fire wasn't the only thing spooking the buffalo. There might be something—or someone—else provoking them. This is becoming quite the mysterious case!

Keep moving to find the buffalo marching onward. Hop onto a buffalo's back and take a ride to the Checkpoint platform. Remember to snag the Score Bubbles dangling in the air.

A Crocodile!?

Make sure you have properly activated the Checkpoint before jumping back onto a buffalo. As soon as you are on the beast, there is no turning back. Hang on tight as the buffalo zooms downhill. Ahead, you notice trails of green Hazardous Gas. Leap up and grab one of the balls hanging from the trees before you reach the source of the gas. From above, you can watch as the buffalo fall one at a time into the hungry mouth of a giant crocodile. Gross!

Swing from ball to ball until you are able to reach solid ground. Moving ahead, you can see more crocodiles looking snappy. If their teeth don't get you, the Hazardous Gas swarming around them certainly could.

Use the balls dangling from the tree branches overhead to swing across the gruesome pit of reptiles. At about the halfway point, you should hear the camera click of your picture being taken. Now you have a photo to remember this daring feat. Once you reach the seventh ball, you should be able to land on safe ground.

Stating the Obvious

Walk up to the talking monkey to the right. He tells you that it was the crocodiles that were actually scaring the buffalo. Oh, really?

Leave Captain Obvious and turn back to the left. Grab the nearest ball of zebra fabric start swinging. Grab the ball closest to you as you swing to the left. Then swing and grab your way over to the right, until you are standing right on top of the crocodile-shaped outcrop. Collect the Score Bubble hidden on the edge, and then pick up the two Prize Bubbles down the rugged path to the right. One bubble holds the **Bear Nose Decoration** and the other contains the **Shield 1 Decoration**.

WATERFALL OF GOODIES

Don't miss the Sticker Puzzle at the end of the path. Open Popit and select the Stylized Antelope Sticker you collected in the previous level, and slap it onto the Sticker Switch. Once the sticker is placed, a waterfall of bubbles—including a Prize Bubble holding the **Crazy Eyes Sticker**—comes tumbling out. Gather them all up and head back to the balls of zebra fabric.

Grab the closest ball and swing as far to the left as possible. You are just able to reach the bubble-filled tree branches. Land on the first branch and hop across to the others, collecting all types of bubbles. These include a Prize Bubble containing the **Green Rope Decoration**, as well as a Prize Bubble holding the **Dangly Motif Decoration**. Once all the bubbles have been collected, jump down to the landing containing a previous Checkpoint.

Worth Some Extra Investigating

Often when you are collecting a string of bubbles, there is an obvious stopping point; a point where the bubbles look like they have run out, and you go along your merry way.

Well, it's at this seemingly obvious stopping point that a lot of Creator Curators like to place another bubble just out of sight. For instance, after collecting the bubbles in the tree branches, you may want to jump down to the area with the Checkpoint and get back to what you were doing. But in reality, you should make sure to take that one extra large leap onto the outwardly uninteresting branch to the left. Once you land, you can see there is actually a Prize Bubble containing the **Large Red Vase Object**. It was worth a little extra investigating, huh?

ZOLA

Burning Forest

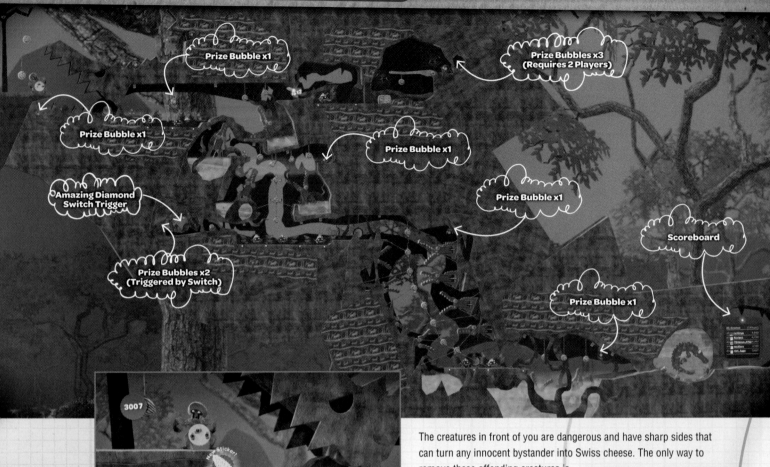

Prize Bubble x1

Prize Bubbles x3 (Requires 2 Players)

Prize Bubble x1

Prize Bubble x1

Amazing Diamond Switch Trigger

Prize Bubble x1

Scoreboard

Prize Bubbles x2 (Triggered by Switch)

Prize Bubble x1

The creatures in front of you are dangerous and have sharp sides that can turn any innocent bystander into Swiss cheese. The only way to remove these offending creatures is by popping the bubbles containing their Creature Brains. Do this to make the creatures disappear.

Pop Goes the Creature

Head back over the pit filled with crocs and land next to Captain Obvious again. Jump down into the mouth of the crocodile outcrop and collect the Score Bubbles and Prize Bubble holding the **Pigeon House Sticker**. After moving right and passing a Checkpoint, your sackperson comes across a frightening thing.

IT'S ALIVE!

SOMETIMES, THE CREATOR CURATORS LIKE TO PRETEND THEY ARE MAD SCIENTISTS AND TRY TO BRING OBJECTS TO LIFE. THEY DO THIS BY ADDING A CREATURE BRAIN, WHICH LOOKS QUITE A LOT LIKE A BUBBLE, TO AN OBJECT. THE RESULT IS A CREEPY MOVING CREATURE, JUST LIKE THE ONE YOU SEE IN FRONT OF YOU. THE CREATURE BRAIN TELLS THE OBJECT HOW IT SHOULD ACT, WHAT WAY IT SHOULD MOVE, AND SO ON. FOR MORE INFORMATION ABOUT CREATURE BRAINS, SEE THE ADVANCED CREATE A LEVEL SECTION.

A Little Help

When you pop a brain, you get a little boost into the air. Use this extra leverage to snag the dangling Prize Bubble containing the **Feathery Spiky Object**. There are other times  in LittleBigPlanet when it is necessary to get a little help from a creature in order to reach a higher bubble. So keep an eye out.

Don't Snap at Me!

Pop the creatures and keep moving to the right. More snapping crocodiles and oozing Hazardous Gas await you just up ahead. Make for  the fabric ball ahead and swing over to the next one. Land at the mouth of a little cave and head inside for a Two-Player Puzzle.

Grab the closest fabric ball and swing until you are between the two crocs. Let go, and drop to the ball of zebra fabric below. Now repeat this two more times. There are three Score Bubbles on each of the balls. It's difficult to get all of them, so just do the best you can. Hanging on the last ball, you dangle above three of those dangerous creatures. Land on the one in the middle, and then pop the creatures on either side.

TAKE TWO

LIKE THE SIGN AT THE CAVE ENTRANCE SAYS, THERE IS A TWO-PLAYER PUZZLE UP AHEAD. BEFORE THE TWO PLAYERS DO ANYTHING, ONE OF YOU NEEDS TO POP THE WANDERING CREATURE BELOW. NOW, HAVE PLAYER ONE STEP ON THE RED BUTTON ON THE HILL BEHIND THE CHECKPOINT. THIS LIFTS A DOOR ON THE RIGHT FOR PLAYER TWO TO PASS THROUGH. PLAYER TWO THEN MOVES THE CUBE OF ZEBRA MATERIAL UNDER THE DOOR, SO WHEN PLAYER ONE JUMPS OFF THE BUTTON, THE DOOR STAYS PROPPED OPEN.

*HAVE PLAYER TWO GRAB HOLD OF THE BALL HANGING OVERHEAD. THIS ACTION PULLS DOWN A LEDGE FAR ENOUGH THAT PLAYER ONE CAN JUMP ON IT. HE OR SHE CAN THEN CLIMB UP THE LEDGE AND COLLECT THE PRIZE BUBBLES THAT CONTAIN THE **TIGER NOSE DECORATION**, THE **ANTLERS COSTUME PIECE**, AND THE **MAHOGANY WOOD MATERIAL**.*

Head back to the snapping crocs and drop onto the platform between the first two. Maneuver down to the second platform (be sure to collect all the bubbles along the way) and grab the fabric ball ahead. Swing from ball to ball until you pass over the head of the croc to the right. Land safely in the small alcove and collect the Prize Bubble holding the **Cardboard Support Decoration**.

DIAMONDS ARE FOREVER

Down the path to the left, a little meerkat leads you to a Sticker Puzzle. Open Popit and select the Amazing Diamond Sticker found earlier in the level. Place the sticker on the Sticker Switch and receive two Prize Bubbles that contain the **Rock the Jungle Audio** and **Orange Stripy Costume**. Of course, there are loads of Score Bubbles, too.

53

Move to the right to find a tunnel of snappy crocs. A row of fabric balls leads down the center of the tunnel. If you can stick to the fabric balls, then you should make it out of this mess alive. But first, there is a Prize Bubble to retrieve.

Run and jump onto the fabric ball, and then quickly hop onto the croc to the right. Collect the Prize Bubble on its back that contains the **Croc King Object**. Once you have it, return to the fabric ball.

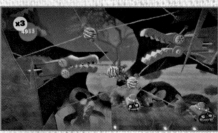

Just like before, grab the first ball and then drop to the next. Keep doing this until you reach the safety of the rocky platform below. While shimmying down between the crocs, another picture was taken and placed in your Photobooth.

Meerkat Attack!

You are finally on solid ground, but not for long. Pop the two wandering creatures to the right, and then use the balls of fabric to swing over another pit of gassy crocs. Don't forget to swing up to the Prize Bubble containing the **Attitude Face Sticker** before you drop to the ground. On the other side, you soon come across a group of angry meerkats attacking a crocodile.

The croc cries out to you, telling you that this Meerkat Mum thinks he ate her son, Stripy Tail. But the reptile swears he's been falsely accused. Maybe you can help solve this mystery as well. Hop on the Scoreboard to the right, and consider yourself on the job!

Story: Chapter 3

The Savannah
The Meerkat Kingdom

The dark underground tunnels the meerkats call home are quite different from the red hot fires of the Burning Forest. Allow some time for your eyes to adjust to this new mysterious place before you go out to find Meerkat Mum's missing son.

Prize Bubble Pick-Ups

Decorations
Brown Stripy Button	

✓ Objects
Big-Belly Meerkat	
Baby Meerkat	
Hanging Snapping Claw	
Jet Cheetah	
Meerkat Popup	
Snapping Claw	
Wooden Flamingo	
Wooden Zebra	

✓ Costume
Red Roman Cape	
Blue Circles Denim	

✓ Materials
Brown Wood
Carved Animals
Carved Heads
Engraved Metal
Green Felt
Orange Weave
Pink Knit
Wallpaper
Wooden Planks

✓ Audio
"My Patch"
"Savannah Int Music"

✓ Stickers
Bat Wing
Big Cute Nose
Birdy Outline
Black Animal Nose
Blue Fish
Blue Wing Graphic
Cat Head
Cow Head
Cow Udders
Crazed Donkey
Growl Face
Mr Beaver Says No
Orange Bird
Red Boy
Red Butterfly
Red Lobster
Rubber Duck
Scary Fangs
Scratch Pattern
Sleeping Elephant
White Butterfly

Level Complete Gifts
✓ Costume
Pink Scarf

Collected All Gifts
✓ Stickers
Red Wolves Concept	

✓ Objects
Red Wolves Concept with Frame	
Meerkat Mum & Scenery	

Aced Level Gifts
✓ Costume
Gold Monocle
Ringmaster Top Hat

Prize Bubble x1

Prize Bubbles x5
(Triggered by Switch)

Fluffy Tree
Switch Trigger

EXPLORE THE UNDERGROUND TUNNELS

THE ROAD LESS TRAVELED

As soon as you pop out of the Entrance Barrel, turn to the right. Although it looks like the path leads to nowhere, it actually takes you into a little cave, with a Sticker Puzzle inside. Open up Popit and select the Fluffy Tree Sticker you collected in Swinging Safari. As you line it up with the Sticker Switch, the walls all around it start to glow. This is a warning. Once the sticker is in place, those walls are going to crumble. But don't worry. The rocks actually fall into the Hazardous Gas pit in front of you, so you won't get hurt. Collect the five Prize Bubbles containing the **Orange Weave Material**, **Pink Knit Material**, **Green Felt Material**, and the **Brown Stripy Button Decoration**, and the **Blue Circles Denim Costume** that drop from above, and then return to the Entrance Barrel.

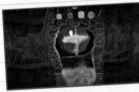

The First Step is a Doozy

Move to the left and pass the Close-Level Post. Ahead, two small meerkats are holding onto a Prize Bubble containing the **Baby Meerkats Object**. Looks like an easy target, except the meerkats get scared and hide when you approach. This sends the Prize Bubble tumbling down the steep tunnel just beyond the animals. Don't let it get away! Say a prayer and jump down after it.

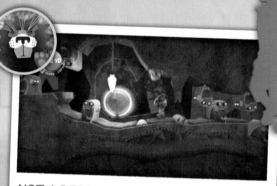

NOT A PEOPLE PERSON

MEERKATS ARE VERY SKITTISH. WHENEVER YOU GET TOO CLOSE, THEY MAKE A RUN FOR IT. THIS MAY SEEM RUDE AT FIRST, BUT IT IS ACTUALLY NOT A BAD THING. MANY TIMES, MEERKATS BLOCK YOUR PATH. WITH OTHER ANIMALS THIS WOULD BE A PROBLEM, BUT WITH THESE SKITTISH UNDERGROUND DWELLERS, YOU CAN JUST SCARE THEM OUT OF THE WAY.

Stumble and fumble down the steep slope until you hit the bottom. The ride down is triggered. Though the rocks may cause a few bruises, they are nothing to worry about; they disappear shortly after you land at the bottom of the first decline. Collect the runaway Prize Bubble, and don't forget to check your Photobooth later, to view a newly added picture of your descent.

Spelunking

Jump down the Score Bubble-lined tunnel to the right and continue the search for Stripy Tail. When you land on the bottom, it's time for a race.

Stand at the Start Gate and get ready to navigate some very narrow tunnels. Follow the trail of Score Bubbles to a labyrinth of little platforms, and collect all the Score Bubbles in sight. Don't worry about reaching a high score multiplier: the bubbles are too far apart to string one together.

There is plenty of time in this race, so take it easy and make sure you have gathered everything. Don't miss the hidden Prize Bubble that holds the **Carved Heads Material**. It's behind the small white material on the right side of the center platform.

You have to pull the material aside before gaining access to the bubble. After all the bubbles have been gathered, head for the Finishing Gate.

Do I Smell or Something?

Keep moving to the right. Soon you come across some more cute little meerkats. Don't they look like they'd be fun to pet? Of course, as soon as your sackperson gets close by, they dive underground. Sheesh, no love.

Walk past all the skittish creatures and pass a Checkpoint. Once you reach the alcove with tree branches sporting balls of zebra fabric, put on the brakes.

WHAT'S OVER HERE?

Ever get the feeling that those sweet innocent meerkats are hiding something? That's only because they are. Take the two meerkats in the upper right, for instance. Swing up to them using the highest tree branch, and you find that the little boogers were hiding three Prize Bubbles from you. The nerve. Grab the bubbles, which contain the **Cow Udders Sticker**, the **Cow Head Sticker**, and the **Crazed Donkey Sticker**.

Swing down to the bottom of the alcove. A load of meerkats are resting under you, hiding underground when you dip down too close for comfort. Why not give them a good scare and land right on top of them? When you are done teasing the meerkats, move to the left to head into a cave full of glorious bubbles.

Wasn't Expecting That

What a wonderful cave! There are bubbles everywhere! There is even a **Challenge Key**! But it's all out of your reach. Sigh. Better move on. But as soon as you step forward, you get launched into the air. Looking down, you can see that it was actually a meerkat who helped you. Now you can collect all the surrounding bubbles. Make sure to aim for the small ledge to the right and grab the Challenge Key and Prize Bubble containing the **My Patch Audio**.

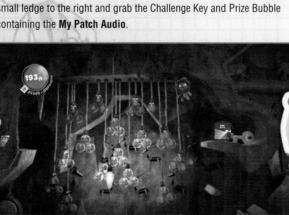

There are two other hidden meerkats who launch you into the air. Use the last one to reach the small ledge on the left and collect the three Prize Bubbles, which hold the **Mr Beaver Says No Sticker**, the **Rubber Duck Sticker**, and the **Carved Animals Material**.

Professional Swinger

Another little alcove with tree branches and balls of fabric lies ahead. By now you are a pro at swinging, so this next bit should be a piece of cake. Swing from the nearest branch to the one on the right. Now swing back to the ledge on the left and collect the Prize Bubble containing the **Growl Face Sticker**.

Grab the same branch and swing back to the right and land on the ledge there. Collect another Prize Bubble holding the **Cat Head Sticker**, then stand on the dissolving rock at the end of the ledge. This drops you down onto more bubbles, including a Prize Bubble, which holds the **Birdy Outline Sticker**. That should do it! Drop to the ground—watch out for the spikes—and head to the left for a Two-Player Puzzle

TAKE TWO

HAVE PLAYER ONE STAND ON THE LEFT EDGE OF THE PLATFORM TO CAUSE IT TO RISE UP. THIS ALLOWS PLAYER TWO ACCESS DOWN THE SMALL TUNNEL UNDER THE PLATFORM. NOW, HAVE PLAYER TWO MOVE TO THE LEFT AND GRAB THE BALL OF FABRIC TO AGAIN RISE UP THE PLATFORM. THIS ALLOWS PLAYER ONE TO JOIN PLAYER TWO IN THE LOWER CAVERN.

WALK OVER TO THE BLOCK OF ZEBRA FABRIC. HAVE PLAYER ONE PULL OUT THE BLOCK SO THAT PLAYER TWO CAN USE IT TO REACH THE UPPER LEDGE. ONCE PLAYER TWO STEPS ONTO THE LEDGE, A BLOCK OF ZEBRA FABRIC DROPS DOWN, ALLOWING PLAYER ONE TO REUNITE WITH PLAYER TWO. NOW THE TWO OF YOU CAN COLLECT THE FOUR PRIZE BUBBLES IN THE ALCOVE BEHIND THE LEDGE. SNAG THE RED ROMAN CAPE COSTUME, THE BLACK ANIMAL NOSE STICKER, THE ORANGE BLOCK STICKER, AND THE SCARY FANGS STICKER.

ZOLA

Belly Hop

The path to the right leads to two very large meerkats. These normally small creatures have grown to an unimaginable size. They are so large that their bellies stick out and they have to lie on their backs. Try jumping on the first meerkat's belly. Did you see that? When you jump on the stomach, the meerkat's head goes flying forward, shooting rocks into the air. If you have someone playing with you, one player could stand on the head while the other player jumps on the tummy. The player on the head could be launched up to the Prize Bubble containing the **Wooden Planks Material**.

If you are playing by yourself, then you're out of luck. There is no other way to reach that bubble.

UP WE GO!

If you have a partner who can launch you off the meerkats, then make sure to fly up to the small ledges located in the ceiling above the second meerkat. There are Score Bubbles up there, as well as a Prize Bubble containing the **Big-Belly Meerkat Object**.

Rocky Road

Up next is a really tricky jump. The jump isn't far, but the ground you land on is very unstable. In order to climb up the rocks and reach the Prize Bubble that holds the **Brown Wood Material**, you need to jump forward as soon as your little sack feet touch the rocky edge. If you fail in reaching the Prize Bubble before you slip down to the next ledge, then the bubble cannot be reached until you play the level again.

Stripy Tail

Prize Bubble x1
(Triggered by Switch)

Voodoo Face
Switch Trigger

Scoreboard

Prize Bubbles x2

Prize Bubbles x3
(Requires 2 Players)

Growl Face
Switch Trigger

Prize Bubble x1

Prize Bubbles x3

Challenge Key

Challenge Key
Prize Bubble x1

Meerkat Mum

Prize Bubbles x3

Not Worth Dying For

In many situations, if you mess up or miss your chance at snagging a hard-to-get bubble, you can try again by opening Popit and holding down the Retry icon. This sends you  to the last Checkpoint for another chance at what you missed. However, in cases like the Prize Bubble at the top of the rocky cliff, you only have one chance to reach it, and no amount of self-destruction is going to change that.

Meerkat Walk

Collect the Prize Bubble on the lower ledge, which holds the **Red Boy Sticker**, then grab the tree branch to the left. Swing down to the row of meerkats and avoid the spikes below. Strut down the catwalk of meerkats and collect all the Score Bubbles in sight.

An older brother-type meerkat stands at the end of the walkway. He's a little bigger than the typical meerkat, but he's not as large as the overgrown ones. Also, like a typical big brother, he's blocking your path. But this can work to your advantage. Hop onto the meerkat's head and

 jump into the little cave overhead. Collect the Prize Bubble inside, which contains the **Jet Cheetah Object**, and then move on.

Mama's House

You finally find Meerkat Mum. She can't help but ask what a no-fur like you is doing underground, but doesn't really complain. The mama

 meerkat has a proposition for you. Find her son, and she might let you pass through her domain. Sounds like a fair deal.

Swing over Meerkat Mum using the red lantern, and take note of the picture in the background. That darling in the glasses is Stripy Tail, the missing animal you are looking for. Follow the arrow to the left and seek him out.

Club Meerkat

First, you come across a stubborn meerkat who won't let you collect the lovely bunch of bubbles behind him unless you find Stripy Tail. Just another reason why you should find him!

Use the meerkat as a stepping stool and climb up to the next level. On the upper platform, you start to see some flashing spotlights. As you move forward to check it out, the music turns funky. Soon you enter a plush underground club, fully stocked with meerkat pole dancers, upholstered walls and lots of bubbles. Could Stripy Tail actually be in a place like this?

PUT ON A GROWL

Before you enter the club, take a peek inside the small alcove before the first cluster of bubbles on the upper platform. Step inside and head to the right to enter a small cave containing a Sticker Puzzle and a Prize Bubble that holds the **Sleeping Elephant Sticker**. Collect the Prize Bubble, then open Popit and select the Growl Face Sticker you found earlier in the level. Place it on the Sticker Switch to release a flow of Score Bubbles, as well as a Prize Bubble containing the **Hanging Snapping Claw Object**.

Before searching for Stripy Tail, why not enjoy yourself a little bit? But going clubbing all by yourself isn't fun, right? So grab a friend and let loose!

TWO, PLEASE

TO GET THE FULL CLUB EXPERIENCE, YOU NEED TO HAVE A FRIEND WITH YOU. USE THE TWO OVERGROWN MEERKATS LYING ON THE GROUND TO LAUNCH EACH OTHER INTO THE AIR AND COLLECT ALL THE SHINING BUBBLES DECORATING THE SCENE. MAKE SURE TO GET THE PRIZE BUBBLE THAT CONTAINS THE **RED LOBSTER STICKER**. IT'S HANGING IN THE AIR NEAR THE CLUB ENTRANCE. ALSO, DON'T MISS THE TWO PRIZE BUBBLES ON EITHER SIDE OF THE OUTCROPPING NEAR THE CEILING ON THE LEFT SIDE OF THE CLUB. ONE CONTAINS THE **BLUE FISH STICKER** AND THE OTHER ONE HOLDS THE **BIG CUTE NOSE STICKER**. USE THE MEERKAT TUCKED INTO THE RIGHT UPPER WALL AS A STEPPING BLOCK TO REACH THAT HARD-TO-GET BUBBLE ON THE LEFT SIDE OF THE OUTCROPPING.

Scandalous

Move to the left side of the club to meet a meerkat bouncer. This tough-looking character blocks off a side path that leads to a Challenge Key. This must be a VIP section. For now, just use the meerkat as a steeping stool to reach the elevated path.

Ahead, you finally find Stripy Tail. But he's not alone. No, the scandalous little meerkat is in a little room with five lady meerkats. My, my. Don't bother asking questions, just grab Stripy Tail and head for the exit.

Make a stop by the meerkat bouncer. As you approach with Stripy Tail, the bouncer steps down. Looks like Mr. Missing Son is on the VIP list. Use this connection to sneak in and collect the Score Bubbles and Prize Bubble containing the **Wooden Flamingo Object**. Return to Stripy Tail and keep moving to the exit.

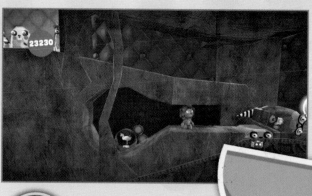

DO YOU SENSE THAT?

SOMETIMES YOU ARE REQUIRED TO DRAG AN OBJECT OR CREATURE AROUND WITH YOU TO COMPLETE A TASK. MANY TIMES, THESE OBJECTS AND CREATURES HAVE SENSORS ON THEM THAT ALLOW SPECIAL PASSAGEWAYS AND DOORS TO OPEN. USUALLY YOU ARE GIVEN INSTRUCTION ON WHAT THE OBJECT OR CREATURE OPENS, BUT SOMETIMES YOU HAVE TO FIGURE IT OUT FOR YOURSELF, LIKE IN THE CASE OF THE MEERKAT BOUNCER.

Returning Home

Keep dragging Stripy Tail until you are just out of the club. At the entrance, stand on top of Stripy Tail to reach the clusters of Score Bubbles hanging from the ceiling. When you're finished, drop to the lower level with Stripy Tail in tow. Remember that stubborn meerkat who wouldn't let you pass without Stripy Tail? Now that you have the runaway with you, the meerkat stands down and lets you collect the Prize Bubble, which holds the **Snapping Claw Object**, and Score Bubbles. There's also

the **Savannah Int Music Audio Object** right next to it. When you're done, take Stripy Tail back to his mother.

How to Make a Meerkat Fly

Stripy Tail is a little bit on the heavy side, and it can be difficult to drag him up the steps to the club's exit. Use the oversized meerkats to launch Stripy Tail over the steps and through the exit.

Meerkat Mum is so thankful that her son is back at home that she lets you pass through her domain. The large door she was holding up is now open for you to walk through. On the other side is a pile of Score Bubbles along with three Prize Bubbles that contain the **Wooden Zebra Object**, the **Wallpaper Material**, and the **Engraved Metal Material**.

Going Up?

Head right and jump across the small pit of spikes. At the end of the path you come across a hidden meerkat. As you pass over it, the meerkat pops you up into the air. You land on a second floor, which has a few Score Bubbles and another hidden meerkat to the right. Step on this meerkat to be launched to the third floor, where there are more Score Bubbles and yet another hidden meerkat. Land over the same meerkat to then fly up to the **Challenge Key** located way overhead. Land on the third floor and pass over

its meerkat to be launched to the fourth floor. Grab the Prize Bubble containing the **Scratch Pattern Sticker** and uncover the hidden meerkat. Use this last meerkat, and the three above it, to jump up to the topmost floor, where there are two Prize Bubbles and a secret Sticker Puzzle area. Collect the bubbles to receive the **Red Butterfly Sticker** and **White Butterfly Sticker**.

VOODOO MAGIC

On the topmost floor, turn to the left and enter a small alcove to find a Sticker Puzzle. Open Popit and select the Voodoo Face Sticker you collected in Swinging Safari. Place it on the Sticker Switch to release a Prize Bubble containing the **Meerkat Popup Object** from a hidden passage.

From the top floor, move to the right and slide down the small tunnel to reach a lower level. Pass by a Checkpoint and collect any bubbles in the area. Use the hidden meerkat to the right to launch up to the next level.

Collect the clusters of Score Bubbles on this floor, and use the final hidden meerkat to reach the last floor.

Vertigo

The last meerkat actually launches you up to the orange hill on top of the final floor. Collect all the Score Bubbles you can reach, then drop down

one plane to grab the three Prize Bubbles containing the **Bat Wing Sticker**, the **Orange Bird Sticker**, and the **Blue Wing Graphic Sticker**.

Just like a Trampoline

Did you notice the Score Bubbles above the orange hill that looked impossibly out of reach? In reality, they are quite easy to collect; you just need to know how to jump up there. Launching mechanisms, like the hidden meerkats, act like a trampoline. Dropping down on them with greater momentum provides greater lift when you launch back off. So, a little hop onto a hidden meerkat results in a short hop. However, when you jump down from something as tall as the orange hill, the meerkat sends you flying. Use this to reach the sky-high Score Bubbles.

Case Closed

With your two soft feet back on solid ground, walk over to one of Zola's monkeys, who is located on the right. He thanks you for your hard work and asks you one last favor: could you help save his friend's wedding? Why not? You're up for it, aren't you? Just step on the Scoreboard to end the level, then take the tunnel and ask for Frida.

The Savannah
Mini Levels!

Flaming Seesaws

RUN AND JUMP ALONG THE SEESAWS OVER FIERY OBSTACLES

How to Unlock: Collect the Key in Burning Forest

Wild Fire

The Savannah is on fire, and not in the good way. In the Flaming Seesaws Challenges, your objective is to get through the course of seesaws as fast as you can without getting burned by the fire pits or the obstacles. There are no bubbles of any kind and no hidden secrets to worry about.

Although it has seesaws like the Castle Climb Challenge, these races are pretty different. You don't have to worry about climbing up a building. Instead, you have to deal with pits of fiery doom. Don't let that get you down, though! You have a whole 60 seconds to navigate the Easy version of the Challenge, 90 seconds for the Medium version, and 120 seconds for the Hard version. Remember,

you must first complete the Easy version before you can take on the Medium one. In turn, you have to complete the Medium one to tackle the Hard Challenge.

General Tips

Take your time when going over the seesaws. You often need the incline to move to the other side of the seesaw. If you rush

across, this won't happen, and you won't have the ramp leading up to the next obstacle.

Remember that touching the fire isn't an instant kill. So if you accidentally fall into the flames, you still have a chance. After

you hit the Hazardous Material, get your little sack tush in gear and just hop out of the flames.

There is more than one way to get the incline you want from a seesaw. Make use of the fabric spheres on the ends of the seesaws and pull down the side you want resting on the ground. This is very useful, and at times necessary, in the Medium and Hard versions of the Challenge.

In the Hard Challenge, there is a pinball flipper that sends you flying into the air. Make the most of this altitude and soar over the next section of fiery obstacles. You should be able to land on the fire-free platform and continue the race with the most difficult section behind you.

Tunnel Plunge

PLUNGE HEADLONG THROUGH THE TUNNEL, AVOIDING THE SPIKES

How to Unlock: Collect the Key in The Meerkat Kingdom

Watch Out Below

The Meerkat Kingdom is a maze of interweaving tunnels, and the Tunnel Plunge Challenge is a prime example of the meerkat's digging abilities.

This is not a straight dive to the bottom; this is a journey of winding S-curves, unstable platforms, spinning rocks, and spike-covered corners.

There are Score Bubbles along the race route. Collecting these bubbles stops the timer for a bit, giving you a little extra wiggle room. But with only 60 seconds on the clock, you don't have much time to make mistakes. So get ready to jump over the edge and into the meerkat's favorite race!

Meerkat Bounce

BOUNCE ON THE MEERKATS AND AVOID THE FIERY COALS

How to Unlock: Collect the Key in The Meerkat Kingdom

Just Bounce with Me

In the Meerkat Bounce Challenge, the objective is to use the meerkats to fly up into the air and collect the Score Bubbles overhead. There is no timer to worry about, but there are clusters of fiery coals that like to throw you off your bubble-collecting groove. As long as you avoid them, you can keep gathering Score Bubbles to your heart's content. So what are you waiting for? Press the red button to begin and start grabbing bubbles!

General Tips

Bouncing is fun, but soaring too high can be dangerous and cause you to miss a lot of bubbles passing below you. Try to keep your bounces steady and even for optimal bubble collecting.

The bubbles come in from both the right and left sides of the screen. Wait for a large number of them to enter the area. Then, bounce to collect a long string of bubbles all at once and gain a score multiplier.

After a while, Venus Flytrap-like creatures come swaying into the scene. When they open their mouths, a fiery coal drops out. Your first instinct is probably to jump over them. In actuality, it's safer to jump under them. If you try to go over, you have to get really high in the air since they are taller than the other objects so far. In addition to this, you have to make sure you properly clear the patch of fire at the top of the creature. Save yourself the hassle, and just jump under them when their mouths are closed.

General Tips

Just go for it. Right from the get-go, you are moving downhill at full speed. Don't try to over think the racecourse; it wastes too much time. Instead, just go with the flow and try to get to the Finish Gate as quickly as you can.

Use the tree branches with the zebra fabric on the end. They're there for a reason, so grab hold and leap forward to avoid obstacles.

Keep to the center of the tunnel. The spikes are located in the corners of the tunnel and can easily be avoided by staying in the center. Remember this tip when you reach the spinning rocks. They try to fling you to the corners, but don't let them!

Mini Levels!

ZOLA

FRIDA

The Wedding

Bienvenido mi amigos! You've arrived at The Wedding, where the lovely Frida is about to enter into nuptials with her longtime fiancé, Don Lu. Unfortunately, in addition to the fact that everyone in the wedding party is muy, muy muerto, you'll soon discover that all is not right, and these forlorn lovers need some help if the wedding day is to go on.

Prepare to explore dark catacombs with the help of a sackperson's best friend (Don Lu's faithful dog, that is), traverse across many deathly hazards, traps, and pitfalls, and stay one step ahead of the fury of a spurned bride and her Skulldozer contraption. Didn't your mother ever tell you not to get in the middle of a lover's quarrel?

Story: Chapter 1

The Wedding
The Wedding Reception

After playing with the meerkats and tunneling all the way from The Savannah, you've finally made it to Frida's wedding. But it doesn't look like everyone is having a good time. What could be the problem?

Materials
- [x] Basket
- [ ] Bevel Concrete
- [ ] Blue Glass
- [ ] Brown Glass
- [ ] Green Glass
- [ ] Purple Glass
- [ ] Red & Gold Cutout Wood
- [ ] Red Glass

Stickers
- [ ] Big Chin Skeleton
- [ ] Bowler Hat
- [ ] Calavera the Wrestler
- [ ] Confused Skull
- [ ] Green Skulls
- [ ] Half Moon
- [ ] Huge Eye
- [ ] Psycho Bunny
- [ ] Purple Skull Torso
- [ ] Purple Stuff
- [ ] Red Coffin
- [ ] Red Cross
- [ ] Saint
- [ ] Skeleton Hat
- [ ] Standing Skeleton

Decorations
- [ ] Bow Tie
- [ ] Glasses
- [ ] Lower Teeth
- [ ] Plastic Ear
- [ ] Plastic Mustache
- [ ] Plastic Nose
- [ ] Springy Arm
- [ ] White Flower
- [ ] Wobbly Leg
- [ ] Yellow Dandelions
- [ ] Yellow Flower

Level Complete Gifts

- [x] **Costume**
  - Fairy Dress
  - Rainbow Dot

Collected All Gifts

- [x] **Stickers**
  - Wrestling Ring Concept

- [x] **Objects**
  - Wrestling Ring Concept with Frame

Aced Level Gifts

- [x] **Costume**
  - Wooden Sword

HELP FRIDA LIVE HAPPILY EVER AFTER

Runaway Groom!

Bienvenidos! But wait, you don't have the proper wedding attire, do you? Luckily, Frida has set out some clothes for you to try on and wear. Grab the eight Costume-filled Prize Bubbles just to the right of the Entrance Barrel. Included in the mix are the **Zombie Boy**, **Zombie Girl**, **Top Hat**, **Wedding Veil**, **Red Wig**, **White Wedding Dress**, **Black Tuxedo**, and **Black Bow Tie Costumes**.

But wait! Alas, the wedding day has gone awry. Frida's groom, Don Lu, has gone missing. It's up to you to find the missing groom and bring him back to Frida's open arms.

Prize Bubble Pick-Ups

Costume
Black Tuxedo
Bow Tie
Farmer's Cap
Red Wig
Straw
Top Hat
Wedding Veil
White Wedding Dress
Fuzzy Scribble
Zombie Boy
Zombie Girl

Objects	
Balloon Launcher	
Bowler-Hatted Skeleton	
Dismembered Hand	
Large Balloon	
Little Butler	
Medium Balloon	
Screaming Skull	
Skeleton Talking Head	

Objects	
Skull Bungee Cord	
Skull Lift	
Small Balloon	
Spiked Screaming Skull	
Stained Glass Bouncy Platform	
Teeter Platform	
Tilting Stained Glass Window	
Wavy Davy Skeleton	

FRIDA

Audio
"Volver a Comenzar"

Prize Bubbles x8

Prize Bubbles x3

Prize Bubbles x2
(Triggered by Switch)

Skeleton Hat
Switch Trigger

Prize Bubbles x4

Prize Bubble x1

Start your quest by entering the skeleton's mouth and dropping down to the platform to the right, avoiding the spikes below in the process. In order to grab the Score and Prize Bubbles atop the platforms along this hallway, jump up and grab the basket material in the middle of each, causing the platforms to teeter and tip over, proffering their goods in the process. You can find the **Bevel Concrete Material**, the **Basket Object**, the **Red & Gold Cutout Wood Material**, and the **Teeter Platform Object inside**.

Jump for Joy!

That suspended platform down to the right not only supports your weight, it also can spring you high into the air if you time your jumps properly. Leap onto it and wait for it to spring upward. As it reaches its maximum height, press ✕ to bounce along with it, just like a trampoline. If you can manage to successfully do this multiple times in a row, your jumping power becomes higher and higher. This is the key to collecting the goodies

inside the Prize Bubbles, which include the **Purple Glass Material**, the **Big Stained Glass Window Object**, and the **Red Glass Material**. Just watch out for those spikes below!

The Wedding Reception

69

HATS OFF!

Use the springboard to launch yourself up to the suspended ledge holding the Prize Bubble with the Red Glass Material. From here, jump across to the high platform to the right to locate a Sticker Puzzle. You soon get the required Skeleton Hat Sticker, in mere moments. When you do, return back here, and use it to reveal two skeleton heads containing two Decorations: the **Plastic Mustache** and **Lower Teeth**.

Watch out for the roving butler on the platform below. He isn't too happy you're tracking dirt all over the floor on the big wedding day. You can send him packing with a well-jumped hop onto his exposed Creature Brain when he opens his mouth. Just make sure you time your jump so the brain is not crackling with lethal electricity (it cycles between lethal and non-lethal every time he opens his mouth), and avoid being launched up into the spikes along the roof.

Leap across and grab the goodie inside the Prize Bubble atop the teetering platform—the **Little Butler Object**.

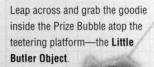

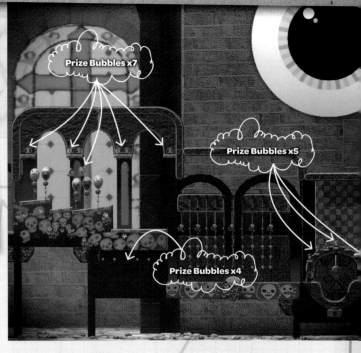

Balloons Away!

Soon inside the wedding hall, you come across some festive balloons secured to the ground by Score Bubbles. You can jump up and grab hold of the basket material underneath the balloon to burst the bubble and float into the air. Just out of sight, up on platforms high above the floor, are a series of Prize Bubbles containing Stickers and one Object. To get all seven, hang on and use the balloons to float up above. Collect them all to receive the **Skeleton Hat Switch Trigger Sticker**, the **Confused Skull Sticker**, the **Red Cross Sticker**, the **Green Skulls Sticker**, the **Standing Skeleton Sticker**, the **Saint Sticker**, and the **Balloon Launcher Object**.

Leaps of Faith

There are a total of five balloons to use to grab all of the goodies above. Once one has been freed from its tether, it floats to the top and does not come back down. However, you only really need one or two, tops. Once you float up to the ceiling and have dropped onto a platform, you can run and leap across to any of the others. There's little room for error, but if you jump just as you reach the end of each platform, you can make it to the next!

Spring into Action!

Jump into this next Score Bubble-filled chamber and prepare to be flung around while hanging onto cloth balls attached to springy, elastic, bungee material. If you let go or fall off one of the bungee balls while attempting to grab another, you can use the protruding skull platform on the ground to launch yourself back into the air. Like the springy platform you encountered earlier, if you jump just as the skull launches you into the air, you can get high enough to grab onto the suspended balls.

Precarious Position

These Prize Bubble-laden steps are not secured by any material, which causes them to fall off the pegs they're resting on when you touch them.

However, with patience and precision, you can quickly hop across as they become unstable, or use the pegs they're resting on to jump from one to the other if they fall off and dissolve. If you fall off and drop into the pit below, use the red button on the floor to launch yourself up to the hanging basket material and swing on out!

RUBBER BAND, AID!

To get into the small opening in the wall on the left, hang from the last, leftmost cloth ball and then press to the left on the left stick as you spring up and down until you can drop inside the opening. There are a handful of Object-filled Prize Bubbles in here, including the **Skeleton Talking Head**, the **Bowler-Hatted Skeleton**, the **Tilting Stained Glass Window**, and the **Skeleton Hand**.

To get onto the series of collapsing steps to the right of the Checkpoint, hang from the last, rightmost bungee ball and then press to the right on the left stick as you spring up and down until you can drop onto the first step.

For your efforts you receive the **Huge Eye Switch Trigger Sticker**, the **Green Glass Material**, the **Skull Bungee Cord Object**, the **Brown Glass Material**, and the **Blue Glass Material**.

Prize Bubble x1

Prize Bubbles x3

Prize Bubble x1 (Triggered by Switch)

Huge Eye Switch Trigger

Prize Bubbles x2 (Requires 2 Players)

Butler Bash

Enter into the next hallway and continue to move to the right. You can ride atop the roving butlers' snapping heads in order to grab the Score Bubbles above. In fact, make sure you ride the second butler all the way to the right, and then jump and grab the cloth ball at the end. Doing so causes it to release a Prize Bubble with the **Spiked Screaming Skull Object** inside.

Two Sack People are Better than One

Just past the area with the butlers is a small chamber containing a Two-Player Puzzle. The key to the puzzle is to work together to bring down the platform with the dangling cloth balls on the right side of the chamber in order to reach the hanging cloth ball attached to the skeleton head floating high above.

Start by grabbing the lowest cloth ball and use your weight to lower the platform down the tiniest bit. While player one is hanging onto the first cloth ball, player two should grab the second, lowering the platform even more than before. Continue this process until you can finally reach the fourth cloth ball at the end of the platform. Have player one grab and hold onto it, and then player two should release his or her grip, allowing player one to swing up and reach the goal. Grab the final cloth ball above to open the skeleton's mouth. The goodies for your troubles include the **Volver a Comenzar Audio Object**, **Straw Costume**, and the **Farmer's Cap Costume**.

Take the High Road

Use the skeleton platform to launch yourself up to the next level. Approaching the skeleton heads along this walkway causes their mouths to open wide, revealing a mouthful of Score Bubbles. Stepping into the third skeleton head tosses you into the air. Instead of pressing to the right to leap up to the next level, press the left stick to the left, and grab the **Screaming Skull Object** inside the Prize Bubble.

I'VE GOT MY HUGE EYE STICKER ON YOU

Want that Prize Bubble suspended inside the box over the middle skeleton's head? In order to get to it, you need to use the Huge Eye Sticker, which you should have acquired when hopping across those precarious platforms just a few moments ago, to solve a Sticker Puzzle. Slap the Huge Eye Sticker on the middle skeleton's left eye to cause the Prize Bubble to drop. You're rewarded with the **Fuzzy Scribble Costume**!

Ride the skeletons' mouths higher and higher until you reach the last one. Instead of hopping off onto the platform to the right, ride the final mouth almost all the way up to the top and then leap off to the right, aiming for the high ledge. From here, hop onto the skeleton head to the left and burst the Prize Bubble. Collect the bubble to receive **Skull Lift Object,** and then hop across the skeletons' heads to the right to collect more Prize Bubbles. You gain the **Bow Tie**, **Plastic Nose**, **Plastic Ear**, and **Glasses Decorations**.

FRIDA

GOODIE GRAB BAG

There are a ton of Prize Bubbles and a **Challenge Key** in this next area waiting to be discovered. To get the batch of five Prize Bubbles in the small catacomb below, carefully drop down off the platform to the right of the Checkpoint and immediately press to the left as you begin to fall. Snag the **Red Coffin**, **Big Chin Skeleton**, **Half Moon**, **Top Hat**, and **Calavera the Wrestler Stickers** from inside the bubble.

Grabbing the Prize Bubbles above requires patience and timing. As you did earlier, hop onto each spring-loaded platforms and jump just as it launches you into the air. Continue to successfully do this a few times in a row to get high enough to grab your prizes. Up here, you get the **Yellow Dandelions**, **Yellow Flower**, **White Flower**, **Wobbly Legs**, and **Springy Arm Decorations**. The key is above the last platform, way up high, and it unlocks a Score Challenge.

Crossing this next area requires you to jump from spring platform to spring platform. Be careful not to fall off and plummet to the spikes below! If you do happen to have a misstep, aim for the skeleton heads in between the spikes, as they can give you a second-chance push back to the platforms above.

Cross the bridge and hop from skeleton head to skeleton head to continue to ascend through the level. Grab the **Small Balloon Object** inside the Prize Bubble in between the two heads, and make sure to jump onto the left platform when you reach the top. Look out for a few more Prize Bubbles up here; these contain the **Psycho Bunny**, **Purple Skull Torso**, and **Purple Stuff Stickers**.

TOP HAT TOUCHDOWN!

While you're up here, why not leap over to the very large and fancy waving skeleton's top hat to the left? The top hat holds three Prize Bubbles and a **Challenge Key** along the brim and top. The key unlocks a Survival Challenge, and the Prize Bubbles contain the **Disco'n'Tinued Audio** and the **Wavy Davy Skeleton Object**. To get the one on top of his hat, carefully move over to the right edge of the brim and jump up when the skeleton tilts its hat to the right.

There are two more Prize Bubbles containing the **Medium Balloon** and **Small Balloon Objects** mixed in with the Score Bubbles up in the air to the right. Use the second of the two skeleton heads to reach them.

Don Lu and the Dark Crypts

Poor Frida can be found up along this walkway, crying her eyes out for her beloved Don Lu. She's heard he went underground into the dark crypts, and needs you to find him. Of course you will! Step in front of the Scoreboard to wrap up this area, and then depart for The Darkness.

The Wedding Reception

73

Story: Chapter 2

The Wedding
The Darkness

Descend into the heart of darkness to find Frida's groom. What could that Don Lu be up to, leaving his lovely bride at a time like this? You better find him and set him straight!

Decorations ✓

Grey Ghost	
Skeleton Arm	
Skeleton Leg	
Skeleton Torso	
Skull	

Materials ✓

Ceramic Mosaic	
Metal Skull Plate	

Level Complete Gifts

✓	**Costume**
	Pink Fairy Wings
	Pink Dot

Collected All Gifts

✓	**Stickers**
	Themed Characters Concept

✓	**Objects**
	Themed Characters Concept with Frame

Aced Level Gifts

✓	**Costume**
	Roman Armor

WHO TURNED THE LIGHTS OUT?! FIND FRIDA'S GROOM DON LU IN THE DARK!

Sackboy's Best Friend

It's dark and spooky down in the catacombs, but luckily, Don Lu's faithful dog is nearby. He carries a light and follows you to light up the path ahead. He can even give you a ride if you hop on his back.

Leap on the furry canine and go for a ride, collecting the Score Bubbles on the ledges found along the path.

PLAY DEAD

YOU CAN MAKE DON LU'S DOG MOVE FORWARD AND BACKWARD BASED ON YOUR PROXIMITY. IF YOU'RE IN FRONT OF THE DOG OR RIDING ON TOP OF IT (POSITIONED NEAR THE MIDDLE OR CENTER), IT MOVES FORWARD. IF YOU'RE BEHIND IT (OR ON OR NEAR ITS RUMP), IT MOVES BACKWARD. YOU CAN ALSO RIDE ON THE DOG'S BACK AND USE IT TO TRAVERSE HAZARDS, SUCH AS SPIKES.

Prize Bubble Pick-Ups

Objects

✓		
	Bull Skull	
	Christmas Light	
	Deadly Bat	
	Fairy Light	
	Picture Frame	
	Red Candle	
	Seated Skeleton	
	Small LED Light	
	Sugar Bone	
	Sugar Skull	
	Torn Cloth	

Stickers

✓	
	Blue Piñata Motif
	Cartoon Bone
	Flower Frame
	Green Piñata Motif
	Piñata Dog
	Pink Piñata Motif
	Pixel Skull
	Purple & Orange Piñata Motif
	Purple Piñata Motif
	Purple Skull Arm
	Purple Skull Skirt
	Red Piñata Motif
	Skeleton Hand
	Skeleton Hip Bone
	Spotty Skull Leg

Costume

✓	
	Cyclops Eye
	Pink Star Sunglasses
	Brown Leather
	Bunny

Audio

✓	
	"The Appliance of Science"

FRIDA

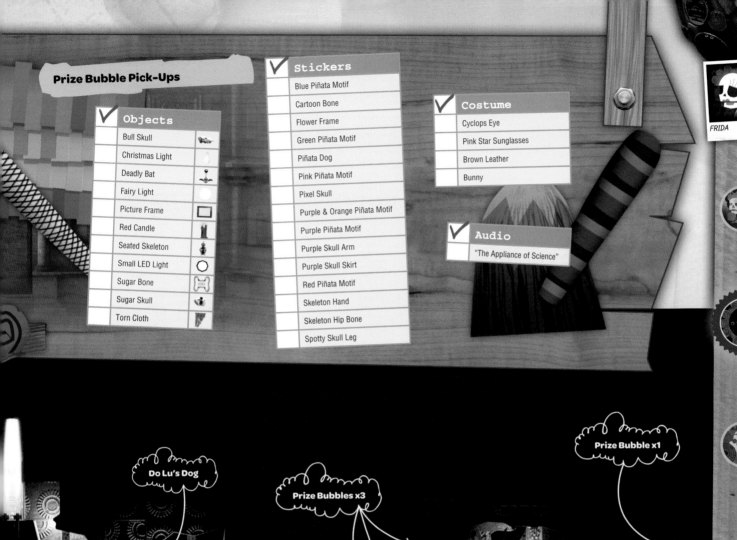

Ride Don Lu's dog across the first small set of spikes and then over the next larger spiked pit. While riding across this set, hop off into the back plane to grab the two Prize Bubbles set in the wall. Don't be tempted to jump into the space between the bubbles, as there are spikes here! Collect the bubbles to receive the **Bull Skull** and **Seated Skeleton Objects**.

As the dog begins to climb up the small slope, leap off to the left in order to grab the Prize Bubble with the **Ceramic Mosaic Material** inside.

Don Lu's dog needs help to get up to the next platform. Hop off its back and jump up to the ledge, then grab the spongy material at the base of this wooden plank and push/pull it to create a ramp for the dog to climb.

Separation Anxiety

Don't be fooled by that innocuous looking-hallway along the top path; it's filled with lethal gas! The safe path is down below. Hop off Don Lu's dog and traverse the lower section while the dog continues along the top.

Be sure to proceed slowly enough so the path is lit in front of you; there is a trio of spike pits along its length. Once you've been reunited with Don Lu's dog, make sure to grab the Prize Bubble and its contents, sitting precariously at the edge of the gaseous hallway. The **Grey Ghost Decoration** is inside.

Down, Boy!

When not riding on Don Lu's dog—and especially when you want to grab a Score or Prize Bubble near a hazard—stand in the back or front planes in order to avoid accidentally getting pushed or knocked into a hazard.

Dead End?

Continue to ride atop Don Lu's Dog's back, making sure to grab the three Prize Bubbles on the pedestals along the path. Collect them all to gain the **Skeleton Hand**, **Skeleton Hip Bone**, and **Cartoon Bone Stickers**.

When you reach the small wall and cannot go any farther with Don Lu's dog, hop off, and leap up to the ledge overhead. The lever up here can be pulled, which raises the platform the dog is standing on. Up top, use the extra height of the dog's back to leap over to the alcove to the left to grab the two Prize Bubbles up here. These bubbles host the **Pixel Skull Sticker** and the **Christmas Light Object**.

The Wedding Crasher

Make sure you leap off Don Lu's dog before reaching the trap door inside this next room. Oh, did we forget to mention the trap door? The poor pup is gobbled up and swept away by a mischievous little man known as The Collector, leaving you to fend for yourself in this dark, dank place.

Ride the skeleton lift upwards, walking off of one platform to another in order to avoid the jagged, spiky teeth inside the roof of each mouth.

HIDDEN SECRETS!

There are a handful of goodies tucked away here and there nearby. To grab the first one, ride the third and final platform of the skeleton lift, and press right on the analog stick as you ascend. There is a semi-hidden opening along the wall that leads to a small alcove. Inside lies a Prize Bubble containing the **Skull Decoration**.

To grab the other Prize Bubble atop the final skeleton head, ascend the final lift and then jump off and up to the left as it nears the top, avoiding the spikes yet quickly pressing to the right on the left stick in order to land on top of the head. It may take a few attempts, but grabbing the **Picture Frame Object** inside is worth the effort.

But wait; there's more! Repeat the jump off the last skeleton platform, this time leaping to the left and grabbing the dangling skeleton head. From here, swing across to the left and drop down onto this tucked-away ledge to find a Prize Bubble containing **"The Appliance of Science" Audio**, as well as a **Challenge Key** that unlocks a Score Challenge.

The final three Prize Bubbles are behind the lattices, just past the next Checkpoint. You can find two of them on either side of the first candle. Hop to the back plane and grab each, being careful not to get snuffed out by the candle's flickering flame. The last one is behind the lattice next to

the second candle. You get three Decoration items—the **Skeleton Arm**, **Skeleton Leg**, and **Skeleton Torso Decorations**.

Those dangling bats are not of the friendly sort. One touch from their lethal bodies sends your sackperson to the great beyond. Dash underneath each as it's rising upward in order to avoid contact. Stop as precisely as you can in between them to grab the **Deadly Bat Object** inside the Prize Bubble hovering overhead.

Carefully traverse this hazard-filled obstacle course, taking your time to cross each pitfall. Wait for the spiked platform to lower before leaping across. Duck underneath the next dangling bird, then jump and grab the hanging skeleton head and swing across the spiked pit to safely reach the other side.

The next spiked pit may look intimidating, but grabbing the skeleton head allows you to ride it across, grabbing the Score and Prize Bubbles along the way. You gain the **Small LED Light Object** item for your troubles.

Prize Bubbles x3
(Requires 2 Players)

Prize Bubbles x2
(Requires 2 Players)

Prize Bubble x1

Prize Bubbles x3

Don Lu

Don Lu, Where are You?

Hop across the small set of spikes to snag the **Red Candle Object** inside the Prize Bubble, and drop down into the next area. There are three more Prize Bubbles containing Stickers down here, just off in the darkness to the left. These Stickers are the **Purple Skull Skirt**, **Purple Skull Arm**, and **Spotty Skull Leg**.

Grab hold of the large sponge block set in the alcove and drag it backwards, revealing the **Sugar Skull Object** inside this Prize Bubble. When you're ready, use the steps to the left to get on top of the sponge. Then, use the sponge to get up to the next ledge. Above, leap over the spiked platform while it's lowering. Grab the Prize Bubble to gain the **Metal Skull Plate Material,** then drop down into this next chamber to find Don Lu, the missing groom.

Don Lu regales you with his sad story of how he became lost and too exhausted to continue on. The only way he can be reunited with his darling Frida is for you to grab hold of him and take him back. Before you do, it's time to grab a friend for a quick distraction.

Are you the rescue party? I got lost and I'm too exhausted to walk another step. Grab hold of me and take me back to my darling Frida!
● Close

Double Trouble

This next area is a Two-Player Puzzle. Grab a friend, and then both of you should grab hold and ride the dangling skeleton head up to the opening to the left. Repeat again with the next skeleton head to get up to the next hallway. Up here, player one needs to hop onto the small block in the back plane, and then player two should jump up and grab the nearby dangling skeleton head to cause the block to rise, allowing player one to hop up to the higher block to the left.

Up here, jump and grab the sponge ball and press to the left, using your momentum to ride it over the set of raising/lowering spiked platforms. In order to collect the Stickers inside the Prize Bubbles, you need to drop down on them from above, which means you must repeat the process three times. However, you receive the **Red Piñata Motif**, **Green Piñata Motif**, and **Blue Piñata Motif Stickers** for the extra effort.

Continue on the Two-Player quest. Player one must navigate the spiked obstacle course below in alignment with player two riding the sponge from above. This must be done together in order for the rider above to light the way. Otherwise, it's just too dark to see the hazards ahead. Once the two of you are on the other side, player two should drop and stand on the button located on the ledge above. Stepping on this button raises a gate, allowing player one to walk underneath. You'll discover a booty of Prize Bubbles inside the chamber beyond, which contain the **Flower Frame Sticker**, and the **Cyclops Eye** and **Pink Star Sunglasses Costumes**.

To escape this chamber of doom, hop up the stone blocks and push the skeleton head off of the ledge and down onto the button where player two is waiting. Return the way you came and head back to Don Lu!

Ball and Chain – Part 1

Don Lu is pretty helpless, but you shouldn't hold it against the poor chap; it is his wedding day, you know. You can start helping him out by dragging/pushing him to the right until he reaches the raised spike pit. Next, leave him be for a moment, and carefully jump, grab, swing, and ride the set of three skeleton heads across the spike pit to get to the other side. The lever here can and should be pulled, which extends a slab of the floor across the pit over the spikes. You now have a safe route to drag Don Lu across. Go get him!

Bring Don Lu into this next room and move him up the small ramp until he can go no farther. Leave him once again and hop onto the button above, which causes a spring trigger to launch Don Lu up onto the platform where you're standing.

FRIDA

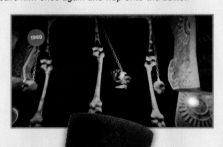

Gruesome Twosome

Before dragging ol' Don Lu into the next room, grab a buddy once more for another Two-Player Puzzle. First, have player one drop down onto the spring trigger used to launch Don Lu moments ago. Next, have player two hop onto the button, causing the trigger to activate. Player one is too heavy to be launched high enough in the air to reach the Prize Bubbles in the alcove above. However, with the correct timing of a jump (just as the trigger launches forward) you should get that extra "oomph" to reach it. Up here, you find the **Sugar Bone Object** and the **Torn Cloth Object**.

The Darkness

79

Ball and Chain – Part 2

Continue to drag Don Lu into the next room. While you're at it, use him to get up and into the small ledges containing the Prize Bubbles. The bubbles contain the **Piñata Dog**, **Blue Piñata Motif**, **Pink Piñata Motif**, and **Purple & Orange Piñata Motif Stickers**.

It looks like Don Lu is too large to fit through this next area. He tells you to go on without him. Heed his words and leave him where he rests. He'll be fine. Ride the skeleton lift upwards and onwards.

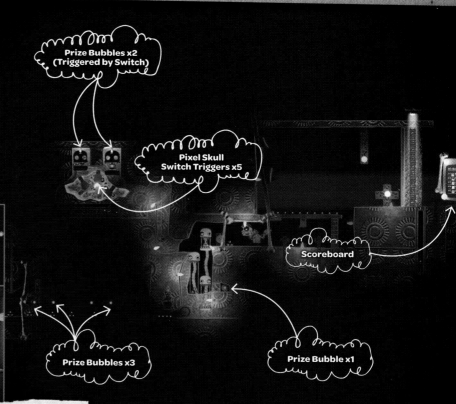

WHAT'S BEHIND WALL #1?

Yes, there's a Prize Bubble inside the wall to the right. However, a simple push against the left stick in that direction as you ride the first platform has negative results. The way inside is with a small hop into the back plane. Just be careful not to jump up by mistake, as there are spikes overhead. For your efforts, you receive the **Fairy Light Object** item.

WHAT'S BEHIND WALL #2?

There is also a Sticker Puzzle nearby. Ride the lift all the way to the top, but instead of continuing to the right, walk off to the left and head into the opening. Ride the hanging skeleton up to the next area, and then access your Popit Menu to find the **Pixel Skull Sticker**. Place it on all five Sticker Switches to solve the puzzle. Two large skull heads lower from above, revealing two Prize Bubbles inside their mouths. Collect both to gain the **Brown Leather** and **Bunny Costumes**!

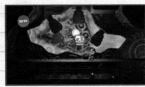

A Woman Spurned

Head up on the ledge to the right of the skull lift to find one of the wedding party, who urgently tells you that Frida's gone off the deep end and is on a rampage with her Skulldozer.

You witness her wrath firsthand as soon as you continue on. Steer clear of her Skulldozer, which crashes through the walls to the right and left—

one touch equals death. Carefully head up the ramps to reach the Scoreboard and the end of the level.

The Wedding

Skulldozer

- -

Never mess with a woman who feels betrayed. Poor Frida's got the wrong idea! Her fiancée never meant to go missing. These things just sort of happen sometimes. But Frida is too far-gone to listen to reason, and now she's going to bulldoze everything in sight.

Hojaldra

Prize Bubble Pick-Ups

✔ **Stickers**

	Bowler Hat
	Graveyard Tux
	Hojaldra
	Los Muertos
	Owl Drawing
	Pirate Skull
	Purple Piano
	Scary Skull
	Treasure Box Body
	Treasure Box Inside
	Treasure Box Lid

✔ **Materials**

	Ceramic Tile
	Paper Weave
	Red Fabric
	Red Stitched Fabric

✔ **Audio**

	"Wedding Int Music"

✔ **Objects**

	Candle Stick
	Real Bone

EL DIA DE MUERTOS

Level Complete Gifts

✔ **Costume**

	Long Bunches Wig

✔ **Background**

	The Wedding

Collected All Gifts

✔ **Stickers**

	Graveyard Concept

✔ **Objects**

	Graveyard Concept with Frame
	Skulldozer

Aced Level Gifts

✔ **Costume**

	Roman Helmet

FRIDA

RUN FOR YOUR LIVES!

Runaway Bride

It's quiet—too quiet, if you ask us. With trepidation, move up the path to meet with a wedding well-wisher who does not bring good tidings (or a present, for that matter). The dapper man tells you that Frida thinks she's been jilted by Don Lu, and is on a rampage of epic proportions. The only thing you can do is run—fast!

JILTED LOVER

THIS LEVEL IS A LONG RACE/CHASE WHERE THE ULTIMATE GOAL IS TO STAY A STEP AHEAD OF FRIDA'S SKULLDOZER WHILE COLLECTING THE SCORE AND PRIZE BUBBLES ALONG THE WAY. THIS IS NOT AN EASY TASK, THOUGH, AS THERE ARE PLENTY OF HAZARDS AND OTHER CHALLENGING OBSTACLES IN YOUR PATH TO SLOW YOU DOWN. TO TOP IT OFF, YOU ONLY HAVE 1:20 TO MAKE IT TO THE FINISH LINE!

Run Sackboy, Run!

Step onto the starting platform to start the race! As soon as the gates open, run! Time is ticking! Stay as far ahead of Frida and her rampaging Skulldozer as possible, but not so far ahead that you can't see or anticipate what is coming in front of you. Jump up the first few sets of platforms to collect the Score Bubbles on top of them.

Haste Makes Waste

Don't bother trying to collect every single Score Bubble—it's nearly impossible to do it and survive. Instead, go for the larger clusters in order to maximize your points!

Prize Bubble x1

Prize Bubble x1

If you manage to stay on top of the platforms, you can leap off the second set and on to the wedding members' heads. Don't miss a Prize Bubble containing the **Red Fabric Material,** located at the third set of platforms; make sure you grab it without slowing down.

Jump up to the highest platform and hop along the second set of wedding attendees' heads, grabbing this next Prize Bubble containing the **Red Stitched Fabric Material.** Repeat once more and hop up to the highest platform on the next set for another Prize Bubble; this one holds the **Ceramic Tile Material.**

Prize Bubble x1

Prize Bubble x1

Prize Bubble x1

FRIDA

Make sure you leap across this lethal pit, hopping onto the low platform on the other side to grab the next Prize Bubble. Collect it to gain the **Real Bone Object**.

NO GOING BACK

IF YOU HAVEN'T NOTICED ALREADY, PERISHING IN THIS LEVEL DOES NOT RESTART YOU AT A CHECKPOINT BEHIND YOU. INSTEAD, IT ONLY RESULTS IN TELEPORTING YOU A FEW STEPS AHEAD OF THE SKULLDOZER. IF YOU DIE ATTEMPTING TO GRAB AN ITEM, THE ONLY WAY TO GET IT IS TO RESTART THE LEVEL.

Cross this next set of fragile bridges. If you're too close to Frida and her Skulldozer, they crumble apart, taking you down with them. Do everything in your power to stay one step ahead! Up here on a platform is a Prize Bubble containing the **Treasure Box Body Sticker**.

To get this next Prize Bubble, you must hop from the last platform onto this wedding party member's head. This bubble holds the **Treasure Box Lid Sticker** inside.

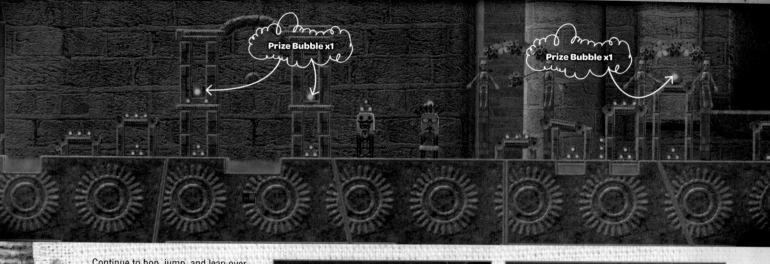

Continue to hop, jump, and leap over the deadly pits and from platform to platform. Make sure to hop up this next set to get up to the Prize Bubble containing the **Candle Stick Object** and **Treasure Box Inside Sticker**. Grab onto the hanging ball, as well, in order to swing across to the next.

Another Prize Bubble lies on the other side. This one is a bit tough to get. Stay way ahead of the Skulldozer in order to reach it atop the wedding member's head before she gets toppled over and it falls by the wayside. Snag the Bubble to receive the **Bowler Hat Sticker**.

Look for a series of platforms that go higher and higher just up ahead. Jump to the third and highest one and grab the Prize Bubble up here, which holds the **Paper Weave Material**.

Continue running! This next Prize Bubble is easier to get with the help of Frida. Let her knock over the wedding member and topple the bubble. As soon as it falls, quickly double back and grab it before the Skulldozer can get you. Your prize is the **Scary Skull Sticker**.

Grab that hanging ball and swing across to grab the Prize Bubble holding the **Pirate Skull Sticker** on top of the head of this wedding member, then grab the next ball and repeat for the next Prize Bubble, which contains the **Graveyard Tux Sticker**.

A set of four tiered platforms is up ahead; the last one holds a Prize Bubble that houses a **Purple Piano Sticker**.

Prize Bubble x1

Prize Bubble x1

Prize Bubble x1

Continue your momentum down and up the next set to grab the Prize Bubble with the **Owl Drawing Sticker** inside. Beyond this is another set of bridges, and another Prize Bubble at the end of them. This one has the **Hojaldra Sticker** inside it.

Glance past the bridges and notice a lone wedding member holds a Sticker-filled Prize Bubble over her head. Either leap onto it to grab it, or let the Skulldozer topple her over to grab the **Wedding Int Music Audio Object** and the **Los Muertos Sticker**.

Just ahead is the finish line, where Don Lu awaits! Keep running and step over it to beat Frida and her nasty Skulldozer. Realizing it was just a silly misunderstanding, all is forgotten, and Frida and Don Lu are reunited in a decorated heart of flowers. The lovely couple is planning to honeymoon in Jalapeño's Canyons, where Don Lu's uncle Jalapeño—master of explosives—resides. Step on the Scoreboard to receive your goodies, and exit the level.

Thank you for saving our wedding! It was all just a silly misunderstanding. We shall honeymoon in Jalapeño's Canyons. Come and meet my Uncle Jalapeño, master of explosives.

Close

The Wedding
Mini Levels!

At the outset of this Challenge, there is only one path to take. However, after the first set of teetering platforms, things begin to get tricky. Don't be tempted to drop down to the bottom of the level to grab some of the extra Prize Bubbles, as it's more of a time waster than point gainer. Keeping your momentum along the top level nets some decent score multipliers.

In fact, staying away from the bottom of the level is a good idea in general. Not only are there fewer Prize Bubbles to be had down here, there are also multiple spiky hazards by which you may die many nasty deaths if you're not careful.

The only real tricky parts are the swinging ball sections that come after and before the teetering platforms. Just make sure you keep holding down ⊗ for long leaps to reach the balls, and don't release **R1** and let go of the balls until you are confident you will land on the next platform.

Wobble Poles

RUN AND JUMP ALONG THE WOBBLE POLES

How to Unlock: Collect the Key in The Wedding Reception

Wobble, but Don't Fall down!

Ready for another challenge, are you? Well then, you've certainly come to the right place. Run and jump as fast as you can along this wobble obstacle course, avoiding spiky traps as you go. Beat the timer (you have 30 seconds, mind you) and get to the finish post as fast as you can for a nice high score.

As with most timed challenges, grabbing Score Bubbles pauses the countdown timer, while also winning you points.

The Dangerous Descent

FALL THROUGH THE HOLES AND AVOID THE HORRIBLE GAS – SURVIVE AND COLLECT POINTS FOR AS LONG AS YOU CAN!

How to Unlock: Collect the Key in The Wedding Reception

Who Cut the Cheese?

What's that smell, you say? Well, it certainly isn't us. It must be the Horrible Gas permeating the entirety of this Challenge level. Pinch your nose with a free hand, and then run left and right to fall through the holes in the platforms. Avoid that Horrible Gas at the top and bottom! Nothing in life is certain, however, and all good (and bad) things must come to an end. You might as well do your best to survive and collect those Score Bubbles for as long as you can before you kick off. When you're ready, hop on the red button to start.

Bubble Labyrinth

PUSH THE SPONGY BITS TO FIND A PATH

How to Unlock: Collect the Key in The Darkness

The Path of Least Resistance

Confused? Confounded? Confuzzled? Not to worry. Just push those spongy bits to find the fastest path through this maze. Aha! You didn't think it would be that easy, did you? You must also avoid the fiery coals AND beat the timer by reaching the finish post before the countdown reaches zero. Did we mention you have 120 seconds to do so?

General Tips

This labyrinth can be a bit perplexing at first, especially when you factor in that the spongy bits can only move so far in either direction. Throw in those fiery coals, which are lethally hot to the touch, and things become much more serious. Don't fret, though, as it's not as puzzling as it seems. The path you seek is along the top two tiers. Just stay on top, dropping to the level below as you come to each coal, and you'll reach the exit in no time flat.

You can go exploring, if you like. However, trying to collect each and every Score Bubble actually nets you fewer points than making that mad dash for the finish post.

If you do get turned around or end up in the lower portion of this maze, quickly take a moment to plot a path back to the top.

General Tips

At first, your biggest challenge is staying above the Horrible Gas lining the bottom of the level. The platforms rise so slowly that you can make an easy mistake and fall through consecutive holes at once, dropping right into the gas below. To avoid this terrible mistake, take your time and steer your sackperson out of harm's way if there happen to be multiple holes lined up one after another.

As things speed up, the challenge becomes more about avoiding the Horrible Gas along the top of the level. A good strategy is to keep an eye on the platforms below, so that you have an idea of the locations of the next few holes and can plan accordingly.

It's also a good idea to keep your sackperson relatively near the center of the platforms. This way, you are centrally located and (in theory) have less space to cover to get to that next hole.

The Canyons

Boom baby! The Canyons are a real blast! Uncle Jalapeño knows how to have a good time—maybe a bit too good of a time, since now he's in the slammer. But it seems like he may have been put there unfairly by the evil Sheriff Zapata. You're the only one who can save him!

Once you set Jalapeño free he shows you the wonderful world of explosives. You learn how to use impact explosives and timed explosives and also how to utilize both new tools to track down the evil Sheriff Zapata and put him out of commission. But getting to him isn't easy, so be prepared for booming towns, run-a-way mine carts, and ancient shrines!

Story: Chapter 1

The Canyons

Boom Town

After saving the day and the wedding, Frida and Don Lu take you along to their honeymoon spot, Jalapeño's Canyons. Apparently, good ol' Uncle Jalapeño knows how to have a blast.

✔ Materials

	Brown Stripy Fabric
	Check Fabric
	Dark Wood
	Green Stripes Fabric
	Orange Wood
	Red Wood
	Red-Painted Wood
	Sandpaper
	Weathered Green Wood
	Weathered Wood
	White Panels

✔ Stickers

	Angry Skull
	Big Spider
	Blue Paint
	Border Bit
	Cactus
	Cactus Arm
	Cactus Body
	Colonial Arch Motif
	Colonial Balcony
	Colonial Door
	Green Face
	Long Colonial Window
	Mexican Door
	Mexican Shutters

✔ Stickers

	Mustard Colonial Motif
	Pixel Cactus
	Red Paint
	Round Orange Face
	Smiley Sun
	Square Colonial Motif
	Square Colonial Window
	Warrior Hand
	Warrior Swoop
	White Paint
	White Window
	Window Semi Circle
	Yellow Corner
	Yellow Paint

✔ Audio

	"Cornman"
	"Cries in the Wind"

Level Complete Gifts

✔ Costume

	Red Flowers
	Fringed Dress

Collected All Gifts

✔ Stickers

	Boom Town Concept

✔ Objects

	Boom Town Concept with Frame

Aced Level Gifts

✔ Costume

	Cowboy Boots
	Leather Gloves

RESCUE UNCLE JALAPEÑO

See ya, Newlyweds

After landing in the newlywed's carriage, get ready for an overload of Prize Bubbles. Jump onto the nearby ledge and grab the two Prize Bubbles resting on the rocky landscape. One bubble contains the **Birds in Tree Object** and the other holds the **White Panels Material**. The **Pixel Cactus Sticker** is right next to it. Then, hop down to the ground and backtrack slightly to snag another Prize Bubble. This time, the bubble contains the **Green Stripes Fabric Material**. Finally, start heading forward and collect the seven Prize Bubbles stacked in front of framed images of local Canyon sackpeople. These bubbles contain the **Seniorita Wig**, **Lace Trim Dress**, **Mexican Wrestler**, **Sombrero Hat**, **Red Poncho**, **Long Mustache**, and **Piñata Costumes**.

Prize Bubble Pick-Ups

TABASCO

Prize Bubbles x7

Prize Bubble x1

Prize Bubbles x3

Prize Bubbles x2

Prize Bubbles x2

Prize Bubble x1

Prize Bubbles x2

Kidnapped

Move forward and start exploring this new world. Soon you come across a happenin' looking amigo who tells you the latest news. The evil Sheriff Zapata kidnapped Uncle Jalapeño, and the amigo wants you to save him. Didn't see that coming, did you?

Hola! The evil Sheriff Zapata has kidnapped Uncle Jalapeño! Please help him!
● Close

Cactus Jumping

Before you set out on this heroic journey, collect the two Prize Bubbles hiding behind the cactus just behind you. They hold the **Fat Cactus**

Object and **Cactus Arm Sticker**. Now head out to save the day—again. Grab the Prize Bubble just past the amigo, which holds the **Cactus Sticker**, and head up to the Checkpoint. Make sure you activate it, because these cacti up ahead are pretty tricky.

Head forward to encounter three cacti with very sharp spikes lined up in front of you. An unstable stack of rocks lies in between each one. Jump from one wobbly rock pile to the next until you reach safe ground. Make sure you pick up those Prize Bubbles on the rock piles too! They hold the **Mexican Rock Scene** and **Large Cactus Objects**.

When to Start Over

This cactus jumping part can be pretty painful if you aren't careful. It can also cost you a lot of lives. Since you're so close to the beginning of the level, maybe you should just decide to start the level over rather than continuing from the Checkpoint. Doing this resets your lives and gives you another chance at winning the "Ace the Level" award. Plus, it doesn't take much time to return to this point.

over near the spiky cacti to the right, which causes the Prize Bubble resting on the large block to fall to the ground. Collect this Prize Bubble (which contains the **Brown Stripy Fabric**) as well as the one behind the small cactus in front of the rock formation behind you (which holds the **Thin Cactus Object**), then use the blocks to jump over the cacti. The **Round Cactus Object** is found floating above the round cacti just to the right of them.

On the ground, move behind the last cactus and collect the two hidden Prize Bubbles; one contains the **Red Wood Material** and the other holds the **Orange Wood Material**. Head out past the Checkpoint to the stack of colored fabric blocks. Move to the right side of the stack and grab the second block, pulling it down. This makes the largest block on top topple

Prize Bubbles x4

Prize Bubbles x2
Challenge Key

Prize Bubble x1

Prize Bubbles x2

Prize Bubble x1

Challenge Key

Luchador

Prize Bubbles x4

Prize Bubble x1

Prize Bubbles x9
(Requires 2 Players)

It's Called Boom Town for a Reason

Walk to the right to discover a red button and what looks like a bunch of boxes stuck in wall. The wall completely blocks your path and there is no way around it. However, there is a way to get rid of it. Try stepping on the red button and see what happens. BOOM! The wall is gone! Those boxes were actually explosives.

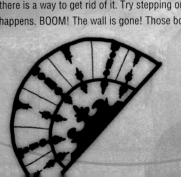

GO BOOM

EXPLOSIVES HAVE BEEN AROUND SINCE ANCIENT TIMES, SO IT'S NO SURPRISE THAT LITTLEBIGPLANET HAS THEM TOO. EXPLOSIVES COME IN VARIOUS SHAPES, BUT THEY ALL HAVE THE SAME DEVASTATING EFFECT WHEN ACTIVATED. EXPLOSIVES LIKE THE BOXES YOU JUST BLEW UP RELY ON SOMETHING TO TRIGGER THEIR DETONATION. IN THIS CASE, IT WAS THE RED BUTTON. THIS IS JUST ONE TYPE OF EXPLOSIVE, AND YOU ARE SURE TO LEARN MORE AS YOU PROGRESS THROUGH JALAPEÑO'S CANYONS.

Wait a second before jumping down onto the charred path. A fireball comes rolling down, stopping just short of the red button. Leap over the fireball and walk up the slope to reach another red button.

Step onto the button and blow open the path again. Watch out! More fireballs come rolling down the slope. Quickly hide in the alcove created by the earlier blast and wait for the first fireball to roll by. When it's gone, hop back out onto the path and collect the Score Bubbles before getting singed by the second fireball. Now that the coast is clear, keep heading uphill.

Cow Tipping

Up the slope, a bull hangs out, dangerously close to the cliff's edge. Normally, you wouldn't want to aggravate a bull, but this time you need him.

Tip the bull over the edge to collect the **Challenge Key** he's wearing around his neck. Then, use him as a stepping stool to reach the Prize Bubble on the rocky edge to the right. This bubble holds the **Sandpaper Material**.

Think Quickly

Back up on the slope where the bull used to be, keep moving to the right and collect the Prize Bubble tucked away in the little dip in the path. This bubble contains the **Hillside Village Object**. Step on the red button ahead and get ready for some quick maneuvering. A large fireball drops right in front of you. The only way to avoid it is by quickly hopping forward and down a plane. Make sure you land on the box below and not the explosive! Then, just as quickly, hop back up to the slope and grab the Prize Bubble trailing behind the fireball. Inside the bubble is the **Check Fabric Material**.

WASHING UP

THIS LAST EXPLOSION WAS A LITTLE TOO CLOSE FOR COMFORT. IN FACT, YOU PROBABLY GOT PRETTY DIRTY FROM ALL THE ASH. YOU DON'T WANT TO STAY DIRTY FOR THE REST OF THE LEVEL, RIGHT? SO WASH UP! OPEN POPIT AND SELECT THE CUSTOMIZE CHARACTER ICON. MOVE TO THE 'MY COSTUMES' PAGE AND SELECT WASH COSTUME TO GET SPIC AND SPAN!

TWICE THE EXPLOSIVE FUN!

A TWO-PLAYER PUZZLE BEGINS ONCE YOU'RE ON THE LOWER PLANE. THIS IS A TRICKY ONE THAT REQUIRES YOU TO THINK AHEAD. FIRST, MOVE THE COLORFUL PLANT OF FABRIC OVER THE GAP TO THE RIGHT, CREATING A RAMP DOWN TO THE NEXT AREA. THEN HAVE EACH PLAYER TAKE HOLD OF A BOMB FROM THE BOX OF EXPLOSIVES. DRAG THEM OVER THE RAMP AND PLACE A BOMB IN EACH OF THE MINE CARTS.

*WITH ONE PLAYER ON EACH SIDE OF THE CART, DRAG IT OVER THE TRACKS AND UP THE HILL. YOU PASS OVER A GAP, BUT JUST HANG ON AND KEEP PUSHING, AND YOU MAKE IT TO THE OTHER SIDE WITHOUT ANY PROBLEM. HAVE PLAYER ONE HOLD THE CART AT THE TOP OF THE HILL, AND THEN HAVE PLAYER TWO PULL THE SWITCH ON THE GROUND TO THE RIGHT. THIS LOWERS A CONVEYER BELT. PLACE THE CART ONTO THE CONVEYER BELT AND LET IT RIDE TO THE TOP, THEN RAISE THE BELT BY PULLING THE SWITCH TO THE LEFT. BEFORE GETTING THE SECOND CART, SNAG THE PRIZE BUBBLE HOLDING THE **WEATHERED GREEN WOOD MATERIAL**.*

NOW GO BACK FOR THE SECOND CART. AGAIN, HAVE PLAYER ONE HOLD IT AT THAT THE TOP OF THE HILL AND HAVE PLAYER TWO LOWER THE CONVEYER BELT. ONCE THE CART IS HALFWAY UP THE BELT, PULL THE SWITCH TO THE LEFT. THIS RAISES THE CONVEYER BELT AND CHANGES ITS DIRECTION, PLACING THE SECOND CART ON THE OPPOSITE SIDE OF THE FIRST.

*WHEN EVERYTHING IS IN PLACE, LOWER THE CONVEYER BELT ONE MORE TIME AND PRESS THE RED BUTTON TO DETONATE THE BOMBS IN THE CARTS. THIS BLOWS OUT THE CEILING AND CAUSES ALL THE GOODIES IN THE BANK ABOVE GROUND TO FALL. COLLECT ALL THE PRIZE BUBBLES TO RECEIVE THE **JUMBO CHILI OBJECT**, THE **WARRIOR HAND STICKER**, THE **POWERED MINE CART**, THE **BUMPY COW OBJECT**, THE **ROUND ORANGE FACE STICKER**, THE **GREEN OCARINA OBJECT**, THE **WOODEN RULER OBJECT**, THE **BLUE PEN OBJECT**, THE **MEXICAN BASKET OBJECT**, THE **LUCHADOR THE WRESTLER**, AND **CALAVERA THE WRESTLER OBJECTS**.*

A Real Blast

The center of town, surprisingly filled with explosives, is located at the top of the slope. Use the colorful block next to the stack of explosives to climb up to the red button. This sets off a massive blast that rips through the town, destroying buildings and causing Prize Bubbles to drop. There are a total of four Prize Bubbles to collect in this first part of town. Snag them all and receive the **Colonial Door Sticker**, the **White Window Sticker**, the **Long Colonial Window Sticker**, and the **Mexican Shutter Sticker**.

There is still more explosive fun to be had in this hill town. Climb up the tattered remains of the blasted buildings and collect the Prize Bubble

near the big red piñata to gain the **Dark Wood Material**. Once you're under the piñata, hop down on the red button and watch the building below go up in smoke.

Now, move back to the left and head up to the platform located between the two large towers. Snag the Prize Bubble containing the **Mexican Door Sticker** before stepping on the red button. Say goodbye to the towers and hello to four Prize Bubbles. They contain the **Yellow Corner Sticker**, the **Colonial Arch Motif Sticker**, the **Square Colonial Window Sticker**, and the **Yellow Paint Sticker**.

Jump from the remains of the left tower and land on the roof of the building next door. Collect the Prize Bubble on the roof, which hold the **Mustard Colonial Motif Sticker**. Now maneuver your way back to the piñata and climb to its top for something special.

PIÑATA PARTY!

Everyone knows that piñatas have lots of goodies inside, and this particular piñata is no exception. Collect the Prize Bubble containing the **Cat Piñata Object** to release a bunch of Bubbles onto the ground, including a Prize Bubble containing the **Cries in the Wind Audio**. There is also a **Challenge Key** in the mix! Collect all the Bubbles at once to receive a x4 score multiplier.

Bubble Bank

Swing from the piñata onto the bank. The bank should look familiar if you did the last Two-Player Puzzle. There are two Prize Bubbles on the roof of the bank. Collect them all to receive the **Narrow Rooftop Object** and the **Colonial Balcony Sticker**. You can also meet Luchador the wrestler, who looks like he's just hanging out.

A LITTLE FART HUMOR

If you think this kind of thing is funny, which you should, you can make Luchador fart just by grabbing hold of him. There are a variety of noises that come along with the gas. You never know just what sound is going to come out next.

TABASCO

Sheriff Zapata

Uncle Jalapeno Prize Bubbles x5

Prize Bubbles x3

Prize Bubbles x5 (Triggered by Switch)

Orange Bird Switch Trigger

Prize Bubble x1

Prize Bubbles x5 (Requires 2 Players)

Jet Pack

Prize Bubble x1

Jump off the bank and collect the Prize Bubble hiding behind the ramp to gain the **Red Ocarina Object**. After snagging the item, walk up the ramp and confront Sheriff Zapata. The sheriff informs you that Jalapeño is stuck in a jail cell and that being evil really rocks. What a jerk! Show that stupid sheriff what's what and bust Jalapeño out of jail.

Surfing on a Rocket

Time to get down to business! Step on the red button to the right to bring out a rocket. Jump on the rocket and hold onto the front to start its engine. The powerful projectile lurches forward and sails over a wide gap. After landing on the other side, try to keep the rocket upright to snag the Prize Bubble dangling overhead. If you manage to collect it, you receive the **Rocket Cart Object**.

Jail Break

After crash—landing the rocket, climb up to the jail. Poor Jalapeño is there and looks like he's been there awhile. He's nothing but skin and bones. Actually, he's only bones. Oh, that's right, he's a skeleton. Move over to the right side of the jail and talk to the amigo. He tells you to go grab the explosives ahead of you and push them back to the "X" in front of the cell.

Before you can reach the explosives, you have to navigate through some scorpions. That's right; that's not a typo. There are four deadly scorpions ahead; one prick from them is enough to send you back to the last Checkpoint. They drop down from the ceiling one at a time. But if you take your time, you can make it through with no problem. Just make sure you also get the three Prize Bubbles resting among the creatures, because these Bubbles hold the **Blue Paint Sticker**, the **Red Paint Sticker**, and the **White Paint Sticker**.

Boom Town

95

Beyond the scorpions is a small cart of explosives along with Frida and Don Lu's honeymoon retreat. They look so cute snuggling in their love nest, don't they? That is until The Collector swoops down and hulls them off to who knows where. It's tragic, but there's no time to worry about the newlyweds. You need to cart that cart back to the amigo.

TARGET PRACTICE

Grab the large colorful fabric block and drag it over behind the cart. Use the cart and the block to reach the upper ledge. This leads to what looks like a sharp-shooting game. Two tracks of duck cutouts rock back and forth. Each cutout has a Sticker Switch on it. Using the Orange Bird Sticker collected in Meerkat Kingdom, stamp each of the five Sticker Switches. Make sure you don't miss. If you do, bombs drop from above and blow you up. If you hit all the targets in a row, five Prize Bubbles drop down as a reward. Grab them all to collect the **Cornman Audio Object**, the **Border Bit Sticker**, the **Cactus Body Sticker**, the **Angry Skull Sticker**, the **Weathered Wood Material**, and the **Window Semi Circle Sticker**.

After you check out all the secrets of this area, grab the cart and pass back through the scorpions. Stop just after the last one and use the cart to reach the three Prize Bubbles located in a small overhead alcove.

These bubbles hold the **Big Spider Sticker**, the **Black Rubber Scorpion Object**, and the **Mexican Vase Object**.

Stop the cart on the "X" in front of the cell. The amigo drops in to thank you for your hard work and to ask you to stand over by the door. Once you're there, the amigo brings down the detonator. When it gets close to the cart, the explosives blow up the cell. Uncle Jalapeño is free! He knows just how to thank you, too. Meet him below for a lesson on impact explosives.

Before you head down, collect the five Prize Bubbles located in the jail. Some of them might be hiding behind some rubble, so make sure you look carefully. In total, you should receive the **Square Colonial Motif**, the **Bandit Toy Solider 1 Object**, the **Bandit Toy Solider 2 Object**, the **Pencil Object**, and the **Wide Rooftop Object**.

Instant Action

Hop down and slide down the slick Score Bubble—lined tunnel. It's hard to get all the bubbles at once, but whatever you don't collect the first time

through, you can go back and get. It may take some expert jumping on the glass surface of the tunnel, but it is possible.

At the bottom of the tunnel, Jalapeño tells you about impact explosives, although it's pretty self-explanatory. He then gives you the task of clearing the tunnels ahead so that the two of you can escape.

IMPACT EXPLOSIVES

THESE ARE BASIC BOMBS THAT EXPLODE ON IMPACT. THEIR EXPLOSION DOESN'T BLOW ALL MATERIALS AWAY. IMPACT EXPLOSIVES CLEAR OUT ONLY MATERIALS SUCH AS BASIC POLYSTYRENE, CARDBOARDS, AND SPONGES.

An Explosive Exit

It's time to blast your way to freedom. Put on the jetpack next to Jalapeño and pick up the impact explosive from the box of bombs. Carefully head through the tunnel and collect the three Prize Bubbles along the way. These bubbles contain the **Green Face Sticker**, the **Red Painted Wood Material**, and the **Impact Explosive Emitter Object**. Once

you get to the pale destructible material blocking your path, drop the impact explosive. Only part of the blockade is destroyed. You're going to need a few more bombs to completely take it out.

Bombs Away!

Each destructible wall should only require two or three impact explosives before it is destroyed. To get the most bang for your buck, drop your impact bomb from as high as possible. The longer the fall, the bigger the explosion on impact.

On the other side of the second obstacle, switch jetpacks and activate the Checkpoint. To the right, the tunnel to freedom continues. A Two-Player Puzzle is to the left.

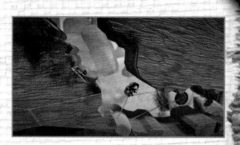

TWO FREEDOM

FIRST YOU HAVE TO BLOW OPEN THE PATH TO THE PUZZLE. HAVE ONE OF THE PLAYERS GRAB AN IMPACT EXPLOSIVE AND BLAST AWAY THE SPONGE BARRIER. FLY DOWN THE FIRST TUNNEL AND HAVE PLAYER ONE STATIONED AT THE RED BUTTON, AND HAVE PLAYER TWO GRAB HOLD OF AN IMPACT EXPLOSIVE. TAKE THE BOMB UP OVER TO THE NEXT TUNNEL. ONCE PLAYER TWO IS THERE, HAVE PLAYER ONE PRESS THE BUTTON TO RAISE THE DOOR BLOCKING THE PATH. TWO DESTRUCTIBLE WALLS BLOCK THE PATH FURTHER DOWN THE TUNNEL. LET THE IMPACT EXPLOSIVE DROP AND BLOW THE OBSTACLES APART. IT TAKES A TOTAL OF FOUR BOMBS BEFORE THE PATH IS COMPLETELY CLEARED. ONCE IT IS, PLAYER TWO HAS ACCESS TO A CAVERN FULL OF GOODIES. HOWEVER, PLAYER ONE CAN JOIN IN THE FUN BY PULLING THE SWITCH IN THE CAVERN TO THE RIGHT. THERE ARE FIVE PRIZE BUBBLES TO COLLECT HERE. THEY CONTAIN THE RINGMASTER TROUSERS, THE PATCHY EYE COSTUME, THE FEATHERED HEAD BAND COSTUME, THE WARRIOR SWOOP STICKER, AND THE SMILEY SUN STICKER.

Move to the right and pick up an impact explosive. Here is where you really have to be careful. Three jagged spikes pounce up and down, ready to brutally skewer anything that stands under them. Be patient and weave through the spikes to reach the other side. Drop your bomb on the destructible wall and then repeat until the wall is cleared.

Once you are through, shake your jetpack off and collect the bubbles below, including the Prize Bubble containing the **Sombrero Hat Object**. If you get them all at once, you can earn up to a x5 score multiplier.

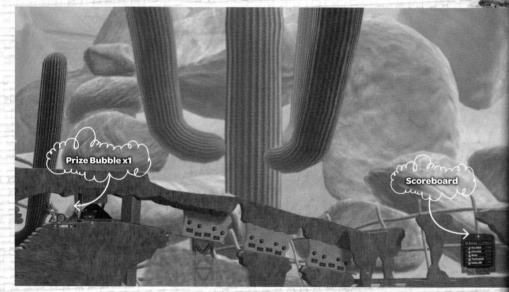

Prize Bubble x1

Scoreboard

After Him!

Climb up the steps ahead and talk to Uncle Jalapeño. He congratulates you for your work and tells you to grab the nearby cart. Hurry, before Zapata gets away!

Snag the Prize Bubble just in front of the cart to receive the **Iron Mine Cart Object**, and then hop in and hold on! The cart takes off and zooms through three exploding walls until it crashes to a halt just past the Scoreboard. Hop out of the cart and finish the level. Don't relax just yet, though. You still need to take care of Zapata.

Story: Chapter 2

The Canyons
The Mines

Sheriff Zapata is on the run, and it's up to you to find him. He thinks he can hide in the mines. Prove him wrong! Meet up with Uncle Jalapeño at the entrance to the mine and get ready for an exciting chase!

✓ Materials

- Basket
- Framed Carved Wood
- Leather Struts
- Red Pattern Fabric
- Red Stripy Fabric
- Wooden Basket

✓ Costume

- Dungarees Bottom
- Rotten Teeth
- Plain Natural

Level Complete Gifts

✓ **Costume**
- Pigtails Hair Wig
- Brown Camo

Collected All Gifts

✓ **Stickers**
- Anteater Concept

✓ **Objects**
- Anteater Concept with Frame

Aced Level Gifts

✓ **Costume**
- Jeans with a Belt
- Cowboy Bandana

NAVIGATE THE MINES

Brains and Wheels and Stickers! Oh My!

Pass through the mine entrance and pop the brains of the two enemies just inside. When the coast is clear, hop down to the next platform and use the enemy to reach the two Prize Bubbles in the little alcove overhead. Pop them to gain the **Red Stripy Fabric Material** and the **Aztec Spiky Object**.

Zapata has headed into the mines! After him!
◉ Close

Just ahead, two large spinning wheels of soft fabric material stand to the right. These wheels move at a fairly slow pace, so you can walk and jump across them without much effort. Make sure you grab the two Prize Bubbles hanging above the wheels. They hold the **Red Pattern Fabric Material** and the **Standing Man Sticker**. Once they are collected, land on the ledge to the right to find a Sticker Puzzle.

Stickers ✓

Apple Heart	
Big Mouth Teeth	
Bottle Logo	
Cactus Quench	
Green Gecko	
Half a Tache	
Mexican Spice	
Mexican Symbol	
Pink Wrestler Face	
Red Explosives	

Decorations ✓

Snake Stone	

Stickers ✓

Red Motif	
Red Wrestler Face	
Sardine Label	
Shouting Mustache Man	
Standing Man	
Standing Man Outline	
Thin Sardine Label	

Audio ✓

"Saregama Sun"	

Objects ✓

Aztec Spiky	
Big Platform Booster	
Cardboard Mine Cart	
Double Sponge Rotator	
Empty Mine Cart	
Jumping Wrestler	
Matchstick	
Mine Cart with Handles	
Powered Chain Platform	
Sardine Can	
Single Sponge Rotator	
Timed Explosive	
White Cotton Bud	

TABASCO

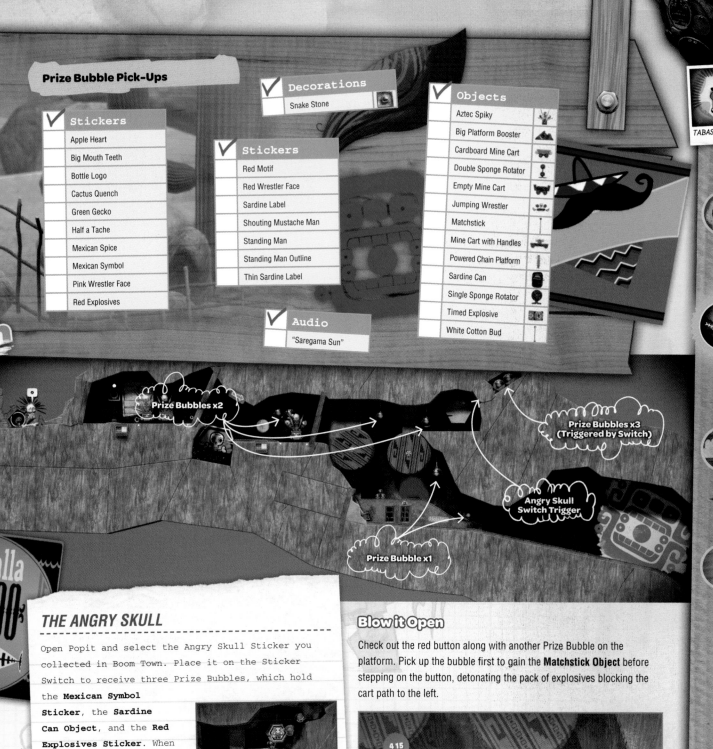

Prize Bubbles x2

Prize Bubbles x3
(Triggered by Switch)

Angry Skull
Switch Trigger

Prize Bubble x1

THE ANGRY SKULL

Open Popit and select the Angry Skull Sticker you collected in Boom Town. Place it on the Sticker Switch to receive three Prize Bubbles, which hold the **Mexican Symbol Sticker**, the **Sardine Can Object**, and the **Red Explosives Sticker**. When you have collected your booty, return to the closest wheel.

Grab the closest wheel and hang on tight. As you slowly spin counterclockwise with the wheel, you reach another Prize Bubble. This one holds the **Red Wrestler Face Sticker**. Snag it, then quickly drop to the platform beneath you.

Blow it Open

Check out the red button along with another Prize Bubble on the platform. Pick up the bubble first to gain the **Matchstick Object** before stepping on the button, detonating the pack of explosives blocking the cart path to the left.

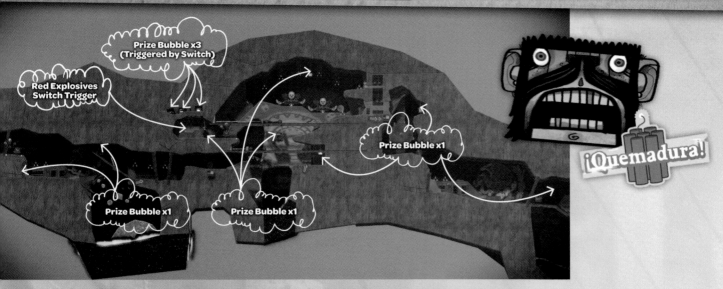

Red Explosives Switch Trigger

Prize Bubble x3 (Triggered by Switch)

Prize Bubble x1

Prize Bubble x1

Prize Bubble x1

¡Quemadura!

With the road cleared, mine carts are able to pass through. Jump on one and ride it downhill and over a fiery pit. When you land on the other side, hop off the cart and keep moving forward.

Two more spiky enemies stand in your way. Bust them up and then move down to another set of mine cart tracks. Like before, a wall of explosives blocks the tracks. But don't clear the path just yet. Instead, go over to the nearby switch and pull it to the right. This causes the drawbridge to the right to lower over the dangerous pit of fire just ahead.

ONE UP, ONE DOWN

THIS BRIDGE IS ALSO PART OF A TWO-PLAYER PUZZLE. AFTER LOWERING THE DRAWBRIDGE, ONE OF YOU STANDS ON THE TIP OF THE BRIDGE, WHILE THE OTHER ONE WORKS THE SWITCH. PULL THE SWITCH BACK TO THE LEFT AND RAISE YOUR PARTNER UP INTO THE AIR. NOW YOUR FRIEND CAN REACH THE PRIZE BUBBLE NEAR THE CEILING AND RECEIVE THE **POWERED CHAIN PLATFORM OBJECT**. RETURN THE SWITCH TO THE RIGHT TO LOWER THE BRIDGE AND YOUR PARTNER BACK DOWN.

Go ahead and step on the red button to blow open the path and then, instead of jumping on the cart that slowly creeps out, head into the tunnel entrance. Inside is a cleverly hidden Prize Bubble, which contains the **Cardboard Mine Cart Object**.

Unloading

Jump on a cart and ride it across the bridge, collecting Score Bubbles along the way. On the other side, leap up to the next platform and head to the large pit of Horrible Gas.

Two buckets trudge back and forth over the pit. The one on the bottom holds burning hot coals, while the one on the top holds a Prize Bubble containing the **Standing Man Outline Sticker**. Grab hold of the switch at the edge of the pit and pull it to the right when the bucket on top is right over your head. The switch causes the bottoms of the containers to open, spilling out their contents, which means the Prize Bubble lands directly on your head. Now close the buckets again by pulling the switch to the left. Then, hop into the bottom container. Ride safely across the pit and jump out at the other side.

Collect the Prize Bubble hanging just ahead to gain the **Cactus Quench Sticker**, and then jump onto the conveyer belt going up to the next area. Before you reach the top, jump off onto the ledge near the upper bucket. Get inside the container and head over to a secret area.

¡QUEMADURA!

The upper bucket takes you to a small area guarded by one spiky enemy. Pop the creature and move to the left to find a Sticker Puzzle and a Prize Bubble containing the **Jumping Wrestler Object**. Collect the bubble and then choose the Red Explosives Sticker from Popit. This Sticker is from this level, so if you haven't found it, you need to backtrack a bit. Place the Sticker on the Sticker Switch and collect the three Prize Bubbles that fall from above. Snag all the bubbles to receive the **Plain Natural Costume**, the **Big Mouth Teeth Sticker**, and the **Big Platform Booster**. When you're done, return to the bucket.

Calavera

Back on the other side of the pit, climb up the hill and collect the Score Bubbles in front of the next Checkpoint. Explosives block the path to the right. You must head to the left and face two new enemies. Their spike—covered bodies look painful, and they move in little hops. Their brains are located between the spikes underneath their bodies — not an easy spot to reach. Use your smaller size to sneak under the enemies when they hop into the air, and then pop their brains before they have a chance to skewer you. When you have destroyed the two creatures, move across to the left.

A launching pad lies ahead. Step onto it and get tossed back across, collecting bubbles, including a Prize Bubble holding the **Thin Sardine Label Sticker**, as you soar through the air. Land on the upper platform and check out the small nearby shaft.

Bombs Away

The shaft houses an impact explosive that is held in place by a sliding panel. This panel extends out into the platform where you are standing. Grab hold of its soft end and pull it out of the shaft. This causes the impact explosive to drop and clear out the wall of explosives that was previously blocking your path. Drop to the lower level and continue through the newly—opened walkway.

On a Roll

Hop down onto the spinning wheel and slowly walk along it to collect all the Score Bubbles. Then jump to the ledge on the right to snag the Prize Bubble to gain the **Basket Material**. When all the bubbles have been gathered, drop down to the lower level to reach another cart path.

Press the red button to clear the tracks, and then get on the first cart that appears. Make sure you are on the front of the cart. This way, when you jump for the Prize Bubble down the path, you land on the back of the cart and gain the **Mine Cart with Handles Object**. If you were already on the back and tried to jump for the bubble, you would fall off and land in the pit of flames below.

The cart continues to roll down the track, leaping over pits, and in general, doing a good job of scaring you. Once you reach the other side, pass the Checkpoint and get ready to feel the heat.

Prize Bubble x1

Challenge Key

Prize Bubbles x2

Prize Bubbles x3

Prize Bubble x1

Elevator of Fire

Step onto one of the platforms attached the conveyor belt. It's just like the one you were on earlier in the level, only this time surrounded by fire. One false move, and back to the Checkpoint you go.

When the first conveyor belt reaches its end, hop to the next one. Repeat the process to reach the third conveyor belt. Make sure you grab the Prize Bubble located between the second and third belt to receive the **Wooden Basket Material**.

At the end of the last conveyor belt, hop onto solid ground and pop the new enemy that stands in your way. It is very similar to the basic spiky enemy, only this time it also has a mace it swings back and forth over its head. Time your jump so you do not get whacked upside the head when you go in for the kill.

Good Timing

Move to the left to reach the Starting Gate of a race. When the gate opens, don't bother charging forward. You can't go very far anyway, since a wall blocks the road. However, this wall is destructible; unfortunately, there aren't any explosives in sight.

Head back toward the gate and press the red button on the small incline to cause a new type of explosive to drop down. The small box with two arrows slowly winding toward each other is a timed explosive. When the two arrowheads meet, the bomb detonates.

TIMED EXPLOSIVES

THESE TYPES OF EXPLOSIVES ARE VERY HANDY WHEN YOUR TARGET IS A LITTLE WAYS AWAY. YOU HAVE UNTIL THE TWO ARROWHEADS ON THE BOX MEET BEFORE THE BOMB DETONATES. JUST MAKE SURE YOU KEEP AN EYE ON THE ARROWS. YOU WOULDN'T WANT TO MISJUDGE HOW MUCH TIME YOU HAVE AND GET CAUGHT IN A DEADLY EXPLOSION.

REWIND

Before you drag the timed explosives toward the destructible wall, pull one back through the gate. Set it in front of the cardboard material near the last conveyer belt. When it detonates, the wall blasts away, revealing three Prize Bubbles. Collect them to receive the **Shouting Mustache Man Sticker**, the **Timed Explosive Object**, and the **Snake Stone Decoration**.

It takes four or five timed explosives before the wall is cleared. Snag the Prize Bubble that was trapped in the wall to receive the **Mexican Spice Sticker**, and move on to the next obstacle.

Flippin' Out

Jump over the two small spike pits and land on the red button at the end of the path. This detonates a stack of explosives that were holding up a wooden platform. The platform flips around and lands miraculously, creating a ramp up to the next level.

Before you reach the top of the ramp, jump up to claim the Prize Bubble above your head to gain the **Apple Heart Sticker**. When you collect the item, return to the ramp and walk to the next level.

Jump onto the red button to the right to make another platform to drop down and form a ramp. Climb to the third level and grab hold of the cart to the right. Be careful not to hit the red button on its bed.

RIGGED TO BLOW

The cart you are holding on to is rigged to blow when the red button on its bed is pressed. It doesn't do you any good to press it now. Instead, push the cart as far to the right as possible, so it's under a ceiling of destructible material. Now press the button and watch as the ceiling is blown away. Loads of bubbles drop onto the ground, including the two Prize Bubbles holding the **Bottle Logo Sticker** and the **Half a Tache Sticker**.

After gathering the bubbles in the secret area, head back to the left and cross the Finishing Gate.

Here We Go Again

Slide down the steep slope after the Finishing Gate to return to the mine cart tracks. Gather the Score Bubbles on the platform next to the tracks, and then jump into the first cart you see.

As the cart rolls down the tracks, leap up and grab as may Score Bubbles as possible. After the first three clusters, keep your feet in the cart to avoid being fried by the fiery walls overhead. You then have four more clusters before another wall appears. Get ready to find a **Challenge Key** and more walls directly after this obstacle.

After this last set of walls, the cart speeds downhill. There are plenty of bubbles to try to grab, but concentrate on snagging the Prize Bubble that contains the **White Cotton Bud Object**. At the bottom of the hill, hop out of the cart and onto solid ground.

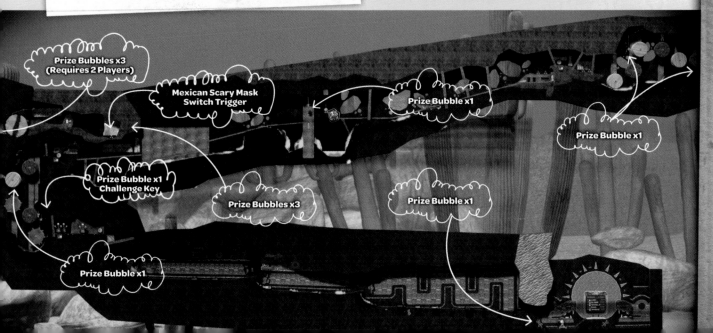

Prize Bubbles x3 (Requires 2 Players)

Mexican Scary Mask Switch Trigger

Prize Bubble x1

Prize Bubble x1

Prize Bubble x1 Challenge Key

Prize Bubbles x3

Prize Bubble x1

Prize Bubble x1

The Mines

The Big Wheels Keep on Turning

Pop the mace-wielding enemy ahead and continue forward until you reach a set of slowly spinning fabric covered wheels. Grab onto the first red wheel; don't let go until you have completed one rotation and have collected the Prize Bubble near the base of the wheel. The bubble holds the **Spikehammer Block Object**.

Leap across the next two wheels and grab onto the fourth one. Hold on until you reach the Prize Bubble to the left, which contains the **Double Sponge Rotator Object**, then let go and drop to the next wheel. From there, you just need to hop over to the last wheel, collect the Score Bubbles there, and then land on the platform to the left.

The First Drop Is Killer!

Move forward until you hit the mine cart tracks, collecting Score Bubbles along the way. Step on the red button to blow open the path and hop into the first cart that appears. Stand near the back of the cart to keep it from tipping over as you roll downhill.

Get ready to jump. At the bottom of the hill, the track suddenly drops off. Leap out of the cart and grab the ball of fabric hanging over the gap. When you grab on, you also manage to collect a Prize Bubble containing the **Empty Mine Cart Object**. Swing to the left and let go. At first it looks

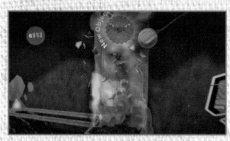

like you are going to land on a small burning pit of fire, but just before you hit the hot coals, a mine cart pops up to rescue you.

The heroic cart takes you down another steep hill and across a track that appears at the last second, finally stopping suddenly at the platform.

Getting Dizzy

Activate the Checkpoint on the platform, then head the left. Although those spinning wheels ahead look awfully tempting, resist them for just a little bit and walk up the hill behind the Checkpoint. There, you find a secret area.

TIME OUT

Take a little time away from the main road and head up the hill behind the Checkpoint. A Sticker Puzzle sits at the top. You need the Mexican Scary Mask Sticker found in the next level to solve the Puzzle. Once you have it, you can place it on the Sticker Switch to reveal three Prize Bubbles and a handful of Score Bubbles. Collect all the Prize Bubbles to receive the **Sardine Label Sticker**, the **Pink Wrestler Face Sticker**, and the **Leather Struts Material**.

BUT WAIT! THERE'S MORE!

Instead of heading back down after completing the Sticker Puzzle, grab a friend and move to up the hill to the left for a Two-Player Puzzle. To start, have player one grab hold of the ball of fabric attached to a small hook. This action allows player two to grab the ball attached to the stone wheel. Pull the ball down to move the wheel clockwise, giving the players access to the next area. From here, have player one grab hold of the first fabric wheel and have player two pull the center switch to the left. This causes the wheel to move clockwise. Player one can then jump to the second wheel. Once he or she has a firm hold, have player two pull the switch farthest from the entrance to the right. Now player one can reach the third wheel. Once player one is there, player two can pull the switch near the exit to the left. This brings player one over the small ledge containing four Prize Bubbles. Collect them all to receive the **Single Sponge Rotator Object**, the **Red Motif Sticker**, the **Rotten Teeth Costume**, and the **Dungarees Bottom Costume**.

After fully exploring the secret area, return to the spinning wheels. Hop from the first fabric wheel to the second, and then hang on for a full rotation to collect the Prize Bubble dangling to the left to gain the **Framed Carved Wood Material**. Move from the second fabric wheel down to a metal wheel covered in Score Bubbles. Walk against the rotation and gather all the bubbles.

Jump from the metal wheel to the next fabric wheel and hang on until you reach the Prize Bubble, which contains the **Saregama Sun Audio** and **Challenge Key** on the right. After gathering the items, drop down onto another metal wheel and walk slowly against its rotation to collect all of its Score Bubbles. When you are done, jump onto the platform to the right.

Goodness Gracious! A Great Ball of Fire!

Pop the three enemies on the platform, and then activate the Checkpoint on the right. Now is a good time to stretch your little sack legs, because you are about to run like your life depends on it.

Step down onto the small platform below the Checkpoint. The floor beneath your feet quickly pulls away, and you fall down a level. As soon as you hit the ground, start running. A giant ball of fire comes hurtling after you. Keep moving your little sack feet and don't look back. Hop over any small fire obstacles in your way, running through a short tunnel and towards your escape from the giant fireball.

Baby Hops

When you're running away from the giant fireball, it's natural to want to take huge leaps over the fire obstacles you come across. If you've been relying on this tactic, you have probably racked up a lot of deaths.

Try taking small hops over the fire instead. You are actually faster when you run than you are when in the air. Also, many of the fire pits are close together, so taking larger leaps means you clear the first obstacle but might accidentally land in the next one.

Let's Get Out of Here

After making your escape, you meet up with Uncle Jalapeño. He informs you that you found the entrance to the ancient Serpent Shrine. Zapata must be inside! Step up onto the Scoreboard and get ready to settle things with Zapata once and for all.

ONE FOR THE ROAD

There is one last Prize Bubble before the end of the level. After talking to Jalapeño, move up one plane. This allows you to enter the small cave inside the hill to the left. Go inside and claim the **Green Gecko Sticker** before finishing the level.

The Canyons
Serpent Shrine

It all comes down to this. Zapata has nowhere else to run. All you have to do is navigate the Serpent Shrine's labyrinthine paths, avoid deadly traps and sudden attacks, and stay alive long enough to bring the evil sheriff brought to justice. Piece of cake, right?

Level Complete Gifts

✓ **Costume**
Frying Pan

✓ **Object**
The Canyons

Collected All Gifts

✓ **Stickers**
The Mines Concept

✓ **Objects**
The Mines Concept with Frame

Sheriff Zapata's Explosive Machine

Aced Level Gifts

✓ **Costume**
Cowboy Hat

Prize Bubble x1

TAKE DOWN ZAPATA

Does it Have to be Snakes?

Talk with Uncle Jalapeño before entering the massive Serpent Shrine. He warns you that there are fiery serpents all throughout the ancient holy grounds. It's easy to get scorched by them, but you must save yourself for your confrontation with Sheriff Zapata.

Cross the Close-Level Post and pull the nearby switch to the right. This raises the ground in front of you to create a stairway to the next level. Before reaching the top of the stairs, turn around and collect the Prize Bubble bobbing from the ceiling to gain the **Raising Steps Object**.

Prize Bubble Pick-Ups

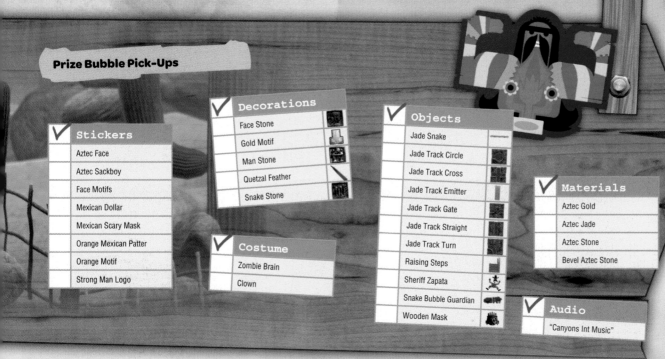

✓ Stickers
Aztec Face
Aztec Sackboy
Face Motifs
Mexican Dollar
Mexican Scary Mask
Orange Mexican Patter
Orange Motif
Strong Man Logo

✓ Decorations	
Face Stone	
Gold Motif	
Man Stone	
Quetzal Feather	
Snake Stone	

✓ Costume
Zombie Brain
Clown

✓ Objects	
Jade Snake	
Jade Track Circle	
Jade Track Cross	
Jade Track Emitter	
Jade Track Gate	
Jade Track Straight	
Jade Track Turn	
Raising Steps	
Sheriff Zapata	
Snake Bubble Guardian	
Wooden Mask	

✓ Materials
Aztec Gold
Aztec Jade
Aztec Stone
Bevel Aztec Stone

✓ Audio
"Canyons Int Music"

On the next level, pass the Checkpoint and leap across the small gap in the floor. Collect the Prize Bubble dangling overhead to gain the **Snake Stone Decoration**. Destroy the spiky enemy on the other side and then take in your surroundings. Jalapeño wasn't lying about the fiery serpents. Look down the gap you just jumped over to see one zooming through

a tunnel. There is also one above your head. They must be all over the place and, by the looks of it—one hit is all it would take for you to burst into flames.

Hop to it!

Don't let all the deadly snakes get you down! Head to the right and use the launching pad to reach a bunch of Score Bubbles and a Prize Bubble located up a narrow shoot. Popping the Prize Bubble awards you the **Aztec Gold Material**. When you've cleared the area of bubbles, move to the right and jump across the gap in the road.

1, 2, 3, JUMP!

You do a lot of jumping in this level, and the shrine's fiery serpents reside in many of the gaps you cross. The serpents zoom down the gaps at rapid speed and if you get caught up

in their path, you're a goner. The trick to staying alive is to wait until a snake has just passed by before jumping. There is a bit of time before the next one appears, so make good use of what little time you are given!

Hop across the next three gaps and collect all the Score Bubbles in the path. After the last gap, step on the launching pad and soar up to the highest platform. Keep on your toes; a new enemy is about to attack!

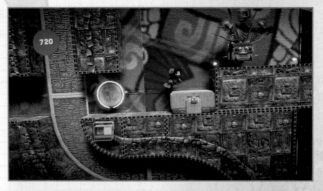

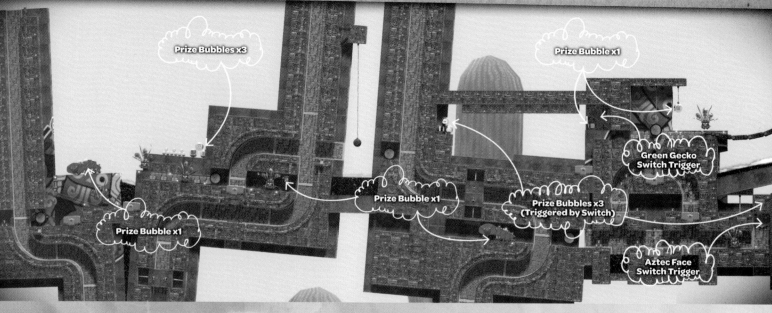

Snakes Everywhere!

A short snake slithers back and forth across the platform. Spikes are attached to its front and backside. There are also three Creature Brain Bubbles on its back. All of the brains need to be popped in order to defeat this new foe. After removing all three, the snake disappears, revealing a Prize Bubble previously hidden in its tummy. Snag it to collect the **Aztec Sackboy Sticker**.

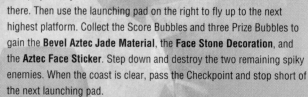

Hop down one level and destroy the spiky enemy there. Then use the launching pad on the right to fly up to the next highest platform. Collect the Score Bubbles and three Prize Bubbles to gain the **Bevel Aztec Jade Material**, the **Face Stone Decoration**, and the **Aztec Face Sticker**. Step down and destroy the two remaining spiky enemies. When the coast is clear, pass the Checkpoint and stop short of the next launching pad.

Swing is your Middle Name

Hop over the launching pad and pop the enemy on the other side. Collect all the bubbles in the area, including the Prize Bubble containing the **Aztec Stone Material**, and then return to the launching pad to be sent flying up to the next level.

Leap across the next gap without getting fried by a fiery snake, and land on the small platform. From here, use the ball of fabric to swing over the wide fire pit. Once on the other side, make sure you activate the Checkpoint.

On the Run

The next bit is tricky. Face the tunnel in front of you and wait for the fiery snake to slither through. As soon as it passes by, jump down the tunnel and into the small gap in the path. Watch out for the spiky snake inside! Pop its three Creature Brains and then collect the Prize Bubble it was keeping in its tummy to receive the **Jade Track Straight Object**.

Keep moving and jump across the next gap. Leap over the fire pit in the path and then hop over the launching pad and second fire pit to find a secret Sticker Puzzle.

AZTEC SECRET

Just past the second fire pit is a small alcove housing a Sticker Puzzle. Open Popit and select the Aztec Face Sticker, which you found earlier in the level. Place it on the Sticker Switch and a door opens behind you, revealing three Prize Bubbles.

Collect the bubbles to gain the **Mexican Dollar Sticker**, the **Strong Man Logo Sticker**, and the **Gold Motif Decoration**.

Up You Go

After checking out the secret area, return to the launching pad. Navigate the next three levels using the launching pads located on every platform. Once at the top, activate the Checkpoint and then turn to the left for a not-so-secretive Sticker Puzzle.

NOT MUCH OF A SECRET

First, collect the Prize Bubble at the base of the Sticker Switch to receive the **Jade Track Gate Object**, and then open Popit. Select the Green Gecko Sticker you acquired in the last level and place it on the Sticker Switch. This causes a series of blocks to lower from the ceiling one at a time. Walk down the blocks as they appear and be careful not to get squished when they rise back up. Once you reach the end of the path, jump

across to the nearby platform and collect the three Prize Bubbles to gain the **Clown Costume**, the **Orange Motif Sticker**, and the **Jade Trace Emitter Object**.

When you're done, drop down to the ground and walk back to the beginning of the area. Use the launching pad at the end of the path to return to the entrance of the Sticker Puzzle cave.

End Secret The Labyrinth Continues

Back by the Checkpoint, move to the right. Climb up to the next platform and use the spiky enemy to reach the Prize Bubble overhead, which contains the **Jade Track Cross Object**. When the area is cleared, walk across the nearby bridge.

Prize Bubbles x3
(Requires 2 Players)

Prize Bubbles x2

Prize Bubbles x3
(Triggered by Switch)

Prize Bubble x1

Orange Motif
Switch Trigger

Prize Bubble x1

Serpent Shrine

109

On the other side, the labyrinth of snake—filled tunnels continues. Hop across the gap in the path and pop the spiky snake ahead. Don't forget to grab the Prize Bubble from its tummy: it contains the **Aztec Jade Material**. At the end of the walkway is a ball of fabric. Grab onto it to be lifted to the next platform. The safest route is to head right, but going down the dangerous left route leads to a secret.

A gap that leads to a lower level lies on the other side of the final jump. Pass over it for a second and collect the Prize Bubble on the right to gain the **Mexican Scary Mask Sticker**. Just peeking out above your head is a ball of fabric attached to a chain. Grab hold of it to reach a secret Two-Player Puzzle area.

FOLLOW THAT SNAKE!

The path to the left leads down one of the tunnels the fiery snakes like to zoom through. Wait until one of the snakes has passed by and then jump down after it. You soon find a ball of fabric anchored to the ceiling in the path. When the next snake nears, the ball raises up to a hidden platform. Step on the launching pad in the secret area to reach two Prize Bubbles that contain the **Quetzal Feather Decoration** and the **Wooden Mask Object**. When you have collected the bubbles, wait for a snake to pass through the tunnel below. As soon as it's clear, hop down to the tunnel and jump through the gap in the path. When you land, you find yourself back where you popped the recent spiky snake. Walk to the end of the path, grab the ball of fabric hanging down, and ride up to the platform.

TWIN SNAKES

Ride up to the next level using the ball of fabric. Once you are there, climb to the launching pad and fly up to the Two-Player Puzzle. Have player one jump across the gap ahead. Watch out for the temple's fiery residents! Set up next to the first red button and wait for player two. As soon as the fiery snake passes through the tunnel again, it's time for player two to run for it. Grab onto the ball of fabric hanging down the tunnel. Once player two has a hold of the ball, player one needs to step on the red button and raise player two out of harm's way. Once a snake has passed, player two can run to the next ball while player one runs to the next button. Have player one raise player two out of the tunnel, and then have both players move on to the final button and ball. Once player two is away from the snakes, he or she can climb up and snag the three Prize Bubbles above. Collect them all to receive the **Zombie Brain Costume**, the **Man Stone Decoration**, and the **Orange Mexican Pattern Sticker**.

Head down the path to the right. Jump over the next four gaps and collect the Score Bubbles along the way. Make sure you remember to time your jumps to avoid the fiery serpents.

Falling Rocks Ahead

Return to the shaft leading to the lower level. Grab hold of the ball of fabric hanging in the middle of the gap and ride it to the platform below. Collect all the Score Bubbles and then move to the right until you are pressed against the wall.

LIKE TRYING TO MOVE A WALL

Push up against the wall and it slowly moves back, revealing a small alcove. Jump in the alcove and move to the right to find a Sticker Puzzle. Open Popit and select the Orange Motif Sticker, which you recently found. Place it on the Sticker Switch and two Prize Bubbles, along with a bunch of Score Bubbles, come pouring out of the serpent statue overhead. Snag the Prize Bubbles to receive the **Canyons Int Music Audio Object**, the **Jade Snake Object**, and the **Jade Track Turn Object**. If you collect all the bubbles at once, you receive a x5 score multiplier. When you are finished, return to the moveable wall.

After investigating the trick wall, head to the left. Jump over the gap in the path and then stop before trying to make it to the next platform. In this section, instead of fiery snakes storming through, rocks avalanche down through the gap. Like the snakes, there is a little bit of free time between the series of tumbling rocks where the path is clear. This is when you make your move. When the rocks stop, jump to the next platform. Use this strategy to clear the next two gaps, one housing a fiery snake, while the other contains falling rocks.

Another Checkpoint is located on the other side of the last jump, but as soon as you get close to it, it falls down the tunnel below. Rush after it and land on the lower floor.

Down in the Snake Pit

Hop up onto the platform on the left and pop the spiky enemy there. Collect the Prize Bubble it was guarding to gain the **Jade Track Circle Object**, and then jump over to the platform on the right. Destroy the spiky snake ahead and steal the Prize Bubble that was hiding in its tummy to receive the **Snake Bubble Guardian Object**. When the area is clear, continue right and leap over the next six gaps in the path. Watch out! Each gap is home to either falling rocks or fiery snakes.

Once you have made it over the last pit, there is no time to take a break. Two spiky enemies are heading your way. Pop the one on the lower level first and then use the one on the upper level to reach the platform overhead. Claim the bubbles there, including the Prize Bubble containing the **Face Motifs Sticker**, and then return to the lowest level.

Prize Bubble x1

Sheriff Zapata

Uncle Jalapeño

Scoreboard

Temple Bridge is Falling Down

Start walking across the bridge to the right and collect the Score Bubbles along the way. Be careful, though. About halfway across, the bridge gives out and drops dangerously close to the fire pit below. Climb up the remaining steps and reach the platform ahead.

Close Calls

The next section calls for patience and precise timing. The only way to proceed is to go through the fire serpent-infested tunnel. Wait for one to go by, then rush down the tunnel until you reach a hanging ball of fabric. Grab hold. Once another fiery snake closes in, the ball jerks you up and out of harm's way.

After the serpent has passed you by, drop back down into the tunnel and move to the next hanging ball. Repeat the process and then drop down the tunnel and hide in a small dip in the path. Activate the Checkpoint in the little hole, then wait for the next fiery snake to pass. When the coast is clear, jump

out and start running. Grab onto the third hanging ball to be yanked out of the path of the upcoming snake. When the snake is gone, drop down and head for the exit.

The tunnel opens up over a large pit of Hazardous Gas. Leap and grab the ball fabric hanging over the pit. Swing to the other side of the gap and land smack in front of the evil Sheriff Zapata. The sheriff threatens to do you in with his timed explosives, but then runs away. What could this guy be up to now?

IN THE EYE OF THE SERPENT

Look behind where the sheriff was standing, and note a broken piece of the tunnel. The broken shards form a ramp that leads into the carved serpent overhead. Climb up into the head and collect the last Prize Bubble of the level to gain the **Sheriff Zapata Object**.

BOSS FIGHT!

High Noon

Cross the Checkpoint and get ready for your first boss fight! Jump down into the pit ahead and prep for some fast footwork. Zapata is hiding behind a wall of Basic Polyurethane, a destructible material. If you had some sort of explosive, you could clear his blockade. Don't wish for them too hard. In just a second, you are going to be up to your sack ears in explosives.

THE DOUBLE RINGED CHECKPOINT

NOTICE SOMETHING DIFFERENT ABOUT THE LAST CHECKPOINT YOU CROSSED? IT HAS TWO RINGS AROUND ITS EDGE INSTEAD OF THE USUAL ONE RING. THIS MEANS THAT YOU HAVE DOUBLE THE NUMBER OF CHANCES TO OVERCOME THE AREA AHEAD. IT ALSO MEANS YOU ARE ENTERING A VERY DIFFICULT SECTION OF THE LEVEL.

Zapata sends three impact explosives your way. One lands back near the Checkpoint, one lands in the middle of the pit, and the other lands close to the blockade. The safest thing to do is stay in the middle of the pit and maneuver back and forth to avoid the bombs. Zapata then throws out a timed explosive. This is just what you were waiting for.

Grab the timed explosive and drag it to the base of Zapata's blockade. You have just enough time to move the bomb and return to the center of the pit before the impact explosives start flying in. Once you have used three timed explosives against the blockade, the wall blasts open, and Zapata retreats behind another barrier.

In the Spotlight

Pass another Checkpoint and hold up for a bit. There's a box cut into three moveable sections up ahead. The first and last sections move opposite of the middle section, so when the middle section moves up, the other two move down and vice versa. Zapata has taken to hiding behind the destructible wall just past the last section of the box. He uses a spotlight to mark his target, and then fires down two impact explosives. After every set of explosives, the spotlight moves. He drops two sets of two bombs, then drops a single bomb. Then he drops two more sets of two bombs before tossing out a timed explosive.

Avoid the spotlights to keep from becoming a pile of ash. Once a timed explosive comes into play, drag it over to the destructible wall as quickly as possible, and then hightail it out of there. Like before, three is the magic number. Set off three timed explosives at the base of Zapata's blockade to defeat him once and for all.

Take Cover

The inside of the box sections make for some excellent cover against Zapata's impact explosives. When you need a break, just head inside one and take a load off. You can stand in there for hours and never get hit. Of course, you'd never get rid of Zapata either.

With Sheriff Zapata put in his proper place, there is only one thing left to do. Take a vacation! And Uncle Jalapeño has just the place. Get ready to take on the big city and meet his friend Mags the Mechanic in The Metropolis. Step on the Scoreboard and away you go!

TABASCO

Serpent Shrine

113

The Canyons
Mini Levels!

Wrestler's Drag

LUCHADOR THE WRESTLER IS LATE FOR HIS MATCH! DRAG HIM TO THE RING!

How to Unlock: Collect the Key in Boom Town

Who Cut the Cheese?

The gaseous Luchador from Boom Town is back in the Wrestler's Drag Challenge. The wrestler is late for his match, and it's up to you to get him there before they disqualify him. You have 180 seconds to bring Luchador to the ring and with no Score Bubbles to collect, every millisecond counts!

The route to the match is mostly downhill, and there are no major obstacles along the way. However, you still have a tubby and gassy wrestler you have to heave around.

General Tips

Don't get crushed by Luchador. He's a pretty big guy and if he lands on you after sliding down a hill, you could be in some serious trouble. Avoid getting squashed by pushing Luchador from behind rather than pulling him from the front. You'll be down wind, but it's a price you'll just have to pay.

Save yourself the trouble of trying to keep up with Luchador on the steep slopes by pushing the wrestler over the edge and catching up with him at the slope's base. This tactic can also save you a lot of time.

Remember to press ⊗ when trying to push or pull Luchador over a steep incline. This gives you the extra "umph" you need to continue forward.

Roller Run

JUMP AND GRAB THE SPINNING ROLLERS TO AVOID THE FIERY FLOOR

How to Unlock: Collect the Key in The Mines

You Spin Me Right Round

The Roller Run Challenge is a fast-paced adventure that sends you over a vast pit of fire. Jump on and grab spinning wheels of fabric and rock as you rush from the Start Gate to the Finish Gate.

There are bubbles found throughout the race. Make sure you collect them to give you a little extra time on the clock.

There are three different Challenges to play: Easy, Medium, and Hard. You must first play Easy before you can play Medium, and you must play Medium to unlock Hard. The Roller Run Challenge does get progressively harder, so make sure you are an expert at the difficulty you are on before trying the next one.

Cowabunga

STAY ON THE COW AND DON'T FALL INTO THE HORRIBLE GAS

How to Unlock: Collect the Key in Boom Town

Ride 'em Cowboy!

If you have always wanted to ride a bucking bull, here is your chance. The objective of the Cowabunga Challenge is to stay on the cow for as long as possible while it tries to knock you off. There is nothing to hang on to, so you must rely on your quick wit and even quicker feet to stay out of the Hazardous Gas below.

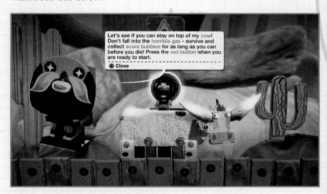

Score Bubbles spring out from behind the cow. Collect as many as possible and get the largest score you can! There is no timer to worry about, just the deadly gas (probably methane). Press the red button to start the Challenge.

General Tips

Stand on the center of the cow. For a while, you don't even have to move; as long as you're in the middle, you won't fall off. However, when things start picking up, you have to make a bit more of an effort to stay on the cow.

Be aware of the cow's movement. There is a certain pattern it follows; the cow always moves left, then right. By knowing this, you can anticipate where you need to be on the cow next and avoid being tossed.

Don't panic. When you get out of your groove, don't try to get it back by overcompensating and jumping around on the cow. Instead, calmly walk along the cow to find the right rhythm again. Only jump if you have to.

General Tips

It's not always necessary to hold on to the wheel. Sometimes the wheels are spinning slowly enough for you to just jump from one to the other. This saves time and effort. This is especially useful during the Easy and Medium Challenges.

On the faster spinning wheels, it can be difficult to judge when to release and fly to the next roller. Allow yourself a few trial runs to practice your timing. Usually you'll want to release a little sooner than you anticipate. It's easier to fly too high and direct yourself back to the wheel than to fly too low and end up roasted by the fiery floor.

Pay close attention to the speed, direction, and material for each wheel. Not every wheel is the same, and misjudging one can cost you a trip back to the last Checkpoint.

TABASCO

Puzzle Wheel
TURN THE WHEEL TO SOLVE THE PUZZLE

How to Unlock: Collect the Key in The Mines

Puzzling

The Puzzle Wheel Challenge is a timed race. You have only 45 seconds to push and pull the switch, rotating the wheel and navigating the three jade stones through the maze. Solve the puzzle before the timer runs out, or you score a big fat zero!

There are no bubbles to collect, no spikes to jump over, and no fire to fall in. In this race, the only thing you are going to exercise is your little sack brain.

General Tips

The switch used to rotate the wheel is actually a three-way switch. This means the switch has three positions: right, left, and center. When you are not pulling or pushing the switch, it automatically goes back to center, stopping the rotation. So if you want to keep the wheel moving, you better keep pushing or pulling in the desired direction.

The exit for the puzzle is in the bottom right of the wheel. It takes a lot of effort to navigate one jade stone at a time through the maze. Instead, collect all the pieces together within the maze first and then lead them through all at once.

Once the jade pieces are through the wheel, the race doesn't stop. You still have to move to the right and cross the Finish Gate. It sounds silly to have this as a tip, but even the slightest hesitation could cost you a lot of time in this short race.

MAGS

Metropolis

Your pursuits in the Canyons have led you to this urban jungle where the lovely and tough-as-nails Mags the Mechanic resides. Mags needs some help with a certain—situation. It's going to be dangerous, indeed, but the payoff is a new set of wheels. Sweet!

Before the day is out, you'll have been tasked with riding atop speeding subway trains, descending deep into the bowels of a sewer system, leaping across dangling girders and over flaming barrels, racing along at blistering speeds inside a flashy hot rod, and engaging in an explosive battle with Mags's longtime nemesis, Ze Dude. Up for the challenge?

Story: Chapter 1

The Metropolis

Lowrider

It's good to be getting out of the dry and explosively hot heat of Jalapeño's Canyons. Don Lu's toasty uncle wants you to take a ride with him to Metropolis to find his friend Mags the Mechanic.

✓ Costumes

- Afro Wig
- American Jacket
- American Trousers
- Baseball Cap
- Basketball Vest
- Big Quiff Wig
- Bouffant Hairdo Wig
- Cannonball Helmet
- Dollar Chain
- Hero Cape
- Mirror Sunglasses
- Tracksuit Bottoms
- Tracksuit Top
- White Sequin Dress

✓ Stickers

- Bacon Slab
- Bobcat
- Coffee Logo
- Dripping Smile
- Fruity Logo
- Graffiti Scrawl
- I Heart LBP
- Ice Cream Sign
- LOLZ
- Pink Blaster
- Pink Donuts Logo
- Red Bicycle
- Route 77
- Skyline 3
- Statue of Liberty
- Wanted Poster
- Yeah

✓ Materials

- Brown Rusty Metal
- Chrome and Velvet
- Concrete Paneling
- Taxi Metal

✓ Audio

- "Metropolis Int Music"
- "Rhythm Trax 07"

Level Complete Gifts

✓ Costume

- School Girl Dress
- Grey Tweed

Collected All Gifts

✓ Stickers

- Early Sackboy Concept

✓ Objects

- Early Sackboy Concept with Frame

Aced Level Gifts

✓ Costume

- Dinosaur Tail

TRAVEL TO THE BIG CITY TO FIND MAGS THE MECHANIC

Jalapeño's Wild Ride

Hop into Uncle Jalapeño's jalopy and drive to the big city, grabbing **Uncle Jalapeño's Car Object** from the Prize Bubble on the driver's seat in the process.

Prize Bubble Pick-Ups

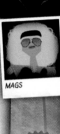

MAGS

✔ Objects

Object	
Bling Curtain	
Custom Sports Car	
Electrified Hazard Sign	
Hanging Traffic Light	
Mags' Car Garage	
Piston Lowrider	
Red Skyscraper Scene	
Scrap Car Lift	
Scrap Cars 1	
Scrap Cars 2	
Scrap Cars 3	

✔ Objects

Object	
Skyscraper Scene	
Spanner	
Spotlight	
Tricycle Wheel	
Uncle Jalapeño's Car	
Wheel Gear	
Wrench	

✔ Decorations

Decoration	
Bling Ring	
Button Eyes	
C Pipe	
Car Bling	
LBP Badge	
Metal Support	
Pipe	
Red Tartan Patch	
Rough Red Tartan Patch	
Toy Car Engine	
Toy Car Exhaust	
Toy Car Spoiler	
Y Pipe	

Prize Bubble x1

**Prize Bubbles x2
(Triggered by Switch)**

Prize Bubble x1

**Route 77
Switch Trigger**

LICENSE TO DRIVE

HAVE A PERMIT TO DRIVE THAT THING? THAT'S OK IF YOU DON'T. HERE'S A QUICK "CRASH" COURSE ON THE BASICS. JUST GRAB AND PULL THE SWITCH TO THE LEFT TO GO FORWARD, AND TO THE RIGHT TO PUT 'ER IN REVERSE. SIMPLE, RIGHT?

ABIDE BY THE SIGNS!

In order to solve the Sticker Puzzle ahead, you need the Route 77 Sticker. While you do get it much later in the level, don't forget to return here during a subsequent playthrough.

Once it's in your possession, place the Route 77 Sticker on the Sticker Trigger to reveal two Prize Bubbles containing the **Fruity Logo** and **Dripping Smile Stickers**. Use Jalepeño's car to get up and grab them!

WANTED
DEAD OR ALIVE
REWARD $500

Lowrider

121

Hold tight and head out on the highway by driving forward into the city. When you arrive, drive up the ramp and don't worry about slamming into the railing up top—Jalepeño's got a low deductible. Throw the car in reverse and back up the next ramp, and repeat by going forward to get to the top level.

Watch that lead foot up top. There's a hanging Prize Bubble containing the **Skyscraper Scene Object**. You should probably grab it before driving off the ledge.

Meet Mags the Mechanic

Hey, it's Mags! She's not feeling Jalepeño's ride, (and is willing to give him a cooler one by heading over to her garage in the scrap yard. Sounds like a deal!

Before you head into the city proper, you should probably dress appropriately. You can find the latest "urban" fashions just to Mags' right. Pop those Prize Bubbles to acquire a bevy of Costume items. You get the **Dollar Chain**, **Baseball Cap**, **Mirror Sunglasses**, **Basketball Vest**, **Tracksuit Top**, **Tracksuit Bottoms**, **White Sequin Dress**, and **Bouffant Hairdo Wig Costumes**.

Use the hot rod to be launched up to the ledge to the right, where another hot rod is located. Repeat the process to continue up to the next ledge above and to the left.

Asphalt Jungle

Leave Jalepeño to chill with Mags, and head out into the city. A tricked-out hot rod sits to the right. Hop on top of its hood and step on the button to be launched into the air. Up above are a series of hanging lights with Prize Bubbles in between them. You can—and should—grab and swing from light to light, popping the Prize Bubbles as you go. You'll get three items from here: the **Y Pipe**, **C Pipe**, and **Pipe Decorations**.

TAXI!

Before you exit this area, you can find a hidden Sticker Puzzle. Solve it to open the gate to the right. From the second hot rod's hood, launch up and grab the hanging light above, then swing into the small alcove to the right. Pull the switch inside to open the gate below and to the right, and then head into this taxi-filled garage. It may look like there's nothing inside here, but once you have the Pink Blaster Switch Trigger Sticker, you can place it on the Sticker Switch between the two vehicles to cause them to hop up and down on their hydraulics. Use this momentum to launch up in the air and grab four Prize Bubbles, containing the **Metropolis Int Music Audio Object**, the **Metal Support Decoration**, the **I Heart LBP Sticker**, the **LBP Badge Decoration**, and the **Wheel Gear Object**.

Use the third hot rod's hood to be launched up into the air. Up above are a series of Score and Prize Bubbles, as well as some lethal, electrically charged hazards. Grab the hanging lights up here to gingerly swing and grab the goodies, which include the **Spotlight Object**, the **Graffiti Scrawl Sticker**, and the **Piston Lowrider Object**.

If you continue to swing to the left, you can also find the **Brown Rusty Metal Material** item inside the Prize Bubble on the top floor of the high rise. To get the **Pink Blaster Switch Trigger Sticker** inside the Prize Bubble in the room below, carefully walk off to the right and immediately press left on the left stick as you fall.

LAND OF THE FREE—PRIZE BUBBLES

MAGS

There are a few more goodie-filled Prize Bubbles to be popped nearby. From the second story of the high rise, carefully drop down into the bottom floor. Next, leap to the left and grab the hanging yellow stoplight with the Prize Bubble underneath it. This bubble houses the **Pink Donuts Logo Sticker**. From here, swing and drop onto the roof of the structure where you grabbed the Costume items earlier; grab the **Statue of Liberty Sticker** from the Prize Bubble here. Next, leap and grab the second yellow stoplight to the left to grab the **Coffee Logo Sticker** in the Prize Bubble hanging underneath.

There are yet still more Prize Bubbles to be discovered. Swing from the second stoplight to the left to drop down onto the roof over Mags. Up here are three Prize Bubbles containing Object items. Collect them all to gain the **Spanner**, **Wrench**, and **Mags' Car Garage Objects**.

Bust a Move!

Now that you have the Pink Blaster Sticker, you can return to the taxi garage and complete that puzzle. Make sure to do so before continuing on.

Put the Pedal to the Metal

When you're ready, use the hood of the third hot rod to be launched up to the right, where a shiny new ride awaits. Before taking it for a test drive, use its hood to grab the Prize Bubbles and **Challenge Key** dangling above. The Key unlocks a Score Challenge, and the Prize Bubbles contain the **Red Skyscraper Scene**, **Red Lowrider**, and

Electrified Hazard Sign Objects. Be sure and avoid the spinning electrical hazards. To get the Score and Prize Bubbles to the right, just move the car a few feet over.

Lowrider

PUSH TO PLAY

There are two more Prize Bubbles up here, inside a small section of the wall to the right. Use the hood of your car to launch yourself up, and then press left to land on the ledge. To get to the goods inside, push the block forward, which causes the bubbles to drop through a hole in the ceiling. Just return to the floor and grab them. The **Wanted Poster** and **Bacon Slab Stickers** are located inside these bubbles.

You can only take your ride so far before it quite literally hits a wall. Hop out and onto the hood, then stand on the button to be launched up to the platform above.

To get the Prize Bubble containing the **Taxi Metal Material** way up high, you can either press ⓧ just as the hood launches you into the air from below, or wait and use the hood once it's driven up this way.

You need to lower that ramp so you can drive your car up to this level. Grab the soft bit of material at the ramp's base and push with all your little big might. It may help to take a running jump at it. Don't forget to grab that Prize Bubble, which has the **Ice Cream Sign Sticker** inside it, as you return to the car.

Hop back into your ride and put it in reverse until it can be driven forward and up the ramp to the next level. Once it's up top, you can use the hood to launch yourself up to grab the switch, which opens the gate to the right. You can also reverse the car to the edge of the ramp and launch up to grab the **Hanging Traffic Light Object** inside the Prize Bubble above the two yellow stoplights.

City Frights

Drive into the next area. Your car can only go so far before it hits a dangerous dead end. In order to continue on, you have to launch yourself up into the air high enough between the electrically charged hazards to be able to land onto the hanging wreck of a car to the right.

Up for the challenge? Just use slight movements, press ✕ at the appropriate time to catch air, and keep in the middle of the hazards. You are rewarded with the **Concrete Paneling Material**.

This next section gets even hairier. In order to grab the spinning Prize Bubbles going round and round above, you must keep up with the slowly spinning tire you're running on by running against it in a counter-clockwise fashion AND hop over/avoid the lethal, electrically charged obstacles.

To start, stay on the trunk of the car and wait for an obstacle to spin by, then jump on to the tire and run in the opposite direction. Time your jumps as the obstacles come around while grabbing the Prize Bubbles in the process. Collect them all to gain the **Route 77 Sticker**, the **Tricycle Wheel Object**, the **Red Tartan Patch Decoration**, the **Scrap Cars 2 Object**, the **Rough Red Tartan Patch Decoration**, the **Skyline 3 Sticker**, and the **Bobcat Sticker**.

Check This!

This last bit of running and dodging can start to whittle away your little big lives in a hurry. If you're about to use up all your lives, hop over to the Checkpoint on the yellow car to the right and activate it for another four!

Get Your Kicks on Route 77?

That Route 77 Sticker you just acquired is required to solve Sticker Puzzle back at the beginning of this level. Don't bother backtracking; just make sure you replay the level and remember to use it on the sign when you start out.

Once you're on the next car, hop over the spinning hazard and grab the **Button Eyes Sticker** inside this next Prize Bubble sitting on the trunk. From here, drop off of the trunk and onto the hood of the car below, then hop over the next hazard and grab a Prize Bubble containing the **Scrap Cars 3 Object** on this car's hood.

You certainly can grab the Prize Bubbles above without the help of a buddy, but to get the hidden ones below, you need some help. First, take a moment to collect all the ones that you can. Do so by riding the moving car upwards and then jumping to grab the goods. Up here you can gain the **Yeah Sticker**, the **LOLZ Sticker**, the **Red Bicycle Sticker**, the **Bling Curtain Object**, the **Scrap Car Lift Object**, the **Chrome and Velvet Material**, and the **Bling Ring Sticker**.

A Couple of City Slickers

Now it's time to call on a friend for a Two-Player Puzzle. Hop over to the upside down car and pull the switch, which drops a car down below to reveal a new path. Both of you should drop down into this new area, grabbing the **Scrap Cars 1 Object** inside the Prize Bubble in the process.

Here's where it gets even more fun! Player one should hop into the car above, and player two should drop down to the platform through the opening in the ground. Here, player two needs to grab onto the sponge ball while player one takes the other for a ride! Wait for the electrically charged dangling object to lower and stretch downward, creating a short window of opportunity to scoot past. Have player two let go of the sponge ball when he or she can safely drop onto the platform. Grab the **American Pants Costume** from the Prize Bubble in the process, and then pull the switch to raise a gate above.

Next, have player one drive up a bit to pick up player two, and then carefully drive past the next two obstacles. Time the pass so that player one is either above or below player two. Find another Prize Bubble, and collect it to gain the **Cannonball Helmet Costume**.

When you reach the wall after completing the Two-Player Puzzle, hop out of the car and jump up to the platform in the back plane where a switch can be pulled. The wall below lowers, allowing both players to continue on. Have player two grab the **Big Quiff Wig Costume** from the Prize Bubble on the next platform, drop off to safety, then ride the sponge ball to be reunited with player one. Up top, there are two final Prize Bubbles. One contains the **Hero Cape Costume** and the other, which is hanging from the roof, contains the **American Jacket Costume**. Return the way you came to continue on.

Wanna Race?

Up top, Mags meets you with your new ride. She even bets you could use it to successfully race against Ze Dude and get her own car back. Apparently, that punk stole it from her. Pull the switch to reveal the new beast. Inside, you even find a Prize Bubble with the **Custom Sports Car Object** sitting in the driver's seat.

LITTLEBIGPLANET MY RIDE

Don't drive out of the garage without first uncovering this devious secret. High above, out of prying eyes, is Mags' very own special stock of Stickers. To get 'em for your very own, just solve the Sticker Puzzle by slapping a Route 77 Sticker

on your new car. You get the **Toy Car Exhaust**, **Toy Car Engine**, **Car Bling**, and **Toy Car Spoiler Objects**.

Hop into your new ride and drive it back and forth down the series ramps until your run into Ze Dude and his bouncer. He challenges you to a race. Show him how it's done, *LittleBigPlanet* style! Just keep that lead sack-foot on the gas and speed forward. It doesn't take long before Ze Dude chokes on your exhaust and plummets off the track and down into the subway.

Take a moment to revel in the glory, and then grab the **Rhythm Trax 07 Audio** inside the Prize Bubble to the left. When you're ready (no one likes a show-off), climb the ramp and speak with Mags, who is in a tizzy because the car Ze Dude was driving was hers! She needs you to go down to the subway and get it back. Oblige the pretty mechanic, and step on the Scoreboard to continue.

The Metropolis
Subway

Mags is not happy about this latest development. Thanks to Ze Dude, her car is in the river! Guess it's up to you to go find it. Step onto the large lift to the right to automatically take a deep dip.

MAGS

Stickers

- [x] Big Burger
- [x] Blue Arm
- [x] Blue Leg
- [x] Blue Star Banner
- [x] Brown Beard
- [x] Cassette Tape
- [x] Chug Lite
- [x] Eagle Drawing
- [x] Eagle Wing Drawing
- [x] Hairy Leg
- [x] Hello Card
- [x] Hut Roof
- [x] Old Guitar
- [x] Old-Timer
- [x] Pink Stetson
- [x] Red Star Banner
- [x] Sackboy Spray Paint
- [x] Scary Mouth
- [x] Skyline 4
- [x] Waffle
- [x] Yellow Fries

Prize Bubble Pick-Ups

Objects

- [x] Airvent
- [x] Double Airvent
- [x] Female Doll Arm
- [x] Female Doll Head
- [x] Female Doll Leg
- [x] Female Doll Torso
- [x] Powered Airvent
- [x] Quadruple Airvent
- [x] Railroad Crossing
- [x] Rollerskate
- [x] Rollerskate Lift
- [x] Straight Subway Tunnel
- [x] Subway Slide Tunnel
- [x] Subway Train
- [x] Triple Airvent
- [x] Ze Dude's Wheels

Costumes

- [x] Pink Hair Wig
- [x] Stitched Button Eyes
- [x] White Weave

Materials

- [x] Blue Deck Chair
- [x] Blue Denim
- [x] Blue Felt
- [x] Blue Knit
- [x] Red Deck Chair
- [x] Rusty Metal Grill
- [x] Shiny Metal

Level Complete Gifts

Costume

- [x] Wellington Boots
- [ ] Green Damask

Collected All Gifts

Objects

- [x] Grabbing Machine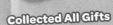
- [ ] Rock God Concept with Frame

Aced Level Gifts

Costume

- [x] Green Sock Puppet

SEARCH FOR MAGS' LOST CAR. MIND THE GAP.

Calling All Cars!

Ride the lift down, positioning over the Prize Bubbles as they pass by. Along the way you can acquire a whopping total of 13. Collect all of the bubbles to receive the **Rollerskate Wheel Object**, the **Rollerskate Object**, the **Blue Deck Chair Material**, the **Blue Felt Material**, the **Female Doll Torso Object**, the **Female Doll Arm Object**, the **Rollerskate**

Lift Object, the **Blue Denim Material**, the **Female Doll Object**, the **Red Deck Chair Material**, the **Yellow Fries Sticker**, the **Female Doll Head Object**, and the **Blue Knit Material**.

Going down?

The moment you step on to the lift, it begins to descend. In order to retrieve every single one of the numerous Prize Bubbles along as it goes downward, you must replay

this section multiple times. It's literally impossible to grab them all in one visit, as oftentimes multiple Prize Bubbles can be at opposite sides of the lift simultaneously. Follow the red piping to get a bead on their locations, and just restart the level as many times as you need until you've collected them all.

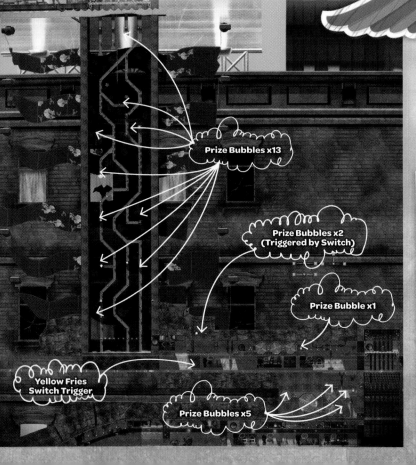

Prize Bubbles x13

Prize Bubbles x2
(Triggered by Switch)

Prize Bubble x1

Yellow Fries
Switch Trigger

Prize Bubbles x5

A Sewer Situation

Say hello to Mags, who meets up with you at the bottom of the lift. It looks as if the tide has carried her car into the sewer entrance. In order to track it down, you need to hop on the train and then find a lift to take you down there. Hope you brought your nose plug. Oh right, you don't have a nose.

EXTRA CHARGE

Those train tracks are crackling with deadly electrical energy. Please do your best to mind the gap.

Train Troubles

Patiently wait for the train to come by; when it does, drop down onto its roof. On the other side of the low ceiling, however, you need to jump up onto the ledge.

FRIES GO WITH THAT SHAKE?

A crafty Sticker Puzzle, this one is. Before continuing on, search the area underneath you between train cars to locate the square cardboard poster affixed to the wall. Carved into its front is the outline of a Sticker in your possession—the Yellow Fries. Place it on the poster to cause two Prize Bubbles to lower from above. Collect both bubbles to gain the **White Weave Costume** and the **Subway Train Object**.

Wiggle your way through the subway's air duct system to get to the other side. Once there, you find a Prize Bubble containing the **Double Airvent Object**. Ride the next train that comes by to the following ledge, and then hop onto the lift in the back plane and yank that switch to the right.

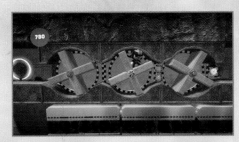

SUBWAY SECRETS

If you look carefully during your descent on the lift, you can spot a small opening along the left wall, just as the lift reaches the second set of electrified tracks. Stop the lift and squeeze through the opening, then start working your way through the air vents, collecting the Prize Bubbles along the way. There are a total of five Prize Bubbles. Snag them all to gain the **Quadruple Airvent Object**, the **Powered Airvent Object**, the **Triple Airvent Object**, the **Airvent Object**, and the **Big Burger Sticker**.

Prize Bubble x1

Prize Bubbles x3 (Triggered by Switch)

Intense Blue Graffiti (Triggered by Switch)

Prize Bubble x1

Continue to ride the lift down into the bowels of the subway until it comes to a stop. When you're ready, hop down onto the roof of a passing train and jump over the posts that could potentially impede your progress (or kill you, if they are of the electrically-charged kind) along the way. Make sure you pop that Prize Bubble and grab the **Straight Subway Tunnel Object**. Take a much-deserved rest at the next Checkpoint. You must hop and duck under a second set of obstacles as the train goes deeper underground. Just keep your jumps short to avoid hitting the charged obstacles above while clearing the ones below until you are back on solid ground.

TICKETS, PLEASE

See that Prize Bubble in the background? It's basically floating in mid-air. The only way to grab it without falling to a toasty death on the tracks below is to jump to the back plane and then quickly use the passing train. Run across its roof and snag the **Subway Slide Tunnel Object**.

As long as you're on the back plane, you might as well hop on the train going back toward the way you came. Ride it to the right as it slopes ever downward and continue to vault over the obstacles as they come. To get past the set of air vents, squeeze underneath the first and last, and hop up and around the middle.

TAG THE WALL!

Before initiating the race through the air vents, take a moment to notice the cardboard cutout on the wall. Yes, that's right—it's a Sticker Switch. Unfortunately, you don't have the correct Sticker just yet. You'll find it in the next level. However, you should make a mental note and come back here to collect the Prize Bubbles it reveals.

When you have the required Intense Blue Graffiti Sticker in hand, place it here to obtain three goodies: the **Shiny Metal Material**, the **Blue Star Banner Sticker**, and the **Red Star Banner Sticker**.

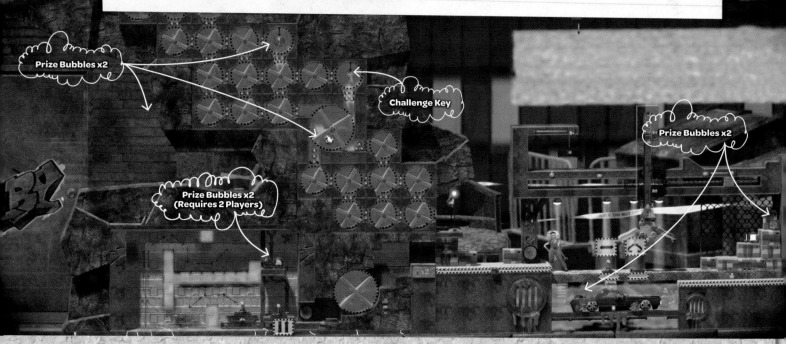

Prize Bubbles x2

Challenge Key

Prize Bubbles x2

Prize Bubbles x2
(Requires 2 Players)

Pachinko Panic

Once you step onto this platform, a race begins. You have 26 seconds to race through the winding maze of spinning air vents and make it to the finish post before the timer runs out for bonus points.

In your haste to blast through this maze, you most likely noticed a handful of Prize Bubbles here and there. If you grabbed them all, as well as the **Challenge Key**, then you are a true *LittleBig* champion. If not, well, there's still hope for you yet—just try again. With diligence and a little elbow grease, you can collect the two bubbles to receive the **Skyline 4 Sticker** and the **Railroad Crossing Object**, in addition to the Challenge Key (which unlocks the Score Challenge).

Try, Try Again

DON'T activate that next Checkpoint if you're looking to grab all those Prize Bubbles in the maze. Instead, you can select the Try Again option from the Popit Menu and take another (or two) run-through to collect the goodies you missed the first time around.

Mags is down here and she's located her car, but before you lend her a hand, tap a friend on his or her shoulder and ask them for a little assistance in this Two-Player Puzzle.

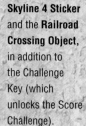

It Takes Two to Make the Sewer Go 'round

The chamber to the left has a large air vent that rotates when activated by standing on the red button above it. Position player one on the button, and then have player two ride  around the rotating vent until it has reached the bottom. When the button down here is pressed, the vent keeps spinning, thus allowing player one to come on down.

Now for the tricky bit (you didn't think it was going to be that easy, did you?). Have player one hop onto the left trolley with the switch, then have player two carefully stand on the platform and operate the nearby switch. By moving the switch to the right, the trolley rises. By moving the switch to the left, it lowers.

First, carefully raise it up until the trolley is safely above the lethal green-colored noxious gas, but not too high that you are downing gulps of it from above.

Next, player one can move the trolley left and right by operating their switch. Pull it to the left to move left, and to the right to move right. Go ahead and try it now by moving to the left, passing the gas below, but not going so far as to run into the gas to the left.

Now, player two needs to lower the trolley down. Have player one pull the switch to the left. Move it all the way to the left so that it now is against the far wall.

We're getting there. Back at the switch to the right, have player two raise the trolley all the way up to the roof. When it's there, it's player one's turn to move the trolley to the right until it is past the gas wall below and to the left.

The final stretch! Lower the trolley a smidge, move it to the right, and then raise it up so both players can grab those beautiful Prize Bubbles on the platform above. It's worth the back and forth, as you gain the **Pink Hair Wig Costume** and the **Stitched Button Eyes Costume**.

Car Catcher

Mags needs you to retrieve her car from the sewage. It's a dirty job, but somebody's got to do it. To pull it out, you can use the switches to her right. Once it's retrieved, she's promising you a Prize Bubble, which is in the trunk.

To retrieve the car, you must operate a button and a switch. There is a large claw hanging overhead and by pulling/pushing the switch to the left and right, you can move the claw in each direction. When you have it in the right position, you can drop the claw by stepping on the button.

Arrange the claw so that it is directly over the top of the car by moving the switch to the left and letting go when it's in position. When you're ready, hop on the button and let the machine do the rest of the work for you!

Once it's out of the sewage, head over and grab your prize from the trunk—the **Ze Dude's Wheels Object**. There's also a second Prize Bubble sitting high atop the stacked boxes to the right. Hop on up and grab the **Rusty Metal Grill Material**.

MAGS

Prize Bubbles x3

Scoreboard

Prize Bubbles x13

Going up!

It's time to head back up to the surface and out of these stinky sewer tunnels. Walk onto the lift and ride it up! The long ascent gives you time to collect some more Score and Prize Bubbles; however, you need to watch out for and avoid the lethal green gas emanating from the vents along the way.

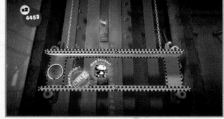

Make sure to pop as many Prize Bubbles as possible, although it's nearly impossible to get them all on one ride up. If you're a perfectionist, you must replay the level to collect each and every goodie inside. When you do, you'll receive the **Blue Arm**, **Blue Leg**, **Cassette Tape**, **Sackboy™ Spray Paint**, **Chug Lite**, **Hut Roof**, **Eagle Wing Drawing**, **Eagle Drawing**, **Pink Stetson**, **Brown Beard**, **Hairy Leg**, **Old-Timer**, and **Old Guitar Stickers**.

Once you reach the top, make sure you topple the stacks of boxes to grab the final three Sticker-filled Prize Bubbles, containing the **Waffle**, **Scary Mouth**, and **Hello Card Stickers**.

Construction Conundrum

Mags still needs your help! Even though you've rescued her wheels, Ze Dude got away, and he's taking out his revenge by wrecking her construction site. Hop on the Scoreboard to exit the level, and head over to the Construction Site.

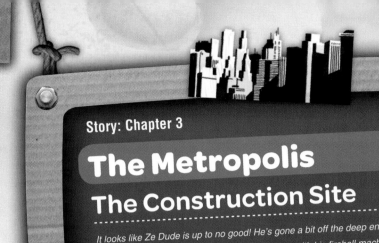

Story: Chapter 3

The Metropolis
The Construction Site

It looks like Ze Dude is up to no good! He's gone a bit off the deep end if you ask us, vandalizing poor Mags' construction site with his fireball machine. It's your duty as one of LittleBigPlanet's most helpful sackpeople to help her out, and take down this dirty rotten scoundrel once and for all!

MAGS

Prize Bubble Pick-Ups

✔ Audio
"Atlas"

✔ Costumes
Dungarees Top
Yellow Builder Cap
Red Flash
White Burlap

✔ Stickers
Electric Guitar
Fragile Warning
Front Red Football Hat
Hat Glasses
Intense Blue Graffiti
Lightning Outline
Plane Silhouette
Red Football Hat
Skyline 1
Skyline 2
Two Arrows Warning
Umbrella Warning

✔ Objects
Basketball	
Basketball Head	
Big Crane	
Boxing Glove Back	
Boxing Glove Front	
Chicken Drumstick	
Crane Hook	
Fiery Coal Emitter	
Long Conveyor	
Power Digger Man	
Red Stiletto	
Spike Hammer Block	
Wheelbarrow Man	
Ze Dude's Private Jet	

✔ Materials
Blue Cardboard Skyscraper
Brown & Cream Concrete
Brown Cardboard Skyscraper
Bumpy Concrete
Checkered Concrete
Dark Grey Concrete
Disco Metal
Flame Motif Metal
Grey Concrete
Knitted Fabric
Polystyrene Packing
Red Cardboard Skyscraper
Rough Concrete

Level Complete Gifts

✔ Costume
Blonde Hair Wig

✔ Background
The Metropolis

Collected All Gifts

✔ Stickers
Boss Concept	

✔ Objects
Giant Concept with Frame	
Monster Truck	

Aced Level Gifts

✔ Costume
Dinosaur Mask

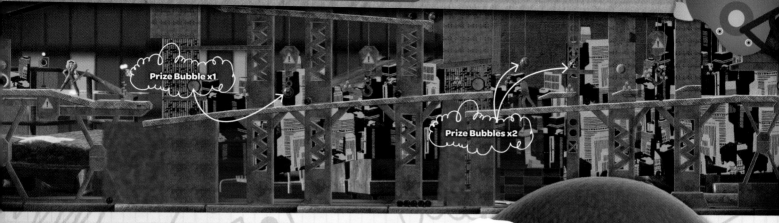

Prize Bubble x1

Prize Bubbles x2

RESCUE MAGS' CONSTRUCTION SITE FROM ZE DUDE ONCE AND FOR ALL!

We've Had Ze 'nough of Ze Dude

Step onto the platform to start a race. When the gates open, you have a mere 33 seconds to make it to the finish post. Of course, it's not as easy as running from point A to point B. Ze Dude's fireball machine is in full force, sending rolling barrels speeding your way that you must avoid and/or jump over.

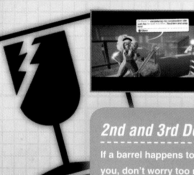

2nd and 3rd Degree

If a barrel happens to run into you, don't worry too much. You are pretty resilient and can take one or two singes before you become burnt to a crisp.

Even though you're in a rush, continue to take your time planning your jumps and hops so that these rolling barrels of fire don't toast you completely. Also, make sure you hop up and pop the nearby Prize Bubble, which holds the **Crane Hook Object**.

When you reach this next area, you can take the short detour to grab the **Skyline 2 Sticker** inside the Prize Bubble on the hanging girder now, or finish the race and return. Either way, use the sponge ball to swing up to it. Just to the left of it is a second Prize Bubble holding the **Wheelbarrow Man Object**. Take a running leap off the girder to pop it!

Let 'em Pass You by!

Here's a nice little secret tip. The rolling barrels are in the front plane, meaning you can position yourself in the center or back planes and let them harmlessly pass you by.

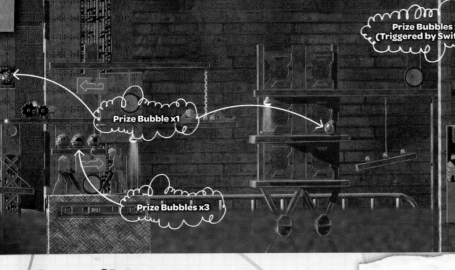

Prize Bubbles x7
(Triggered by Switches)

Prize Bubble x1

Prize Bubbles x3

Skyline 2, Skyline 3, and Skyline 4
Switch Triggers

MAGS

Beware of Dog

Carefully navigate over the hanging girders in this next area; you don't want to fall off and into the lethal, burning heat below. When you reach this last girder, weigh it down to cause its right end to angle up by standing toward the back end, then make a mad dash up its length and leap up to the higher girder to reach the three Prize Bubbles. Collect them all to gain the **Two Arrows Warning**, **Umbrella Warning**, and **Fragile Warning Stickers**.

Step onto the button on the next platform to lower a girder to the right. It looks as if you caught one of Mags' men sleeping on the job. Pay him no mind and leap across, then use the next hanging girder to get up to the higher platform by weighing it down and running up its length. Another Prize Bubble is located up here, and this one contains a **Power Digger Man Object** item. Step on the button up top to raise Mr. Lazy back up to continue on.

PAINT THE TOWN RED

You can use the girder Mr. Lazy is on to also find this next secret. Instead of continuing to the left, weigh the girder's left side down, and then run to the right and leap up onto the ledge (this may take a few tries to be successful). Up here, run to the right, pass the Checkpoint, and hop onto the moving girder. There is a large Sticker Puzzle containing six Sticker Switches that need decorating. At this point (and if you've been following this walkthrough), you should have the three Stickers required in your Popit.

Use the bottom row of skyline as a guide, and start slapping those Stickers. Here's how the should go:

Bottom Row from Right to Left:
- Skyline 2 (flipped)
- Skyline 3
- Skyline 4 (flipped)

Top Row from Right to Left:
- Skyline 4
- Skyline 2
- Skyline 4

Once all the Stickers are in place, a second girder lowers into place with seven Prize Bubbles sitting along its length. Snag them all to gain the **Skyline 1 Sticker**, the **Red Flash Costume**, the **White Burlap Costume**, the **Red Football Hat Sticker**, the **Front Red Football Hat Sticker**, the **Electric Guitar Sticker**, and the **Lightning Outline Sticker**.

The Construction Site

135

Return to Mr. Lazy, and then use his girder to cross over to the platform to the left. One of Ze Dude's guard dogs watches you up here. Wait for its spiked head to retract to the opposite side of where you're facing, and

then take the opportunity to hop onto its exposed Creature Brain before it turns back the other way. If you want that **Spike Hammer Block** Object inside the Prize Bubble above in the small alcove to the left, you should also time your attack so that the dog is underneath the bubble, and press ⊗ to jump off the Creature Brain to reach it.

Use the dangling sponge balls to swing across this gap, and then hop up and grab one of the balls on either end of the next girder to lower it down enough for you to hop on. Grab and hang on to this last sponge ball to be carried up to the ledge high above.

Prize Bubble x1

Prize Bubble x1

Pants of Fire

Dropping down onto this next platform activates a new race. You have 180 seconds to make it to the finish post before the timer expires. Start by hopping over the rolling barrels as you make your way up the slope. There's a **Chicken Drumstick Object** inside the Prize Bubble hanging from the ceiling.

Drop down to the next slope and quickly duck into the small area to the right to grab the Prize Bubble containing the **Basketball Object**, then pop back out and continue before a rolling fire barrel gets you.

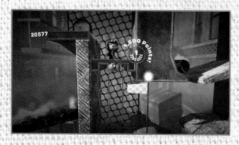

To beat the clock and win the race, just use the final two sponge balls to swing to safety and hit the finish line. Congratulations!

Strange Days Indeed

The small lift takes you to this next area where a very strange basketball head rolls your way as soon as your weight tips the girder on which you stand. There is a Prize Bubble stuck in the center of its head, but getting it requires you to jump between the flaming barrels attached to key positions around its radius. Wait for an opening, and then jump through! Snag the bubble to gain the **Basketball Head Object**.

GET IN THE BACK

To get this Prize Bubble sitting behind the construction wall, you just need to scoot to the back plane. Stand in front of the Checkpoint and hop back, and then walk behind to grab it! The bubble holds the **Intense Blue Graffiti Sticker**, which also happens to be the required Sticker for a Sticker Puzzle in the Subway level. Make sure that, once you've wrapped things up in the Construction Site, you return to the Subway and use the Graffiti Sticker to get the remaining Prize Bubbles.

Prize Bubbles x6

Prize Bubbles x4

Prize Bubbles x6
(Requires 2 Players)

Destroy the guard dog along this next platform, and then use the girder beyond to get up to the higher ledge. The next hanging girder to the right offers up two possible paths: to the left is a Two-Player Puzzle. To the right, the level continues. Before moving out, grab a friend and head to the left.

Heavy Machinery X2

Up inside this area, player one needs to position himself or herself on the hanging girder to the far left, while player two hops inside the cab of the crane. Next, have player one pull the switch to the left to move the girder across the gap and to the small ledge to the left.

Once the girder is against the ledge, player one can move off of it. Grab the square rubber object and pull it onto the girder. When both sackpeople and the square object are securely in place, have player two operate the crane and bring the girder all the way back to the right.

Finally, have player one move the block over to the right and position it in front of the Checkpoint. Use the block to get up on the roof of the crane's cab and grab the Prize Bubbles here. These hold the **Red Stiletto Object**, the **Yellow Builder Cap Costume**, the **Boxing Glove Front Object**, the **Dungarees Top Costume**, the **Atlas Audio Object**, and the **Boxing Glove Back Object** inside. You can also use the hanging sponge ball to swing over to the right and grab the **Big Crane Object** located in that direction.

Careful Crossing

The path continues to the right, but to move on, you must first take out another one of Ze Dude's fearless guard dogs.

OFF A DOG'S BACK

There are some goodies up on the platforms above, but to reach them, you need the help of Ze Dude's guard dog. Wait for it to approach the left end of the platform, and then jump off its Creature Brain and grab the dangling sponge ball above. The ball carries you up to the higher level where you find multiple Prize Bubbles. Collect them all to gain the **Knitted Fabric Material**, the **Flame Motif Metal Material**, the **Grey Concrete Material**, the **Brown & Cream Concrete Material**, and the **Checkered Concrete Material**. Make sure you also snag the **Challenge Key** that unlocks a Survival Challenge. To get to the Prize Bubbles and key on the hanging girders, just throw your weight around. Jump on the very end of the girders as they rise upward to

make them rock back and forth. After a few times, you should get enough air to leap up to the next.

Continue by hopping across the next set of hanging girders to the right. Once back on solid ground, you encounter more rolling barrels of death. These come in sets of three and cover all planes, so there's no sneaking by them.

Wait for a set to come "barreling" down the ramp and then quickly give chase after them, leaping and grabbing the four Prize Bubbles dangling above as you go. This set holds multiple Material items: the **Dark Grey Concrete**, **Bumpy Concrete**, **Rough Concrete**, and **Polystyrene Packing Materials**.

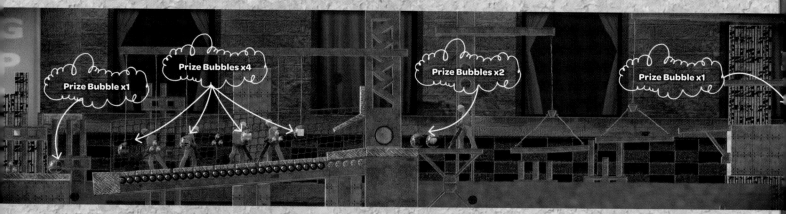

Take a breath, grab the **Long Conveyor Object** from the Prize Bubble here, and steel yourself for this next dangerous bit. When you're ready, hop over to the conveyor belt and start slowly moving up its length, hopping over the barrels as they come. Along the way, be sure to jump up and pop the Prize Bubbles. Snag all of them to receive the **Brown Cardboard Skyscraper**, **Blue Cardboard Skyscraper**, **Red Cardboard Skyscraper**, and **Disco Metal Materials**.

You're not out of the fire yet. Grab the **Plane Silhouette** and **Half Glasses Stickers** from the Prize Bubbles next to the Checkpoint, and then leap from girder to girder while hopping over the rolling barrels. The easiest way to get across without getting burned is to jump to a girder and then wait for a barrel to come, leaping over it in a vertical fashion as it passes by, then continuing to the next girder and repeating. You can find a Prize Bubble with a **Fiery Coal Emitter Object** inside once you reach the opposite end.

BOSS FIGHT!

Ze Dude

Scoreboard

Hi-Scores (1 Player)

Prize Bubble x1

Burning Bouncer Bash

You've found Ze Dude, but he's not ready to go against you face-to-sackface just yet. In order to do so, you must first get past his two burly bouncers.

To take out his bouncers, you need to grab the contraption along the track and then position it under each bouncer as it drops flaming barrels. If done correctly, the contraption bounces the barrel back at the bouncer and hits the button between his legs for a nice explosive surprise.

Taking down the first bouncer is a piece of cake compared to his buddy. Just stay close to him while avoiding any random barrels that get past you. He moves fairly slowly and is an easy target.

The second bouncer is tough. This guy drops an almost never-ending stream of barrels, making it difficult to avoid getting hit. It's easier to combat him from the right side of the contraption (you can grab onto either end) and chase him back and forth, staying behind/in front of him and his fiery falling projectiles as he moves left and right. Do your best to spring the barrels directly back up to the button between the bouncer's legs. With determination and skill, he goes out in a "blaze" of glory.

Once the two bouncers have been eliminated, it's Ze Dude's turn to enter the fray. Compared to the two bouncers, he is extremely tough to take out. Not only does he move much faster than either of them, dropping multiple barrels at a time, but you also have to contend with the floor rolling back and forth, which likewise causes the barrels to roll—right toward you!

Stay on your toes and follow Ze Dude as closely as possible. Bouncing the barrels back up and hitting the button is tough, as he moves so fast that by the time a barrel has been launched back at him, he's already out of position. If a barrel hits the ground nearby or rolls your way, quickly evade it before it explodes.

Don't fret too much if you don't get him right away. Defeating him often takes multiple tries, but you have an extra four lives (for a total of eight) in which to do it …eventually, you'll get him.

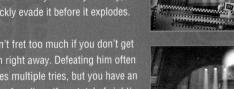

Martial Artist

Ze Dude, under the pressure of defeat, acknowledges you're a worthy foe. He even offers up his private jet for you to take to Grandmaster Sensei's Islands and train under his teacher. Why not take him up on the offer?

Before you go, hop into the back plane and grab the **Ze Dude's Private Jet Object** inside the Prize Bubble. Hop up on the steps and onto the plane to jet to the next level!

The Metropolis
Mini Levels!

The Drag Race

GRAB THE SPONGE TO BOOST YOUR SPEED

How to Unlock: Collect the Key in Lowrider

It's a Drag

Ready to burn some rubber? Hop into your souped-up racer and get ready to pull some Gs! The cars are automatic, but to get some boost, you need to grab the sponge on the dash. However, keep in mind that you have very limited boost, so you must only use it when it counts!

General Tips

You don't have to race in one particular car—they are both available to hop into and ride. However, make sure you don't get left behind when the gates open. If you mistakenly hop in between the cars or fall out, you'll have to restart the race.

You have approximately 20 seconds to race to the finish post. Even if you don't use any boost, you should make it before the timer runs out with even a few seconds to spare. However, racing with the back (blue) car without using your boost results in a loss.

You have approximately five seconds of boost before it runs out. It's up to you when and how to use it, but just be careful not to apply too much on jumps, as it's possible for your car to hit a bump as it lands and topple over.

The Discombobulator

RUN AND JUMP TO AVOID THE FAST FOOD AND FIERY COALS

How to Unlock: Collect the Key in Subway

You've Been Discombobulated!

Ready for another Challenge, are you? In this one, you have to keep running to the right, jumping over the fast food and avoiding the Horrible Gas and fiery coals or, like the man says, it's game over. When you're ready to start, step up to the switch and push it to get going.

Elevation

RUN LEFT AND RIGHT TO AVOID THE HORRIBLE GAS EMANATING FROM THE VENTS

MAGS

How to Unlock: Collect the Key in Subway

A Gassy Situation

This Challenge requires you to survive a series of Horrible Gas-filled lifts, avoiding the gas vents as you descend and ascend, while collecting as many Score Bubbles as you can for the high score.

General Tips

You have 180 seconds to ride three lifts and make it to the finish post to the left of the scoreboard. As long as you are collecting even a fraction of the Score Bubbles, you should have plenty of time to make it to the end.

The first lift is a breeze, with very little in the way of gaseous obstacles to hinder your progress. Just concentrate on looking for the lines/clusters of the most Score Bubbles to maximize your points and multipliers.

The second lift is a bit more of a challenge, but shouldn't pose too much of a problem. It moves a bit faster than the first, and is going up instead of down. Just keep an eye out for approaching gas vents, and plan your route accordingly.

The third and final lift is the most challenging. It speeds downward at a good clip, and there are lots of gas vents to avoid. Continue to scan the area below with one eye to anticipate any potential traps. Also, don't get greedy, not unless you're absolutely sure you can grab that Score Bubble directly underneath that gas vent without getting killed.

General Tips

This Survival Challenge is deceptively difficult. It starts out easy enough, but as the conveyor belts speeds up, and the food and fiery coals begin to clog its path, you must really apply precision timing to your jumps to avoid getting killed.

Both the sushi and chicken drumsticks can be grabbed and pulled. If you find them clustered too close to coals or need to create some space, grab and move them out of the way.

Collecting Score Bubbles is surprisingly hard—especially when the conveyor belt begins to move at warp speed. Even though you want to rack up a high score, staying alive is more important. Don't go for those few bubbles right next to a fiery coal unless you're absolutely certain you can get them. It's not worth the risk!

SENSEI

The Islands

   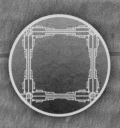

Konichiwa! Welcome to Grandmaster Sensei's Islands. The Islands are a beautiful yet dangerous place full of stealthy ninjas, razor sharp shuriken, massive sumo wresters, and terrible fire demons. Sounds exciting, doesn't it?

Grandmaster Sensei's castle has been stolen by Sumo—the large and in charge bad guy with a nasty temper. After defeating him, you must take to the sky in Sensei's own personal flying machine and head to the volcano lair of the Terrible Oni. Sumo wrestling and demon fighting? Can we count you in?

Story: Chapter 1

The Islands

Endurance Dojo

Ze Dude was so impressed by your combat abilities that he gave you the keys to his private jet. Now here you are at his Sensei's Islands, ready for the biggest endurance trial of your life. Can you survive the Sensei's grueling training?

Stickers

- Black & Blue Tie
- Black Japanese Text
- Daruma San
- Fried Egg
- Geisha
- Japanese Angry Eye
- Lemon Graphic
- Moshi Moshi Logo
- Pink Cupcake
- Pink Microchip Motif
- Pink Sundae
- Pink Umbrella Top
- Play
- Straight Whiskers
- Triple Cone
- Wavy Beige Motif
- Wooden Cane

Materials

- Black & Gold Leaves
- Green & Gold Pattern
- Green Mosaic
- Rough Stone Bricks

Decorations

- Gold Charm
- Green Flower Button
- Jumbo Flower Button
- Piñata Cloth
- Red Charm
- Red Flower Button

Level Complete Gifts

Costume
- Dungaree Dress
- Escaped Convict

Collected All Gifts

Stickers
- The Islands – Temple Detail Concept

Objects
- The Islands – Temple Detail Concept with Frame
- Mystical Dragon

Aced Level Gifts

Costume
- Japanese Festival Robe

BEGIN YOUR NINJA TRAINING

We Have Reached Our Destination

You land Ze Dude's jet at Sensei's Endurance Dojo, the first stop on your way to becoming a ninja. Step out of the jet, and collect all the Score Bubbles in the area.

Prize Bubble Pick-Ups

✔ Objects	
Blue Wave Fan	
Clockwork Box	
Coat Hanger	
Domino Platform	
Double Rocker Platform	
Egg Sushi	
Egg Sushi Monster	
Grab-Swing Platform	
Long Fence	
Long Rocker Platform	
Prawn Sushi	
Prawn Sushi Monster	

✔ Objects	
Quadruple Rocker Platform	
Red Lantern	
Rotating Wheel Platform	
Salmon Sushi	
Salmon Sushi Monster	
Samurai Fan	
Short Fence	
Short Rocker Platform	
Tall Prawn Sushi Monster	
Tilting Kanji Platform	
Wooden Tower Platform	

✔ Audio
"Girly Goodie Two Shoes"
"Islands Int Music"

✔ Costume
Ninja Scarf
Ninja Skin
Red Kimono
Wooden Wig

Move left and collect the four Prize Bubbles resting in the little costume hut. Collect them all to gain a load of Costume items, including the **Ninja Scarf**, the **Red Kimono**, the **Wooden Wig**, and the **Ninja Skin**. Then, pass the Close-Level Post and cross the bridge. Find the torii, or sacred shrine gate, located on the other side of the bridge. There is a Prize Bubble on a small platform in front of the torii as well as a cluster of Score Bubbles on either side. Snag the Prize Bubble to gain the **Geisha Sticker**. To reach the Score Bubbles, grab hold of the red lantern to the left and swing up to the platform. Keep an eye out for The Collector, as he makes off with a few items in the background.

Grandmaster Sensei

After gathering all the bubbles, continue left to meet the Grandmaster Sensei. The warrior woman tells you that you must hone your skills to defeat the Terrible Oni. Wait, Oni? Who said anything about fighting demons!? Looks like you have no choice but to get stronger.

Hands off the Ride

The Grandmaster Sensei has one of the best anti-theft systems in all of *LittleBigPlanet* guarding her ride. So don't even think about touching her magical cloud, or you won't live to regret it.

Just Swing It

There are lots of platforms and ledges in the Endurance Dojo that can only be reached by swinging onto them. Make use of the red lanterns hanging all throughout the dojo; they are light, easy to grab, and located everywhere. Swing on them to reach high platforms and collect the bubbles.

Mind the Gap

Leave Grandmaster Sensei and head to the left. There is a large gap between the platform you are on and the next one. Luckily, there are two red lanterns you can use to swing across the pit. Be careful not to fall, because the floor below is covered in Horrible Gas.

While on the second lantern, make sure you have a lot of momentum going. When you're ready, fly up on to the high ledge on the next platform. Snag the two Prize Bubbles containing the **Gold Charm Decoration** and the **Red Charm Decoration,** and then continue to the next platform using the red lantern to the left.

¡Moshi Moshi!

Your Biggest Fan

Activate the Checkpoint on the new platform and then collect the two Prize Bubbles peeking out from behind the stone pillar. Popping them gives you the **Red Lantern Object** and the **Wooden Tower Platform Object**. To the left are two large fans with two little platforms attached to each one; Prize Bubbles rest in between the platforms. Grab both to gain the **Samurai Fan Object** and the **Blue Wave Fan Object**.

As you jump onto the first platform, the fan starts to fall toward you. Looks like these aren't the sturdiest footholds. Hop to the next platform and allow the fan to dip a little. This closes some of the distance to the next fan, making the leap a little less dangerous. All that's left is to hop across the second fan and land safely in front of the torii.

Collect the Score Bubbles in front of the torii, and then keep moving. A tricky little obstacle consisting of a fan and a fabric wheel lies ahead. First, hop onto the fan's second platform, then leap to the fabric wheel and hold on. The wheel is loose, and you plummet down. Use the momentum from this fall to launch over onto the next platform. Be sure not to stay on the wheel too long; just like the fans, it's not a stable place to hang out.

HIGH JUMP

The Prize Bubble containing the **Thin Wooden Tower Platform Object** located on the high ledge of the platform is extremely difficult to get. First, you must make sure that as soon as you hit the second platform on the large fan, you jump onto the fabric wheel. You have to land on the top of the wheel, or else you won't make it to the bubble. From the wheel, immediately leap as far as you can to the left. This should be enough to reach the elusive Prize Bubble.

Run, Ninja, Run!

Cross the bridge ahead to reach the platform. This one holds two Prize Bubbles behind its wooden pillar. Collect them to gain the **Egg Sushi Object** and the **Prawn Sushi Object,** then get ready for some ninja running. Sprint across the thin wooden planks to the left. Don't worry, you won't fall unless you slow down. Once you reach the next platform, gather the Score Bubbles there and then continue over the next set of planks. On the last plank, jump and try to land on the top of the nearby fabric wheel, snagging the Prize Bubble there to receive the **Domino Platform Object**. Then, without hesitation, leap to the red lantern and swing to the ledge holding a Prize Bubble. Collect the bubble to gain the **Tilting Kanji Platform Object**. Now you can hop down and collect the Score Bubbles on the platform below. What a workout!

These Fish are Getting Fresh

The next area hosts an array of sushi monsters that are looking to start something with you. Hop onto the teetering platform to the left and show the first sushi monster who's boss by popping his Creature Brain. Use the lift you get from popping the monster to reach the Prize Bubble overhead containing the **Egg Sushi Monster Object**.

Wait for the platform to tilt so you can jump to the next one on the left. Gather the two clusters of Score Bubbles and then use the sushi monster to reach the Prize Bubble dangling above. Popping it gives you the **Prawn Sushi Monster Object**. When the creature is destroyed, collect the last bunch of Score Bubbles before jumping onto the third teetering platform.

Here, use the sushi monster to reach the Prize Bubble overhead, which contains the **Moshi Moshi Logo Sticker,** and then hop onto the platform to the right. Two Prize Bubbles are just lying there waiting for you to grab them. Pop them to gain the **Pink Cupcake** and **Triple Cone Stickers**. When you're done, move to the platform in front of the torii to the left.

Geisha
Switch Trigger

Prize Bubbles x3
(Triggered by Switch)

Prize Bubbles x3

Prize Bubble x1

Prize Bubble x1

Prize Bubbles x2

Swing down Low

Collect all the Score Bubbles in front of the torii, and then head to the left. The only thing standing between you and the next platform is a series of fabric wheels. Jump for the first one and snag the Prize Bubble at its base, which contains the **Green & Gold Pattern Material**. Swing over to the next wheel and gather the Prize Bubble at its top, which holds the **Salmon Sushi Object,** and make sure to snag the Score Bubbles hanging out underneath. Leap onto the third wheel and swing down to the platform, collecting Score Bubbles along the way.

Reaching the platform on the other side of the rotating steps causes the Grandmaster Sensei to float down. She instructs you to grab onto her staff to be taken to an even greater challenge.

Step on up

Up ahead, you see five rotating steps with bubbles attached to their top and bottom. Jump on the first step and collect the Prize Bubble there to gain the **Black & Gold Leaves Material**, then wait for it to turn. As soon as it starts to move, jump. By the time you land, the step is stable again. Continue this for the rest of the steps, and don't forget to get that Prize Bubble on the last one. It holds the **Green Mosaic Material**.

Serious Obstacles

Sensei takes you up to a new platform, with a bridge to the left. Head across and pop the three sushi monsters blocking your path.

Prize Bubble x1

HOP TO IT

After destroying the sushi monsters, turn back to the right and step on the small wooden box. Now, hop onto the little ledge and continue jumping across the series of narrow platforms in front of you. On the last one, collect the Score Bubbles, and then leap to the red lantern on the right. Swing to the next lantern, land on the narrow pillar, and collect the Prize Bubble there. This bubble holds the **Straight Whiskers Sticker**. Hop from pillar to pillar, collecting all sorts of bubbles along the way, including two Prize Bubbles, which hold the Tall **Prawn Sushi Monster Object** and **the Blue & Black Tie Sticker**.

After the last pillar, jump onto to the wooden platform. A stone wall separates you from another Prize Bubble. This one holds the **Rotating Wheel Platform Object**. But don't be fooled; you can actually step behind it. So go ahead and move behind the wall to get the bubble. From there, leap out and grab the red lantern to the right. As soon as you have a hold on it, the lantern swoops down for you to collect two more Prize Bubbles and two Score Bubbles. If you managed to snag all the bubbles, you receive the **Japanese Angry Eye Sticker** and the **Play Sticker**. At the end of the ride, you land back where Sensei dropped you off.

Keep moving left to come across a fabric wheel lined with Score Bubbles. Swing down off of the wheel and land on the platform below, where a Sticker Puzzle waits to the left.

THE STICKERED LADY

You soon find a Sticker Puzzle to the left of the platform. Luckily, the Sticker you need is from earlier in the level. Open Popit and select the Geisha Sticker. Place it on the Sensor Switch and three small platforms drop down, each holding a Prize Bubble. Collect all the bubbles to gain the **Pink Sundae Sticker**, the **Black Japanese Text Sticker**, and the **Short Fence Object,** and then return to the original platform on the right.

Head to the right and grab the Prize Bubble on the path before reaching another fabric wheel. This bubble gives you the **Rough Stone Bricks Material**. Swing down from the wheel and land on the next platform, collecting Score Bubbles along the way. Watch for a long stretch of wooden planks for you to run across, located to the left.

Make a run for it and collect all the Score Bubbles in your path. Once you reach the next platform, get ready to meet some more sushi monsters. The first monster is located on the teetering platform to the left. Pop its bubble and send it packing. Repeat the action on the next platform to the left. When the coast is clear, jump up to the teetering platform on the right, and get ready for a Two-Player Puzzle.

Prize Bubbles x4

Prize BubbleS x3
(Requires 2 Players)

JUST LIKE A HAMSTER

From the top teetering platform, jump to the right and land near the launching pad. Step onto it and fly to the Two-Player Puzzle area. A switch and a small stand are right in front of you. Have player one step onto the stand and have player two pull the switch to the right. The switch raises player one up to the next platform. While player one is checking out the large wheel on the upper platform, move player two to the wooden pillar on the lower platform.

When player one jumps in the wheel, make sure they move to the left. This lowers the next wooden pillar, allowing player two to move forward. If player one keeps moving left, so can player two. Soon enough, player two is able to access the small room housing three Prize Bubbles. Snag them all to receive the **Salmon Sushi Monster Objec**t, the **Piñata Cloth Decoration**, and the **Pink Microchip Motif Sticker**. Next, have player one run to the right inside the wheel to allow player two back across to the beginning platform. Now have player one collect the three Prize Bubbles inside the wheel to gain the **Fried Egg Sticker**, the **Pink Umbrella Top Sticker**, and the **Wooden Cane Sticker**.

After finishing the Two-Player Puzzle, return to the second teetering platform and step onto the small Checkpoint station on the left. Hop to the next teetering platform to see another set of rotating steps.

Move from step to step, collecting all the Score Bubbles, and then land on the platform in front of the torii to the left. There's a Start Gate in front you!

Stepping Stones

Once the gate opens, you have 120 seconds to navigate this small obstacle course. There are nine stone pillars you must jump across. The trick is to take your time; you have plenty of it. Just be sure to pick up the four Prize Bubbles located throughout the course. Collect them all to receive the **Short Rocker Platform Object**, the **Long Rocker Platform Object**, the **Double Rocker Platform Object**, and the **Quadruple Rocker Platform Object**.

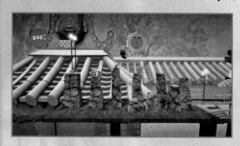

When you have finished the race, cross the bridge ahead of you and step onto the launching pad on the other side to be sent up to a new obstacle.

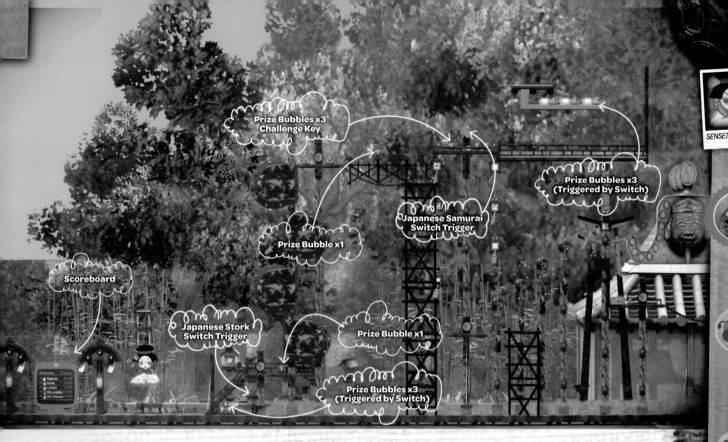

Prize Bubbles x3
Challenge Key

Prize Bubble x1

Japanese Samurai
Switch Trigger

Prize Bubbles x3
(Triggered by Switch)

Scoreboard

Japanese Stork
Switch Trigger

Prize Bubble x1

Prize Bubbles x3
(Triggered by Switch)

SENSEI

To and Fro, Stop and Go

Grab the **Islands Int Music Audio Object** and head over to your left. A series of four fabric wheels lay before you. Jump and grab onto the first one. Swing down the second wheel, collecting Score Bubbles along the way. Repeat this action until you reach the platform beyond the last wheel.

There is a switch on the platform, which can be pulled to the right to raise the platform and to the left to lower it. There's nothing but Horrible Gas below you, so just pull the switch to the right.

Stop the platform once you reach a small wooden box on the left. Hop from your little elevator onto the box and collect the Score Bubbles there. Return to the platform and continue up until you reach another wooden box, this time on the right. Collect its bubbles, and then keep heading upward. Make one more pit stop for the two upcoming wooden boxes. Once you've grabbed all the bubbles in the area, take the elevator all the way up.

At the top, collect the Score Bubbles in front of the Checkpoint, and then walk across the bridge. Gather all the Score Bubbles in sight before continuing.

Endurance Dojo

151

IN NEED OF SAMURAI

Instead of continuing left, turn back to the right and jump onto the little wooden ledge. Hop from ledge to ledge, collecting bubbles along the way, including a Prize Bubble containing the **Red Flower Button Decoration**. When you get to the last ledge, leap onto the platform housing a Sticker Puzzle. Before solving the puzzle, grab the **Challenge Key** and the three Prize Bubbles at the base of the Sticker Switch. The bubbles hold the **Jumbo Flower Button Decoration**, the **Daruma San Sticker**, and the **Girly Goodie Two Shoes Audio**. Unfortunately, you don't yet have the Japanese Samurai Sticker needed for this puzzle; you won't receive it until the next level.

Once you have it, you can place it on the Sticker Switch to make three red lanterns to drop from above. Each one has its own Prize Bubble, so make sure you get them all to gain the **Long Fence Object**, the

Clockwork Box Object, and the **Wavy Beige Motif Sticker**. Once you're done collecting as many of the bubbles as you can, drop over the platform to the left, and cross back over the bridge.

Let It Fly

Check out the fabric wheel lined with Score Bubbles up ahead. Swing down the wheel, letting go once you reach the base to fly to the next wheel. Swing down and collect all the bubbles, then fly over to the third wheel. Repeat once more for the fourth wheel, and then land on the platform below.

Collect the Prize Bubble holding the **Green Flower Button Decoration**, then cross the Checkpoint. Slide down the steep slope to reach Grandmaster Sensei and the end of the Endurance Dojo. It appears Sensei has one more task for you: save her flame-throwing cat from the evil Sumo who has also taken over her castle. Perform this task, and you will be ready for the Terrible Oni.

Move past Sensei to reach the Scoreboard and end the level.

AS THE STORK FLIES

Before talking to Grandmaster Sensei, take a peek behind the steep ramp you just slid down. Directly under the ramp are a Sticker Puzzle and three Prize Bubbles, which contain the **Lemon Graphic Sticker**, the **Coat Hanger Object**, and the **Grab-Swing Platform Object**. The Sticker required is the Japanese Stork Sticker. You don't receive this until you reach the third level of The Islands. Once you have it,

you can place it on the Sticker Switch, which raises the ramp up enough for you to run under and grab the Prize Bubbles.

Story: Chapter 2

The Islands
Sensei's Lost Castle

Here you are at the foot of Sensei's Castle, which was recently ransacked and hijacked by the evil Sumo. You're going to need to use all of your Ninja Skills to take on this new foe and his deadly minions.

SENSEI

✓ Costume
	Flip Flops
	Metallic Tunic

Prize Bubble Pick-Ups

✓ Stickers
	Big Cute Eye
	Blue Mountain
	Dragon Eye
	Dragon Scale
	Grass Doodle
	Japanese Fish
	Japanese Samurai
	Japanese Wave
	Pink Warrior Mask
	Red Japanese Text
	Sakura Flower

✓ Decorations
	Gold Charm	
	Pink Flower Button	
	Sakura	
	White Flower Button	
	Yellow Button	

✓ Materials
	Pale Green Wood
	Red Wicker
	Screen

✓ Audio
	"Song 2"
	"Tricky Business"

✓ Objects
	Big Rotating Sponge	
	Brushcloud	
	Brushcloud with Sponge	
	Cherry Blossom Tree	
	Daruma San	
	Diagonal Large Wheel	
	Diagonal Small Wheel	
	Fat Ninja	
	Green Bamboo Stick	
	Little Doll	
	Mini Sumo	
	Shuriken	
	Shuriken Tower	
	Spiked Rotating Wheel	
	Swinging Ninja	
	Thin Ninja	
	Wooden Catapult	

Level Complete Gifts

✓ Costume
	Angel Halo
	Rainbow Squares

Collected All Gifts

✓ Stickers
	The Island Concept	

✓ Objects
	The Island Concept with Frame	
	Big Sumo	

Aced Level Gifts

✓ Costume
	Googly Eye Glasses

USE YOUR NINJA SKILLS TO CLIMB THE FORTRESS

Prepare for Takeoff

Step away from the Entrance Barrel to meet up with Grandmaster Sensei. She tells you that you need to get over the castle wall before you can

even think about reclaiming the fortress for her. The catapult to the right ought to help you out.

Before you can use the catapult, you need to position it correctly. If you just hop in now, you get launched right into the side of the wall. Move to the switch located on the back of the machine and pull it to the right. This sets it in motion toward the castle. Let go of the switch right as you line up with the small fire pit at the base of the wall. Now, step onto the red button to be launched over the castle wall and into a small alcove of bubbles, including two Prize Bubbles. Collect them both to gain the **Japanese Wave Sticker** and the **Wooden Catapult Object**.

Behind Enemy Lines

Jump out of the alcove to try to collect the stream of bubbles positioned on the adjacent tree. Aim for the Prize Bubble rather than the Score Bubbles. If you can manage to snag the Prize Bubble, you are rewarded with the **Cherry Blossom Tree Object**.

Hop up the steps to the right to enter the fortress, where you immediately discover two sprightly ninjas hopping all over the place. Be careful not to get caught by the spikes located on their undersides. Pop their Creature Brains, and then collect all the Score Bubbles in the area before heading up the stairs to the right.

At the top of the stairs, turn left and jump onto the bubble-lined platform. Be on your guard, because an assassin drops out from behind the screen in front of you. Take him down, and then continue to the end of the platform.

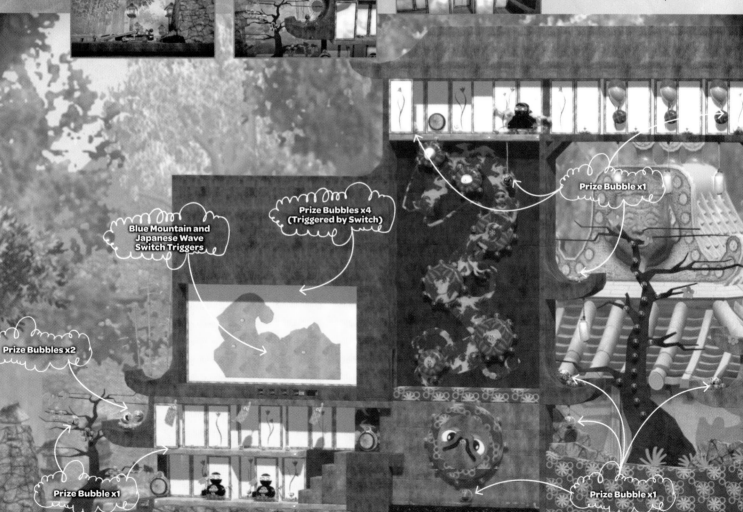

Prize Bubbles x4 (Triggered by Switch)

Prize Bubble x1

Blue Mountain and Japanese Wave Switch Triggers

Prize Bubbles x2

Prize Bubble x1

Prize Bubble x1

WHAT'S BACK HERE?

Behind the screen, all the way at the end of the platform, is a Prize Bubble containing the **Screen Material**. It's completely hidden, but it is there!

Going for a Spin

Return to the top of the steps and head to the right. A giant spinning wheel stands in front of you. Jump onto it and grab hold. Spin down to the base of the wheel to collect the **Blue Mountain Sticker** inside the

Prize Bubble there, and then do your best to walk along the top of the wheel to collect all the Score Bubbles.

Use the momentum of the large wheel to fling your little sack body up to the platform above. There are a series of spinning wheels overhead.

SCENIC PORTRAIT

Head left on the new platform to sneak through a small door. On the other side of the door is a room housing a Sticker Puzzle. You need both the Blue Mountain Sticker and the Japanese Wave Sticker to solve the puzzle. You just picked both of those Stickers up. How lucky can you get? Select them from Popit and place them on the appropriate Sticker Switch. Completing the puzzle causes four containers to drop from above. Pull on the soft material dangling below each container to open them and collect the Score Bubbles and Prize Bubbles they hold inside. Gather up all the bubbles to receive the **Pink Warrior Sticker**, the **Big Cute Eye Sticker**, the **Little Doll Object** and the **Green Bamboo Stick Object**.

Grab the first spinning wheel and use its momentum to fly up to the next wheel. Repeat this process with the next four spinning wheels. Be careful on wheels number three and four; they are not completely covered in fabric, so only certain sections of their surfaces are suitable

for holding on to. Once you get to wheel number five, make sure you fling yourself over to the right and collect the Prize Bubble holding the **Dragon Eye Sticker**.

Walk It out

There are lots of spinning wheels in Sensei's Lost Castle, and nearly all of them are lined with bubbles of some kind. The best way to collect them all is by positioning yourself at

the top of the wheel, and then just walking against its rotation. Before you know it, you've snatched up all the bubbles!

Floating through Life

At the last wheel, hop up onto the upper platform and collect the Score Bubbles there. Move behind the screen to the left to find a hidden Prize Bubble containing the **Pale Green Wood Material**. To the right is a beefy

ninja with spikes on both his sides and bottom. His Creature Brain is located between the spikes on his bottom, so sneak in there once he jumps up and give him a good pop. When you're done, keep heading right and jump from platform to platform, collecting all the Score Bubbles in sight. Make sure you also grab the Prize Bubble on the last platform, since it contains the **Gold Charm Decoration**.

SENSEI

Sensei's Lost Castle

155

Now return to one of the small platforms between the three grey balloons. Grab one of the balloons and start floating down. There are a lot of bubbles to snag in this area, but getting them all is a bit tricky. First, sway over to the small ledge on the left and collect the bubbles there, including the Prize Bubble holding the **Sushi Material**. Then, move to the right and grab the line of Score Bubbles along the ledge. Remember not to let go of your balloon! Now sway back over to the left to reach a ledge that's lower down. This one has one Prize Bubble containing the **Sakura Flower Sticker** and a slew of Score Bubbles. Finally, head to the right for the last ledge and collect another Prize Bubble, this time holding the **Fat Ninja Object**, and more Score Bubbles. When you're done, let go and drop to the ground.

Climb up the rocks on the left to collect the Prize Bubble hanging from the ledge above before you head further into the castle. This bubble contains the **Grass Doodle Sticker**.

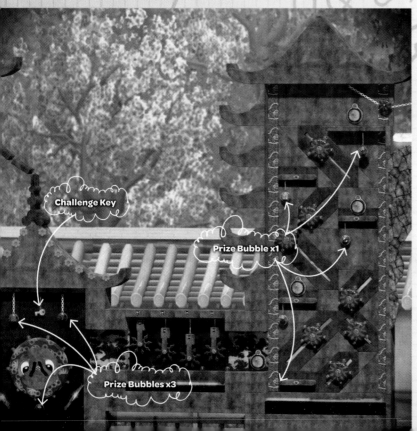

Challenge Key

Prize Bubble x1

Prize Bubbles x3

Shuriken Run

Next up, you find a chamber housing a large spinning wheel, three Prize Bubbles, and a **Challenge Key**. Jump onto the wheel and spin down to snag the first Prize Bubble at its base to receive the **Brushcloud with Sponge Object**. Ride up to the top of the wheel and jump up to collect two more Prize Bubbles and the Challenge Key. These bubbles grant you the **Shuriken Tower Object** and the **Spiked Rotating Wheel Object**. It may take a few tries to collect everything, so stick with it!

Land on the other side of the chamber and face a deadly row of shuriken, or ninja stars. Each shuriken drops down to the narrow path in an attempt to slice you to pieces. Don't become another victim! Wait until the first shuriken rises before stepping forward. Once you take that first step, don't stop. The shuriken are timed so that as soon as one rises, the next one starts heading up, creating a wave effect and giving you just enough room to sneak by.

Climbing Higher

If you thought the spinning wheels before were tricky, then just wait until you reach the next obstacle. A series of spinning wheels slide back and forth along the walls, many of them covered in Score Bubbles.

Step down onto the wobbly platform and grab the bubble-covered wheel to the right. Collect all its goodies and then, when the wheel gets close to the next one overhead, make the jump. From there, snag all the Score Bubbles and jump to the wheel to the left. Wait until you can set yourself up at the top of the wheel and then leap to the left and collect the Prize Bubble dangling down. Pop it, and you gain the **Shuriken Object**.

You should be able to land safely back on the walkway or wobbly platform. Either way, return to the wheel you were just on. When it gets close enough, jump to the wheel positioned up and to the right of you. Collect the Score Bubbles on this wheel and then move on to the next one located up and to the left. Once you have a good hold, drop to the nearby wobbly platform and activate the Checkpoint.

Return to the last wheel and gather all of its Score Bubbles. Once it gets halfway up its diagonal path, leap out to the right and snag the Prize Bubble hanging underneath the next wobbly platform to gain the **Diagonal Large Wheel Object**. You land on the wheel to the right of the last Checkpoint. Return to the last wheel.

Jump up to the next wheel overhead and activate the Checkpoint to the right. Then, return to the same wheel and leap out to the left to collect another Prize Bubble. Snag it to gain the **Red Japanese Text Sticker**. You land on a lower wheel, so make your way back up to where you were.

Jump up to the last wheel and use it to reach the final Prize Bubble in the area, located to the right. Pop it, and you are rewarded with the **Diagonal Small Wheel Object**. Then, work your way back up to the last wheel and out into the open air.

Prize Bubble x1

Challenge Key

Prize Bubbles x4 (Requires 2 Players)

Prize Bubble x1

Prize Bubbles x2

A Storm is Brewing

Two storm clouds full of electricity hover at the top of the pagoda. The clouds rise up and down, and if you touch either of them, you're a goner. Use the ball of fabric on the chain above to swing past the clouds.

Make sure to only go over them when they are lowered, or you can expect to get quite a shock. Collect the Prize Bubble containing the **Brushcloud Object** and Score Bubbles as you slip on by.

Quite the Ride

Past the clouds, a fabric ball is attached to a rolling pin. You must use the rolling pin to navigate your way down to the next area. Grab hold of the fabric and swing down the path to the right. As you drop to the next area, swing to the left and collect the Prize Bubble holding the **Dragon Scale Sticker** along with the Score Bubbles there.

Head back to the right and drop again. Swing to the left and collect all the bubbles under your feet, including the Prize Bubble containing the **Japanese Fish Sticker**. On your final drop, swing up to the right just as you hit the bottom, flinging yourself up to a fabric ball hanging nearby. Once you grab on, you also collect the Prize Bubble attached to the ball, holding the **Red Wicker Material**. Use this ball to reach a Two-Player Puzzle.

Hide and Seek

Back below the Two-Player Puzzle, activate the Checkpoint and move to the right. The area ahead is lined with hidden alcoves where ninja assassins sit, ready to attack. Pop each ninja on sight, but pay attention to the two ninja assassins that drop from the ceiling; they are beside an alcove holding a Prize Bubble. Use the last ninja assassin to reach the Prize Bubble and set of Score Bubbles overhead. Collecting the Prize Bubble grants you the **Daruma San Object**.

HEAVY LIFTING

Access to the Prize Bubble in the enclosed alcove is completely cut off. The only way to gain the **Thin Ninja Object** inside the bubble is to do some heavy lifting. Remember that fabric ball you pulled back and forth in the Two-Player Puzzle? Well, you have to drag it all the way down to the magnetic switch next to the alcove. This, however, is no easy task. You sackpeople were made for pushing and pulling objects, not heaving them into the air. Just the same, you need to push it up over the small wall and drop it down onto the platform below. Drag it over to the magnetic switch and the bottom of the alcove drops out, allowing you to snag the Prize Bubble.

I'll Take the High Road, You Take the Low

First of all, both players need to be up in the Two-Player Puzzle area. If one of you didn't make the jump up there, then have the other one stand on the red button closest to the edge of the platform to lower the fabric ball. Then the other player can grab hold and ride up to the puzzle area.

Have player one grab onto the fabric wheel overhead, and have player two stand on the red button to the right to make the wheel spin. Once player one is able to reach the upper platform, player two can step off the button. Player one gets to chill out for a second while player two moves to the right and grabs the fabric ball on the ground. The ball has a switch on it that causes the spinning shuriken above it to rise up and slow down. Have player two drag the ball to rest under the shuriken closest to player one. Then the both of you can move across the areas, dodging the shuriken. At the end, player one can leap over and collect the four Prize Bubbles hanging past the last ninja star. You gain the **Flip Flops Costume**, the **Metallic Tunic Costume**, the **Sakura Decoration**, and the **Tricky Business Audio**.

Here a Sumo, There a Sumo

Use the spinning wheels ahead to fling yourself up to the next platform. Make sure you grab the Prize Bubble containing the **Big Rotating Sponge Object** at the base of first wheel. Collect as many Score Bubbles in a row as you can while flying from wheel to wheel to land yourself a score multiplier. When you are on the last wheel, jump onto the fabric ball hanging from the ceiling. Make sure you land on top of the ball so you can reach the **Challenge Key** just above it. Don't forget the **Song 2 Audio Object** to the left of the key.

Prize Bubble x1

Prize Bubbles x5

Move to the right and get ready to face some of Sumo's henchmen. Two junior sumo wrestlers land on the platform, and begin hopping around, trying to crush you.

Pop the Creature Brains on their heads to send those sumo wrestlers back to their mommies. Continue to the right and get ready to face the big, bad, evil Sumo. He drops down from above and starts pounding the ground with his feet. There are a total of five Creature Brains you have to pop in order to defeat Sumo.

Start with the brains on his bottom. Sneak under one of Sumo's feet when it is raised, and be careful not to be crushed when the foot comes stomping down. After popping the two brains on the bottom, move back out from under Sumo. Step onto one of his feet and let it fling you up to his head. Once you're up there, pop the brain on his head and the ones on either shoulder. Then, POOF! He's gone.

Thanks for the Lift

You can use the two sumo wrestlers to reach the alcoves way overhead. Hop onto their arms and jump when they leap into the air. This is enough to send you flying up into the alcoves. Collect the Prize Bubble and Score Bubbles. Inside the Prize Bubble is the **Mini Sumo Object**.

Swinging Ninja

Ahead, a ninja greets you with a warm welcome. It looks like they didn't like being the servants of Sumo. The ninja tells you to grab hold of his fellow ninjas and they shall take you to the roof where Grandmaster Sensei's flame-throwing cat is located.

Grab onto one of the two ninjas attached to chains. As soon as you have a hold of one, you scamper together up the wall. There are plenty of Score Bubbles to collect, but with how fast these ninjas move, it is hard to gather them all. Move from ninja to ninja, taking whatever route you'd like up the wall. Just make sure you stop by the third triangle on the right. It holds a Prize Bubble containing the **Swinging Ninja Object**.

At the top is none other than the flame-throwing cat. To set it free, just step on the red button. The cat thanks you for your kindness and floats off in a hot air balloon.

Sliding Home

After freeing the cat, grab the fabric ball to the right and use it to glide through the treetops. Make sure you collect all the bubbles under each tree branch as you slide down to the end of the level. There are a total of five Prize Bubbles to collect in this small area, so make sure you get them all. If you are successful, you gain the **Pink Flower Button Decoration**, the **Purple Button Decoration**, the **Yellow Button Decoration**, the **White Flowers Button Decoration**, and the **Japanese Samurai Sticker**.

At the last tree, let go of the fabric ball and chat with Grandmaster Sensei. She thanks you for freeing her castle and her cat. You are now ready to take on the Terrible Oni. Step on the Scoreboard, and get ready to face the demon at his volcano lair.

Story: Chapter 3

The Islands
The Terrible Oni's Volcano

There you are, standing outside the demon's lair in the dead of night. Can't you just feel the dramatic climax building? With the aid of Grandmaster Sensei and her flame-throwing cat, it's time to slay the Terrible Oni and free The Islands.

Prize Bubble Pick-Ups

✓ Objects	
Bonsai Pot	
Dagger	
Japanese Coin	
Long Vase	
Ornate Bridge	
Pointing Grandmaster Sensei	
Rainbow Tree	
Rustic Vase	
Spike Trap	
Wind Up Teeth	
Wind Up Teeth - Bottom	
Wind Up Teeth - Top	
Wooden Pagoda	

✓ Decorations	
Cream Marble Button	
Dark Wooden Button	
Square Blue Button	
Wind Charm	
Wooden Button	

✓ Stickers
Black Waveform
Bouncy Cloud
Dragon Tooth
Japanese Pattern
Japanese Samurai 2
Japanese Stork
Green
Japanese Sun
Kimono Outline
Old-Fashioned Specs
Pretty Leaf

✓ Materials
Beige Wood
Ceramic
Golden Wood
Illuminated Screen
White Wood

✓ Costume
Fairy Star Wand

Level Complete Gifts

✓ Costume
Pink Hair with Feathers Wig

✓ Objects
Flying Machine
The Islands

Collected All Gifts

✓ Stickers	
The Islands – Mini City Concept	

✓ Objects	
The Islands – Mini City Concept with Frame	
Terrible Oni	

Aced Level Gifts

✓ Costume
Japanese Festival Headband

FLY THE AIRSHIP INTO THE FIERY MAW OF THE MOUNTAIN

The Great Flying Machine

Step down the stairs to the right and collect the small cluster of Score Bubbles. Once you reach the first landing, jump to the nearby red lantern and swing left to collect Score Bubbles, and right to snatch a Prize Bubble holding the **Japanese Pattern Sticker**.

Gather the last bit of Score Bubbles on the ground, and then meet up with Grandmaster Sensei. She instructs you to use her flying machine to reach the Terrible Oni's volcano.

FLYING LESSONS

USE THE THREE SPONGES ON THE FLYING MACHINE TO SOAR THROUGH THE AIR. HOLDING THE SPONGE ON THE RIGHT PROPELS THE AIRSHIP RIGHT, HOLDING THE LEFT SPONGE MOVES THE AIRSHIP LEFT, AND HOLDING THE CENTER SPONGE MOVES THE AIRSHIP UPWARD. THE ROCKETS ATTACHED THE SPONGES ARE SENSITIVE, SO IT ONLY TAKES A LITTLE SQUEEZE TO ACTIVATE THEM.

Hop into the flying machine and grab the center sponge to be propelled upward. Nine banners fly overhead, and each banner has either a cluster of Score Bubbles or a Prize Bubble attached to one of its three decorative disks. Use these to practice handling the airship. Gently direct the flying machine to the bubbles on each banner. When you get to the last one, you should have a pretty good understanding of how to navigate the airship using the three sponges. You should also have collected two Prize Bubbles to gain the **Japanese Sun Sticker** and the **Ornate Bridge Object**.

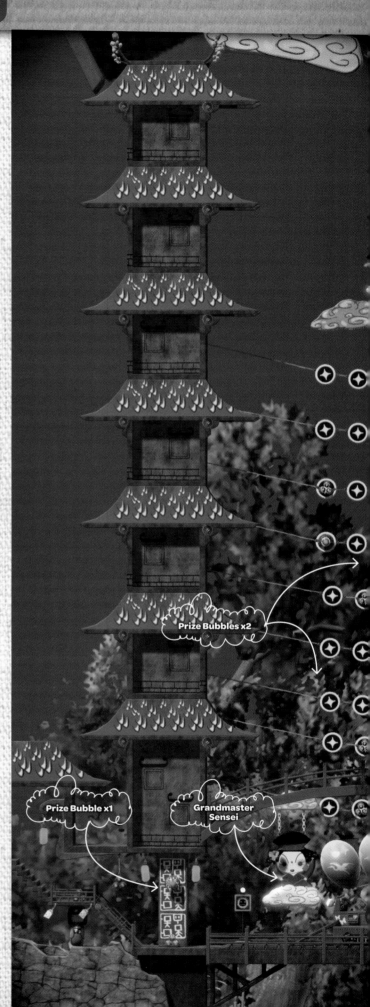

Prize Bubbles x2

Prize Bubble x1

Grandmaster Sensei

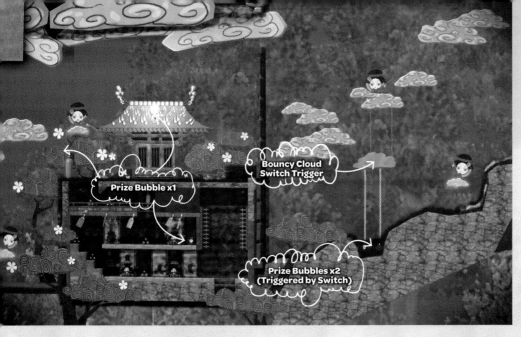

Prize Bubble x1

Bouncy Cloud
Switch Trigger

Prize Bubbles x2
(Triggered by Switch)

Follow the Pointing Sensei

After the last banner, Grandmaster Sensei points you in the direction of the Oni's volcano. Follow her directions (as well as the three pointing Sensei that follow) to reach a castle tower. The tower's gate blocks your flying machine's path. Grandmaster Sensei informs you that you must enter the castle and lower the gate yourself. Before landing on the tower, swoop down under the talking Sensei to collect the Prize Bubble containing the **Long Vase Object**.

No Parachutes

Try to stay on the flying machine unless you absolutely have to exit. You aren't equipped with parachutes, and the ground below is most likely covered in Horrible Gas. There are some areas that are only safe when the airship is nearby. Normally, the top of the tower is covered in black Horrible Gas; it's only when the flying machine has touched the roof that the tower becomes safe to walk on. So don't go hopping off the airship carelessly! You only have the Checkpoint located onboard for most of the level.

Have Fun Storming the Castle

When the flying machine has landed on the tower roof, jump off and climb inside the castle. Right away, two clusters of Score Bubbles can be collected at the entrance. Leap down into the gap under the hanging red lantern to enter the castle interior.

Whoa, this place is heavily guarded. Ninjas and booby traps are located everywhere. Move to the right and pop the sprightly ninja's Creature Brain. With him out of the way, you can easily collect the Prize Bubble he was guarding to gain the **Square Blue Button Decoration**.

Head back to the left and rush under the set of three falling spikes. Watch out! One prick by those sharp blades sends you back to the Checkpoint on the flying machine. Descend the stairs to the next level, and pop the two ninjas there. Collect the two clusters of Score Bubbles they were protecting, and keep moving right.

Soon, you notice a launching pad at the end of the hall. This might lead to where you can open the gate. However, you must first survive the series of spikes that dart out to skewer anything that dares to pass them. But you have to get that gate open, so leap onto the launching pad and cross your fingers that none of the spikes stab you!

More than Luck

Actually, more than luck, you just need a little bit of thought to get past the spikes. Stay in the center of the path and they are guaranteed to miss you. However, if you move to the sides, then they are guaranteed to hit you.

After you safely land above the row of spikes, pull the switch on the wall down to lower the tower gate. This also lowers stairs that lead to the roof. Climb up and return to the flying machine.

Return to the Sky

Fly straight up into the air to collect the Prize Bubble containing the **Wooden Pagoda Object** before you move out to the right. More pointing Sensei guide you forward to the next castle tower.

CLOUDY DAY

Between the two towers and just above the swirls of Horrible Gas covering the ground is a Sticker Puzzle. Unfortunately, the Bouncy Cloud Sticker that is required to solve the puzzle isn't found until later in the level. Once you have the Sticker, you can place it on the Sticker Switch to raise two

 Prize Bubbles from the gas below. Collect them to receive the **Fairy Star Wand Costume** and **Wind Charm Decoration**.

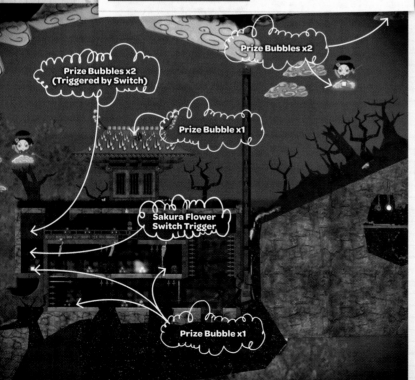

Prize Bubbles x2

Prize Bubbles x2 (Triggered by Switch)

Prize Bubble x1

Sakura Flower Switch Trigger

Prize Bubble x1

Castle Crasher

Land on the tower roof and enter the castle. This time, three clusters of Score Bubbles line the entrance. Drop into the interior via the gap under the red lantern to find more of those deadly spikes.

There are lots of bubbles to collect on this floor. Grab the Score Bubbles in between the two sets of jabbing spikes, and then slip under the spikes to the right to collect the Prize Bubble holding the **Spike Trap Object**. More Score Bubbles, as well as a small room containing a Prize Bubble

 and Sticker Puzzle, lie past the spikes, to the left. Make sure you pop the Prize Bubble and gain the **Illuminated Screen Material**.

SAKURA, SAKURA

This Sticker Puzzle is a simple one to solve. Open Popit and select the Sakura Flower Sticker, which you collected in the previous level. Place it on the Sticker Switch, and two Prize Bubbles drop from above. Collect them to receive the **Rainbow Tree Object** and the **Pretty Leaf Sticker**.

Be careful when you drop to the next level. A row of spikes dart out periodically, obstructing your path. Wait for them to recede, and then hop down. As soon as you land, move back to the furthest plane. Not only

 does this put you out of the spikes' range, but you can also then snag the Score Bubbles and Prize Bubble containing the **Japanese Samurai 2 Sticker**.

Continue to the right and leap under the set of spikes dropping from above. This action also brings you over a small fire pit. Shortly after this obstacle is another fire pit with a set of spikes just past it, rather than on top of it. You must time your jump carefully if you want to safely cross both the fire and the spikes.

At the end of the hall, another launching pad shoots you through a row of darting spikes. When you have landed on the platform above, pull the switch down to lower the tower's gate. Like before, this also lowers an exit to the roof.

Flying into Danger

Once again, fly straight up from the roof to collect a Prize Bubble. This one holds the **Golden Wood Material**. Move out to the right. Stop briefly at the first pointing Sensei to collect another Prize Bubble and gain the **Beige Wood Material**. Keep flying up to reach a batch of clouds and a Prize Bubble containing the **Dragon Tooth Sticker**.

The route gets steeper ahead, and you're almost to the mouth of the volcano. In your rush to meet the Terrible Oni, don't forget to collect the Prize Bubble between the second and third pointing Sensei, and the Prize Bubble at the base of the third Sensei. Snag these two bubbles to receive the **Bouncy Cloud Sticker** and the **Pointing Grandmaster Sensei Object**.

The Wild Blue Yonder

Don't bother flying off course. There isn't anything to explore beyond the castle towers and volcano. But hey, isn't that enough? If you try to fly off on your own, you run into a barrier of Horrible Gas and clouds. Maybe that's Grandmaster Sensei's way of making sure you don't run off with her flying machine.

Into the Belly of the Beast

Descend to the bottom of the volcano. Try to land so you have access to the five Prize Bubbles hiding in the furthest back plane. You might have to move the flying machine around a little bit in order to get them all, but if you do, you receive the **Kimono Outline Sticker**, the

Japanese Stork Sticker, the **Old-Fashioned Specs Sticker**, the **Black Waveform Sticker**, and the **Wooden Button Decoration**.

After gathering all the bubbles, take a look around. There are two paths to choose from. Go right to continue toward the Terrible Oni, or wander left to reach a Two-Player Puzzle.

Prize Bubbles x2

Prize Bubble x1
(Triggered by Switch)

Prize Bubbles x2

Prize Bubbles x2
(Requires 2 Players)

Pink Parlor Mask
Switch Trigger

Prize Bubble x1
(Requires 2 Players)

Prize Bubbles x2

We Did Stop the Fire

Have player one hop up to the higher platform while player two passes by the Checkpoint on the ground floor. When player one steps on the nearby red button, a small ledge appears to the left, blocking a stream of red hot coals from falling down into player two's path. Now, player two can safely hop across the gap in front of them. Have player two walk up the path and jump up onto the platform overhead. Collect the Prize Bubble holding the **White Wood Material**, and stand on the red button there to block the coals from the other side. Player one can now reunite with player two.

Cross the Checkpoint and have player two move to the switch on the left. Once he or she approaches the nearby ball of fabric, it lowers to a mine cart. Have player one grab hold of the ball and land on the cart. Once settled, player two can pull the switch to the switch to the left to move the cart forward. Let go of the switch when it approaches the falling coals up ahead. As soon as the last coal falls, have player two move the cart again, and have player one collect the two Prize Bubbles containing the **Cream Marble Button Decoration** and the **Japanese Coin Object**. But you two aren't out of trouble yet!

Now, have player two pull the switch to the right to move the cart back towards the beginning of the tracks. Once there, player one can grab hold of the fabric ball. Player two needs to move away from the switch in order to raise player one up to the same platform. Now you two are free to return to the main road!

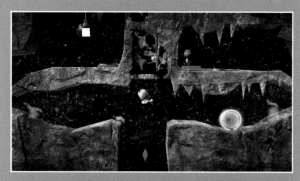

We Have Reached Our Destination

Cross the Checkpoint to the right, and hop over the gap in the path. Be careful when taking the jump: fiery coals pop up from below and try to smite you. Collect the Score Bubbles on the other side, and then leap over hot coals.

A bit of danger lies ahead of you, where a stone wheel spins behind a pedestal. Two balls of fire are attached to the wheel. You must leap over the balls of fire as they pass along the ground. Make sure to time your jumps carefully! Just past them is a cluster of Score Bubbles; collect

 them before leaping out onto the pedestal. Jump directly from there to the ledge just to the left.

PUT YOUR GAME FACE ON

Pass the stone pillar to the left to find a hidden Sticker Puzzle. Open Popit and select the Pink Warrior Mask, and place it on the Sticker Switch to release two Prize Bubbles. Collect both to gain the **Dark Wooden Button Decoration** and the **Bonsai Pot Decoration**.

Climb up the path to the next spinning wheel of doom. This time, there are many more fiery balls on the wheel. In fact, there are only two small paths you can jump through in order to reach the two pedestals in front of the wheel. Time it just right, and you can collect the Prize Bubbles on the pedestals. You gain the **Ceramic Material** and the **Rustic Vase Object**.

BOSS FIGHT!

Prize Bubbles x2

Scoreboard

Terrible Oni

As soon as the Terrible Oni slams down his blade, jump onto the first step. Then, when he lifts the weapon, leap from the second step to the upper platform. Book it to the switch and pull it to the right. Soon enough, the Oni starts blasting fire at you. Stay strong! Most of the fire flies over your head; only the last few cause you any danger.

Fight Fire with Fire

To the right is none other than the Terrible Oni himself. The large beast seems pretty ticked off. Every five seconds, he chops down his terrible blade and spews out terrible balls of fire. It's very terrifying. Good thing Grandmaster Sensei's flame-throwing cat is there to help you out.

Ahead are two wobbly steps that lead up to the upper platform where a switch is located. This switch controls the cat. If you can move the cat close enough to the Oni, then the cat can take him down. The only problem is getting to the switch.

Get me closer to him using that switch - I'll do the rest!
⊙ Close

When those last few balls of fire come flying your way, let go of the switch and rush to the right. When they have disappeared, return to the switch. Keep this up until Sensei's flame-throwing cat is close to the Terrible Oni.

BOOM! This cat is more powerful than it looks! Just by getting close enough to the Oni, it is able to send it sky high! After blasting the beast to smithereens, the cat lowers a bridge for you. He's courteous too! What a cat. Cross the bridge to collect four Prize Bubbles. This rewards you with four Objects: the **Dagger**, the **Wind Up Teeth**, the **Wind Up Teeth-Bottom**, and the **Wind Up Teeth-Top**.

You have done well. Fly to The Great Magician's Temples and get yourself a flame-throwing cat from the shopkeeper.
⊙ Close

You've Done Well, Young Grasshopper

The Grandmaster Sensei floats down to congratulate you on your work. Now, you may fly to the Great Magician's Temples. There, seek out the Shopkeeper and get a flaming robot cat for yourself. A robot, eh? That explains why the cat could talk.

Step on the Scoreboard, and start packing for an exotic trip to The Temples!

The Islands
Mini Levels!

Wheel of Misfortune

RUN AND JUMP AROUND THE WHEEL, AVOIDING THE FIERY PITS AND PILLARS!

How to Unlock: Collect the Key in Sensei's Lost Castle

The Hot, Hot Island Hop

Platform jumping is an important skill to have. For anyone who dares to test his or her hopping grit, the Wheel of Misfortune is the place to be. Weave, jump, and dart your way over the fiery coals and Horrible Gas.

Snatch up the Score Bubbles along the Wheel of Misfortune. Collect as many bubbles as you can while the wheel speeds up to gain the highest score possible. Keep those sack feet moving and hop over the burning coals, leaping from plane to plane as the wheel turns. But make sure not

get too close to that Horrible Gas. Remember, the longer you stay hopping, the more bubbles you can collect!

General Tips

As soon as the stage begins, leap onto the platform and fall right smack onto the Wheel of Fortune. Don't take your time once you've landed. Gather up as many bubbles as you can before the Wheel of Misfortune really gets moving, because once that pesky spinner starts picking up speed, it becomes harder and harder to stay alive, let alone collect bubbles.

Stay fixed in the center and hop from plane to plane, avoiding the obstacles. This really gives you the edge in avoiding those fiery coals scattered throughout.

Keep to the center of the wheel. That helps stay clear of the gas at both ends of the challenge.

Roller Castle

JUMP AND GRAB THE SPINNING ROLLERS TO GET TO THE TOP OF THE CASTLE.

How to Unlock: Collect the Key in Sensei's Lost Castle

Spin It 'til You Win It!

Hold on to your stuffing when you're riding up the spinning halls of the Roller Castle Challenge. Grab and release the rollers to launch yourself from one tier to the next, all the way to the finish line.

Snatch those Score Bubbles as you whirl through the air from one soft, spongy wheel to the next. But watch out for those spikes along the way: one poke, and you're done for! And remember, to make it easier on yourself, collecting bubbles temporarily pauses the timer.

Daruma San

MAKE YOUR WAY OVER THE DARUMA DOLLS

How to Unlock: Collect the Key in the Endurance Dojo

Balancing Act

Scale the Daruma Dolls and race against the clock to be declared champion of the Daruma San race. Just remember to keep your balance, or else you may find yourself unpleasantly buried or wedged between piles of Daruma dolls!

Collect the Score Bubbles as you race. Remember, the more bubbles you collect, the more time you buy by temporarily pausing the timer. And you better believe that extra time is a huge help. With only 32 seconds on the clock, you have to hustle.

General Tips

Keep moving! Don't fret too much about missing some bubbles. There are plenty! Just keeping running and jumping through the level to make sure you beat the timer. Besides, there's a juicy bonus for winning the race.

If you've got your sights set on all those shiny bubbles, then remember, it's all about balance. Keeping centered on the stacks of Daruma Sans not only increases the speed at which you traverse the level, but you also reap the rewards of dozens more bubbles.

Watch what plane you are on. When you reach the flag at the halfway point of the level, hop back to the farthest plane and push that little Daruma San into the large one. This helps insure that you don't waste time with missed jumps.

General Tips

Don't rush it. On this challenge, you have 120 seconds to get to the top. Carefully aim yourself at the spinning rollers you'd like to grab; don't worry too much about the bubbles. One good spin on the rollers, and you collect several.

Avoid the spiked walls. Keep to the center of the spinning wheels. Even though the rollers beside the spikes move slowly, they still put you in far too much danger.

If at first you don't succeed: re-spawn! Reach the second tier of green rollers, and you can activate a Checkpoint. If you find that you can't make it all the way up the level on your first try, use the Checkpoint to take a second.

Mini Levels!

169

MAGICIAN

The Temples

Flaming cats, blue colored yoga dancers, meditating swamis, a huge, lumbering elephant, dangerous serpents, and a Great Magician are just some of the things you'll encounter during your trek through The Temples. Don't let the pulsing, rhythmic movements of the dancers and the vibrant cycling colors lull you into a hypnotic state—you must keep those sack eyes on the prize (bubbles), you know.

This magical place is as dangerous as it is beautiful, and its nooks and crannies hold many surprises and secrets for you to discover if you dare. Steel your nerves and get ready for a magical adventure!

Story: Chapter 1

The Temples
The Dancers' Court

Welcome to the Great Magician's Temples. Your first goal is to seek out the Shopkeeper and procure the Magician's latest creation—the flame-throwing robot cat. You know you want one. Nothing in life worth getting comes easy, however, and it's going to take some little big effort to get one of these fire-spewing robot kitties for your own.

✓ Stickers

	Cobra Head
	Girl Arm
	Girl Body
	Girl Face
	Prince Arm
	Prince Face
	Sara Sama
	Temple
	Tiger

✓ Decorations

	Fabric Hair Wig

Level Complete Gifts

✓	Costume
	Dotted Line
	Green Goggles

Collected All Gifts

✓	Stickers
	Background Environment Concept

✓	Objects
	LittleBigPlanet Concept with Frame

Aced Level Gifts

✓	Costume
	Chicken Beak

THE DANCERS ARE AS DANGEROUS AS THEY ARE BEAUTIFUL

Keeping Shop

You don't want to show up to the Dancer's Court looking shabby, do you? Pop those Prize Bubbles near the Entrance Barrel to get six new

items to help you dress to impress. These include **Baggy Silk Trousers**, **Blue Sari**, **Sherwani**, **Turban**, **Blue Headscarf**, and **Beard Costume**.

Up ahead is the Shopkeeper. Take a moment to speak with the altruistic entrepreneur, and he reveals the prize of which you seek. But in order to acquire the flame-throwing cat, you must find a way to get up to it.

Before making the trek, take a moment to collect the Prize Bubbles inside this room. There are two that are easily acquired—one on top of the basket hanging from the ceiling, and another on top of the counter in the corner. To knock the one above down, first jump up and grab the small ball attached the underside of this shelf to weight it down. This causes a small pack of cats to slide off the shelf and onto the floor. Next, use the kitties to hop up onto the shelf, and then leap over and grab the basket, which causes the Prize Bubble to fall out and join the felines on the floor. For the other, use the kitties to hop on top of the counter and claim the prize. These bubbles house the **Flame-Throwing Cat Attack** and **Flame-Throwing Cat Objects**. Don't forget to grab the **Shopkeeper Object** behind the shopkeeper's head

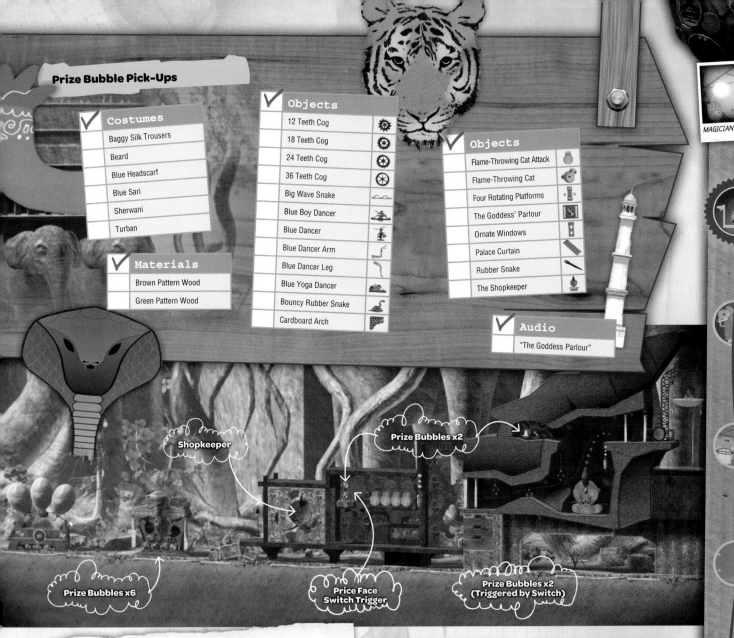

Prize Bubble Pick-Ups

✓ Costumes

- Baggy Silk Trousers
- Beard
- Blue Headscarf
- Blue Sari
- Sherwani
- Turban

✓ Materials

- Brown Pattern Wood
- Green Pattern Wood

✓ Objects

Object	
12 Teeth Cog	⚙
18 Teeth Cog	⚙
24 Teeth Cog	⚙
36 Teeth Cog	⚙
Big Wave Snake	～
Blue Boy Dancer	🕺
Blue Dancer	💃
Blue Dancer Arm	
Blue Dancer Leg	
Blue Yoga Dancer	
Bouncy Rubber Snake	🐍
Cardboard Arch	

✓ Objects

Object	
Flame-Throwing Cat Attack	
Flame-Throwing Cat	
Four Rotating Platforms	
The Goddess' Parlour	
Ornate Windows	
Palace Curtain	
Rubber Snake	
The Shopkeeper	

✓ Audio

- "The Goddess Parlour"

MAGICIAN

Shopkeeper

Prize Bubbles x2

Prize Bubbles x6

Price Face Switch Trigger

Prize Bubbles x2 (Triggered by Switch)

A FACE ONLY A PRINCE COULD LOVE

There is a Sticker Puzzle inside this room, but you currently are not in possession of the Prince Face Sticker required to solve the puzzle. Once you have this princely Sticker in your Popit, return to the shop and place it on the wall above the shelf to reveal the two Prize Bubbles behind the small counter in the corner. The **Ornate Column** and **Cardboard Arch Objects** are located inside.

Inside the next room, grab the cloth material at the base of the wall to the right and yank it to the left to extend a small set of platforms—now you can use them to get up to the next level. Up here, collect the Score Bubbles hanging from the ceiling, ascend the ramp, and hop on the swami's head to be propelled up to the next section of the level.

SWAMI SAYS, "JUMP"

The swami is in deep mediation, but even in his relaxed state, he's happy to lend a helping hand. Use his springy head to leap up and into the alcove to the left in order to grab the two Prize Bubbles nestled inside. Pop 'em both to receive the **Palace Curtain Object** and the **Tower Sticker**.

The Dancers' Court

173

Prize Bubble x1

Prize Bubble x1

Prize Bubbles x3

Namasté

Carefully navigate across the moving platforms suspended over the hot coals. The first few just require a bit of timing to successfully jump or walk off of one to another. However, the final set requires you to leap over toasty obstacles. Make sure you get enough air to clear them.

To get past this lovely lady, you need to run up the length of her left leg as she rises, and leap into the alcove to the right, grabbing the **Temple Sticker** from the Prize Bubble in the process. When she ducks back down, quickly hop onto her back and run down it to grab the Score Bubbles on the ledge to the left. To get the Prize Bubble dangling above, hop back onto her back and wait for her to rise, then leap off and grab the prize inside— the **Blue Yoga Dancer Object**.

Platform Peril

This next set of moving platforms is a bit more challenging than the last. Take your time and use precise movements and hops to get across

without getting singed. Jump from one to another until you reach the next Checkpoint.

In order to grab the Prize and Score Bubbles hanging from the ceiling in this next section of the level, you must use the help of the dancing ladies' forearms. Wait for each to lower their arms down and then jump/ walk onto them, then ride them up and leap off when they have risen as high as they go to grab the bubbles. Inside the three Prize Bubbles are the **Prince Arm Sticker**, the **Blue Dancer Object**, and the **Fabric Hair Wig Decoration**. As with all of the hazards and obstacles in this level, taking your time and exercising caution means the difference between staying alive and having to restart the level.

Deadly Downward Dog

Be careful when running up the lady's legs. She may be a beauty, but looks can be deceiving. If you get caught in between her leg and body as she bows down, you are instantly crushed!

The moving platforms after the Checkpoint with the snake begin to reveal just how deviously challenging this level is. Ride the first one diagonally up, then quickly walk onto the one to the right as it connects with the one on which you're currently standing. Walk onto the next and hop over the fiery obstacle, then leap onto and ride the vertically rising platform until it reaches the top, and jump down to the next. Ride this platform all the way to the top and then jump onto one of the platforms of the rotating contraption.

Find Your Inner Balance

Don't stray too far off in one or the other direction while riding this rotating contraption. A bolt in the contraption's center attaches the platforms, which allows them to stay level. However, this also means that

they can be weighted down if you happen to move onto the outer edges, causing you to slip off and fall to a fiery death below. To make things a bit more interesting, the center of the contraption is flickering with fire. One or two brushes with it, and you're toast.

IF YOU DARE

The brave of heart only need to apply to grab this Prize Bubble, tucked away in an alcove to the right of the four rotating contraptions. To get it, ride one of the platforms around and jump into the

opening as the platform rotates into the four o'clock position. Inside is the **4 Rotating Platforms Object**.

It doesn't get any easier as you progress. After the next Checkpoint, carefully walk onto the moving platform when it touches the ledge, ride it all the way to the right, and then drop down to the one below as they both begin to move to the left. The following topsy-turvy platforms make for some precarious jumping. Be careful, and execute a few precise hops from one to the next, aiming for the center of each in order to keep yourself from falling off.

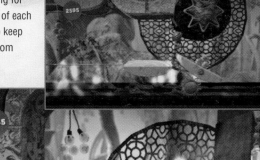

Drop down onto the next platform as it lowers toward the pit of flaming coals. Ride it up to the top and wait for the large flaming hazard to being to drop, and then leap over it and onto the next platform. Repeat once more to make it to the safety of the next Checkpoint. You can stop holding your breath now.

This next bit looks daunting, but you can dash through the crushing platforms fairly easily, as long as your timing is right on. Wait for the first set to crush together, and then start running to the right as they open. You should be able to get through the lot of them without so much as a scratch. To get over this next set of flaming platforms, ride the non-flaming platforms up to their apex and leap over the flames to the safety of the next.

Snake Charmer

The undulating cobra makes for an interesting crossing. While it's easy enough to cross its rippling back, the real challenge is getting up to the two Prize Bubbles dangling from the dancing lady's arms. Ride the snake's waves and leap upward as each one crests until you are able to burst the bubbles and acquire the **Cobra Head** and **Prince Face Stickers** inside.

This next section requires you to ride a set of rotating platforms. Take a moment to wait until the platform with the Prize Bubble resting on it comes by and hop on. You get a **12 Teeth Cog Object** for your troubles.

To get from one to another, ride the first set of counter-clockwise rotating platforms until the one you're standing on approaches the second set of platforms moving in the opposite direction. As soon as they almost touch, carefully hop over.

Rotating Redux

Don't worry if you can't time the rotation to get the **18 Teeth Cog Object** inside the Prize Bubble on this set of clockwise rotating platforms. In a few moments, you can easily drop down on to it from the Checkpoint ledge above.

Repeat the process to get onto the third counter clockwise rotating platforms. There are two Prize Bubbles to get on this set. One is sitting on one of the platforms; just time your jump to get it. The other is dangling from the ceiling as you reach the top of the rotation. Jump up straight to pop it, nabbing the **24 Teeth Cog** and **36 Teeth Cog Objects**.

Four's Not a Crowd

The hidden area beyond to the right requires a total of four players to unlock its secrets. To start, three players need to hop onto the blue platforms on the back plane (two on one and one on the other), and then the fourth player must jump on the button to raise them up.

Next, the two players on one side should stand on the next platform, while the other third player steps on the button here to raise them up. From this position, one of the two players can jump up to the center ledge and grab the **Blue Dancer Head Object** from the Prize Bubble, as well as stand on the button to raise the final platform up to its highest point. From here, the final player not standing on a button can leap over and grab the **Blue Dancer Arm Object** from the Prize Bubble, then jump up to the highest ledge and run across the top level, using the snake to bounce up to get and grab the **Bouncy Rubber Snake Object** inside the Prize Bubble above it. A final Prize Bubble can be found on the platform to the left, and it contains a **Blue Dancer Leg Object**.

This next large dancing boy can help you reach the three Prize Bubbles high above his head. To get them, run up his left leg, hop onto his torso, and then get up to his chest. From here, climb up each of his arms and use the momentum as he waves them around to leap upwards and grab the prizes inside, which include a **Brown Pattern Wood Material**, a **Blue Boy Dancer Object**, and a **Green Pattern Wood Material**. You can also grab and hold onto the soft parts of his body, arms, and wrist to help you

in your endeavor. And don't worry if you fall off— unlike every other part of this level, there is no fire waiting for you below.

Prize Bubbles x3
(Triggered by Switch)

Temple and Tower
Switch Trigger

Prize Bubble x1

MAGICIAN

Prize Bubbles x2

Scoreboard

Prize Bubble x1

Ride of Your Life

Ready for another challenge? Step onto the platform to start a race and ride this precarious platform across the flaming coals. You've got approximately 180 seconds to make it to the finish post before the timer runs out.

Time your start so that the gates open as the platform appears, and then jump onto it before it moves too far to reach. Jump over the flaming obstacles as each approach, and then onto the platforms blocking your path, running across them and dropping back onto the one you're riding when it appears on the other side.

When you reach the platform with the snake, take a moment to grab the **Tiger Sticker** inside the Prize Bubble above it. You can use the snake's springy skin to get up to it by timing your jump just as it springs you

upward. Don't worry if the platform moves away, as there is another right behind it.

A series of carefully timed, precise jumps is the only way to make it over and across this set of fiery obstacles. Short, concise hops over each should get you to the other side unscathed. Hop, drop, and jump through this mini-maze, and then continue your ride to the finish post. Even with a handful of

stops and starts, you should make it to the end with plenty of time to spare. Hey, isn't that The Collector who just swooped up the dancing girl?

TRIM THE TAJ MAHAL

Before continuing on through the rest of this fiery obstacle course, take a moment to notice the large Sticker Puzzle to the right of the Checkpoint. The cardboard cutouts of a temple and series of towers can be decorated with their accompanying Stickers, which you should have in your Popit Menu. Use the Temple Sticker on the center piece, and then slap four Tower Stickers on the four tower pieces to reveal three Prize Bubbles containing **Girl Face**, **Girl Body**, and **Girl Arm Stickers**.

Feel the Heat from below

The obstacle course continues with a series of moving platforms that you must drop down onto while avoiding the flaming hazards. Patiently wait and time your drops so that the next platform is right below. The first few are fairly easy, but it gets trickier and trickier as you go. Snag the **Sara Sama Sticker** above the wave section. At the bottom, ride the undulating slope until you reach the safety of the next Checkpoint below.

Steel your nerves to get past this next obstacle. The rippling snake is completely engulfed in flames, which makes crossing its back impossible. Instead, you must dash underneath it and keep up with the arching body so as not to get crushed by its fiery belly. Wait until its head rises high enough for you to have a safe opening and then run underneath, not stopping until you reach the opposite end.

Prize Bubble Sanctuary

The triangle-shaped hole in the wall with the Prize Bubble inside offers a safe place to rest out of harm's way. Make sure to jump inside it and into the back plane, allowing you to grab the **Big Wave Snake Object** as well as giving you a quick breather before attempting to finish the ducking underneath the remainder of the snake.

Psychedelic Surprise

Beyond the next Checkpoint is the six-armed Goddess who delivers a request from the Great Magician. He needs your help to bring sharing back to *LittleBigPlanet*. You must go see him. His palace can be found beyond the Elephant's Temple. Grab the **Rubber Snake Object** from the Prize Bubble at her feet, as well as the **The Goddess Parlour Audio Object** near the exit, and run through the collapsing walls to find the Scoreboard on the other end.

Story: Chapter 2

The Temples
Elephant Temple

Your quest for an audience with The Great Magician leads you to this ancient temple, where all is not as it seems. In order to reach The Great Magician, who happens to be the master of emitters, you must survive the diabolical booby traps of the perilous Elephant Temple.

Prize Bubble Pick-Ups

✔ Stickers

Crown	
Jewel Crown Motif	
Monkey	
Pink Elephant	
Straight Cobra Body	
Tiger Patterns	

✔ Decorations

Crystal Earring	
Elephant Mosaic	
Emerald Jewel	
Green Fabric Star	
Green Star	
Ruby Jewel	

✔ Objects

Double Oscillating Platform	
Elephant Head Statue	
Extendable Stairs	
Five Section Wave Platform	
Large Wave Platform	
Mechanical Stone Elephant	
Oscillating Platform	
Puzzle Platform	
Six Section Wave Platform	
Sliding Block Platforms	
Stone Elephant	

✔ Costumes

Mini Sackboy
Short Sleeved Shirt
Brown Burlap
Brown Carpet

✔ Materials

Blue Wood
Bollywood Collage
Gold Metal
Gold Sequin Fabric
Green Fabric
Latticed Stone
Silk Pattern
Stone
Temple Stone

Level Complete Gifts

✔ Costume

Life Ring
White Knit

Collected All Gifts

✔ Stickers

Copyright Costumes Concept

✔ Objects

Costumes Concept with Frame

Aced Level Gifts

✔ Costume

Chicken Tail

Prize Bubbles x3
(Triggered by Switch)

Blue Elephant
Switch Trigger

BEWARE OF THE DEVIOUS TRAPS IN THIS ANCIENT TEMPLE

Temple Terrors – Part 1

The Swami forewarns of what's to come. If you can manage to overcome the dangerous and deadly obstacles of this terror-filled temple, then you just may locate The Great Magician.

Drop down onto the series of rising and lowering platforms and carefully make your way across, jumping over the hot coals atop the one in the center.

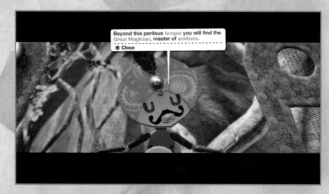

AN ELEPHANT NEVER FORGETS

There is a Sticker Puzzle on the platform above. Unfortunately, you don't have the required Sticker to solve it at the moment (you won't get it until the next level, but you should make a mental note of it and return when you do).

Once you have the Blue Elephant Sticker, return to this platform and place the Sticker on the Sticker Switch to raise the entire platform. Once it's stopped, jump to the ledge to the right to find three hidden Prize Bubbles resting on top of an adjacent platform. Hop down and grab your prizes, which include the **Jewel Crown Motif**, **Crown**, and **Tiger Patterns Stickers**.

While you can't solve the Sticker Puzzle just yet, you can grab the prize inside the Prize Bubble on the small platform to the right of it. To get up there, hop onto the rising and lowering floor to the right, and then leap off towards the left corner as it elevates. You find a **Stone Elephant Object** inside the bubble.

Quickly run through the hallway as the floor lowers, ducking under the hot coals on the ceiling in order to not get burned / crushed. Speaking of not getting crushed, ride the next platform up into this chamber, and

 then hop up and over each of walls as they extend toward you. When you reach the top, jump up and out to the right.

Prize Bubbles x3
(Triggered by Switch)

Prize Bubble x1

Monkey
Switch Trigger

Prize Bubble x1

MAGICIAN

Up top, grab the cloth material at the base of the wall to the right and yank it to the left to extend a small set of platforms. Like the last level, you can use them to get up to the next section.

Hop onto the rising platform and use the ledge above to grab the **Monkey Sticker** inside the Prize Bubble. Continue across the automatically raising floor—each piece raises to meet your footsteps—and collect the Score Bubbles as you go. Once again, pull the cloth material to extend the next set of platforms, and then jump to the left from the topmost one to pop the Prize Bubble and acquire the **Switch Activated Bridge Object** inside.

Drop into this next small chamber to reveal its many secrets. To start, you can get that Prize Bubble dangling above by first grabbing and pulling the soft material attached to the large block and dragging it to the left. Next, pull and extend the platforms to the left to create a series of steps to get up and over to the top of the large platform and then leap across and claim your prize: the **Bollywood Collage Material**.

MONKEY SEE, MONKEY DO

There are other secrets to be found in this chamber. The first is obvious, and the second more obtuse. By pulling the large block to the left, you should have revealed a small opening in the wall behind it. Hop into it and then move to the right until you appear inside the small alcove with the Prize Bubble. Pop it to gain the **Extendable Stairs Object**.

The second secret is right in front of your eyes. See the carved silhouette of a monkey on the large platform? This, of course, is a Sticker Puzzle. You already should have the key to unlocking it—the Monkey Sticker. Slap it on the platform to reveal three Prize Bubbles that drop down from the ceiling. These hold the **Pink Elephant Sticker**, and **Brown Burlap** and **Brown Carpet Costume.**

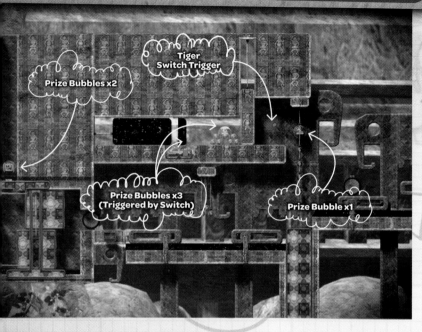

Short hops get you over this set of three coal platforms leading to the next chamber, which contains two large blocks that rotate around each other. You need to run across the tops of them quickly in order to make it through without getting crushed against the ceiling. Before you do, ride up and into the small opening in the ceiling on the left side to grab the two goodies inside the Prize Bubbles. You get the **Temple Stone Material**, and **Puzzle Platform Object**.

Temple Terrors - Part 2

Dash across the rising floor leaping over the hot coals in the center, and then jump over to the square platform in the middle of this next chamber with the button in its center. In there, there are two Prize Bubbles (one atop the ledge high above to the left, and another inset in the rising/lowering block to the right). Wait for this block to begin ascending, and then leap across to the ledge and dash underneath it in order to reach the switch just beyond.

Pulling the switch causes the square platform in the center of the chamber to unfold, allowing you access to the button. Hop into the inset and grab the **Gold Metal Material** from the Prize Bubble, then dash back underneath the block and press the button, which raises the entire center platform.

Hopping off the button results in the floor retracting, but you can jump straight up and grab the large cloth ball and use it to swing over to the Prize Bubble to the left before it drops down. An **Elephant Head Statue Object** lies inside. Use the ball once more to swing over to the top of the block and exit this area.

Cross the next set of horizontally moving platforms, and then use the rising vertical one to launch yourself up to grab the **Double Oscillating Platform Object** inside the Prize Bubble just off screen.

EYE OF THE TIGER

There's also a Sticker Puzzle up here. Launch yourself up and onto the hidden platform to the left, and then use the Tiger Sticker to raise the wall and reveal a secret passage beyond. The first Prize Bubble is up for grabs out in the open—the **Green Star Decoration**. The second two are in a small hole in the floor that is guarded by an extending and retracting block of deadly flaming coals. Wait for the block to begin to retract and then quickly run after it, dropping into the hole in the process. Grab the **Straight Cobra Body Sticker** and the **Oscillating Platform Object** from the Prize Bubbles inside, and then leap back out when it's safe to do so.

Getting across these moving platforms takes a bit of timing. Watch how each set moves and interacts with another, only jumping, dropping, or running to the next when it's safe.

The fiery chamber beyond has a switch located at the far end, and another up top. Hop over the coals to get to the first, and pull it to the right to raise the two platforms in the center. Leap from platform to platform to get to the switch above and pull it to raise the right-most platform even higher. Now, just leap back over the two platforms (and the coals at the end) to get up and out of this death trap.

Prize Bubble x1

Temple Terrors – Part 3

Remember these rotating blocks? Get across them just as you did before by making a mad dash as soon as the left one drops below the opening. When you reach the wall to the right, continue to press to the right in order to drop down and run into the small nook with the Prize Bubble below. Inside is the **Stone Material**. To get out of this chamber, follow the block as it moves to the left.

Down in this next section, you find three sets of undulating floorboards occupying the back, middle, and front planes. Getting across them is a relative breeze; just avoid the two pieces that are on fire. Also, grab the **Six Section Wave Platform Object** from inside the Prize Bubble set inside the very first floorboard in the center plane.

Dash through the section where the floorboards and ceiling come together, and grab the **Five Section Wave Platform Object** from the back floorboard on the opposite side. There are a few more pieces on fire in this next section, but they are easily avoidable as long as you leap over them from a higher vantage point.

KEYS TO THE KINGDOM

Be sure to duck into this small hidden alcove at the end of the floorboard section. You soon find a **Challenge Key**, which unlocks a Score Challenge, and you also discover a **Large Wave Platform** Object.

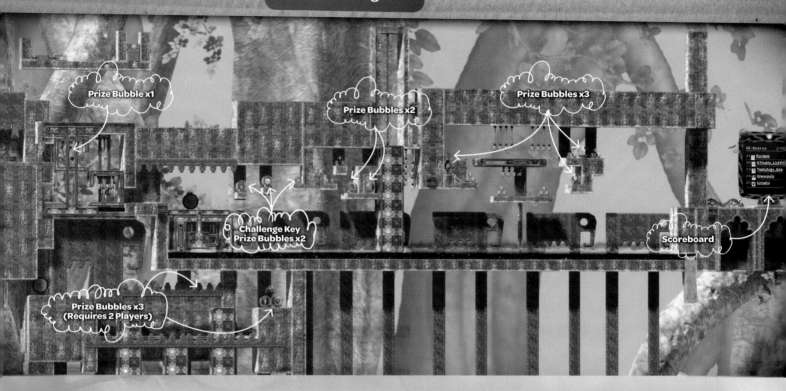

Two for a Drop in the Bucket

Grab a friend to solve this next Two-Player Puzzle. Each player should jump up and grab the soft, spongy material attached to the poles above, and weight them down. Doing so sets a large platform behind them to drop and rise. Hop onto it and ride it down to the chamber below, then player one should jump into the background and run behind the wall to locate a switch and two hidden Prize Bubbles. These contain the **Short Sleeved Shirt Costume** and **Green Fabric Star Decoration**.

To cross this fiery pit, player one needs to operate the switch, which raises and lowers the platforms along its length. To start, player two should hop onto the first platform and then player one should pull the switch. As soon as the switch is pulled, make sure player two leaps off the lowering platform and onto the next. Repeat another two times to get to the goodies inside the Prize Bubbles at the end. These include the **Mini Sackboy Costume**, as well as **Emerald Jewel** and **Ruby Jewel Decorations**. Return the way you came, being careful not to get crushed by the rising platform on the way back up.

Another set of rotating blocks awaits you in this next chamber. However, these are a bit different, as they are hollow inside. Wait for the block with the opening on its left side to rise up and dash in, grabbing the Score Bubbles inside. When it moves to the right and lowers, it lines up with the opening on the opposite block; be ready to run in as soon as the opportunity presents itself. In here is a Prize Bubble containing the **Green Fabric Material**.

Elephant Envy

The moment you drop down onto this elephant's back, it begins to move to the right. As it lumbers forward, you find two Prize Bubbles and a key on a set of platforms above. You have a small window of opportunity to get them, because if you miss or fall off, the elephant continues to move, as does the Checkpoint along with it. Quickly jump up to the first platform to grab the **Gold Sequin Fabric Material**, then hop from this to the next for the **Silk Pattern Material**, and once again for the **Challenge Key**, which unlocks a Survival Challenge. From here, you can drop back down onto the elephant's by hopping into the back plane.

There are a few more Prize Bubbles to the right. Hop up onto the small ledge to grab the **Latticed Stone Material**, then step on the button to open a gate, which allows the elephant to continue its march forward. Once the gate is open, carefully drop down to the right and hop into the small alcove to the left to get the **Mechanical Stone Elephant Object**.

Continue to ride on the elephant's back. Once it passes underneath the low overhang, quickly jump off it and up the steps to the left to get the **Crystal Earring Decoration** inside the Prize Bubble. From up top, run across the large moving platform and grab the **Blue Wood Material** from the Prize Bubble at the opposite end, then drop down into the alcove below to pop this next Prize Bubble, which contains the **Elephant Mosaic Decoration** inside it.

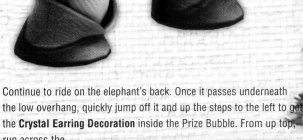

The elephant arrives at its destination—the Scoreboard at the end of the level. Hop off, bid it farewell, and step on the platform to see how you did. Next stop—the Great Magician's Palace.

The Temples
Great Magician's Palace

Your adventure across LittleBigPlanet has led you to Great Magician's Palace. Even though you've faced many perils, seen many wondrous things, and met some of the most interesting Curator Creators along the way, nothing can prepare you for this last leg of The Temples. With dogged determination and a little derring-do, you must survive a deadly obstacle course of emitters.

Stickers

- ✓ Blue Elephant
- Cobra Tail
- Curvy Cobra Body
- Elephant Motif
- Indian Motif
- Yellow Motif

Level Complete Gifts

- ✓ **Costume**
  - Green Swimsuit
- ✓ **Background**
  - The Temples

Collected All Gifts

- ✓ **Objects**
  - Craft Cosmos Concept with Frame
  - Great Magician's Magic Box

Aced Level Gifts

- ✓ **Costume**
  - Chicken Wings

Well, there's no reason to just stand around. Let's tackle the palace head on, shall we? The first obstacle presents itself almost immediately. To cross this dissolving bridge of blocks over that pit of coals, just wait for the first block to drop in place and then dash across as the others follow suit. Make sure you leap up and pop those two Prize Bubbles as you go—inside them are the **Gold Earring Decoration** and a **Small Magic Bridge Object**.

WHAT DOES THE GREAT MAGICIAN HAVE UP HIS SLEEVE?

Dissolving Blocks

The Great Magician challenges you to the death by having you face his palace of emitters. And if you survive, then, and only then, are you worthy to face your greatest challenge…

If you can make it through my palace of emitters, then you are worthy to face your greatest challenge…

● Close

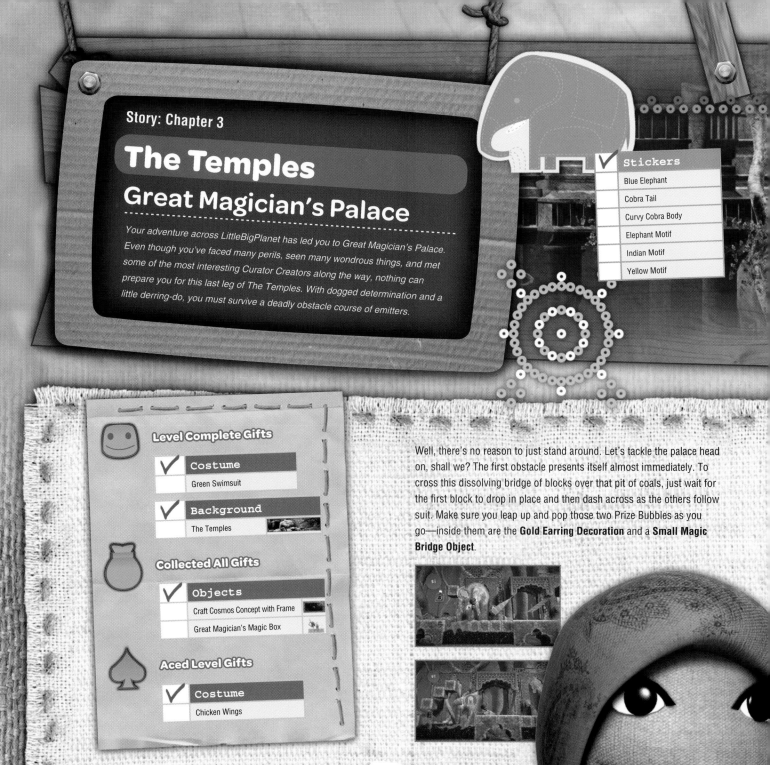

Prize Bubble Pick-Ups

✓ Costumes

Brown Felt
Cardboard Mask
Cartoon Eyes
Green Felt
Grey Side Parting Wig
Trainers

✓ Decorations

Cream Handkerchief	
Gold Coin Chain	
Gold Earring	
Gold Swirly Chain	
Golden Sun	
Green Tassels	
Oval Jewel	
Sackboy Symbol	

✓ Audio

"New Delhi Dawn"
"Temple Int Music"

✓ Objects

Descending Stone Barrier	
Fire Pit Swing	
Fire Pit Double Jump	
Fire Pit Triple Jump	
Grab-Bridge	
Large Magic Bridge	
Magic Flower Bridge	
Mechanical Magic Bridge	
Medium Magic Bridge	
Ornate Arch	
Pink Straw	
Shehnai	
Small Magic Bridge	
Stone Block Emitter	
Sun & Moon	

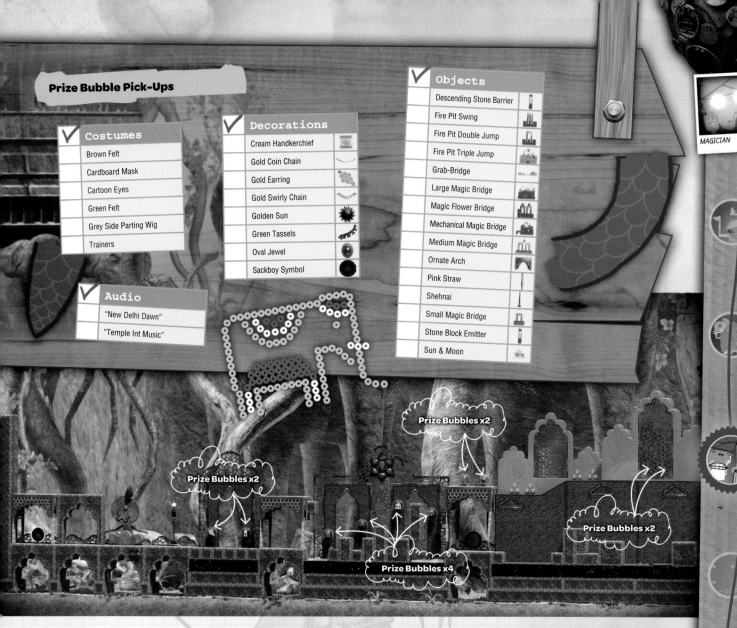

Prize Bubbles x2

Prize Bubbles x2

Prize Bubbles x2

Prize Bubbles x4

Repeat the process over this next pit, except this time the blocks drop a bit slower and are of various heights and sizes. Follow them slowly across as they drop, hopping up to the higher ones, and taking the time to pop the three Prize Bubbles along the way. The real trouble spot is the last three blocks, because if you fall down onto the small middle one, there is no way of getting back up. Make sure you execute a small hop over it. Inside the set of Prize Bubbles, you find **Elephant Motif** and **Indian Motif Stickers**, as well as a **Medium Magic Bridge Object**.

It's obvious where The Great Magician gets his name. This next set of magic blocks appear out of this air as you approach each. Slowly move forward, hopping up each block until you reach the highest point. The path to continue keeps going to the right, but take a quick detour by hopping up to the ledge to the left to grab a few more Prize Bubbles sitting on the rooftop. You get the **Golden Sun Decoration** and **Shehnai Object**.

WHAT'S BEHIND DOOR #1?

Don't drop back down to the magic blocks just yet. There are a few semi-hidden Prize Bubbles up top along this ledge to the right, which are now yours for the taking. Follow the ledge, staying on the back plane, and run behind this wall. Back here, you find the **Large Magic Bridge** and **Sun & Moon Objects**.

Prize Bubbles x2

Prize Bubble x1

Prize Bubble x1

Drop back down to the blocks and continue to cross them slowly until you reach the next Checkpoint. Before continuing across the next obstacle, take a moment to grab the **Magic Flower Bridge Object** inside this Prize Bubble below. To get to it, carefully stand on the left-most edge of the first dissolving block from the Checkpoint platform, and wait for it to disappear. Once it does, as quickly as possible, press the left stick to the left to steer yourself into the small opening and grab that prize. To continue, wait for the dissolving blocks to fall again and slowly follow them across.

Dropping Blocks

This next area is comprised of a series of small, falling blocks that you must cross without getting crushed. The task is simple but dangerous, as to collect the Score and Prize Bubbles, you must use the blocks as stepping stones. Since they are continually falling, doing so can be a bit of a challenge.

Carefully duck underneath the first set and position yourself between the first and second, then jump onto a block as it reaches the floor and quickly vault off it to pop the first Prize Bubble, which contains the **Descending Stone Barrier Object**. Repeat this process at the opposite end to get the second Prize Bubble. This one holds the **Stone Block Emitter Object**.

Dash across this next set of dropping blocks, ducking underneath or hopping over the descending stone barrier to get safely across. There is another Prize Bubble to pop along the way; this one holds the **Pink Straw Object**.

Bridging Blocks

At first look, this pit seems impassable. Upon closer inspection, you find the switch in front of the Checkpoint operates some sort of machine along the ledge above. Upon even closer inspection, you notice that there is a button set on the ceiling just to the right of the switch. To solve this perplexing puzzle, jump up and hit the button with your head (ouch!), which causes a small block to drop from the machine and begin to create a bridge. Next, pull the switch to the right just a touch to move the machine over a bit, and press the button again. Another block drops in place. Repeat this over and over until you've got a safe passage across the coals. Word to the wise—you need two blocks stacked atop one another to get out of the pit. And don't forget to grab the **Mechanical Magic Bridge Object** inside the Prize Bubble here while you're at it.

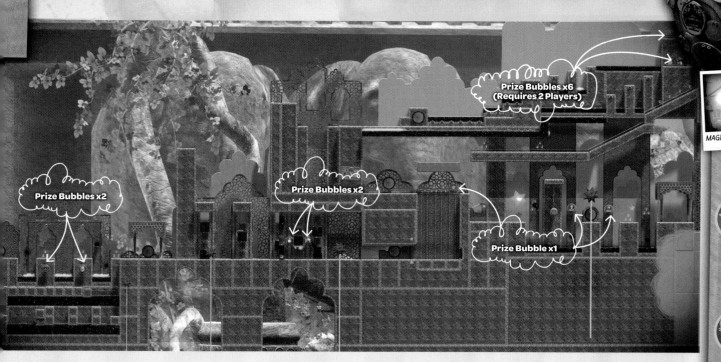

Prize Bubbles x6
(Requires 2 Players)

Prize Bubbles x2

Prize Bubbles x2

Prize Bubble x1

Flaming Blocks

Don't be swayed by the intimidating appearance of this next set of emitter obstacles. Ignore the falling/dissolving set above and concentrate on the lower portion for the moment. As soon as a fresh set of blocks fall in place in front of you, start slowly hopping up and across them. When you reach the end to the right, jump up to the higher set and follow them back to the left, taking just a moment to pop the two Prize Bubbles to grab the **Oval Jewel** and **Sackboy Symbol Decorations** from inside them.

These small fire pits have popping fiery logs that literally "pop" up and out of the pits at steady intervals, creating flaming obstacles of death. The only way across is to time your leaps so that you jump over them. Wait for each to drop down, and then quickly jump. The last pit is the trickiest, as there are two logs to contend with. Wait as before and get a running start to clear them both.

To get through this toasty challenge, you must be quick yet precise. These descending blocks happen to be on fire, and as you know, one or two touches equals one crisp sackperson. Wait for an opening as each set dissolves when it reaches the floor, and then quickly duck underneath, stopping immediately before the next set to catch your breath and wait for the next opening. You also find two Prize Bubbles in between burning barriers. These house the **Cream Handkerchief Decoration** and **Ornate Arch Object**.

Building Blocks

This next chamber presents a unique challenge. Pressing the button on the far right locks you inside and starts a chain of falling blocks to drop from above, filling the chamber in the process. To keep from getting squashed and climb your way out, you need to continually hop up onto the falling blocks as they drop. Up top, you get the **Cobra Tail Sticker** from inside the Prize Bubble for your efforts.

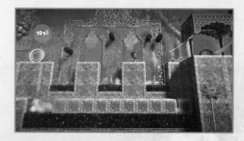

Trip for Two

The path to the left leads to a Two-Player Puzzle. Call on a friend to help, and get ready for a challenging experience. To start this puzzle, player one needs to run back and forth,

continually pressing the left and right buttons to drop blocks on either side, while player two hops up them. Be careful not to get crushed while also being quick enough to get to the top before the blocks begin to dissolve.

Once player one is up top, you must wait for all the blocks to dissolve and then repeat this process using the two buttons above

to get player two up to the top. Be careful not to crush player two, and make sure to work in tandem with him or her so you are aware your friend's position.

Once both players are up top, one player needs to run along the bottom path and trigger a series of blocks to fall and create a

walkway over the pit for the other player to cross. You should both do this at the same time and in a quick fashion, as the blocks dissolve quickly.

It's the player on top's turn to return the favor and create a path for the player on the bottom path by jumping from one platform to the other, before the tables are reversed once again.

When you both reach the top of each path, you find what you're looking for—a whopping six Prize Bubbles. The contents inside are the **Gold Coin Chain**, **Grey Side Parting Wig**, **Grey Trainers**, **Cardboard Mask**, and **Cartoon Eyes Costumes**, as well as a **"New Delhi Dawn"** Audio. Take a ride on the glassy ramp to return back to the bottom.

Pits on Fire

The first portion of this large fire pit has two popping logs at each end and a hanging ball in the center. To get safely to the Checkpoint, wait for the first log to descend and leap over it, grabbing the ball in the process. Don't start swinging just yet! Stay stationary and hang here until the next log passes by on

its descent, then quickly swing over to the Checkpoint, grabbing the **Fire Pit Swing Object** from inside the Prize Bubble as you go.

The next section has a leaping fiery log that continually shoots from one section of the fire pit to another and back again. Wait for it to shoot to the right, and quickly follow after it, stopping at the platform in the center. There's another Prize Bubble to pop here, which nets you the **Fire Pit Double Jump** Object. To continue, wait for the leaping log to shoot over your head to the left, and then hop over the gap.

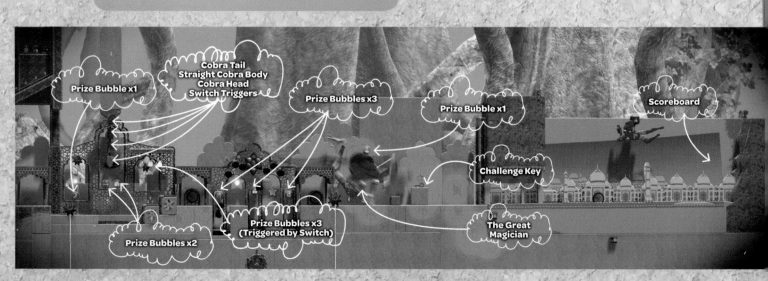

Prize Bubble x1

Cobra Tail
Straight Cobra Body
Cobra Head
Switch Triggers

Prize Bubbles x3

Prize Bubble x1

Scoreboard

Challenge Key

Prize Bubbles x3
(Triggered by Switch)

Prize Bubbles x2

The Great Magician

Jump from the ledge of the yellow colored floor to get up into this windowsill and grab the **Curvy Cobra Body Sticker** from inside the Prize Bubble here, then drop down to the ground. Grab the soft material of the large block at the right side of the room and drag it to the left, which creates a series of small blocks behind as you go. Hop up to the left and then onto the large block, then drop back down to the right and repeat the process with the second large block, dragging it as far to the left as you can. You now have enough height to get into the middle windowsill to grab the items from inside the two Prize Bubbles. These are the **Blue Elephant Sticker** and the **Grab Bridge Object**.

The Elephant Knows

That Blue Elephant Sticker you just collected is the key to unlocking the final Sticker Puzzle back in the Elephant Temple. Make sure you return and solve it once you've completed this level!

SNAKE IN THE GRASS

You may be wondering how to get those three hanging Costume items from the roof in this area. Here's some help! A quick check of your Stickers in the Popit Menu reveals three Switch Triggers—all pieces of a Cobra. Start by selecting the Cobra Tail Sticker and slap it on the small cardboard Switch Trigger found inside the middle windowsill. Doing so lowers the cutout a bit, revealing a second piece of the snake's body. Next, select the Straight Cobra Body Sticker and place it on the second section of the Switch Trigger. Repeat again using the Straight Cobra Body to reveal the snake's head. Select the Cobra Head Sticker and apply it to complete the

 puzzle and lower the Prize Bubbles, which yield the **Brown Felt** and **Green Felt Costumes**. This section also contains the **"Temple Int Music"** Audio Object.

Crossing this next hazard is easier than it looks. The leaping sets of logs go back and forth in intervals—twice to the right, then twice to the left. Wait for them to go to the right and then follow them by hoping from platform to platform until you reach the safety of the next Checkpoint. You also get three Prize Bubbles along the way, which contain the **Green Tassels Decoration**, a **Fire Pit Triple Jump Object**, and the **Gold Swirly Chain Decoration**.

Into the Wild

You've made it! The Great Magician has thrown his toughest obstacles your way, which you overcame with courage and valor. Now that you've proved yourself, you must seek out the greatest challenge of all and save *LittleBigPlanet*! The Collector is stealing all of the Curators' creations and not sharing them with the world. You must go to The Wilderness to find them.

MAGIC TRICKS

The Great Magician has a few last tricks to show you. Every time he pulls up the box he's holding, something different appears from underneath it. There is an order to what is revealed however. It goes from a burning triangle, to a burning log, to a green block, to nothing at all, then it repeats the cycle. Wait for the block to appear and then quickly grab and drag it to the right out from underneath the box. Once you've got it in your possession, you can use it to get up to the blue platform to the right and grab the **Challenge Key**, which unlocks a Score Challenge.

There is also a Prize Bubble sitting atop the Great Magician's turban. To get up and grab it, leap onto his hand from the blue platform and then use its momentum as he raises the box upward to jump up and over to his head. Inside the Prize Bubble is the **Great Magician's Magic Box Object**.

With a wave of his hand, The Great Magician transforms the desert palace level into a snowy oasis, revealing the Scoreboard in the process. Hop on to exit the level and embark to The Wilderness.

The Temples
Mini Levels!

Pillar Jumping

WATCH THE PILLARS AND TIME YOUR JUMPS WELL

How to Unlock: Collect the Key in The Elephant Temple

Alley-Oop

Hike up your trousers or dress, and get ready to bounce. Activate the challenge by jumping into the red button on the far right. Then, leap across the stone pillars as long as you can before you fall into the pit.

Collect as many Score Bubbles as you can before you die. Every time a pillar rises, two bubbles rise with it. Grab them as you pass from pillar to pillar, but concentrate on staying alive for as long as you can.

General Tips

Time your jumps and notice that the pillars raise three at a time, which means you should try to hop from the newest appearing pillar to the latest appearing pillar. This way, you have the most time to collect the bubbles.

Go for the easiest bubbles. Since this is not a timed challenge, you have ample chances to go for the bubbles. Keep on your toes and stay alive as long as you can.

This one may seem obvious, but don't over-jump. Over-jumping can lead to sliding off of the pillars. Instead, aim for the center platform and go for the easy hop, instead of those leaps of faith.

Fire Pits

JUMP OVER THE FIRE PITS AND TRY NOT TO GET TOASTED!

How to Unlock: Collect the Key in The Great Magician's Palace

Fire Walker

Down in the belly of The Great Magician's Palace, the flames of the Fire Pits lick the ancient stones. Race through the obstacles that lie before you, gathering up dozens of bubbles for extra points. Careful though, don't fall into the coals, or you'll be toast!

You have 120 seconds to traverse the Fire Pits before the race finishes. In accordance with other races, collecting Score Bubbles stops the timer temporarily. But the really tricky part is sticking all those jumps onto the narrow platforms. Watch out!

The Shifting Temple

TRY NOT TO GET SQUISHED AS YOU FIND YOUR WAY THROUGH THE MOVING BLOCKS

How to Unlock: Collect the Key in The Elephant Temple

Tight Squeezes

Slip through the manically devious Shifting Temple by traveling through a moving maze and gathering up all of the Checkpoints before the timer runs down. Avoid the fiery coals and mashing blocks by timing your jumps and dashes.

You have 180 seconds to reach the Finish Gate before the race ends. There are no Score Bubbles to pause the timer, so you have to make sure that you keep up a good, but careful, pace.

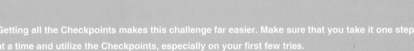

General Tips

Some of the moving blocks shift very fast, so make sure that you give yourself enough breathing room to leap from one moving block to the next. Remember, when you hit the coals, you're not automatically toast; you'll have a brief second chance to skedaddle.

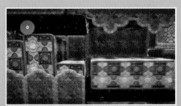

Pacing is key. Time your jumps and dashes well, until you memorize the motions of the blocks. It may take a few tries before you can confidently move from one shifting area to the next.

Getting all the Checkpoints makes this challenge far easier. Make sure that you take it one step at a time and utilize the Checkpoints, especially on your first few tries.

General Tips

Take your time. Make one jump after the other, but don't rush it; the timer may be running, but there is still plenty of time to get through the level.

Hot coals sometimes equal second chances. Remember, you don't instantly die if you touch the hot coals; in fact, there are several places in this challenge where it's nearly impossible to squeeze through without a little singed sack-tushy.

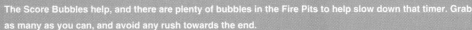

The Score Bubbles help, and there are plenty of bubbles in the Fire Pits to help slow down that timer. Grab as many as you can, and avoid any rush towards the end.

Mini Levels!

THE COLLECTOR

The Wilderness

From the toasty Temples to the wild chill of The Wilderness, this land of ice and snow is the home of the thieving Collector. The Collector has a nasty habit of stealing all the Curators' creations and keep them for himself. Hasn't he ever heard of sharing?

The Collector is prepared for any sort of invasion. His armies roam over The Wilderness. You must defeat them to reach the captured Curators and free them from their complex expanding jail cells. It's an exciting journey with racing sleds, missile attacks, and a boss battle the likes of which you've never seen!

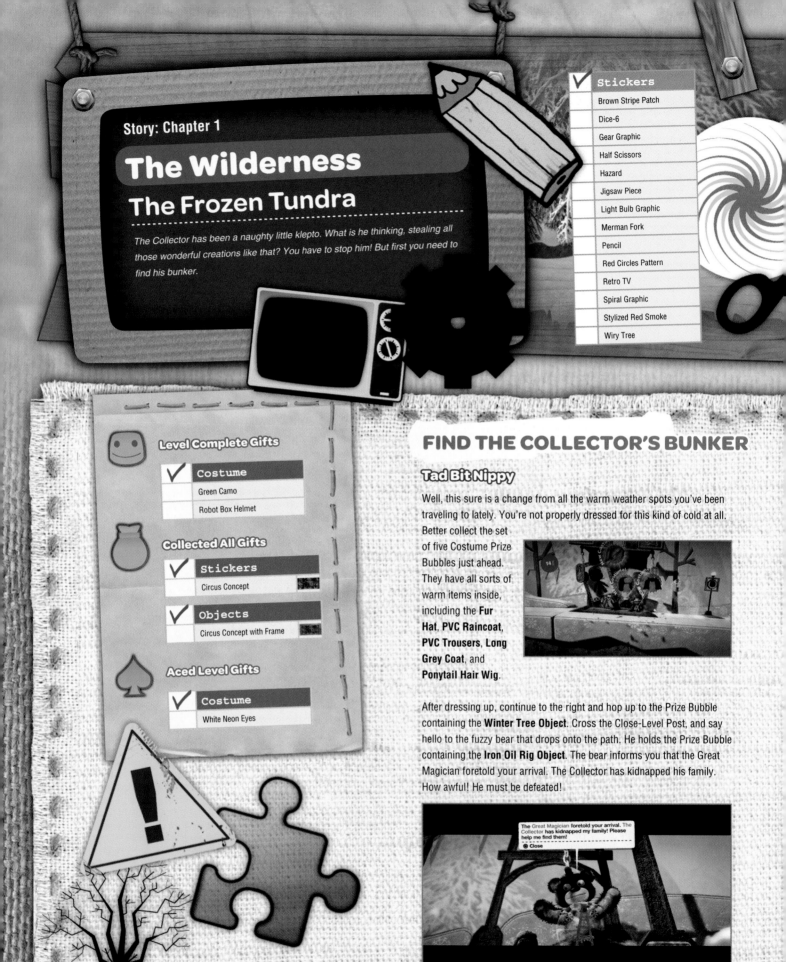

Story: Chapter 1

The Wilderness
The Frozen Tundra

The Collector has been a naughty little klepto. What is he thinking, stealing all those wonderful creations like that? You have to stop him! But first you need to find his bunker.

✓	Stickers
	Brown Stripe Patch
	Dice-6
	Gear Graphic
	Half Scissors
	Hazard
	Jigsaw Piece
	Light Bulb Graphic
	Merman Fork
	Pencil
	Red Circles Pattern
	Retro TV
	Spiral Graphic
	Stylized Red Smoke
	Wiry Tree

Level Complete Gifts

✓	Costume
	Green Camo
	Robot Box Helmet

Collected All Gifts

✓	Stickers
	Circus Concept

✓	Objects
	Circus Concept with Frame

Aced Level Gifts

✓	Costume
	White Neon Eyes

FIND THE COLLECTOR'S BUNKER

Tad Bit Nippy

Well, this sure is a change from all the warm weather spots you've been traveling to lately. You're not properly dressed for this kind of cold at all.

Better collect the set of five Costume Prize Bubbles just ahead. They have all sorts of warm items inside, including the **Fur Hat**, **PVC Raincoat**, **PVC Trousers**, **Long Grey Coat**, and **Ponytail Hair Wig**.

After dressing up, continue to the right and hop up to the Prize Bubble containing the **Winter Tree Object**. Cross the Close-Level Post, and say hello to the fuzzy bear that drops onto the path. He holds the Prize Bubble containing the **Iron Oil Rig Object**. The bear informs you that the Great Magician foretold your arrival. The Collector has kidnapped his family. How awful! He must be defeated!

The Great Magician foretold your arrival. The Collector has kidnapped my family! Please help me find them!

● Close

Prize Bubble Pick-Ups

✓ Costume

	Devil Tail
	Devil Trousers
	Fur Hat
	Long Grey Coat
	Ponytail Hair Wig
	PVC Raincoat
	PVC Trousers
	Red Dress
	Red Horns
	Pink Splat
	Red Devil
	Tree

✓ Objects

	Breakable Ice Platform	
	Falling Icicle	
	Grenade Toy Soldier	
	Gun Turret	
	Iron Bridge	
	Iron Oil Rig	
	Level Ice Slide	
	Lone Double-Wiper Enemy	
	Lone Wiper Enemy	
	Missile	
	Narrow Hammer	
	Relaxed Toy Soldier	

✓ Objects

	Rocket Dog with Sled	
	Shooting Toy Soldier	
	Short Ice Slide	
	The Last Stand	
	The Soldier	
	Triple-Decker Enemy	
	Winter Tree	

✓ Audio

	"Wilderness Int Music"

✓ Materials

	Bunker Stone
	Cream Concrete
	Newspaper
	Snow Paper

Prize Bubbles x5

Prize Bubble x1

Prize Bubble x1

Giddy up, Little Doggie

A set of dog sleds can be found further up the hill. Hop into the top one and grab the front of the sled. Before you know it, you're speeding over a hilly ice-covered course! A Prize Bubble containing the **Rocket Dog with Sled Object** lies just a bit down the track. You can only reach it if you are in the top sled. Aren't you glad we told you to choose that one? As you travel along the icy path, a picture is taken for your Photobooth. Check it out later to see how marvelous you look.

Down, Boy

These dogs are fast. What, are they propelled by rockets or something? Oh, that's right! They are! Remember Grandmaster Sensei's flying machine? You only needed to give the controls a little squeeze for the airship to take off. Well, this is the same. Only take hold of the front of the sled for a little bit at a time, because holding it too long can result in reckless and dangerous driving.

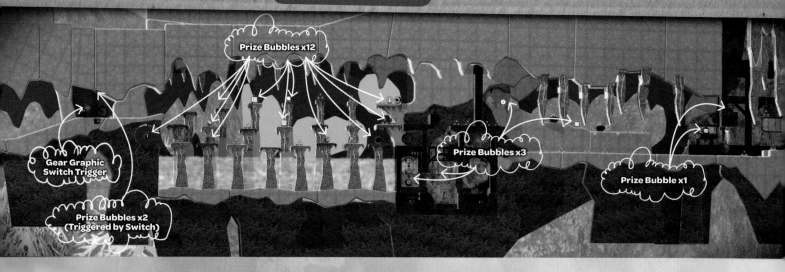

Hop out of the sled after crashing into a wall of soft snow. Watch your step. A new dangerous creature is wandering about. This little military vehicle must be one of The Collector's minions. Pop the Creature Brain on its top, but just don't get shocked by its electric arm.

GEARED UP

Up the hill is a Sticker Puzzle. Too bad you can't solve it right now. The required Gear Graphic Sticker isn't found until later in the level. Once you have it, you can place it on the Sticker Switch to receive two Prize Bubbles. They contain the **Tree** and **Pink Splat Costumes**.

Icicle Madness

A path of icy platforms stretches out before you. Every landing holds either a Prize Bubble or a Score Bubble for you to collect. However, getting to all of them isn't going to be easy. See those icicles hanging overhead? As soon as you step out onto a platform, they come crashing down.

Start on the furthest back plane. Jump from platform to platform until you reach the safe ledge on the other side. The icicles fall quickly! If you hesitate at all during your jumps, you won't make it to the other side. Once you've cleared the back row, move to the middle plane and head back to the left. At the end, leap inside the small cave before turning back to tackle the last set of platforms. You can breathe a sigh of relief. The front row doesn't have any icicles crashing down on them. Feel free to take it easy. Believe it or not, if you have reached all the platforms and ledges, you

gain a whopping 12 Prize Bubbles. That means 12 different items! For Stickers, you receive the **Jigsaw Piece**, the **Dice-6**, the **Hazard**, the **Retro TV**, the **Brown Stripe Patch**, the **Pencil**, the **Merman Fork**, the **Half Scissors**, and the **Gear Graphic**. For Objects, you gain the **Falling Icicle** and the **Breakable Ice Platform**. Last reward is the **Snow Paper Material**.

WATCH OUT BELOW

After crossing the back row of platforms, hop to row two. After activating the Checkpoint, give the block of metal to your right a good shove over the side of the ledge. It falls to the next floor and crashes through to a hidden underground passage. Leave it to traverse the middle and front row of icy platforms. When you are back near the broken path, hop down and check out the Prize Bubbles to the left. Use the launching pad to reach the bubbles containing the **Red Circles Pattern Sticker**, the **Stylized Red Smoke Sticker**, and the **Iron Bridge Object**. Land on the small window ledge to collect the Prize Bubbles holding the **Relaxed Toy Soldier**, **Shooting Toy Soldier**, and **Grenade Toy Soldier Objects**. Drop down and use the launching pad on the right to leap back up to the main path.

That's Some Hail

More icicles drop onto the path. If they land on you, they can crush you, but these giant chunks of ice do have some use to you. The last icicle drops down to create a ramp up to a high-up Prize Bubble containing the **Newspaper Material**.

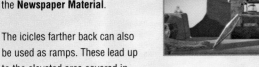

The icicles farther back can also be used as ramps. These lead up to the elevated area covered in bubbles. There are two of The Collector's minions you have to destroy, but once they are out of the way, you can easily snag the three Prize

Bubbles up there. They contain the **Cream Concrete Material**, the **Spiral Graphic Sticker**, and the **Lone Wiper Enemy Object**.

Six more icicles fall into your path. This time, they create a path of cool platforms leading up to the next area. There are loads of Score Bubbles to collect around here, but don't forget about the lonely Prize Bubble hanging out near the third icicle. It contains the **Narrow Hammer Object**.

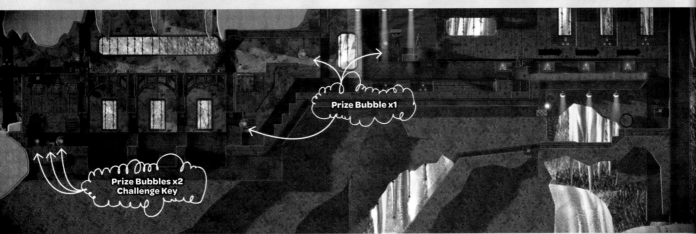

CHARGE!

You must be getting close to the bunker! You soon come across a soldier retreating to the left in the back of a truck. As you run after him, more icicles crash down, this time right through the floor! Do everything you can to avoid falling in!

Once you've made it to the other side, pop the soldier and the vehicle by destroying the Creature Brain. Move to the right and collect the dangling Prize Bubble. This one holds the **Gun Turret Object**. Now you can head down to the area penetrated by the recent run of icicles. Collect the **Challenge Key** and three Prize Bubbles holding the **Light Bulb Graphic Sticker**, the **Bunker Stone Material**, and **The Last Stand Object**. When you're done, return to the upper road.

The Enemy Line

You are going to want to make sure to activate this next Checkpoint, because things are about to get ugly. Missiles fire overhead as soon as you near the short red-tipped wall. Once one missile flies past, hop over the wall and dive into the foxhole on the other side. Repeat this action.

Now it's a straight run from your current foxhole to the enemy combatants. As soon as a missile shoots by, dive out and ram into the red button at the base of the weapon. BAM! Those soldiers won't be giving you trouble anymore.

You're not out of the frozen woods yet. Another missile launcher is active overhead, and retreat is not an option. You must destroy the weapon to proceed. Jump up to the upper path and dive into the first foxhole. This next part may sound like a suicide mission, but if you are up for the challenge, you will be greatly rewarded.

Wait for a missile to fly over, then leap out and race toward the weapon. Jump as high as you can over the oncoming projectile and land on top of the missile launcher. Press the red button on the left wall to send the terrible thing sky-

high. Now the path is completely clear, and you don't have to worry about diving from foxhole to foxhole. Before you continue on your merry way, snag the Prize Bubble by the red button. It contains the **Missile Object**.

Collect all the Score Bubbles in the remaining foxholes, then dive down to the next area. Past the Checkpoint is a Start Gate. When the doors open, get ready for a slippery slide like no other.

WEEEE!

Down you go! Score Bubbles line the path as you slip and slide along the icy slopes. After the first jump, the path makes a sharp right turn. Leap to the back plane so you don't miss the turn. Soon, the slide turns back to the left. Jump planes again to stay with the action. The downward momentum flings you over the jump ahead, allowing you to collect the two dangling Prize Bubbles. They hold the **Long Ice Slide Object** and the **Short Ice Slide Object**.

Continue down the hill and over the next jump. From here things get a little tricky. Multiple paths begin to appear, starting with the one taking up the back plane. It comes into view just after the last jump. Hop back onto this path and allow yourself to be flung over the Horrible Gas. Make sure you end up on the middle path to retrieve the Prize Bubble containing the **Wiry Tree Sticker**. When the new item is in your possession, hop down to the foremost path and snag the **Wilderness Int Music Audio Object**. Follow the curve down to the next level and jump from path to path, collecting as many Score Bubbles as possible.

Go with the Flow

The ice you are sliding around on is a fun material. You can gain some wicked speed, but it's hard to slow down. Backtracking isn't very fun either. Just let the momentum carry you through the race. Flow with the curves and jumps, and don't try to think about the course too much.

Leap into the air as you cross the Finish Gate to collect the Prize Bubble hanging over a set of soldiers. If you pop it, you gain the **Level Ice Slide Object**.

Prize Bubbles x5
(Requires 4 Players)

General

Prize Bubbles x2

Scoreboard

An Enemy's Enemy

Just beyond the soldiers is the General. He's not too happy with The Creator, and is willing to show you the way to his bunker. Just drag him along and he gets you there, no problem.

Take hold of the General and pull him to the Four-Player Puzzle. Don't worry; you are going to hear about that puzzle later. For now, concentrate on popping the Creature Brains of the two new enemies in front of you. More of The Creator's minions, we bet. As you give them a good pop, leap up and collect the Prize Bubbles above their heads. You gain the **Lone Double-Wiper Enemy Object** and the **Triple-Decker Enemy Object**.

Four of a Kind

Welcome to another Four-Player Puzzle. Have all four players stand on the four red buttons in front of the puzzle sign. This lifts the elevator up to the next level. As soon as it jolts to a halt, have all four players jump off the lift. To the right is the main puzzle.

There are four images on the wall. Past that are four wheels with the same four images above each one. The trick is to have the arrow on the first wheel point to the first image listed on the wall, the arrow on the second wheel point to the second images listed on the wall, and so on. Once all the wheels are pointing to the appropriate images (Skull, Egg, Target, World), a door on the right opens up.

Enter the new room and have all four players jump on the small metal platform. This causes the large finger underneath the platform to press a red button. Explosions blast overhead, and five Costume Prize Bubbles come crashing down. Collect them all to gain the **Red Devil**, **Red Dress**, **Devil Trousers**, **Red Horns**, and **Devil Tail Costumes**.

All that's left is to slide down the exit to the right and collect the Prize Bubble containing the **Soldier Object**.

Drag the General through the cleared path, and he opens the entrance to the bunker. From here on out, you're on your own. Step on the Scoreboard, and get ready to strike at the enemy from within.

Story: Chapter 2

The Wilderness
The Bunker

You're really in deep now, sitting inside The Collector's Bunker. But be brave. It is true that there are creatures and machines lurking about that are more deadly than anything you have ever seen before, but you must have courage. All of LittleBigPlanet is looking to you to stop The Collector!

✔	Stickers
	427 Motif
	Faces in Circles
	Mellow Sun
	Red Clown Nose
	Russian Banner
	Russian Border
	Scary Head
	Spiral Doodle

Level Complete Gifts

✔	Costume
	Neon Wireframe
	Box Robot Body

Collected All Gifts

✔	Stickers
	Bad Witch Concept

✔	Objects
	Bad Witch Concept with Frame

Aced Level Gifts

✔	Costume
	Neon Helmet

INFILTRATE THE COLLECTOR'S WAR FACTORY

Goodbye, My Friend

After bursting from the Entrance Barrel, talk to the General. He wishes you good luck. Apparently, you are going to need it. He's right. This is one of

the toughest levels so far, but don't worry. We're here to make sure you come through with flying colors.

Before you leave the General's side, have him help you out one more time. Pull his head down to the left so that it is pressed against the wall. Use his noggin as a stool and hop up to the small platform housing two Prize Bubbles. Collect the bubbles to gain the **Rubber Tongue Decoration** and the **Pink Pin Decoration**.

Sensitive Sides

Move out to the right and cross the Close-Level Post. Down the stairs, a platform rises, shooting out electric arms as it comes from the ground. The platform then lowers back down, tucking its electrical arms back in. Stand on the platform when it is even

with the ground. When it rises, leap into the air and grab the Prize Bubble containing the **Multi-Spear Machine Object**. Then, pop up one more time and land on the ledge to the right to collect the **Black Boot Object**.

THE COLLECTOR

Prize Bubble Pick-Ups

Decorations

1008 Bottle Top	
5 Coin	
Decayed Metal Plate	
Dog Tag	
Green Tartan Patch	
Old Bottle Top	
Pink Pin	
Red Bottle Tip	
Sackboy Coin	
Star Bottle Tip	

✓ Costume

Cardboard Hat
Collar and Tie
Soldier's Helmet
Blue Shellsuit
Grey Camo
Yellow Damask

✓ Materials

Barbed Wire
Blue Concrete
Camouflage
Grey Rusty Metal
White Speckle Concrete

✓ Objects

Black Boot	
Egg Carton Back	
Egg Carton Front	
Egg Carton Side	
Flip-Top Enemy	
Free Range Egg	
Iron Scaffold	
Iron Scaffold Base	
Metal Spear	
Multi-Spear Machine	
Rotating Hemisphere	

✓ Objects

Rotating Iron Bridge	
Spinning Electric Platform	
The Scientist	
Tin Can	
Twisty Platform	

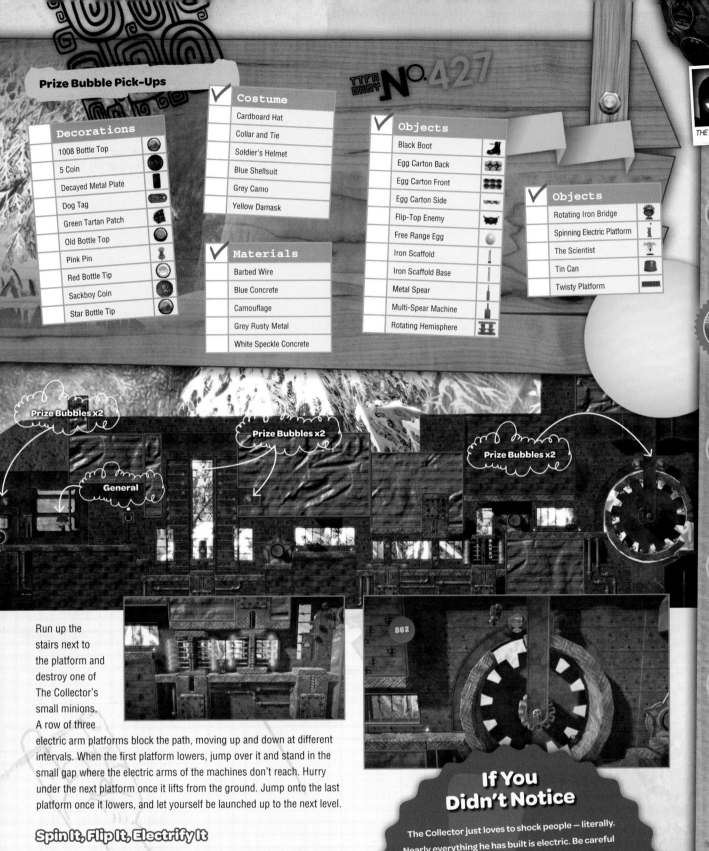

Prize Bubbles x2

General

Prize Bubbles x2

Prize Bubbles x2

Run up the stairs next to the platform and destroy one of The Collector's small minions. A row of three electric arm platforms block the path, moving up and down at different intervals. When the first platform lowers, jump over it and stand in the small gap where the electric arms of the machines don't reach. Hurry under the next platform once it lifts from the ground. Jump onto the last platform once it lowers, and let yourself be launched up to the next level.

Spin It, Flip It, Electrify It

Pop the small minion, and then enter the large rotating wheel. Collect all the Score Bubbles inside by walking along the walls of the object. There are two openings, which you probably noticed. These openings can be used to reach the two Prize Bubbles on top of the wheel. Stay to the left wall and when an opening rotates toward you, stand on the lip. Once you reach high enough, jump from the opening's lip to the outside of the wheel. Now you can pop the bubbles and gain the **Barbed Wire Material** and the **Rotating Iron Bridge Object**.

If You Didn't Notice

The Collector just loves to shock people — literally. Nearly everything he has built is electric. Be careful when leaning up against walls, landing on platforms, or even just walking around.

The Bunker

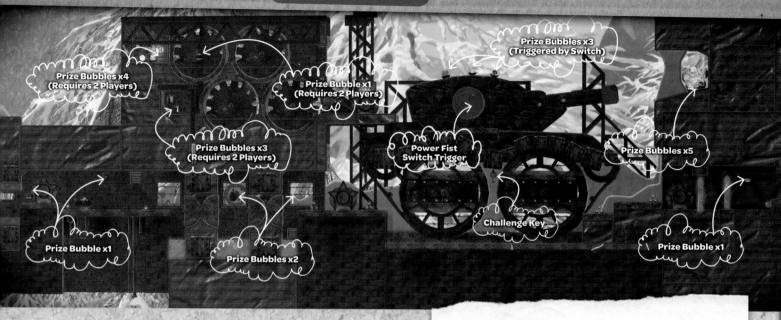

Pass the Checkpoint and find a flipping walkway. The path is made up of six platforms placed side-by-side. Once the first one flips up, then the next one follows, creating a wave effect. Wait for the first platform to flip to a horizontal position, then run to the next one, which is just

landing in a horizontal position, and the next one, and so on. Soon you find yourself safe on solid ground and popping a Prize Bubble. This bubble gives you the **Twisty Platform Object**.

Moving Targets

Observe the next creature carefully. It's a timid thing. Every few seconds it hides its Creature Brain, replacing it with an electric covering. Wait for it to show its brain, then pop it. Use the momentum of the pop to be lifted up to the Prize Bubble containing the very same **Flip-Top Enemy Object**.

At the end of the walkway, four semi-circles swivel back and forth. When they are horizontal, they create a path for you to continue on. When they are vertical, well, there's nothing really helpful about them when they're like that. Wait for the semi-circles to lay flat, then run across and grab the camouflage ball hanging from the ceiling. The semi-circles swing vertical and then go back to horizontal. That's when you book it to stable ground on the other side.

OUT THE WINDOW

Did you see those two Prize Bubbles on the other side of the windows when you were hanging on the camouflage ball? It's tricky to reach them, but if you know this little secret, then you can get them without any trouble at all. On the other side of the semi-circles, step behind the next Checkpoint. There, you find a snow-covered block. Push the block out under the small cluster of Score Bubbles on the snow bank behind you. Jump onto the snowy platform and walk to the left. Soon enough, you reach the two Prize Bubbles behind the windows. Grab both to gain the **Camouflage Material** and the **Rotating Hemisphere Object**.

Not Ready to Go Steady

Pass the Checkpoint and look out over the next area. A platform, lined with bubbles, rotates so that the ceiling is now the floor. Then after a short period of time, it rotates back. Jump inside the platform once it is horizontal and snag all the Score Bubbles. Once it starts to rotate, run up the incline and then fall naturally. The platform is rotating fast enough that

you land on what was previously the ceiling before you slide out. It doesn't hurt to give a little hop once you hit the new floor, just to make sure you have solid footing.

Leap to the next rotating platform and grab the **Challenge Key** hanging between them. Stick to the same strategies you used on the first rotating platform, and you are sure to do just fine.

TANKS A LOT

Climb up the small snow bank on the other side of the rotating platforms to find another snow- covered path leading to the left. A Sticker Puzzle waits for you at the top of the hill. It looks like you need to solve this puzzle to reach the three Prize Bubbles above the camo tank. Too bad you don't get the required Sticker until the next level.

Once you do have the Power Fist Sticker, return to this spot. Stand on the metal platform and place the Sticker onto the Sticker Switch. This makes the platform you are standing on spring up, sending you up to the top of the tank. While you are up there, snag the Prize Bubbles containing the **Spiral Doodle**, **Russian Border**, and **Faces in Circles** Pictures.

Don't hop down just yet! Walk across the tank and stomp on the red button on top of the cannon. This releases an impact explosive that goes hurtling into the nearby wall of snow. Blast it a few more times to reveal five Prize Bubbles. They all go fluttering down to the lower level. Jump off the tank and claim your rewards! You receive the **Yellow Damask Costume**, the **Blue Shellsuit Costume**, the **Russian Banner Sticker**, the **Scary Head Sticker**, and the **Metal Spear Object**.

TWO'S A DATE, THREE'S A PARTY!

To the left of the Sticker Puzzle is a Two-Player Puzzle that actually turns into a Three-Player Puzzle. Sounds interesting, doesn't it? First, have player one climb into the first wheel on the bottom platform and pull the switch. This rotates the wheel so that its opening is now facing the other direction. Climb into the next wheel and pull its switch to make rotate to the left. This switch also moves the first wheel on the upper platform. Now its opening is facing right, allowing player two to hop inside.

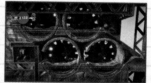

Once player two is settled, have player one pull the switch in the second wheel of the bottom platform. At the same time, player two should be pulling his or her switch to cause the second wheel to rotate. Now the upper platform's wheels have their openings facing each other. Have player two move into the new wheel and collect the Prize Bubble inside. This bubble contains the **Egg Carton Side Object**. Have player two step on the red button in his or her wheel to raise the wall that was blocking player one from a pile of Prize Bubbles. Collect them all to gain the **Collar and Tie Costume**, the **Soldier's Helmet Costume** and the **Decayed Metal Plate Decoration**.

This is where player three comes in. Player one needs to backtrack to the second wheel of the lower platform and pull the switch so player three can access the first wheel of the upper platform. Have player three pull the switch inside to allow player two access to four Prize Bubbles. Grab them all to gain the **Dog Tag Decoration**, the **Grey Camo Costume**, the **Cardboard Box Hat Costume**, and the **Mellow Sun Sticker**.

Now that you have all the prizes, you still need to somehow get out of this puzzle. Once player two is back in the second wheel of the upper platform, have player three pull the switch. Now, player two and player three are both in the same wheel. Player one has to pull the switch in their wheel to let players two and three out of the puzzle. Then, player one can work the switches all alone to reunite with his or her friends.

Shocking Point

Down the path, a series of electric spikes dart across the hall. Sneak under the first one once it lifts up, and then hop over the second one once it lowers down. Be careful not to hop too far. You don't want to hit the spike that juts out along the floor. Leap onto the platform above this last spike, and then quickly turn around and jump back to the left to grab the Prize Bubble containing the **Egg Carton Front Object**.

Back on the platform, run under the next spike as it lifts up, and leap over the last one as it dips down. Cross the Checkpoint and prepare to take on some of The Collector's minions.

Outnumbered

Three minions block the path. Pop their Creature Brains one at a time and be careful of their electric bits. Use the center minion to reach the Prize Bubble above its head. Inside is the **Iron Scaffolding Base Object**. When popping the last minion, hop up to the snow bank to find the Prize Bubble containing the **Iron Scaffold Object**. Keep walking up to the right to find two more Prize Bubbles, as well as a bunch of Score Bubbles. Collect the bubbles to gain the **Green Tartan Patch Decoration** and the **427 Motif Sticker**.

Return to the main path and hop onto the small green cart rolling back and forth over an electric floor. Ride the cart safely across the dangerous ground, and then collect the Prize Bubble containing the **Tin Can Object**.

The Electric Hop

The next obstacles to overcome are the three platforms ahead. They don't look too tricky, but the intervals at which the electric cylinders travel around them makes things a bit more difficult. When jumping from one platform to the next, you must jump high enough to avoid the cylinder coming up from below you, but not so high that you hit the cylinder just above your head.

Pop the minion ahead and step on the lip of the rotating wheel. Ride it up to the first snow bank on the left. Collect the Prize Bubble there, which contains the **Spinning Electric Platform Object,** and then hop onto the outside of the wheel.

Immediately leap to the upper snow bank and grab the Prize Bubble holding the **1008 Bottle Top Decoration**. Don't forget about the Score Bubbles up there too! Jump back onto the outside of the rotating wheel and then leap to the upper right snow bank to collect four Prize Bubbles plus a few Score Bubbles. You gain the **Red Clown Nose Sticker**, the **Red Bottle Top Decoration**, the **Old Bottle Top Decoration**, and the **Star Bottle Top Decoration**. But you're not done yet! There is one final Prize Bubble. Drop down to the next level and collect it to gain the **Rotating Barbed Wire Cage Object**.

Enter the wheel once the opening spins toward you. You find three electric cylinders inside; make sure you hop over them when they approach! Gather all the Score Bubbles inside the wheel, then drop through the bottom exit.

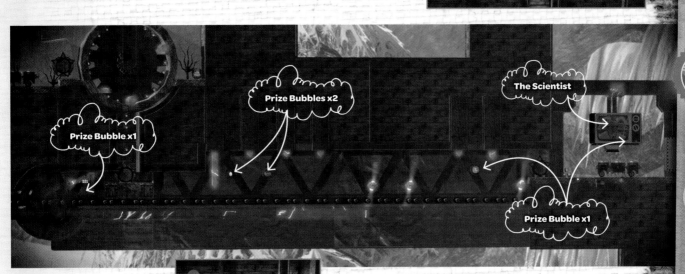

Prize Bubble x1

Prize Bubbles x2

The Scientist

Prize Bubble x1

Walk this Way

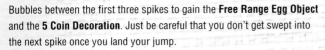

Step out onto the conveyor belt in front of you and walk against its movement for a short bit to gain the Prize Bubble containing the **Egg Carton Back Object**. Now, go with the flow and wander to the right. Watch out for the electric spikes stabbing down onto the belt. Take a moment to hop up to the Prize Bubbles between the first three spikes to gain the **Free Range Egg Object** and the **5 Coin Decoration**. Just be careful that you don't get swept into the next spike once you land your jump.

After the spikes are two electric searchlights. Hop over them to avoid getting fried. Next are two more spikes and another searchlight. Don't miss the Prize Bubble holding the **Sackboy Coin Decoration**. It's in between the spikes.

What's up, Doc?

After the last spotlight, you reach a room with a bristly man trapped inside a TV. Take care of the minion wandering around under the TV before you investigate any further. Pull the switch on the right wall to free The Scientist. The Collector has been forcing him to create all sorts of horrible inventions. You had better keep an eye out for them.

Tossed like a Rag Doll

The switch not only freed The Scientist, but it also caused the giant wheel to the right to start moving. To see what this enormous contraption is all about, follow the yellow arrow behind the switch. Don't forget to grab the Prize Bubble next to The Scientist before you go! It contains **The Scientist Object**.

Prize Bubble x1
Prize Bubbles x2
Scoreboard

Short and Sweet

When jumping around inside this huge rotating wheel, keep the height to a minimum. The larger your jump, the more time it takes for you to get your feet back on the ground. And when the ground is moving like this, you need to keep them planted as firmly as possible.

Move all the way to the right and activate the Checkpoint. The rotating metal wheel is really a large maze you have to navigate. Jump into the center of the wheel and land on the camouflage platform. Move to the right, collecting Score Bubbles as you go. Hop from one camouflage platform to the next until you reach the entrance to the next ring of the wheel. Hop down and keep moving against the wheel's rotation. Don't step off the camo! The floor has a strong electric current.

Grab the ball of camouflage and swing quickly to the next platform. A wall is in your path! Wait until there is a steep enough decline that you can

hop over the wall, and then grab the next ball of camo. Quickly let go and land on the safe platform. Run to keep up your balance and dive past the Checkpoint, landing in the outer ring of the wheel.

Things really pick up in the outer ring. You have to run fast to make sure you don't fall too far behind. If you do, you end up being tossed around like a rag doll inside the wheel. Hop over all the electric cylinders in the path while collecting all the bubbles in sight. Don't bother going back for one you've already passed.

Soon you have to start hopping onto wooden platforms. Move from platform to platform until you reach the highest one, which happens to contain a large Prize Bubble holding the **White Speckle Concrete Material**. Snatch the bubble, and then drop through the maze exit.

Against the Tide

The maze shoots you out onto a backward-moving conveyer belt. Move to the right as soon as you land to avoid being cooked by the spotlight on the left. However, the only way to grab the Prize Bubble over the spotlight is to bite the bullet and take one for the team. For your valiant effort, you are awarded the **Grey Rusty Metal Material**.

Keep to the right and leap over the next spotlight to pop the Prize Bubble containing the **Blue Concrete Material**. Pass under two electric spikes and hop over another spotlight. Jump off the conveyer belt and onto the Scoreboard. Congratulations on surviving The Bunker!

The Wilderness
The Collector's Lair

The Collector's Lair is a labyrinth of twisted and rotating metal cages. Inside this horrible prison are all the friends you've made during your journey around LittleBigPlanet. You, a simple little sackperson, are their last big hope.

THE COLLECTOR

Prize Bubble Pick-Ups

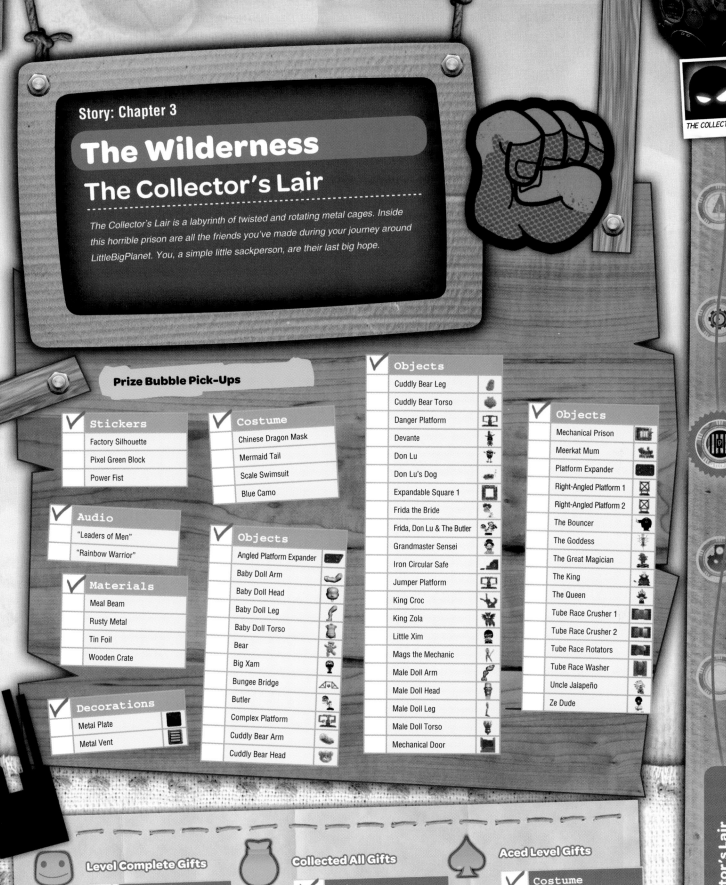

Stickers
- Factory Silhouette
- Pixel Green Block
- Power Fist

Audio
- "Leaders of Men"
- "Rainbow Warrior"

Materials
- Meal Beam
- Rusty Metal
- Tin Foil
- Wooden Crate

Decorations
- Metal Plate
- Metal Vent

Costume
- Chinese Dragon Mask
- Mermaid Tail
- Scale Swimsuit
- Blue Camo

Objects
- Angled Platform Expander
- Baby Doll Arm
- Baby Doll Head
- Baby Doll Leg
- Baby Doll Torso
- Bear
- Big Xam
- Bungee Bridge
- Butler
- Complex Platform
- Cuddly Bear Arm
- Cuddly Bear Head

Objects
- Cuddly Bear Leg
- Cuddly Bear Torso
- Danger Platform
- Devante
- Don Lu
- Don Lu's Dog
- Expandable Square 1
- Frida the Bride
- Frida, Don Lu & The Butler
- Grandmaster Sensei
- Iron Circular Safe
- Jumper Platform
- King Croc
- King Zola
- Little Xim
- Mags the Mechanic
- Male Doll Arm
- Male Doll Head
- Male Doll Leg
- Male Doll Torso
- Mechanical Door

Objects
- Mechanical Prison
- Meerkat Mum
- Platform Expander
- Right-Angled Platform 1
- Right-Angled Platform 2
- The Bouncer
- The Goddess
- The Great Magician
- The King
- The Queen
- Tube Race Crusher 1
- Tube Race Crusher 2
- Tube Race Rotators
- Tube Race Washer
- Uncle Jalapeño
- Ze Dude

Level Complete Gifts

Costume
- Robot Trousers

Object
- The Wilderness

Collected All Gifts

Stickers
- Very First *LittleBigPlanet* Concept

Objects
- Jumping Tank
- Very First *LittleBigPlanet* Concept with Frame

Aced Level Gifts

Costume
- Neon Dress

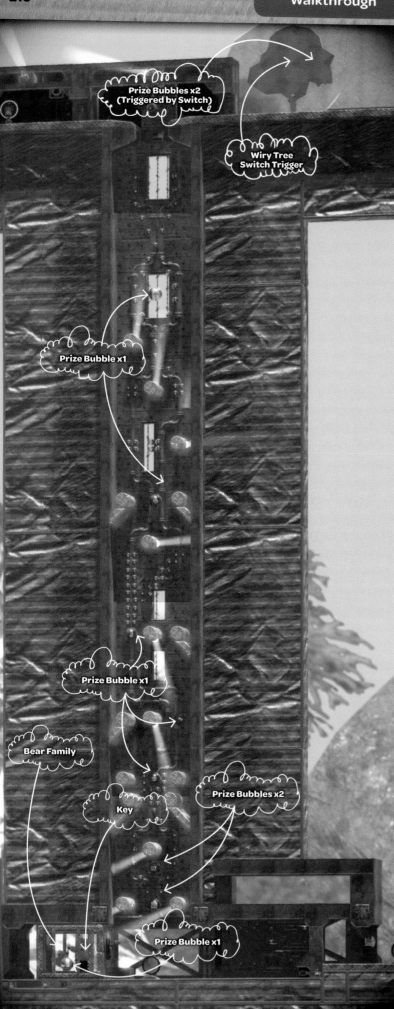

Prize Bubbles x2
(Triggered by Switch)

Wiry Tree
Switch Trigger

Prize Bubble x1

Prize Bubble x1

Bear Family

Prize Bubbles x2

Key

Prize Bubble x1

FIND THE COLLECTOR IN HIS STEEL LAIR AND RELEASE YOUR FRIENDS!

Welcome to My Evil Lair

Spotlights sweep over your burlap body as soon as you enter The Collector's Lair. Cross the Close-Level Post, and then bypass the group of camouflage balls to reach a Sticker Puzzle.

OFF TO A GOOD START

The Sticker Puzzle in this area is an easy one to solve. Open Popit and select the Wiry Tree Sticker. Place it on the Sticker Switch and, just like that,

two Prize Bubbles burst out of the puzzle. Collect them to gain the **Mermaid Tail Costume** and **Scale Swimsuit Costume**.

Down the Hatch

Grab one of the camo balls and ride down the narrow tunnel. Follow the trail of Score Bubbles to pick up as many points as possible. Always keep an eye out for Prize Bubbles; they tend to be located in the center of the shaft.

The first Prize Bubble you come across is in the middle of the path. It contains the **Bungee Bridge Object**. The next Prize Bubble is also in the center, but a bit further down. Collect it to gain the **Cuddly Bear Torso Object**. Over to the left is the Prize Bubble holding the **Cuddly Bear Leg Object,** and a little further down and to the right is the Prize Bubble housing the **Cuddly Bear Arm Object**. Move back to the center to gain the **Cuddly Bear Head Object** from the Prize Bubble there. The last two Prize Bubbles hold the **Rusty Metal Material** and the **Mechanical Prison Object**.

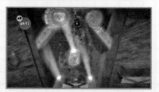

Let My People Go

Let go of the ball and turn left to face a rusty cage. Inside, you spot the kidnapped family members of the bear in The Frozen Tundra. They tell you to open the cage. If you do so, they shall give you the key to saving the other *LittleBigPlanet* inhabitants.

Open the cage by pulling down the switch attached to its side. Run inside and collect the Prize Bubble holding the **Bear Object**. Take the prison key and drag it over to the far wall. It fits! Now you have full access to The Collector's Lair.

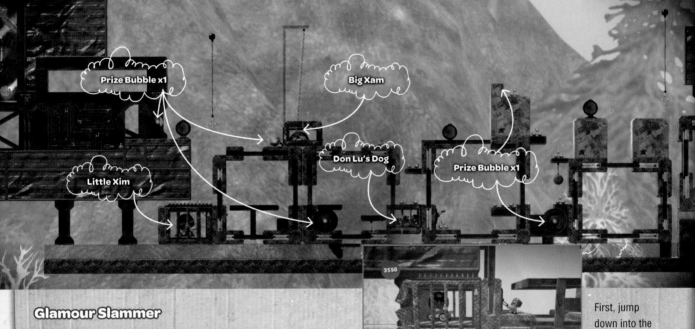

Glamour Slammer

Enter the main part of the prison and head to the right. Grab the Prize Bubble holding the **Mechanical Door Object,** and look over at the moving platform next to you. This is part of the prison? How advanced.

First, jump down into the expanding square by dropping through the gap that appears when the square is stretched out. To the left is Little Xim, ruler of the Score Challenges. The tiny tyke is all locked up. When the square expands, drop to the lowest level and pull the switch on the left. Little Xim is free! But don't celebrate too long. You still have lots of rescuing to do.

Big Xam, You're up!

It's time to return to Big Xam. Return to the middle platform within the expanding square, and then move to the neighboring square when both are fully stretched. From here, you can see a trapped Prize Bubble containing the **Tin Foil Material** and Don Lu's Dog in a small cage. Hang

Leap out onto the moving platform and you find it's actually an expanding square. Before doing anything else, hop over to the Prize Bubble containing the **Expandable Square 1 Object**. Next door is poor Big Xam, the head of the Survival Challenges. You can't help him out of his cage now, but hang in tight! You reach Big Xam shortly.

in there, doggie! You shall be free soon enough!

Leave both the bubble and the dog for now and gather all the Score Bubbles above the dog's cage. Jump onto the small ledge in this area and wait for it to rise up. When it does, jump over to the expanding square on the left. From here, you can reach the switch to Big Xam's cage. That's two down!

Gotta Bust a Move!

All the surfaces in this level just can't keep still. They expand, rotate, sway—you name it, this lair does it. It can be hard to keep up with all this jiving around. The best way to keep from losing the groove is to be patient. Of course you want to save everyone right away, but if you rush through this level, you'll end up running out of lives. Then what's going to happen to all the inhabitants of LittleBigPlanet? Get an idea of how each object in the area moves and works together before you go charging in on your metaphorical white horse.

A Game of Fetch

Wait until the expanding square to the right is lower than you, then jump over and activate the Checkpoint. Drop into the square and pull the

switch on the left to free Don Lu's Dog. The dog is on a lower level, but he still follows you as loyally as ever. Use this to gain access to the Prize Bubble locked away to the right.

Move out of the expanding square and over to the trapped bubble. As you move, so does the dog, until it's pressing up against the red button in front of it. This unlocks the Prize Bubble, granting you the **Iron Circular Safe Object**.

Grab hold of the dangling sponge and swing over to the small Score Bubble-filled ledge on the left, then hop to the ledge on the right. When the expanding square on the left is lower than the one you are on, leap onto the upper platform.

FOLLOW THE LEADER

Don Lu's pooch can help you reach the locked Prize Bubble you saw earlier. But first, you have to manage to get back to where that bubble is. From this upper platform, leap down to the left and land in front of the Checkpoint. Drop onto the small ledge below, then drop once more to land on top of the dog's former cage. Look there! The doggie has followed you back! Move into the expanding square to the left and stand right next to the locked Prize Bubble. The dog presses against the red button under the bubble, releasing the lock. Now you can gather up the **Tin Foil Material**. When you're done, navigate back through to where you were first standing on that upper platform.

Prize Bubble x1

Zola

Prize Bubbles x4

Mags & Ze Dude

Challenge Key & Prize Bubbles x3

Freeing the Zoo

Next on the list are King Croc and Zola, along with one of Zola's servant monkeys. From the upper platform, jump out to the Checkpoint on the right. Keep hopping until you reach the next Checkpoint on the metal expanding square.

Wait for the electric square next to you to lower down, then jump onto the small platform holding the two Score Bubbles. If you stand on the platform farther back, you get squished once the square stretches up to the ceiling.

Move to the next platform holding two Score Bubbles. Keep hopping along the Score Bubble-filled platforms, but make sure not to lose your footing! You know how The Collector is; everything has to be electric. Once you reach the tall narrow platform next to the Prize Bubble containing the **Metal Beam Material**, hop over and grab the Material, then return to the narrow platform. Move to the grey metal beam to the left to find King Croc trapped inside a dismal cage. Set him free by pulling down on the cage's switch.

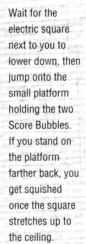

Leap back to the narrow platform. Keep moving, and soon you reach a set of four moving platforms. Aim for the one that has two Score Bubbles on it. Then, jump up to the one with three Score Bubbles. When this platform reaches its peak height, soar through the air and grab the switch on the right wall. Now Zola and his servant monkey are free! But there are still many more to save.

WORDS OF ENCOURAGEMENT

THIS IS A VERY DIFFICULT LEVEL. IN FACT, IT'S ONE OF THE HARDEST. YOU ARE BEING TOSSED, SQUISHED, AND ELECTRIFIED ALL THROUGHOUT THE LAIR. BUT DON'T GIVE UP! ALL THE INHABITANTS OF LITTLEBIGPLANET ARE DEPENDING ON YOU AND, ONCE YOU SET THEM FREE, THEY CHEER YOU ON TO RESCUE THE OTHERS. SO STICK WITH IT! BY THE END, YOU'LL BE THE BIGGEST LITTLE HERO THIS PLANET HAS EVER SEEN.

A Tough-Looking Damsel in Distress

Cross under Zola's opened cage and you can see Mags the Mechanic, Ze Dude, and the Bouncer all trapped inside another one of The

Collector's cages. To reach them, you need to cross over the electrified floor to your right.

Use the swiveling metal right-angles to stay above the deadly floor. Step into the first angle and pop the Prize Bubble containing the **Factory Silhouette Sticker**.

LET IT FLY

You can fling yourself with the help of a swiveling platform to reach the Prize Bubble attached to the second right-angle on the top row. When the first angle on the bottom is facing to the left, stand on the left edge. When it rotates, get ready to be flung up to the Prize Bubble, which contains the **Metal Plate Decoration**, and land on the second right-angle on the bottom row.

Move to the next angled platform and fling yourself to the upper right again to gain the Prize Bubble containing the **Pixel Green Block Sticker**. This time grab and hold onto the sponge in the corner of the right-angle platform. Hang on as the platform swivels up to pop the Prize Bubble holding the **Right-Angled Platform 1 Object**.

To get all the Score Bubbles along the top row of platforms, hop along the angled ledges after snagging the last Prize Bubble. Just be sure to watch which way the platforms swivel.

Hold It!

When you travel around inside of the right-angles, hang on to the little bits of camouflage fabric to keep from being flung around.

From the last angle on the bottom row, drop to the next section of swiveling angled platforms. When the angle you land in is facing up, hop over to the ball of camo and sway over to the next angle. Land on the top of this new platform when its angle is facing left. Hop along the tops of the next few angles until you reach the side of Mags' cage. Leap from the last angle platform to collect a **Challenge Key** and a Prize Bubble holding the **Leaders of Men Audio**.

Pull the switch on the wall to set Mags, Ze Dude, and the Bouncer free. They, of course, give you their gratitude in the coolest way possible. Move to the lowest row of right-angle platforms and navigate your way to solid ground. Don't forget to snag the two Prize Bubbles along this route. Pop them to receive the **Wooden Crate Material** and the **Right-Angle Platform 2 Object**.

Freeing a Magician

It's time to free The Great Magician. The Collector must have some really high-tech cells to keep this magician trapped. To reach him, first pass the Checkpoint near the right-angle platforms, and then move out to the right. Collect the Score Bubbles along the path. Once you reach the end, hop down into the moving box. It slides back and forth over a floor of molten metal. When the box moves to the right, run under the protruding metal pillar and over the short wall.

Grandmaster Sensei

Great Magician

Prize Bubble x1

Meerkat Mum

Prize Bubbles x2

Uncle Jalapeño

Prize Bubbles x2

Hop backwards to reach another moving box. This one has a rotating plank covered in fire to overcome. Stay on the left side of the box. When it slides to the right, sprint under the spinning plank. Don't stop running until you've reached the box's far right wall.

Jump forward into the next box and stand on the right edge of its little metal ramp. When the box moves to the left, hop off the ramp and press against the platform on the left side. When the box moves to the right, jump up onto the platform.

Leap backward into the moving box behind you to activate the next Checkpoint. This box moves brings you up to The Great Magician. Pull the switch on the side of his cage to set him free.

The Student Saves the Teacher

Head to the left and leap over the pit of fire to collect the Prize Bubble containing the **Complex Platform Object**. Move to the back platform, and then head over to the next moving path, collecting Score Bubbles as you move.

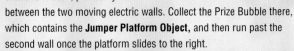

Stay against the right wall of this new moving platform. When it slides to the left, position yourself between the two moving electric walls. Collect the Prize Bubble there, which contains the **Jumper Platform Object,** and then run past the second wall once the platform slides to the right.

Hop to the back platform and walk over to Grandmaster Sensei's cell. Pull the switch to open the cage. She praises your work as she flies away.

A Family That's Caged Together, Stays Together

Grab the camouflage ball near Sensei's cage and ride it down to the next area. Be sure to collect the Score Bubbles that line the route! Land in front of the Checkpoint, and then move onto the extending platform to the right.

These types of platforms stretch in one direction and then recoil back in the other.

Collect the Prize Bubble on the platform to gain the **Male Doll Head Object** before stepping onto the next platform, which moves up and down rather than left and right. This one has the Prize Bubble holding the **Male Doll Arm Object**. Move to the extending platform lined with Score Bubbles to reach another switch. Pull it to open the cell housing Meerkat Mum and her babies.

Drop to the lower level to collect the Prize Bubble containing the **Power Fist Sticker**. Step out onto the extending platform and then ride the next platform up. Hop onto the platform extending to the left and move across to another one stretching out to the right. Navigate the next two platforms before hoping onto stable ground. Don't forget to collect the two Prize Bubbles along the way. They grant you the **Male Doll Torso Object** and the **Male Doll Leg Object**.

Going out with a Bang

Up next is Uncle Jalapeño. Looks like you have to blast him out of prison yet again. You have a little way to go before you can reach him, so get moseying!

Move to the right of the Checkpoint and hop down onto the extending platform. Jump to the next platform and run up its side. There in the

 rusty metal cell is Uncle Jalapeño. This is a familiar sight. But it looks like the amigo is in there too. Pull down the cell's switch to blast them out of there!

SNEAKING UP FROM BEHIND

Before you move to bust out Jalapeño, jump up onto the vertically extending platform near the previous Checkpoint. Not the one in front of you, the one behind you. This brings you up to the one in front. Now you can collect the Prize Bubble atop the large vertically extending platform, as well as the one near the ceiling. For your efforts, you are rewarded with the **Platform Expander** and **Angled Platform Expander Objects**.

Prize Bubble x1 (Requires 4 Players)

Don Lu & Frida

Goddess

Prize Bubbles x2

Prize Bubble x1

Prize Bubbles x3

Scoreboard

The King and Queen

Prize Bubbles x19

Prize Bubbles x2

Releasing the Goddess

Move to the right and hop into the rotating box. Navigate over to the right side, of course snagging all the Score Bubbles along the way, and jump back onto the rising platform. When it reaches the top, hop out onto the stationary platform. To the right is a Four-Player Puzzle and the trapped Goddess. Pull the switch to set her free.

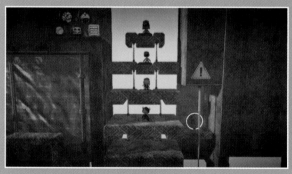

The Magnificent Four

Grab hold of the hanging ball and ride up to the Four-Player Puzzle. For the complexity of The Collector's Lair, this puzzle is surprisingly easy.

Have player one stand on the red button at the very top of the stairs. This elevates the platform he or she is on, but only a little bit. Now have player two land on the next red button. This raises both platforms a little higher. Player three can now stand on the third red button. That pile of Prize Bubbles up to the left is in sight! When player four stands on the last button, player one can now reach the bubbles. Here's where it gets a little tricky. Once player one moves from his or her button, the platform he or she was on moves down, crushing player two. To prevent this tragedy, as soon as player one jumps up to the bubbles, have all the other players move forward, out of harm's way.

After collecting the **Chinese Dragon Mask Costume**, the **Head Dress Costume**, the **Blue Camo Costume**, the **Metal Vent Decoration**, the **Danger Platform Object**, and the **"Rainbow Warrior" Audio Object**, have player one jump down and reunite with the others.

Freeing the Wedding Party

Climb up the next extending platforms and gather all the Score Bubbles along the way. Frida, Don Lu, and the Butler are imprisoned at the top! They're all tightly packed together inside a cage. Pull the switch to open the cage doors. They give their thanks before jetting off. Maybe it's time for a second honeymoon?

Rescuing the King and Queen

You're almost there! Only the King and the Queen remain locked away. From the Goddess's cell, drop to the lower level and move left. Grab one of the hanging camo balls and ride into the tunnel below. Follow the trail of Score Bubbles to navigate the narrow shaft. It's impossible to collect all the Score Bubbles, so just do the best you can.

What you should be really focusing on are the numerous Prize Bubbles found in the tunnel. If you stay to the center of the path, you should be able to collect them all with little effort. The first one you come across

is the Prize Bubble containing the **Baby Doll Head Object**. It's stationed between two moving electric platforms. But, as said before, if you stay central you can retrieve it without getting shocked.

Next up are the bubbles holding the **Tube Race Washer** and the **Tube Race Crusher 2 Objects**. It's a bit more difficult to get both of these in one go, since they're attached to a rotating wheel. If you miss one, you may have to try going through the tunnel again.

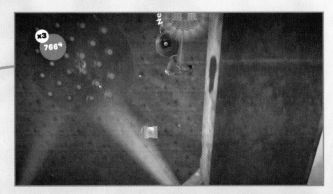

Proceed a little further down to find Prize Bubbles containing the **Baby Doll Torso Object** and **Baby Doll Arm Object**. They are both located between

moving electric platforms. Remember to stay in the center of the tunnel, and you collect them without any damage.

Past the spinning electric wheels is the Prize Bubble containing the **Tube Race Rotators Object**. After that are the Prize Bubbles holding the **Baby Doll Leg Object** and the **Tube Race Crusher 1 Object**. These last two are found between the rows of moving electric platforms. You guessed it: stay in the center of the tunnel to collect them without being electrocuted.

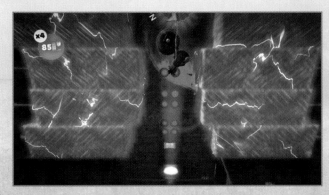

Finally, you reach the end of the tunnel and—look at that! To the right is the switch that frees the King and the Queen! Better go give it a yank. The Queen graciously thanks you for your deeds.

A Hero's Welcome

You did it! You saved everyone! And they would like to properly thank you. Hop down into the Queen's chariot to collect the Prize Bubble holding **The Queen Object**. Move back to the King to snag the bubble holding **The King Object**. Now just sit tight as you pass all the happy (and free) inhabitants of *LittleBigPlanet*. Each one gives you a Prize Bubble holding the Object of his or herself. Humbly accept them all to receive the **Don Lu's Dog**, **Mags the Mechanic**, **The Bouncer**, **Ze Dude**, **Big Xam**, **King Zola**, **Little Xim**, **Grandmaster Sensei**, **The Great Magician**, **Meerkat Mum**, **King Croc**, **Don Lu**, **Frida the Bride**, **The Butler**, **Uncle Jalapeño**, **Devante**, **The Goddess**, and **Frida, Don Lu & The Butler Objects**.

The only thing left to do now is confront The Collector. Step on the Scoreboard to end the level, and prepare to fight for the future of *LittleBigPlanet*!

Story: Chapter 4

The Wilderness

The Collector

This is the final fight, the battle royale, the big one. It's just you versus The Collector. You've made it this far, and there is no stopping you now!

✓ Audio
"The Battle on Ice"

Level Complete Gifts

✓ Objects
The Collector
The Collector's Boss
The Collector's Pod

Aced Level Gifts

✓ Object
The Wilderness

✓ Costume
Yellow Head

BOSS FIGHT!

BATTLE THE COLLECTOR IN THE FINAL SHOWDOWN

Them's Fightin' Words

Exit the trolley and enter the dark and sinister home of The Collector. Enter the security room on the right to come face-to-face with the little thief. He has the nerve to call you puny? HA! At least you're not hiding behind a bunch of scrap metal.

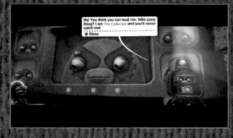

As soon as you approach the little squirt, he runs away! Shortly after The Collector's exit, the floor moves under you, bringing you down to your first battle.

Round One! Ding, Ding!

Follow the evil laughter to the right to enter an electric arena. That big guy to the right is one of The Collector's machines. From the control booth in the upper left, The Collector is able to move his machine left, right, and to the center. There are two Creature Brains, one located on each side of the mechanical beast.

The Rule of Three

This first machine is pretty simple to defeat, as long as you know how to avoid its vicious downward attacks. It moves in a specific pattern: left, then right, then center.

After popping the first two Creature Brains, the bottom of the machine opens and spews out three rounds of electric projectiles. Be careful you don't get hit, or prepare to be sent packing back to the Checkpoint. Your targets are the same two Creature Brains that you previously destroyed: they're back and ready for more.

Another Set of Three

The projectiles are easy to work around if you know where they will be coming from next. Before the machine stomps down on the left, it shoots the electric projectiles to the right. Before it slams down on the right, it fires to the left. Before it lands in the center, it shoots the projectiles along the center.

Pop the two Creature Brains again, and The Collector's great and powerful machine crumbles.

Only the Beginning

The Collector claims that this is only the beginning. HA! Bring it on! The ground moves once more and brings you up to another arena with an even bigger machine.

The heaping pile of metal and gears has a pair of arms that each release one of The Collector's minions. They follow you everywhere. Pop their Creature Brains right away, and then turn your focus to the big guy. Once the minions are destroyed, the machine throws a fit and starts pounding its fists on the ground. This is when you should target the two Creature Brains on either side of the arms. Careful not to get crushed by the smashing fists!

After the second round of minions have been destroyed, the arms open up to reveal two more Creature Brains, one inside each limb. Once these two brains are popped, the arms fade from the machine.

Big Danger in a Small Package

Just because the limbs have faded, it doesn't mean the fight is over. The machine now has a Creature Brain on each of its sides, plus one near its head. Seems like easy picking, right? Wrong.

Watch Where You're Pointing That Thing

The sides open up, and four more Creature Brains are revealed. Don't go for them right away! Electric projectiles fire directly at your head. They seem impenetrable, but if you know the trick, you can get around them without any trouble.

Stay to the far right or left wall and let the machine fire a round. When it's spent, move to stand directly in front of it. When the sides open again, you are out of the range of the machine's fire, and can successfully attack the brains.

After its sides open up and unleash a round of fire, the robot stomps on the ground, causing a stream of electric cylinders to fall from above. Avoid them while trying to stay even with The Collector's creation. Soon, a block

falls into the arena. Grab it and pull it in front of the machine. Once it opens its sides, you can use the block to reach the remaining brains. After each of the five brains are popped, the machine breaks apart.

A Broken Little Man

The Collector speeds away from his final contraption, darting off to the right. Don't let him get away. As the thief retreats, the remnants of his defeated creation break apart, piece by piece, until there is nothing left but the shell of a tiny man. Grab the **"Battle on Ice" Audio Object** as you walk around the statue.

The Collector hides, ashamed of his behavior. He only kidnapped people because he didn't have any friends. Is that all? Well, that's easy to fix! The King and the Queen offer to be his friends. In fact, all the inhabitants of *LittleBigPlanet* offer their hand in friendship. Take their hand, and begin a new life of fun and adventure!

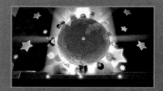

The Wilderness
Mini Levels!

Alpine Rider

HOLD ON TIGHT AND RIDE THE TOBOGGAN ALONG THE ICY TRACKS

How to Unlock: Collect the Key in The Frozen Tundra

The Amazing Electrical Ice Race!

Jump onto the toboggan and race down the ice-laden ramps. But don't fall off, because some of those ramps are electrically charged; use the [R1] button to hold on and the left stick to throw your weight around, so the toboggan doesn't flip in midair.

If you have enough momentum on your side, you can slide all the way up the electrical ramp at the halfway point, and collect a whole row of Score Bubbles.

General Tips

Stick to the center of the toboggan. By staying in the center, you can really keep your balance as you slide down the ramps towards the finish line. But don't forget: if you're holding on, you can manipulate where you throw your weight with the left stick on your controller.

Momentum is momentous. The faster you're able to safely go, the better chance you have of getting all those bubbles at the top of the electrical ramp at the level's halfway point.

Now here's a doozy. Once you've leaned forward and the toboggan tips into a full slide down the electrical ramp, don't hold on. Instead, let go of the controller, and let gravity race for you. Stay in the middle of the toboggan and glide safely from one ramp platform to the other, all the way to the finish line.

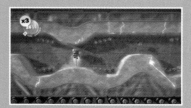

Rotor Tubes

TIME YOUR START WELL TO GET THROUGH THE ROTATING PLATFORMS

How to Unlock: Collect the Key in The Bunker

Sackboy Derring-do

Timing is everything in the perilous Rotor Tubes. Leap from one rotating platform to the next, collecting Score Bubbles and striving to keep from falling into the electric pit.

Keep in mind that you have a time limit and the clock is ticking with about 180 seconds total. Grab bubbles when you can to temporarily pause the timer, but don't focus on the bubbles. Getting to the finish line before the clock runs out gets you a nice reward.

Jetpack Tunnel

USE THE JETPACK TO NAVIGATE THE ELECTRIFIED TUNNELS

How to Unlock: Collect the Key in The Collector's Lair

Rock 'em, Sock 'em Rocket!

Leap down the tunnel and use the jetpack to navigate through the shockingly electrical, wintery world of The Wilderness. Avoid the electric floor and ceiling and the Horrible Gas of the tunnel as long as you can.

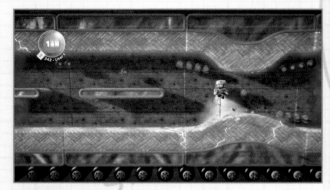

As the level speeds up, try to stay alive as long as possible. Fly around, zooming through the dips and weaves of the tunnel. And remember, beware the Horrible Gas that lurks in front of and behind you—one touch, and poof! You're a goner.

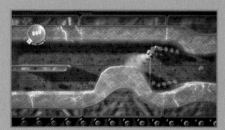

General Tips

Slow it down a tad. Pull back just slightly on the left stick to slow down your jetpack and progress through the tunnel. You don't have control of the tunnel's speed increases, but you can brake and boost yourself. Just be aware of the Horrible Gas in front and behind you.

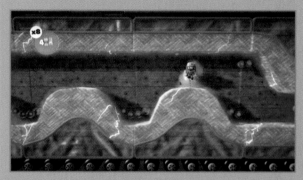

Stay close to the upper tier of the tunnel. There are lots of dips to overcome, but if you stay above the little barriers, you can avoid bumping into sudden curvatures in the tunnel.

Forget about the bubbles here; only grab those that are easiest. Avoid the ceiling and floor, and don't get greedy and risk it all for a row of four. The longer you survive, the easier it's going to be to reach the Score Bubbles you're trying to collect.

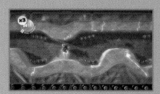

General Tips

Timing is key; wait and watch to see how the platforms move, which direction they move in, and how long their rotations are. Once you've got an idea of the timing, hold your breath and jump!

Keep on top. When you make your jumps, try to stay on the platform's rising side; that way, you can jump and land on the highest point. From there, you can leap onto the platform's outer area and proceed.

Forget about the bubbles. Stay focused on the platform leaps, and grab bubbles only when you can absolutely afford to.

Mini Levels!

221

Create!

SCARY TREES!!

MAYBE A SPIDER WEB?

BAT BROTHERS WILL SWING
ACROSS THE GORGE

HAVE THEM SWING ON CHAINS AND ROPES

BOILING PITS!!

DRAW CASTLE HERE

SKELETONS EVERYWHERE!!

Creating a Level:
The Basic Basics

The Creator Curators certainly are a clever bunch, but then again, so are you. And here's your chance to prove it. Dangling just to the right of LittleBigPlanet is My Moon. Don't be fooled; it may look like a barren landscape, but that's just because you and your sack person have yet to pay it a visit. So what are you waiting for?

Objectives

Ground Control

Not a Tadpole

Goodies Bag

Tools Bag Basics

New Pause-abilities

Using Materials to Make Walkways

Interactive Objects and Simple Problem Solving

Moon Landing

Use the navigation controls in your Pod to select "My Moon" from your available destination options. Choose any landing location that tickles your fancy and select it by tapping ✖ over the "Create" command.

GROUND CONTROL

One Small Step

When your sack person bursts out of the Entrance Barrel on the lunar level of your choice, they are perfectly poised to start creating a level of their own. In "Create Mode," your sack person has a few new abilities to help in this endeavor. The first skill (as evidenced by their continued suspension) is the ability to hover. Flight is now possible at any time, without restriction.

Unique Create Mode Controls	
Button	Action
Directional Button Down	Hover Mode on / off
Directional Button Left	Undo
Directional Button Right	Redo
Directional Button Up	Pause / Un-Pause
Right Stick	Zoom In / Out

IN CREATE MODE L1 AND R1 DO NOT AFFECT YOUR SACK PERSON'S ARM CONTROLS.

How to Hover

As your sack person continues to float, the narrator chimes in to explain your new abilities. Most new abilities are accessible via the directional buttons. Hover Mode can be toggled on and off by  tapping the directional button down. While hovering, your sack person is free to roam the skies in the same way they would using a Jetpack. Hold down ✗ to increase your hovering speed.

Time Lord

The other three directional buttons give you control of time. The right and left directional buttons function much like fast-forward and rewind. If, in a creative misstep, you make a tiny booboo, or even a catastrophic one, simply tap the directional button left until the offending addition has been completely undone. If then you think, "hmm, maybe that wasn't so bad," tap the directional button right to Redo your earlier Undo. You may also Pause the action on screen by tapping the directional button up; tap it once again to Un-Pause.

Changing Perspective

You should also note the new ability of your right stick. Holding it down allows you to zoom your camera out, and by holding it up you can zoom back in. Use this ability to find the perfect perspective to aid in your upcoming construction. Regardless of the camera's zoom level, it remains centered on your sack person.

CREATE MODE TUTORIALS

AS YOU EXPLORE EACH NEW FEATURE AND ITEM WITHIN THE POPIT MENU IN CREATE MODE, BOTH THE NARRATOR AND THE QUEEN OF THE GARDENS WANT TO ENSURE THAT YOU AND YOUR SACK PERSON POSSESS THE KNOWLEDGE TO USE EACH FEATURE TO ITS FULLEST EXTENT. AS SUCH, THE FIRST TIME YOU ATTEMPT TO SELECT A NEW MATERIAL OR TOOL YOU ARE PROMPTED TO A SHORT TUTORIAL. UPON ITS COMPLETION, YOU CAN FREELY USE THAT ITEM OR FEATURE.

New Planet—New Popit

Having mastered your sack person's expanded control options, take a few seconds to explore the surrounding alien terrain. It should only take a few seconds, because there is nothing to see. Why? Because you have yet to create anything! Use ⊙ to open the Popit Menu. Behold! The Popit Menu has some fancy new additions, doesn't it? The narrator speaks up to help you learn how to use your new tools to create a level.

You can also move your creations forward and backwards. Use **L1** to move the object forward between the three available planes, and **L2** to move the object backward. **R1** increases the depth of the object, whereas **R2** decreases it. By pressing **L3**, your object is copied and may be placed repeatedly. Lastly, by pressing **R3**, the object becomes inverted. Though this may seem a daunting tool, your mastery of it is sure to grow along with your level building skill.

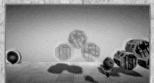

THE THERMOMETER

BEFORE YOU BEGIN YOUR CRUSADE OF CREATIVITY, TAKE A MOMENT TO NOTE THE LARGE THERMOMETER RUNNING UP THE COURSE OF THE LEFT SIDE OF THE SCREEN. THIS DEVICE DOES NOT MEASURE THE TEMPERATURE OF YOUR LEVEL, BUT RATHER THE QUANTITY OF STUFF YOU HAVE IN IT. WHEN YOU REACH THE TOP, YOUR LEVEL IS FULL AND NO MORE CAN BE BUILT.

New to the Popit

In Create Mode the Popit menu has three additional options. First is the Popit Cursor, which allows you to select and affect objects. Next, the Goodies Bag is where to find all of your building materials and creations. Finally, the Tools Bag holds all of your assorted gadgets and tools.

② NOT A TADPOLE

The first new tool is the Popit Cursor. Once selected, you can steer it with the left stick. With this cursor, you are able to grab almost any item you please. To select an object, press ⊗ once the cursor is hovering over the desired item. To choose multiple objects, hold down ⊗ and drag the cursor over any cluster of objects you wish to highlight. Once chosen, your selection is outlined by the cursor, and you can move it with your left stick and rotate/transform it with the right stick—the same way you would with Stickers.

③ GOODIES BAG

Directly below the Popit cursor is the Goodies Bag. This name is quite fitting because as soon as you open it, you say, "Oh, Goodie!" Within the Goodies Bag are four windows. The first window contains all the raw materials you and your sack person have collected throughout your journeys around *LittleBigPlanet*. Next, you can find the first My Objects page, which holds all of your collected characters and Curator Creator creations. The third window is likely quite bare. The second My Objects page is reserved for your personally created objects. The final window, Community Objects, holds the creations sent to you from your many friends.

CREATE MODE TUTORIALS

AS YOU AND YOUR SACK PERSON PROGRESS FURTHER INTO THIS SECTION, IT IS ASSUMED YOU BOTH HAVE TRAVELED JUST AS FAR IN THE CURATOR CREATORS LEVELS AND COMPLETE MANY TUTORIALS.

Living in a Materials World

Everything in *LittleBigPlanet* is composed of base materials. The more materials your sack person collects, the more you can create with. There are several types of materials, each with its own characteristics and qualities that can be used to your benefit. Scroll to the Basic Materials section on the first window of your Goodies Bag to view the most basic forms of different materials you have collected. Most materials fall into one of these categories and behave in the same way as their basic counterpart. Unique materials (like Dissolve) that do not fall into a basic category are also found in this subsection. These items are covered in the next chapter.

Basic Materials

Basic Material	Material Name	Description	Able to Grab
	Cardboard	Very Light	No
	Glass	Slippery	No
	Metal	Heavy	No
	Polystyrene	Very Light	Yes
	Rubber	High-Traction (Good for Wheels)	No
	Sponge	Light	Yes
	Stone	Heavy	No
	Wood	Basic Building Material	No

Craft Material Basics

Once you select a material you would like to build with, the Choose Shape menu options opens in the Popit. Cycle between the shapes you have collected and press ✕ to select the shape you would like to build with. Get your hard hat ready because you are now set to build. You can control the material with the Popit Cursor in much the same way you control objects, but with a few new available options. Position your material with the left stick and rotate / adjust with the right stick. Stamp the material down with ✕. By holding down ✕ you can drag the material along. Holding down ⚪ erases existing materials. If you place a new material on top of an existing one, the new material carves itself into the existing material.

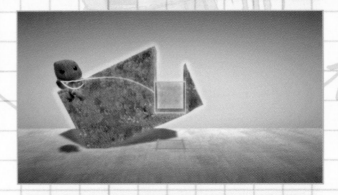

Planes & Depth

Remember; use L1 and L2 to move the material through the planes and R1 and R2 to adjust depth.

From Stone to Sponge

Your Material Changer tool is also found in the Choose Shape menu of the Popit. This helpful fellow allows you to transform any placed material into another material. Select the material you would like, then choose the Material Changer under Functions. Guide the Popit Cursor to the material you would like to transform and tap ✕, then faster than you can say, "Abracadabra Allakhazam," your selected material changes before your very eyes.

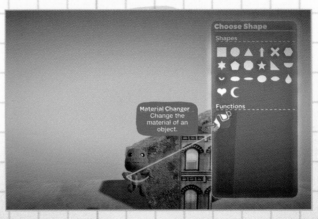

Creative Creations of the Creator Curators

In addition to simple raw materials, the Creator Curators have also given you access to a number of their ingenious inventions. The inventions you have found so far are available for use in Create Mode, located in the second window of your Goodies Bag. To place one in your level, select it from the Popit and place it with the Popit Cursor.

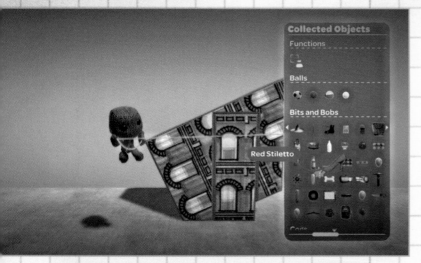

Tweaking Pre-made Creations

Any switches, and most creature pieces, in place on items from the My Objects windows are adjustable to ensure the item behaves how you want it to.

Personally Perfected

The third page of your Goodies Bag is reserved for the goodies you have made yourself. If, while marveling over some of your masterworks, you feel that a particular dinosaur-spaceship is truly outstanding, you may want to save it for future use. The Capture Object tool under Functions on the third page of your Goodies Bag lets you do just that. Once selected, the Capture Object tool appears as a box at the end of the Popit Cursor. Control the box's dimensions with the right stick. Surround your selection and tap ⊗ to save it in you Goodies Bag. Once saved, the object is available in the My Objects section on the third window of your Goodies Bag.

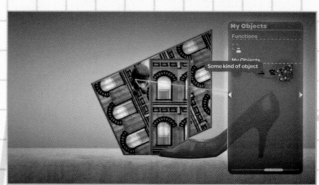

Pass It On

As you have well learned, LittleBigPlanet is a very social place. You can even share your favorite creations and stickers with your friends. To upload to another user, tap ◉ over the desired object or sticker and select the Send To My Friend option. Choose whether you would like your item to be sharable, then select a lucky comrade and tap ⊗. Enter a message, then send your object to its thankful recipient.

If another player sends an item to you, simply tap △ to download the gift when prompted.

④ TOOLS BAG BASICS

The final new Popit tool at your disposal just happens to be the Tools Bag. If the world of *LittleBigPlanet* is made out of the crafts found in your Goodies Bag, then the tools in the Tools Bag are certainly what holds that world together. Within the Tools Bag there are six windows: Tools, Gadgets, Gameplay Kits, Audio Objects, Backgrounds, and Global Controls. This chapter covers some of the most basic functions of the gadgets found in your Tools Bag.

In the Bag

The first window of the Tools Bag has several unique editing and altering tools. It also brings together many of the Function tools from other Popit windows in one place; isn't that handy? This menu's unique tools include all of the ominous-looking danger tools you've collected, as well as the Corner Editor.

Corner Editor
Edit individual corners of an object.

Tools of Destruction

You are no doubt already quite aware of the devastating effects many hazards have on your poor sack person. Now, with the help of the danger tools, you are able to be the one putting in the peril. Select the appropriate hazard for your level and any object you apply it to. If your conscience gets the better of you, you can return any lethal object back to its inert state using the Unlethalise Tool found to the right of the danger tools.

Different Dangers

Note that the different danger tools affect sack people differently. Using the Electric Tool or the Horrible Gas Tool means an instant end to any sack person who touches the hazard. However, objects imbued with fire by the Flame Tool singe a sack person before they destroy completely, allowing for some narrow escapes.

Got You Cornered

The Corner Editor is an amazing tool that allows you to make precise adjustments to the shapes you have made. Select it from the Popit window, and tap ✗ over the object you wish to adjust. The Popit Cursor is now restricted to the borders of the object you have selected. Move your cursor along the edge of the object until you reach the point you wish to alter. Tap ✗ again, and you are able to pull and push the dimensions of the edge you have selected. Tap ✗ once more to set the alteration.

You can effectively change the shape of the object by introducing multiple vertices on the object. Simply select a side of your object and push/pull the corners (once again, but tapping ✗) until you have created a shape you desire. Using this method, almost anything can be created. Check out the scary trees in the *Building a Level* section for a great example!

Gadgets

Moving to the next window in your Tools Bag brings you to your Gadgets section. These are the elements that hold *LittleBigPlanet* together and help fill it with amazing characters and thrilling action. As with everything, you need to start somewhere, so why not let that somewhere be Bolts, Strings, and Rods?

Hooked on Bolts

Want to make something with moving parts? Then you might want to check out the Bolt. The noble Bolt is your most basic form of connector. Bolts allow you to join one item to another and can help you do anything from make a teeter-totter to attach a branch to a tree. To use a Bolt, select it from the Tools Bag and place it over the object you wish to bolt. Next, exit out of the Tools Bag and bring out the Popit Cursor. Select the object you wish to bolt and place it over the object you want to bolt it to. Once placed, the Bolt connects the two objects. You may also pre-place the two objects with the Popit Cursor, then select a Bolt from your Tools Bag and place it over the two to connect them.

It Don't Mean a Thing if You Ain't Got That String

String is another basic connector. It allows you to tie two objects together. To attach String, first select it from the Popit Menu and attach it with ✗ to one of the objects you want to connect. Pull the other end of the String to the second object, and tap ✗ once more. Build a small structure and attach a few sponges to the ceiling to get the swing of it.

BASIC TWEAKING

BOLTS, STRINGS, AND RODS ARE YOUR FIRST EXPERIENCES WITH ADJUSTABLE ITEMS. TWEAKING ALLOWS YOU TO ADJUST THE SETTINGS OF A TOOL SO IT BEHAVES THE WAY YOU WOULD LIKE IT TO. TO OPEN THE TWEAK WINDOW, PLACE THE POPIT CURSOR OVER AN ADJUSTABLE TOOL AND TAP ⊙. YOU CAN ALSO BRING UP THE TWEAK WINDOW BY HOLDING DOWN ⊗ WHILE PLACING THE TOOL. INSIDE THE WINDOW, YOU GAIN ACCESS TO ALL ADJUSTABLE FEATURES OF A TOOL.

BOLTS ALLOW YOU TO SET THEIR STRENGTH. THE HIGHER THE STRENGTH SETTING, THE LESS THE BOLT CAN BUDGE. STRINGS AND RODS LET YOU ALTER THEIR LENGTH. STRINGS CAN BUNCH UP SHORTER THAN THE LENGTH YOU SET, BUT CANNOT STRETCH ANY LONGER. RODS CANNOT BUNCH OR STRETCH OUTSIDE THEIR LENGTH SETTING.

BOLTS, STRINGS, AND RODS REPRESENT SOME OF THE SIMPLEST ADJUSTABLE ITEMS; MORE COMPLEX TWEAKING IS COVERED IN THE FOLLOWING CHAPTERS.

Rod

Rods work much like String and are wonderful for connecting all sorts of objects together. However, unlike String, once you set a Rod's length, that's that; it cannot bunch or stretch. "Is It Stiff?" is another interesting option found in the Rods Tweak Menu. When switched on, the selected Rod is set to its anchor without any pivot in its hinges.

Go on and give it a try. Place a block of sponge just over your sack person's head. Attach one end of a Rod to the floor and the other to the sponge. Open the Rods Tweak Menu and try stretching out the Rod and turning the stiffness on. Upon leaving the Popit Menu, your Rod grows in length and remains standing straight. Turn off stiffness, and the sponge falls to the floor.

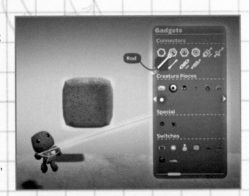

Glue

Glue is a function of your Popit Cursor, not a tool. Glue creates a solid connection between two objects or an object and the floor. To use Glue, select an object with the Popit Cursor and move it where you would like to place it, either against another object or on the floor, and hold down ⊗. When the Popit Cursor detaches from the object, the glue is set. To separate the objects, select one with your Popit Cursor and tap ⊙. Be careful: if you tap ⊙ twice, your object is deleted.

Gameplay Kits

The third window in the Tools Bag houses your Gameplay Kits. These tools allow you to make your creations into a level. Here you find everything from Checkpoints to Goal Posts and everything in-between. Start out by trying the tools in the Basic Kit.

Making an Entrance

Each blank level starts out with only one object in place, the Entrance. If in a creative storm you happen to delete the Entrance, simply replace it.

Bubbles

Score Bubbles are a little reward for those sack people kind enough to play your level. They also provide a nice incentive to fully explore this masterwork you are creating. So go ahead, drop some down here and there.

Making Progress

Checkpoints allow a sack person to resume a level partway through. This is perfect for those who are unfortunate enough to perish before they finish the level. Place them along your path, especially around difficult sections. Double Checkpoints are an advanced version of Checkpoints. This allows players to retry eight times instead of the normal four.

Keeping Score

As unfortunate as it may be, all good things must come to an end, and the Scoreboard is the perfect ending to your level. Once placed, you can use the Tweak Menu to distribute prizes based on a sack person's performance in your level. You may award up to three gifts per Scoreboard achievement, which include Level Complete Gifts (awarded when a sack person reaches the Scoreboard), Aced Level Gifts (awarded if a sack person completes a level without losing a single life), and Collected All Gifts (awarded if a sack person collects all the gifts placed thought the level).

Prizes Galore!

Prize Bubbles are one of the sack people's most favorite things in all of *LittleBigPlanet*. Not only are they worth the same as five normal bubbles, but they can also be loaded up with Stickers, Objects, Decorations, Tools, and all sorts of goodies.

Assigning Gifts

To assign a prize to the Scoreboard or a Prize Bubble, tap ⊗ over one of the gift fields in the Tweak Menu and choose an item from the My Objects or My Pictures sections of your Popit. Any lucky sack person who earns this gift can then find your prize in their Popit.

With or Without You

The Close-Level Post can help eliminate all kinds of confusion. Once a sack person passes this post in Play Mode, no additional players are allowed to enter the level. You wouldn't want some late arriving sack person dropping in halfway through and confusing everyone else, would you? Just drop the post down near the beginning of your level, and save all those friendly sack people the headache.

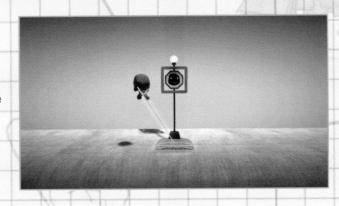

Backgrounds

The fifth window of the Tools Bag is the location all of the Backgrounds you have collected. By setting a Background, you can transform your level into a picturesque garden or a desolate desert. Tap ⊗ over the theme of your choice, and watch the transformation.

Giving You the Time of Day

Global Controls is the sixth and final window of the Tools Bag. Here, you have the ability to alter the look of the level you are creating. You have the power to adjust your level's Lighting, Darkness, Fogginess, Fog Color, and Color Correction. Use either the directional buttons or the right stick to toggle the options. Try adjusting the different selections to create the optimal setting for the level you are creating. There's nothing like a little mood lighting to put a sack person in the proper frame of mind.

④

AUDIO OBJECTS

THE FOURTH WINDOW IN THE TOOLS BAG CONTAINS YOUR AUDIO OBJECTS. AUDIO TOOLS CAN BE PLACED LIKE OTHER OBJECTS, BUT REQUIRE ADVANCED TWEAKING AND ARE COVERED IN THE NEXT CHAPTER.

The Basic Basics

More to Your Menu

⑤ NEW PAUSE ABILITIES

The Popit is not the only thing to have gone through a little transformation. Your Pause Menu has a few new items in it as well. New features can be found in the Change to Play Mode, Save Level, About My Level, and Settings options.

Play Time

The first option available in the Pause Menu is Change to Play Mode. This option lets you, obviously enough, play your level. While Play Mode is active, your controls revert to those of standard play and you are able to interact with the level. Be sure to switch to Play Mode often to ensure all of your creations function correctly.

Save Level

Save Level lets you save the progress you have made on your creations. Save frequently; you don't want to lose any of the genius you put into your level.

About My Level

Select About My Level to give your level a name, personalize the look of your levels seal, and add a description that lets interested sack people know what to expect.

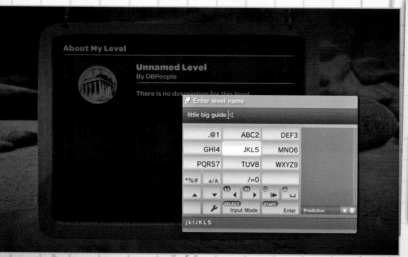

Settings

Perched atop of the Pause menu are a few special options. The grid options allow you to set either a small, medium, or large grid that appears around any item or object you have selected. The grid can help you keep your lines straight and your plans in order. Additionally, you have the ability to toggle your view between Game View, which tracks your sack person from a slightly raised perspective, and Front View, which changes the perspective to dead-on.

Tutorials

Before moving on to the next chapter, it is a good idea to try to put everything you have just learned into practice. The Tutorials section is also useful as a quick reference guide on how to build several basic level elements.

KEEP WHAT YOU MADE

WHILE WORKING THROUGH THESE TUTORIALS, YOU MIGHT COME TO THINK THAT ONE OR TWO OF THE THINGS YOU HAVE MADE ARE QUITE SPIFFY. REMEMBER, YOU DON'T HAVE TO LOSE YOUR WORK. USE THE CAPTURE OBJECT TOOL AS OFTEN AS YOU LIKE TO SAVE THE BEST OF YOUR WORK TO USE IN LATER LEVELS.

⑥ USING MATERIALS TO MAKE WALKWAYS

You can create many imaginative walkways and scenes by using and combining craft materials in different ways. These techniques can help you create a simple obstacle or incredibly complex maze.

RAMPS AND ELEVATED WALKWAYS

To create a simple ramp, try choosing the Basic Wood craft material out of your Goodies Bag. Select the right-angle triangle from your Shapes Menu. Adjust the triangle's size and depth to make a two planes deep upward slant, and stamp it down. Return back to your Shapes Menu and select the square. Use the right stick to match the height of your incline and then ensure that it matches the ramp's depth. Stamp down the block and drag it along until you have a short walkway. There now, that looks so nice any sack person would certainly be inclined to walk up it.

STAIRS

Try using the square shape to generate stairs and level inclines. Again, using Basic Wood, stamp down several squares in diagonal progression and then fill in the base. Or you could stamp down a ramp and use the Delete function with the square shape to carve out several small steps.

Create a more gradual stair incline by dragging your material on a linear plane and either increasing its height incrementally or dropping increasingly shorter planes, one on top of the next. Don't worry, exhausted sack people, the next chapter covers elevator technology.

GAPS

Once you have created an elevated walkway, you can create gaps as minor obstacles. Fortunately, gaps don't require a whole lot of work. Choose any material out of the Goodies Bag and select the shape you wish your gap to be. Use ⊗ to cut the shape out of your walkway. This technique can also be used to create decorative features within the walkway.

TUNNELING

When you can't go over, go under. Tunneling is an incredibly useful technique in level building. It allows you to cut out shapes and walkways from one material using another. Try making a large block, three layers deep, out of Basic Metal. Then choose Basic Glass from your materials and select the square shape. Adjust the size to something slightly larger than your sack person and set it to the back-most plane. Next, ensure your glass is only one plane deep. Starting from the base of the metal structure, stamp down your glass and move it across the bottom of the metal block. This should result in the formation of a tunnel running through the base of the metal.

MORE THAN ONE WAY TO THE TOP—ONE

To practice, try to make a path your sack person can use to get to the top of the metal structure. Use different techniques to reach your goal. Both diagonal tunnels and level based paths can help you get your sack person to the top.

PLATFORMING

Using Basic Metal once again, create another large block of approximately the same size as what you created for the tunneling tutorial. However, this one should only be one layer deep and placed on the farthest back plane. Return to your material selection window and choose Basic Cardboard and select the square shape. Adjust your cardboard so that it is approximately the height and width of your sack person and set its depth to cover all three planes. Stamp several blocks into the metal to create a series of platforms.

You can also drag the cardboard across the metal to create a solid path.

MORE THAN ONE WAY TO THE TOP—TWO

To practice, try to create another path your sack person can use to get to the top. Use several shapes and methods to help achieve this goal.

ROCKING WALKWAY

Try adding a little wobble to your walkway by creating sections that rock. Select Basic Cardboard and choose the teardrop shape. If you have yet to earn the teardrop, you can create it using the circle and triangle shapes. Turn the teardrop on its side and adjust its depth to one layer. Make its size roughly three times taller than your sack person at its highest point, and stamp it down. Return to the shape selection window and

select the triangle. Increase its size and rotate it to cover the top arc of the teardrop you just placed. Tap ⬤ to delete the covered section. Next, select Basic Sponge from the Materials window and set its shape to circle. Make the circle roughly the size of your sack person's head, and line the top of the teardrop as well as the top lip.

⑦ INTERACTIVE OBJECTS AND SIMPLE PROBLEM SOLVING

Creating sections that allow your sack person to interact with the level adds a new layer of depth to the scene you are creating. These strategies can be used to create great obstacles, as well as the solutions needed to cross them.

OVERCOMING OBSTACLES—PART ONE

Even with the most athletic jump, there are some walls that are just a bit out of your sack person's reach. Often the easiest way to overcome these challenges is to add a sponge step to help your progress. Build a wall about two and a half times the height of your sack person, then place a sponge square a few paces away. Next, pull the sponge to the wall and use it to get over the obstacle to confirm that your little puzzle works. Afterwards, reset the block to its starting position.

OVERCOMING OBSTACLES—PART TWO

If a bump in the road is not what you're looking for, try a tower. Make a wall about five times the height of your sack person. Next, using Basic Polystyrene (a grab-able material much lighter than sponge), create a large ramp of sufficient size to overcome the wall and place it a few paces away. Next, delete the bottom tip of the ramp to give your sack person a place to grip. Try pushing the ramp into place to insure you are able to use it to get over the wall. After that, reset the block to its starting position.

SWING

One of the best ways to get by an obstacle is to swing over it. Select Basic Wood to form the stand for a sponge. Construct a small base, column, and support bar. All can be achieved with the square shape. First, construct a small base, and then narrow the size of your square and drag the wood upward from the center of the base to create your column. Lastly, when the column is of a sufficient height, increase the wood's depth and stamp it down to create the support beam. Return to the Materials window and select Basic Sponge. Choose the circle shape and place it midway up the column on the layer beneath your support beam. Exit out to the main Popit menu and scroll down to your Tools Bag, select String, and attach one end to the sponge and the other to the support beam.

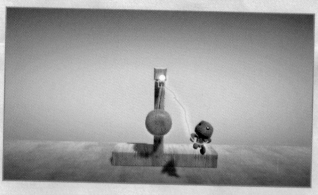

SWINGING TO SAFETY

To create a small trial for your swing, pick it up with the Popit Cursor and use L3 to copy it. Place four swings in a row roughly the same distance apart, and return to the Materials window. Use Basic Metal and select the circle shape. Drag a thin strip of metal across the base of the swings and use the Electric Tool out of your Tools Bag to add a little spark to the metal panel you have created. If everything is lined up correctly, you should be able to swing across the danger.

RUNNING THROUGH HOOPS

Rolling hoops can be a fun and useful tool in your level construction. Use Basic Cardboard to make a large circle one layer deep. Shrink the circle's proportions slightly and use ⊗ to carve a smaller circle out of the larger one you just placed. Your sack person can then jump inside and travel over hazards, or just roll around.

SEESAW

The Seesaw is another basic level element you can modify and use repeatedly in your levels. To create a simple seesaw, use Basic Cardboard to place a triangle on one of the back planes. Swap to the square shape and create a plank on the plane in front of your triangle. Exit out to the main Popit Menu and scroll down to your Tools Bag. Select the Bolt and place it in the center of your beam. If you pre-placed the beam then it automatically attaches to the triangle. If not use the Popit Cursor to position your beam, it attaches when you release your cursor. You can attach beams in this way to larger structures such as walls as well.

TEETER-TOTTER TO THE TOP

Using the techniques from the Seesaw tutorial, try to generate a scalable wall with the aid of several seesaws. First, build a tall wall one layer deep on the third plane back. Next, create a plank out of Basic Cardboard a little less than half the width of the wall. Place a Bolt in the center. Use L3 to copy the plank and then make two columns of seesaws running up both sides of the wall in an ascending pattern. Before you call your creation a success, you might want to test it out for yourself. You can also try different strength settings for the bolts to see how the adjustments affect each seesaw.

Creating a Level:
Going Deeper

Objectives

More Goodies in the Goodies Bag

Get Moving with Gadgets

Adding an Element of Danger

Sounds Good

A Bounce in Your Step

Up, Down, and Side-to-Side

Bolting Away

Attention All Sackpeople: Danger Ahead!

Put It Together

Popit Revisited

The Popit is truly an amazing tool. The more you fill it, the more you are able to create. Once full, your only constraint is your imagination. So open your Popit once again and dive deeper into the creative tools you have collected.

Popit Cursor

MORE GOODIES IN THE GOODIES BAG

If building with the basic Materials in your Goodies Bag begins to feel, well, a little basic, do not worry. There are a few unique materials that should put a bit more zest in your construction. So roll up your sleeves and prepare to get crafty.

Unique Materials

Unique Material	Material Name	Description	Able to Grab
	Dissolve	Very light material that dissolves when triggered.	Yes
	Dark Matter	Unmovable Material.	No
	Peach Floaty	Material that floats away if not tethered.	Yes
	Pink Floaty	Material that floats where placed.	Yes

Vanishing Act

Dissolve is a truly magical material. Select it from the Basic Materials section of the Materials window in your Goodies Bag. Try dropping down a few small shapes and let your sack person drag them around a bit. Dissolve has the same basic characteristics as Polystyrene. Next, choose the square shape and place a wall of insurmountable height in your sack person's path. Leave the wall in place and continue on. Like all good magic tricks, anticipation fuels amazement, and this trick is sure to leave you stunned.

Staying Put

Dark Matter is not as scary as it sounds. In fact, once you start using it, you're bound to think it's quite lovely. Dark Matter is not constrained by the laws of Physics; it is unmovable, it is gravity defying, it is just darn cool. Wherever you place Dark Matter is where it stays. So go ahead and place it mid-air, deep in the base of a wall, or anywhere else you can imagine. The only thing in all of *LittleBigPlanet* that has the power to affect it is your Popit Cursor. Quite handy, don't you think?

1

Going Deeper

Buoyant Bubble

If you need to add a little levity to your level, Peach Floaty is just the material for you. This grab-able wonder is quite literally lighter than air. Try placing it somewhere to see what happens. Just remember to tether it down with a little String.

Picking up the Pieces

If you happen to exit the Popit menu prematurely, causing your carefully placed but unconnected objects to fall or float off, there is an easy way to fix it. Rather than taking hold of each item with the Popit Cursor and returning it to its proper place, simply Pause Create Mode with a tap of the directional button up, then hit Undo and immediately thereafter hit Redo. Everything is restored to its proper place and frozen there until you have had a chance to glue, bolt, and tether the objects to their proper place.

Float on

Pink Floaty is another interesting material, to be sure. It is said to be the most impartial of all materials. This is probably because it always stays neutral, or at least neutrally buoyant. Pink Floaty stays exactly where you place it until it is bumped, then, well, you know what Newton said about objects in motion.

Tools Rules

Now that you have had a chance to experiment with the last few remaining materials, it's time once again to visit the Tools Bag. Here, you can hone your level building skills.

② GET MOVING WITH GADGETS

The Gadgets Window of your Tools Bag is destined to become one of your most invaluable recourses. Whether you're looking to add a little up and down to your level or give one of your creations a voice of their own, this is where you need to be.

Creative Connectors

There's a lot more to connectors than just basic Bolts, Strings, and Rods. If you're looking to add a bit of a wobble or maybe even some side-to-side action to one of your creations, then one of these more advanced connectors is sure to fit into your plans.

ADVANCED ADJUSTING: CONNECTORS

WHEN YOU START DELVING INTO THE MORE CUSTOMIZABLE CONNECTORS, YOU'LL FIND THEIR TWEAK MENU LITERALLY TEEMING WITH MORE OPTIONS. HERE'S A BREAKDOWN OF THE NEW CONNECTOR OPTIONS AND THEIR EFFECT.

Connector Adjustments

Adjustment Type	Adjustment Name	Effect
Basic Settings	Set Angle (Bolt)	Set Bolt's resting position angle. Toggle between 0º and 360º
	Set Speed (Bolt)	Controls the speed of a Bolt's action. Toggle between 0.0 and 12.0.
	Set Number of Turns (Bolt)	Controls the number of Revolutions a Bolt terns before resetting.
	Set Maximum Length (Winch and Piston)	Set connector's maximum length.
	Set Minimum Length (Winch and Piston)	Set connector's minimum length.
Timing	Set Time Taken	Set the amount of time it takes a connector to complete its action.
	Set Pause Interval	Set the amount of time before a connector repeats action.
	Set Movement Phase	Set to synchronize the movement of all the mechanized, motorized, and winchized objects in your level.
Direction (Bolt)	Clockwise/Counter-Clockwise	Set direction of a Bolt's movement.
	Is it Stiff? Yes/No	Determines whether connecting angle is solid or loose.
	Flipper Motion (Winch and Piston) Off/In/Out	Establishes direction of motor force.

Bouncing back

A Sprung Bolt works like a normal Bolt, but adds a little bounce. Create a basic seesaw, but this time use a Sprung Bolt. Open the Tweak menu and adjust the resting angle. The orange marker in the center of the Bolt represents the new resting angle. The strength setting determents just how much spring is in your Sprung Bolt. Try adjusting the Bolt several times until you're comfortable with its properties.

Sprung Bolt Adjustments
Set Strength
Set Angle

Round and round She Goes

The next bolt in your arsenal is the Motor Bolt. This handy little connector can put a spin on things. Build another basic seesaw ensuring that your fulcrum is high enough to allow your lever to fully rotate. Place your lever near the top, then anchor it to the fulcrum with a Motor Bolt. Hold down ✕ to bring up your Tweak Menu. While this menu is open, the orange marker on your bolt displays the current rotation and speed of the connector. Try adjusting the strength, speed, and direction of your Bolt, and then leave the Tweak Menu to see the results. Voila, your seesaw is now a basic windmill.

Motor Bolt Adjustments
Set Strength
Set Speed
Clockwise / Counter-Clockwise

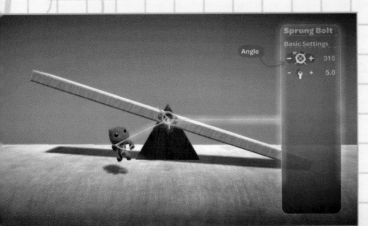

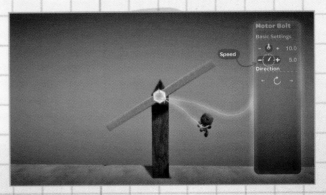

A Shaky Connection

The final bolt at your disposal is the Wobble Bolt. This fine specimen, obviously enough, adds a bit of wobble to your level. Replace the Motor Bolt from the windmill you just created with a Wobble Bolt. Open the Tweak Menu and behold all the adjustments that can be made. The orange marker once again displays the motion of you bolt. Additionally, the Wobble Bolt has three green markers. The two outer markers display your Bolt's range of motion. As you increase the Bolt's number of turns from the Tweak Menu, these markers move accordingly. Each time you add a complete revolution to the motion, the Bolt's outline becomes more opaque. The bolder green centerline shows the Bolt's resting angle.

Under the Timing options, you can adjust the amount of time it takes the Bolt to complete its action. By adjusting the pause interval, you can also affect how long the Bolt waits before repeating its action. Toggle between the Flipper Motion options to test their effects. Now, try experimenting with several settings to see how changing one option alters your Bolt's behavior.

Wobble Bolt Adjustments
Set Number of Turns
Set Angle
Set Strength
Set Time Taken
Set Pause Interval
Set Movement Phase
Flipper Motion

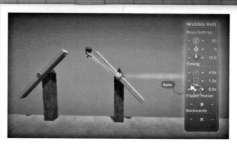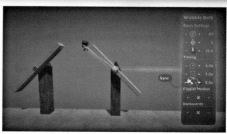

SET MOVEMENT PHASE

THE SET MOVEMENT PHASE OPTION WITHIN THE TWEAK MENU OF MANY OF YOUR GADGETS HELPS SYNCHRONIZE THE MOVING PARTS IN YOUR LEVELS. PICK UP THE SEESAW YOU MADE USING THE WOBBLE BOLT AND PRESS R3 TO COPY IT. NEXT, OPEN THE TWEAK MENU FOR EACH AND SET THEIR MOVEMENT PHASE TO IDENTICAL NUMBERS. YOU CAN ADJUST THE SET MOVEMENT PHASE OPTION BETWEEN 0.0 AND 30.0. NOW, TRY SETTING THE WOBBLE BOLTS TO DIFFERENT NUMBERS TO SEE THE EFFECT.

Flipper Motion (Bolts)

It is important to understand how activating Flipper Motion affects your Bolts when setting the angle and motion. Once on, the resting angle marker becomes the outside border for your Bolt's range of motion.

Think of it like a clock. By default, your resting angle is set to noon with your range of motion between eleven and two. By setting your Flipper Motion to Clockwise, your resting angle remains noon but your range of motion is now between noon and three.

Stretch it out

If you feel your level is lacking a little bounce, why not add some Elastic? Elastic works just like String with one major exception: it's elastic. This connector can be bunched up shorter than its length setting and also stretched out further. Just how stretchy it is depends on its strength setting. The stronger you make your Elastic, the less it can be stretched. To test this flexible connectable, build a basic swing, attaching the sponge to your support beam with Elastic. Grab hold and swing around. Try different strength settings to see their effect.

Elastic Adjustments
Length
Set Strength

A Bouncing Bound

If bounce is more what you were looking for in your stretching connector, then Spring is the tool for you. Similar to Elastic this connector behaves just like Rod but, rather obviously, springy. Replace the Elastic connector on your newly built swing with a Spring and test it out. Remember, as with Rod, you may also make a Spring stiff.

Spring Adjustments
Length
Set Strength
Is It Stiff?

JUST HOW LONG IS IT?

WHEN ADJUSTING STRETCHY CONNECTORS, THEIR LENGTH IS DISPLAYED WITH A WHITE AND ORANGE LINE. WHITE IDENTIFIES THE ACTUAL LENGTH OF THE CONNECTOR, WHEREAS ORANGE SHOWS HOW MUCH IT IS BEING STRETCHED. THIS IS IMPORTANT TO THINK ABOUT WHEN SETTING THE STRENGTH OF YOUR CONNECTOR. BE CAREFUL NOT TO SET ANYTHING TO TAUT.

Expandable Strength

It is important to understand the effect of a strength setting for your stretching connectors. When set to 0.0, your connector has no elasticity and provides no resistance. If set to 10.0, your connector behaves almost identically to its non-stretchy counterparts (e.g. String or Rod).

Let's Reel This in

The Winch is another example of String like connectors, but the difference here is this tool has been mechanized. Use a Winch to replace the Spring connector on your swing and pull up its Tweak Menu. Winches have two length options under basic settings: Maximum Length and Minimum Length. The three green marks on your Winch represent its movement based on these length settings. The first green marker, paired with the orange marker, identifies the Winch's base. The center green marker shows its Minimum Length and the final marker displays Maximum Length. As always, your strength setting determines the integrity and power of your connector. Tweak away to see the effect of different settings.

Winch Adjustments
Maximum Length
Minimum Length
Set Strength
Speed
Pause
Sync
Flipper Motion

A Powerful Piston

The final connector at your disposal is the trusty Piston. This tool is a cross between Winches and Rods. Its Tweak Menu has all the same features as the Winch, with the additional stiffness setting. This connector is ideal for controlled up / down or side-to-side motion. To test the Piston, attach a block to the floor and create three more blocks around it (one on top and one on either side). Attach each block to the base with a Piston. Try adjusting each differently to examine the effects.

Piston Adjustments
Maximum Length
Minimum Length
Set Strength
Speed
Pause
Sync
Is It Stiff?
Flipper Motion

Flipper Motion (Winches and Pistons)

The way activating Flipper Motion affects the motion of your connectors is essential to understand. The In and Out options are in relation to the connector's base, identified by the orange marker. If used incorrectly, your connection breaks.

THINGS FALL APART

BE SURE TO FIND A BALANCE WHEN ADJUSTING YOUR CONNECTORS. IF THE ACTIONS YOU HAVE SELECTED ARE TOO FAR OUTSIDE THE REALM OF POSSIBLE BEHAVIOR FOR YOUR OBJECTS, YOUR CONNECTION EVAPORATES.

Switches

Your sack person is not merely a casual observer of the actions going on around *LittleBigPlanet*. Switches give you the ability to decide how, when, and why adjustable objects function. Once you stamp one into the world, simply grab the Connector Tab (the green and yellow wires connected to the Switch) with the Popit Cursor and attach it to the adjustable objects (such as Wobble Bolts or Pistons) you wish the Switch to control. Scroll down to the Switches section of your Gadgets window to start exploring your activation abilities.

ADJUSTING: SWITCHES

SWITCHES HAVE A VARIETY OF HUGELY HANDY ADJUSTMENTS. HERE IS A BREAKDOWN OF ALL THE OPTIONS AVAILABLE WITHIN THE SWITCHES TWEAK MENU.

Switch Adjustments		
Adjustment Type	Adjustment Name	Effect
Behavior	On / Off	Triggering the Switch causes affected objects to activate.
	Direction	Alters the direction of affected objects when activated.
	One-Shot	Affected objects perform action once.
	Speed	Controls speed of affected objects (when trigger is fully activated, affected objects reach speed set in their Tweak Menu).
	Set Minimum Length (Winch and Piston)	Set connector's Minimum Length.
Item	Item Selection Field	Select activation item from either your Stickers or Decorations window.
Trigger Radius	Set Trigger Radius	Controls certain Switches' activation area.
Magnetic Key Color	Toggle between color options for Magnetic Keys.	Sets color of Switch.
	Inverted (Yes / No)	When activated, Switch inverts action of affected objects.
	Visible? (Yes / No)	Determines whether the Switch is visible in Play Mode.

Proximity Performance

The Sensor Switch is the most basic proximity-based Switch. Whenever a sack person gets close to it, the Switch activates. Just how close they need to be is up to you. Now, remember that wall you built when you learned about Dissolve material? Well, the magic trick is about to begin. Place a Sensor Switch on the Dissolve wall and attach its Connector Tab to the wall. Open the Tweak Menu and set the Switches Behavior to On / Off. Next, set the Trigger Radius to just outside the border of the wall. Have your sack person walk up to the edge of the wall, and prepare to be amazed. Without any warning, a material called Dissolve disappears before your very eyes.

Sensor Switch Adjustments

Behavior Options: On/Off, Direction, One-Shot, Speed
Trigger Radius
Inverted?
Visible?

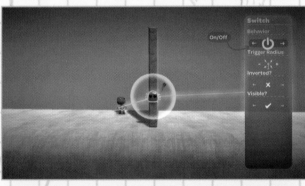

Birds of a Feather Activate Together

Magnetic Key Switches activate whenever a magnetic key of a corresponding color is near. Build a windmill using a Motor Bolt and set its speed to 6.0. Place a Magnetic Key Switch a small distance away and attach its Connection Tab to the Motor Bolt. Open the Tweak Menu and set the Switches Behavior to On / Off and make note of the its Trigger Radius. Now, create a small sponge block and place a magnetic key on it. Pull the block into the Trigger Radius of your Switch to test the results. Re-open your Switches Tweak Menu and try different adjustments to see their effect. See how much you can alter the behavior of the Bolt without adjusting its settings.

Magnetic Key Switch Adjustments

Behavior Options: On/Off, Direction, One-Shot, Speed
Trigger Radius
Magnetic Key Color
Inverted?
Visible?

Magnetic Key Switch Adjustments

Magnetic Key Color

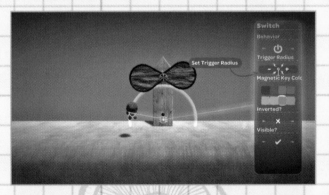

Calling all Colors

Magnetic Key Switches only respond to keys of the same color. Be sure to match the correct key and Switch when designing your levels.

Sticker Starter

Sticker Switches are certainly a crafty bunch, and to activate them, you're going to have to get crafty as well. Sticker Switches work like any other proximity-based Switch, but the key in this case is a specific Sticker or Decoration. Swap out your Magnetic Key Switch for a Sticker Switch and once you have attached the new Connection Tab to the Motor Bolt, open your Tweak Menu. The first item in the window is the Items option. Select it and, much like with Prize Bubbles, you are directed to your Stickers and Decoration Windows. By selecting your favorite Sticker, you create an activation key for your Switch. Adjust the other options to your preferred settings and exit the Tweak Menu. Simply place the Sticker you selected on or near the Switch to activate it.

Sticker Switch Adjustments
Item
Behavior Options: On / Off, Direction, One-Shot, Speed
Trigger Radius
Inverted?
Visible?

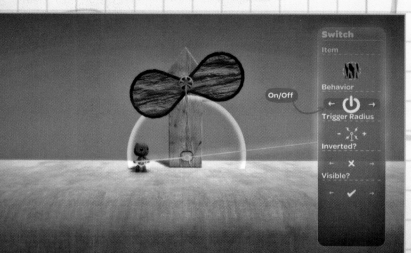

DIFFICULT DEDUCTION

STICKER SWITCHES CAN BE A BIT TRICKY TO FIGURE OUT; THIS MAKES THEM PERFECT FOR OPENING THE WAY TO BONUS GOODIES AND OPTIONAL LEVEL ELEMENTS. BUT, WHATEVER YOU CHOOSE TO USE THEM FOR, BE SURE TO GIVE SACK PEOPLE PLAYING YOUR LEVEL A CLUE OR TWO. WHAT FUN IS A SWITCH IF YOU CAN'T FIGURE OUT HOW TO USE IT?

Trigger Radius

Each proximity-based Switch allows you to adjust the size of the Trigger Radius around the Switch. When toggling this option, the radius is shown as a glowing circle around the Switch. If the behavior of your Switch is set to speed, then the affected objects move faster the closer the catalyst is to the Switch.

Grab and Go

Something's bound to happen if you can just hold on. Attach a Grab Switch to any grab-able material and activate it by grabbing that material. Pretty straightforward really. Grab Switches have all the adjustments you have come to know and love in a Switch, so go ahead and give it a Tweak.

Grab Switch Adjustments
Behavior Options: On / Off, Direction, One-Shot
Inverted?
Visible?

Easy as Flipping a Switch

You are likely already very familiar with 2-way Switches. Pull one out of your Tools Bag and attach it to the floor. When your sack person pulls on the Switch's Lever to the right, it activates. Once turned on, the Switch stays on.

2-way Adjustments
Behavior Options: On / Off, Direction, One-Shot, Speed
Inverted?

Pulled to Perform

Though the 3-way Switch may look awfully similar the 2-way Switch, this fine lever functions a bit differently from its twin. 3-way Switches start standing straight up. Pull it in either direction to activate the Switch. Release the lever to reset it and deactivate the Switch.

3-way Adjustments
Behavior Options: On / Off, Direction, One-Shot, Speed
Inverted?

Is It Coming or Going?

Setting a 2-way and 3-way Switch's behavior to Direction has a unique effect. The Switches are active when pushed to the right and inverted when set to the left.

2

A Pressing Reaction

Buttons are another Switch that should look rather familiar. When a sack person jumps on a Button, they activate the Switch. The Button stays active as long as the sack person is perched atop it.

Button Adjustments

Behavior Options: On / Off, Direction, One-Shot

Inverted?

ADDING AN ELEMENT OF DANGER

③

The Gameplay Kits window of your Tools Bag holds a bit more than just the Basics. Use the Dangerous Kit to help add a new layer of intrigue to your level.

Dangerous

Tucked away in the darkest corner of your Tools Bag lurks the nefarious Dangerous Gameplay Kit. These items don't need any help from the hazard tools to have a lethal impact. If you'd like to add a bit of a boom to your level or you're just looking to make a point, this is the place to go.

Get to the Point

As you can imagine, spikes and sack people are not the best of friends. They can, in fact, knock the stuffing right out of the poor sack people. Place a spikes strip down wherever you'd like to see a little peril. Spikes come in two convenient sizes, small and large. If you'd like to test their lethality, drop a spike down and have your sack person jump aboard.

Under Pressure

Impact explosives are one of the most high-strung tools you're ever going to meet. Add just a little pressure and BOOM, they blow up in your poor sack person's face. Your sack person can grab impact explosives, but remember to handle them gingerly. If dropped or tussled too hard, they blow up.

Wired to Blow

Trigger explosives need a bit more incentive to go KABOOM. That incentive comes in the form of Switches. Simply attach any Switch's connector tab to a trigger explosive and as soon as the Switch is activated, so is the bomb.

COLLATERAL DAMAGE

WEAKER MATERIALS LIKE CARDBOARD, POLYSTYRENE, SPONGE, PINK FLOATY, PEACH FLOATY, AND DISSOLVE ARE DESTRUCTIBLE. IF AN EXPLOSIVE GOES OFF NEAR ONE, THEY CAN BE PARTIALLY OR EVEN FULLY DESTROYED IN THE BLAST. WATCH OUT, YOUR SACK PERSON IS ALSO DESTRUCTIBLE.

4 SOUNDS GOOD

Audio Objects allow you to add some acoustic authenticity to the beautiful level you are creating. These tools can add a soundtrack to a sack person's progress as well as add sound effects to the actions on screen.

ADJUSTING: AUDIO OBJECTS

AUDIO OBJECTS HAVE THE ABILITY TO BE FINELY TUNED. HERE IS A BREAKDOWN OF ALL THE OPTIONS AVAILABLE WITHIN AUDIO OBJECTS TWEAK MENU.

Audio Objects Adjustments

Adjustment Type	Adjustment Action	Effect
Mixer	Toggle interactive music elements prominence.	Select between different music elements, such as Percussion or Melody, and set its prominence in musical track.
Volume	Set linear track volume.	Set the volume of an audio object.
Start Point	Toggle tracks starting point.	Determines the point from which a track will begin playback, but only when a track first starts.
Item	Item Selection Field	Select activation item from either your Stickers or Decorations window.
Trigger Radius	Set Trigger Radius	Controls Audio Objects activation area.
Choose Sound	Select sound option.	Cycle between available sounds. Those marked with an (*) are looping sounds.
Trigger Mode	Set activation method.	Toggle between Player Proximity, On Destruction, By Switch, or On Impact.
Modifier	Alters sound.	Change the sound in marvelous ways.
Visible?	Yes / No	Determines weather the Audio Object is visible in Play Mode.

Setting the Soundtrack

While traveling throughout the Curator Creators' levels, your sack person is likely to come across some marvelous tunes. You can add many of those same songs to your own level. Look to the Music section of your Audio Objects window to see the Music options you have collected. Leave the cursor over any option you would like to hear a sample of. Once you have chosen a song, simply place the music box wherever you want it to be heard. From the Tweak Menu, you can determine the track's overall volume, as well as where in the song it begins. Set the Trigger Radius in the same way you would a Sensor Switch.

Music Adjustments

Volume
Start Point
Trigger Radius
Visible?

Manipulative Music

Just as each Curator Creator's area has a unique themed Background, so too do they have a unique musical theme. There are eight of these interactive music elements, one for each Curator Creator. What makes these musical elements special is just how much you can customize them. Open the Tweak Menu and start toggling Mixer options. Bring up the Melody or drop out the Drums and Bass until it sounds just the way you want.

Music-Interactive Adjustments

Mixer
Start Point
Trigger Radius
Visible?

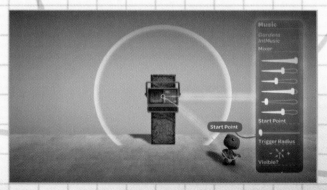

Hear What You See

Silly sound effects never get old. The Sound Effects tools can attach an air of reality to your scene by adding some mechanical noises to your machines. You can also go for a laugh by adding a burp sound effect just about anywhere. Choose the type of sound you want from the Tools Bag, then place it and open its Tweak Menu. First things first, select the specific sound you want to hear. Next, set its trigger and then play with the Modifier until it sounds just right.

Sound Effects Adjustments
Choose Sound
Trigger Mode: Player Proximity, On Destruction, By Switch, On Impact
Modifier
Visible?

Sounding Right

Sound Effects give you an amazing amount of freedom when it comes to activating them. Make sure to take advantage of all the different Trigger Mode Options.

Tutorials

By combining the basic building principles you've learned and some of the more advanced tools and techniques just covered, you can begin building larger scenes and level elements. Again, these tutorials should be used as both learning aids and as a quick reference guide to assist with building your own levels.

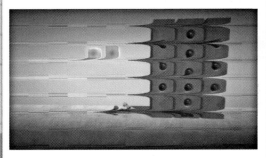

SAFETY BLOCKS

THE BEST WAY TO TEST YOUR CONSTRUCTIONS IS TO SWITCH TO PLAY MODE. IF, HOWEVER, YOU WOULD LIKE TO QUICKLY CHECK A LEVEL ELEMENT IN CREATE MODE, YOU SHOULD START OUT BY DROPPING A SAFETY BLOCK. SAFETY BLOCKS CAN BE ANY MATERIAL OR ITEM THAT IS NON-ESSENTIAL TO YOUR LEVEL. ONCE THE SAFETY BLOCK IS STAMPED DOWN, YOU CAN TRY OUT YOUR CONSTRUCTION AND EASILY RESET IT BY TAPPING REWIND (WHICH RETURNS YOU TO BEFORE YOUR SAFETY BLOCK'S CONSTRUCTION).

5 A BIT OF BOUNCE IN YOUR STEP

Use of flexible connectors can help add a bit of bounce to your levels. Use them to augment your path or provide a challenge for your sack person.

SPRINGBOARD

To create a springboard, place two squares of Dark Matter at the same height. Separate the squares by the width of the springboard you would like to create. Run a plank of cardboard across their base at your desired height. Finally, attach one end of a Spring to a piece of Dark Matter and the other end to the edges of your plank. Adjust the strength of the springs to give more or less bounce to your board. Place Springboards at the base of tall platforms to get the most bounce out of your board.

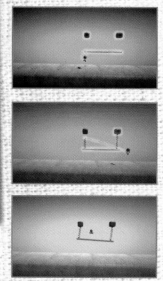

WOBBLE POLES

Wobble poles provide a bit of instability and challenge to your levels. Start by building a tall wooden structure one layer deep on the backmost plane of your level. Next, build a wooden beam with a circle at its base. Use the semi-circle shape to create a platform at the top of your beam. Place the completed pole in front of the wooden structure and connect it with a Sprung Bolt. Be sure to attach the Sprung Bolt to the base of your pole in the center of the circle. Open your Bolts Tweak Menu and ensure that its resting angle is set to 0° (or 360°). Now, adjust the Tightness. The looser you make the Bolt, the more wobble you're going to have in your pole. Set the Tightness to 5.0 for a shaky platform, or as low as 2.0 for a pole that can swing to the floor.

6 BOLTING AWAY

Using mechanized Bolts is often an excellent way to get around obstacles. Try using Motor Bolts and Wobble Bolts to create spinning and flipping level elements.

SPINNING SPONGE — PART ONE

Spinning sponges are very useful items and found throughout *LittleBigPlanet*. Start by constructing a base for your sponge. Your base can be a simple column or triangle, or you can construct something a little more ornate using different shapes. Next, stamp down a medium-sized sponge circle and use a Motor Bolt to attach it to your base. In the Tweak Menu, adjust the Bolts Tightness to 10.0 and set the speed you wish it to revolve at. When setting the speed, remember to take the comfort of your sack person into account. Setting the speed to anything above 5.0 creates a very rough ride and can even cause your sack person to come apart at the seams.

SPINNING SPONGE — PART TWO

Try using similar techniques to build a windmill. As before, start by constructing the base; a tall metal column works perfectly. Next, construct a cardboard cross and attach it to the metal column with a Motor Bolt. Attach sponge to the end of each end of the cross. Use Glue for a basic connection, use standard Bolts if you would like the sponges to rotate in relation to the windmill's motion, or attach with Motor Bolts or Wobble Bolts to add another layer of motion to your construction. The same speed constrictions apply. See if you can use the rotation of Spinning Sponge Part One to get your sack person onto the windmill you just completed.

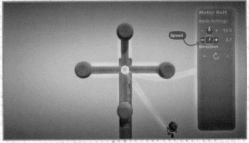

SPINNING SPONGE — PART TWO

Try using similar techniques to build a windmill. As before, start by constructing the base; a tall metal column works perfectly. Next, construct a cardboard cross and attach it to the metal column with a Motor Bolt. Attach sponge to the end of each end of the cross. Use Glue for a basic connection, use standard Bolts if you would like the sponges to rotate in relation to the windmill's motion, or attach with Motor Bolts or Wobble Bolts to add another layer of motion to your construction. The same speed constrictions apply. See if you can use the rotation of Spinning Sponge Part One to get your sack person onto the windmill you just completed.

CATAPULT

To construct a catapult, first build a flat triangular base. Attach your base to the floor on the second plane forward. Now build an arm for your catapult out of cardboard. The arm should extend a good distance from the base on one side. Construct a scoop-shaped tray and place it at the end of the arm. Attach the arm to your base with a Wobble Bolt. Open your Bolts Tweak Menu and set it to create your desired projectile speed and trajectory. To cause your projectile to leave the catapult at moderate speed, running parallel to the ground, toggle the Number of Turns to 0.2, position its angle to 315°, and set the Time Taken to 2.0s. If your sack person is the desired projectile, place a Sensor Switch on the scoop and attach its Connector Tab to the Wobble Bolt. Go ahead and jump in to give it a try.

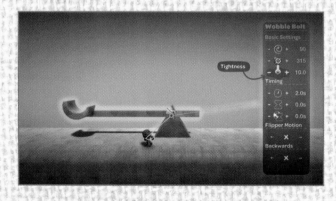

7 UP, DOWN, AND SIDE-TO-SIDE

Use moving connectors and Switches to create unique and fun moving parts like elevators and catapults. These elements can help sack people move through your levels, give them puzzles to solve or just provide a good scare.

RISING WINCH

Winches can help your sack person make it to the top or bottom of anything. To make a simple rising winch, place a square of Dark Matter well above your sack person's head. Place a sponge circle below it within reach of an athletic jump and connect the two with a Winch. Open the Winch's Tweak Menu to determine its Minimum and Maximum Length as well as its speed and pause interval. Once everything is set to your liking, pull a Grab Switch from your Tools Bag and apply it to the sponge. Attach its Connector Tab to the Winch. Now all your sack person must do for a ride up is jump and grab it.

ELEVATORS AND MOVING WALKWAYS

Basic elevators and moving walkways are another simple way to help a sack person go from one place to another. Build a large platform, then place a small cardboard plank next to the structure so that it runs parallel to the top of the platform. Now, get a Piston from your Tools Bag and connect one end to the floor and the other to the center of your cardboard plank. Open the Piston's Tweak menu and reduce its Minimum Length to 2.5 (the Maximum Length should be fine because the plank was set to its intended height). Adjust the speed of the Piston relative to its maximum height. For a comfortable ride, try to give between 0.5s and 1.0s for every 10.0 of space traveled between Maximum and Minimum Height. Next, add a small Pause if you would like to give your sack person a larger window to board and exit the elevator. Lastly, choose to make your Piston stiff. Your sack person can now travel to the top of the platform with ease.

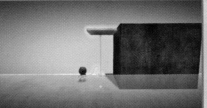

You can use the same technique on the other side of the platform to make a moving walkway. Create a second cardboard plank and place it off the non-elevator side of your platform. Connect it to the platform with a Piston and perform the same adjustments as before. Once set, you have created some lateral transportation to compliment your up-and-down.

Now try adding Sensor Switches to the center of each plank and attach their Connector Tabs to the relevant Piston. Adjust their Trigger Radius to the border of the plank. Each moving component now only functions while a sack person is riding it.

6

7

Going Deeper

257

LAUNCH PAD

You can also use Pistons to create launch pads. Utilize cardboard to create a base for your launch pad. Use the octagon shape, embedding the cardboard in the floor so only the top three sides are above floor level. Next, use the square shape to delete a space for your launch pad. Fill the space you have made with a cardboard plank. Place one end of a Piston on the center of your base and the other on the bottom of the plank. Open the Piston's Tweak Menu and set its Minimum Length to 2.5 and its Maximum Length 5.0. Your Piston's speed setting affects just how far your sack person is launched. Set between 10.0s and 20.0s for a controlled boost, and 20.0 to 30.0 for a major blast off. Turn Stiffness on and set Flipper Motion to Out. Now, attach a Button to the plank and fix its Connector Tab to the Piston. Lastly, adjust the Button's Behavior to One-Shot. Leave the Button's Tweak Menu and have your sack person jump onto the Button to test its boosting ability.

Quick Switch

It is always wise to use Switches whenever you create something that requires quick motion and precise timing to work correctly. For example, without a Switch, the launch pad still works, but it is much harder for your sack person to board it and to receive the full power of the boost.

(8) ATTENTION ALL SACK PEOPLE: DANGERS AHEAD!

Adding dangerous elements to your levels is a sure-fire way to keep things interesting. By combining dangerous elements with techniques you have already learned, you can generate some small scary stretches and some huge treacherous trials.

SIMPLE CRUSHERS

Use the same techniques employed in elevator construction to create crushers. Start by making a simple crusher. Run a strip of Dark Matter above your sack person then build a wooden block and rest it on the floor below the Dark Matter Strip. Attach the block to your strip with a Piston. Open the Piston's Tweak Menu, leave the Maximum Length set to its current height and adjust the Minimum Length to its shortest possible setting. Now, activate Stiffness and set Flipper Motion to Out. Any unfortunate sack person caught underneath is going to be crushed. To add a little flair to your crusher, try using the Flame Tool to set it ablaze, or add a row of spikes to its base.

ADVANCED CRUSHERS

If you want to go really advanced, try turning your crusher on its side to create a squishing obstacle. Build a crusher as before, but attach it to a wall rather than a ceiling structure, causing the crusher to shoot out at a 90° angle rather than downward. Highlight your creation with your Popit Cursor and copy it, then use the R3 to invert the crusher. Place the copied construction so the two crushers meet when fully extended. To ensure your timing is right, open each Piston's Tweak Menu and set their Movement Phase to 1.0. When you exit the Popit, your two crushers should now be moving in and out in tandem, transforming the two crushers into a squasher.

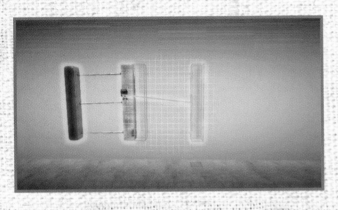

EXPLOSIVES

Explosives are as handy as they are deadly. To start getting a feel for their destructive power, place a trigger explosive near the base of a large cardboard structure. Embed several impact explosives into the cardboard, ensuring that each is close enough to another to cause a chain reaction. Place a Button on the floor nearby and attach its Connector Tab to the trigger explosive. Have your sack person activate the Button to see just what a blast explosives really are.

PUT IT TOGETHER

Try using aspects of all the tutorials just covered to build a sample scene for your sack person to navigate. This scene is composed of four elements working together to form one unified section.

ELEMENT ONE

Near the Entrance of an empty level, build a tall polystyrene column three layers deep. Use Dissolve to create a slim column starting just above the top of the polystyrene and continuing a quarter of the way down. Embed an impact explosive in the top of the Dissolve, then several more incrementally down the length of the column. Place a 3-way Switch near the base of the column and adjust its Behavior to On/Off, and then attach its Connector Tab to the Dissolve.

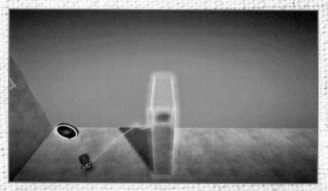

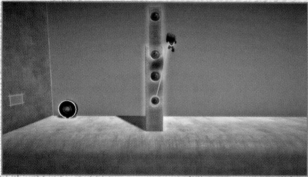

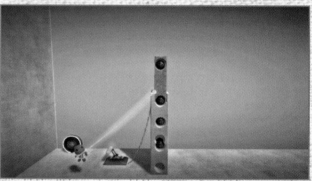

ELEMENT TWO

Build a launch pad to the right of your polystyrene column. Adjust it to give your sack person a decent amount of vertical air travel. Test how high your launch pad launches your sack person, and then create a sponge circle just within reach. Attach the sponge to a rising Winch using a Grab Switch to activate the connector.

ELEMENT THREE

Use metal to create large base with raised columns on either side. Select a sponge material and make six identical columns that fill the base snugly. Lift the six sponge columns and attach each to the base with a Piston. Set each Piston identically with Stiffness on. Vary each Piston's Movement Phase 0.5 apart. You have now created a repelling walkway. Adjust the height of the metal border column on the left side of your walkway to correspond with the sponge on the rising Winch. Copy your rippling walkway and place one on each of the three layers. Tweak the Movement Phase on the central rippling walkway to disjoint the motion, or leave it as is to keep the motion synchronized. Use more metal to extend both metal columns, making them into platforms your sack person can jump onto. Next, add a Checkpoint to each Platform. Now, cover your work by creating a thin piece of metal and gluing it to your rippling walkway's base. Finally, use the Electric Tool to add an element of danger to several columns within the rippling walkway.

ELEMENT FOUR

Use Dark Matter supports to help create a springboard to the right of the rippling walkway. Place the springboard so an athletic jump is needed to reach it. Have your sack person jump from the rippling walkway onto the springboard several times to see how big a bounce it can get off of the board, then construct another platform just within range. Place a block on the floor between the two platforms and use the Horrible Gas Tool to lethalize it. Lastly, place a Score Board on the final platform. You can now switch to Play Mode and have your sack person test its skills.

Creation

Creating a Level:
Let's Get Crafty!!!

Objectives

A Touch of Life

1

Special Gadgets

2

Character Enhancements

3

Racing

4

Camera Controls

5

Creature Construction: Friendly / Non-collectable

6

Creature Construction: Dangerous / Collectable

7

Vehicles

8

Advanced Obstacles

9

Beyond Tools Rules

That endless repository of amazement known as the Tools Bag has a few more amazing apparatuses that can help transform the variety of bits and bobs you create into unique environments of fun and excitement.

① A TOUCH OF LIFE

Open the Gadgets window of your Tools Bag, and behold the magic and mystery of the assorted creature pieces. These tools allow you to give a voice to your creations, let them see the world, and even give them a mind of their own.

Speaking—Laterally

The Magic Mouth allows you to give voice to your level and the interesting creatures that inhabit it. Attach a Magic Mouth the same way you would a Decoration. Once you have placed a Magic Mouth in a somewhat mouth-like location, open its Tweak Menu to see all the amazing customization therein.

Magic Mouth Adjustments		
Adjustment Type	Adjustment Name	Effect
Basic Settings	Enter a Speech	Enter desired speech text
	Speech	Toggle between voice options for mouth's audio output
Trigger Radius	Set Trigger Radius	Set Mouth activation area
Cutscene Camera	Yes / No	Enable or disable cutscene when Mouth activates.
Visible?	Adjust Target	Set Cutscene camera angle when cutscene is activated.
	Yes / No	Determines weather the Mouth is visible in Play Mode.

From inside the Tweak Menu, use the Enter a Speech option to enter the text you want to issue from your Mouth's speech bubble. The Speech option lets you select how you would like your Mouth to sound. Sample your voice options and select the appropriate one in the same way you would a Sound Effect. The Magic Mouth's Trigger Radius functions are exactly like that of a Sensor Switch. Set your preferred radius and, as soon as a sack person enters the perimeter, the mouth speaks. If you enter a particularly informative message, you may want to enable the Cutscene Camera. Once active, the Adjust Target option appears. To set the camera angle for the cutscene, select this option with ✕, which brings up a sample cutscene screen. Use the left stick to pan the camera, the right stick to tilt its angle; both **R1** and **L1** zoom the camera out, where **R2** and **L2** zoom in. Once you have adjusted the scene to your liking, tap ✕ to confirm the cutscene or ● to cancel the action. Finally, toggle the visibility option to determine whether or not your mouth is visible in Play Mode.

Here's Looking at You

Magic Eyes are likely the most observant of all the tools in *LittleBigPlanet*. Whenever a sack person draws near, they cannot help but check it out. Magic Eyes are also placed in the same way as Decorations. Select one out of your Tools Bag and place it in your level. Try having your sack person walk by it a few times to see how it looks.

Getting a Leg up

Legs are one of two forms of creature-controlled locomotion. They can be placed on any material or object, at least one layer in depth, which is not attached to the floor. When paired with a brain, Legs can both walk and jump in accordance with their brain's commands. Legs are inert on objects without brains.

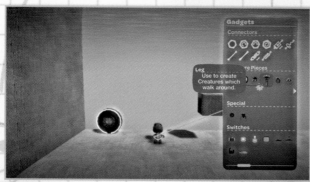

Rolling away

Wheels are the second form of creature-controlled motion. Just like Legs, Wheels can only be attached to non-anchored, single-layered objects. Wheels are also inert on objects without brains.

Traction

Remember that a creature sporting Wheels travels along many different materials, which also have different levels of traction. Glass, obviously, provides the least amount of traction, whereas Rubber gives your Wheels the most grip.

A Vulnerable Mind

Creature Brains allow many of your sack person's greatest enemies and dearest friends to behave with seeming autonomy within the levels of *LittleBigPlanet*. Bubbles power Unprotected Creature Brains. When your sack person collects one in Play Mode, the brain is destroyed along with the object it is attached to, and your sack person receives some points to boot. Stamp a Creature Brain: Unprotected, into your level and open its Tweak Menu to see all the adjustments that go into its apparent sentience.

Creature Brain Adjustments

Adjustment Type	Adjustment Name	Effect
Behavior	Ignore / Follow / Flee	Determines general behavior and motion of creature
	Awareness Radius	Establishes area of creature perception (set like Trigger Radius)
Timing	Movement Speed	Set speed of your creature
	Jump Interval	Set time in-between jumps on creatures with Legs
	Jump Phase	Set to synchronize the movement of all jumping creatures in your level

To sample the actions and behaviors of created creatures, try constructing a box with two Legs and a Creature Brain: Unprotected. Open the Tweak Menu and toggle different options to see the effect on your creation. Try each behavior and select different settings under the Timing options to view their effect. When you are happy with the results, switch to Play Mode and see if your sack person can collect your newly constructed creature's bubble.

TWO MINDS ARE SOMETIMES BETTER THAN ONE

WHEN YOU ATTACH MORE THAN ONE BRAIN TO A CREATURE, ALL OF THEM MUST BE COLLECTED BEFORE THE CREATURE FALLS. IF YOU CONSTRUCT A CREATURE HELD TOGETHER BY CONNECTORS, AN ATTACHED CREATURE PIECE OBEYS THE BRAIN CONNECTED TO ITS SECTION OF THE CREATION. IF THERE ARE MULTIPLE BRAINS ATTACHED TO A SINGLE OBJECT, THEN CREATURE PIECES RESPOND TO THE BRAIN MOST RECENTLY TRIGGERED.

Creating Invulnerability

Unprotected Creature Brains are only vulnerable in Play Mode. To truly test out your creature creations, you must transport your sack person out of Create Mode and face your creation in Play Mode.

Un-pop-able Creatures

The Creature Brain: Unprotected is terrific for enemies set to prowl your level; the Creature Brain: Protected, however, is reserved for those whose brains your sack person would prefer not pop. Put simply, if a creature is constructed using a Creature Brain: Protected, then they are protected from brain collection and the resulting destruction. In all other respects, the Creature Brain: Protected works like its Unprotected counterpart.

Coming or Going

Every creature creator worries about where their creations might wonder off to. By setting Creature Navigators you can rest easy. Place these handy tools like a decoration and whenever a creature encounters one they are forced to reverse direction.

② SPECIAL GADGETS

Hidden at the bottom of the Gadgets Window is a group of invaluable tools under the heading "Various." These tools can propel your creations to unheard-of speed, or create objects out of thin air. Scroll down to discover their power.

That Came out of Nowhere

The emitter is a unique tool indeed. It can be used to surprise, excite, or scare the stuffing out of your sack person. Pull an emitter from your Tools Bag and place it in your level. It won't do anything until you adjust it in the Tweak Menu, so go ahead and open it up.

Emitter Adjustments

Adjustment Type	Adjustment Name	Effect
Object	Choose Object	Set the item you wish to emit and its emitted location
Item Settings	Linear Speed	Establish speed emitted; items travel as soon as they are created
	Spin Speed	Set spin rotation on emitted items
Timing	Frequency	Set time in-between creation of emitted item sets
	Lifetime	Establish duration of time before emitted item dissolves
	Total Emitted	Set the total number of items the emitter can create
	Maximum emitted at one time	Determine total number of items emitted in a set between Frequency setting

Once you select the Choose Object option, you have access to both of your My Objects windows, as well as limited access to items in the Gameplay Kits window (bubbles and explosives). Once you select an item to emit, it appears at the end of a second Popit Cursor issuing from the emitter. Control its placement and proportions as you would an object. To set the area from where it is emitted, tap ⊗. Returning to the Tweak Menu, you may now use the Item Settings adjustments to establish how fast and with how much spin your item is to be spat out. Toggle the timing options to make sure your items emit in the amount and intervals you wish, and then leave the Tweak Menu to see the results of your adjustments.

Control the Flow

Like many other Tools, emitters respond to Switches. So if you do not want objects spat out willy-nilly, be sure to attach a Switch to your emitter.

Flying High

If it's a little get-up-and-go you're looking for in your level, there's no better place to look than Rockets. When you place a Rocket in your scene, you have the option of embedding it into the desired object or gluing it in place after it has been stamped down. Rockets default to "Off" when set. So, they won't launch until activated. Once a Connector Tab is attached, the Rocket only fires when the Switch is active. Rockets have a simple Tweak Menu that can help ensure you get just the right amount of zoom for your scene.

Rocket Adjustments

Adjustment Type	Adjustment Name	Effect
Boost	Set Boost Strength	Toggle the Rocket's Power
On / Off	No / Yes	Toggle between Rocket activation states

To get more "oomph" out of your Rocket, crank up the boost gauge, or bring it down a bit for a more controlled blast. Once again, the Rocket's native state is to "Off", regardless of the setting of the On/Off option.

Resetting Rockets

Once a Rocket with the On / Off setting set to 'Yes' has been activated by a Switch once, it behaves the same way as a Rocket set to 'No' would. So even though the Rocket began active, as soon as a sack person turns on the Rocket's Switch, it deactivates and only reactivates when the Switch has also been reactivated.

③ CHARACTER ENHANCEMENTS

The Character Enhancements section of your Gameplay Kits window holds only one item; but it's a good one.

A Lesson in Aviation

You and your sack person have likely become quite accustomed to flying whenever the urge strikes you here in Create Mode. Unfortunately, flight is not as simple as tapping the directional button down in Play Mode (which could be the reason your sack person gets so sad when it tries). To add flight to a level, place a Jetpack as you would a Decoration. Once your sack person gets close enough, it is equipped with a Jetpack of its own. Jetpacks include only one adjustable option within their Tweak Menu: Set Tether Length. This option allows you to set the maximum length of the tethering chain attached to the Jetpack. Adjust the setting the same way you would set the Trigger Radius on a Sensor Switch.

4 RACING

The Character Enhancements section of your Gameplay Kits window holds only one item; but it's a good one.

On Your Mark... Get Set... GO!

If you feel the need to create a sense of urgency in your level, why not try adding a race kit? Race kits are composed of two items from your Tools Bag: the Start Gate and the Finish Gate. Place a Start Gate where you would like your race to begin and a Finish Gate where you think it should end. In the Start Gate's Tweak Menu, find the Time Allowed option. Adjust this option to an appropriate amount of time to complete the course. Try to be fair; no sack person wants to get into a race it cannot win. Once the time is set, have your sack person try the course itself a few times in Play Mode.

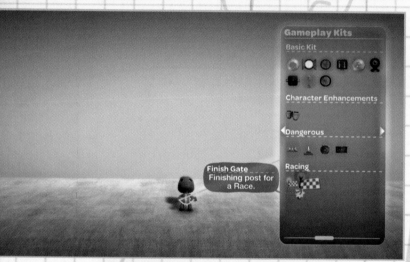

Rewarding Fast Footwork

The more time remaining upon completion of a racecourse, the more points your sack person racks up at the finish line. If more than one sack person is racing, then placement also affects the total points earned. Keep both these facts in mind when designing your course and setting its time.

 # 5 CAMERA CONTROLS

The two cameras within your Basic Kit are the final tools left to learn. You should be quit proud of yourself.

Say Cheese

The Photo Booth is a fun tool indeed. Set one anywhere you would like to create a wonderful sack person candid snapshot. Once set, whenever a sack person comes into range of your Photo Booth in Play Mode, a picture is taken that can thereafter be found in the My Pictures window of its Stickers & Decorations Popit icon. Each Photo Booth lets you customize how, where, and when a picture is taken. To adjust these options, open the Photo Booth's Tweak Menu.

Photo Booth Adjustments

Adjustment Type	Adjustment Name	Effect
Photo Booth	Angle & Zoom	Adjust / Set Photo Booth camera angle
	Zone	Set Photo Both activation area
Countdown	Countdown	Set Photo Booth timer

Adjust the Photo Booth's Angle & Zoom setting in the same way you would a Magic Mouth's Cutscene Camera. The left stick controls your pan, while the right stick adjusts the tilt. Use L1 to Zoom Out and L2 to Zoom In. When the shot looks just right, tap ✕ to confirm the selection. Unlike most other sack person-triggered objects, the Photo Booth's activation zone is not anchored to the tool. Use the left stick to position the target area and the right stick to adjust its size. Once you are satisfied, tap ✕. Finally, the Countdown option allows you to set a delay before the photo is taken, giving sack people a bit of time to strike a pose.

Camera Zone

For as sharp and attentive as the standard in-game camera is, it sometimes doesn't quite capture a scene you have created just the way you've envisioned it. In these situations, feel free to don a director's hat and set the camera yourself. Using the Camera Zone tool, you can control the zoom level and camera angle of the in-game camera. Place a Camera Zone in your level like a Sticker, then open its Tweak Menu.

Camera Zone Adjustments

Adjustment Type	Adjustment Name	Effect
Camera Zone	Angle & Zoom	Adjust / Set Camera Zone angle and zoom level
	Zone	Set Camera Zone activation area
Track Player	Adjust player tracking	Set the level to which the camera tracks a sack person within the Camera Zone

Adjust both the Angle & Zoom and the Zone settings in the same manner as with a Photo Booth. While setting Angle & Zoom, the left stick pans the camera, the right stick tilts it, and **L1** and **L2** Zoom In and Out respectively. While setting the Zone, the left stick adjusts target area and the right stick sets the trigger size. Use the Track Player option to decide how much the camera follows your sack person. The lower the Track Player dial is set, the less the camera moves while your Camera Zone is active.

④

⑤

SNAP!

BOTH THE PHOTO BOOTH AND THE CAMERA ZONE TOOLS ARE UNIQUE ITEMS. PHOTO BOOTHS DON'T INTERACT WITH OTHER ITEMS OR OBJECTS. A CAMERA ZONE CAN BE ATTACHED TO A SWITCH FOR A BIT OF FUN!

Tutorials

You should now have a solid grasp of how each item and object in your Popit works. These final tutorials are designed to help you better grasp the tools just covered, as well as make advanced level elements and create cohesive scenes.

DECORATE!

THE WAY YOU DECORATE AND THEME THE LEVELS YOU CREATE IS ALMOST, IF NOT EQUALLY, AS IMPORTANT AS WHAT YOU BUILD WITHIN THEM. BEFORE BUILDING, THINK ABOUT THE STORY YOU WANT TO TELL AND THE LOOK YOU WANT TO CREATE. THE BEST LEVELS ARE NOT JUST OBSTACLES PLACED ONE AFTER THE NEXT; THEY FLOW AND CONNECT. DECIDE WHERE YOU WANT YOUR LEVEL TO BE AND BUILD IN THAT STYLE. ADD LOTS OF STICKERS AND DECORATIONS. BE ARTISTIC! TO SEE JUST HOW CREATIVE YOU CAN GET, TAKE THE KING OUT OF YOUR GOODIES BAG AND USE THE STICKERS & DECORATION EDIT TOOL TO SEE JUST WHAT STICKERS WERE USED TO TRANSFORM SOME CARDBOARD AND BOLTS INTO THE VENERABLE KING.

Adding Light to a Situation

While creating your levels, you are likely to dip heavily into the items and objects you have collected in the first My Objects window of your Goodies Bag. Some very useful items therein are the lights you have found. Place a light wherever a bit of brightness would be beneficial. Many of the lights you have access to even have their own Tweak Menu to further help incorporate them into your scene.

Light Adjustments

Adjustment Type	Adjustment Name	Effect
Color	Choose Light Color	Select light color from available options
	Zone	Set Camera Zone activation area
Brightness	Adjust Brightness	Adjust how bright the light is
Style	Normal / Foggy / Shadows	Select style / quality of luminosity emanating from your light

6 CREATURE CONSTRUCTION: FRIENDLY / NON-COLLECTABLE

LittleBigPlanet is chock-full of friendly creatures that offer your sack person good advice and often a helping hand (or paw, or hoof, or — you get the idea.) Constructing helpful characters adds kindness to your levels, and is often the best and most creative way to provide solutions to your most inventive puzzles.

JUST SAY SOMETHING

Often the best way to convey fun or important information about your level is by building a character to tell curious sack people the pertinent info as they pass. This can be as simple as adding a Magic Mouth and Magic Eyes to a face Sticker, or as complex as creating your own Curator Creator. Start simple; use basic shapes and uncomplicated connections to generate your gabbing guide, then use Stickers and decorations to personalize its look. Finally, attach some Magic Eyes and a Magic Mouth to give it life. Use the Mouth's Tweak Menu to add text and input an appropriate voice.

TRAVELING COMPANION

By placing a Creature Brain: Protected at the tail end of a mobile buddy (who has creature- controlled Wheels or Legs attached), you can create a friendly traveling partner to help your sack person overcome obstacles. To create a basic traveling partner, stamp down a cardboard rectangle long enough to attach two creature Wheels to its base. Once the Wheels are on, place a Creature Brain: Protected to its left side and set it to follow. You now have a rolling friend who follows your sack person and can be ridden to pass various obstacles like spikes or lethalised terrain. Be sure to decorate your friend appropriately.

7 CREATURE CONSTRUCTION: DANGEROUS / COLLECTABLE

As you and your sack person have undoubtedly discovered, not all the creatures in *LittleBigPlanet* are friendly. In fact, some are downright mean. Drop some of these villainous constructions into your level wherever you feel a little extra danger is needed.

BASIC ENEMY: PART ONE

The most basic enemies require very little to be dangerous. Try stamping down a cardboard block. Attach an Unprotected Creature Brain to the top and a Wheel to its base. Set the brain to follow, and crank up the Movement Speed. Add an element of danger by attaching a spike strip to one side. Use a Leg instead of a Wheel to allow your creature to walk and jump rather than roll. Try increasing the size of your main block and adding extra Legs or Wheels. Decorate your enemy to transform a simple-looking opponent into an ominous adversary.

BASIC ENEMY: PART TWO

Use a combination of the Lethalise Tools and connectors to add another level of danger to your creations. Start with the same basic wheeled enemy as before. Create a flat arm on the layer behind your enemy and attach a cylinder one plane thick to its top. Attach the arm to your enemy with a Wobble Bolt and set its Number of Turns to 0.5, and then set both its Time Taken and Pause Interval to 2.0s. Use your preferred lethal additive on the cylinder, and presto! You have created a much more lethal foe. Add to the terror by attaching two more basic wheeled enemies with short Rods to either side of your elemental enemy (ensure the Rods are long enough to allow the elemental arm to move freely). To complete your triple threat, adjust each brain to the same settings so that they do not work against one another. Try different combos and attachments to build a legion of terrifying fighters.

All Brawn and No Brains

Not every enemy you create needs to utilize Creature Brains. Decorate squashing or lethalised level elements to transform them into ferocious beasts in their own right. By using Sensor Switches to activate these monstrosities, you can even make their attacks seem deliberate.

BIG MEANIES

THERE ARE A FEW CREATURES IN LITTLEBIGPLANET THAT ARE TRULY MONSTROUS. USE OF THESE MASSIVE MEANIES SHOULD BE LIMITED; ONLY PLACE ONE WHEN YOU WANT TO INTRODUCE A MAJOR CHALLENGE. BY COMBINING SKILLS YOU HAVE ALREADY LEARNED AND SOME CLEVERLY PLACED CONNECTORS AND SWITCHES, ALONG WITH SOLID DECORATIONS, YOU CAN BUILD A BRUTAL BRAWLER OF YOUR OWN. REMEMBER THAT THE MORE BRAINS YOUR CREATURE HAS, THE HARDER IT IS TO TAKE DOWN.

Double Your Chances

Given the terrifying and difficult nature of big meanies, it's only fair to give the brave sack people slightly better odds before they step up to challenge your leviathan. Just before the battle zone, place a Double-Life Checkpoint to increase the number of tries given.

(8) VEHICLES

All the hurrying about from level to level can get quite exhausting for your poor sack person. Why not add a few friendly creatures and vehicles to help it along its way?

BASIC TRANSPORTATION

The most basic form of vehicle requires only three elements — a platform and two wheels. To construct one, simply create a plank out of cardboard one plane thick. Now create two wheels of appropriate size out of rubber. Use standard Bolts to secure each wheel to either end of the plank. Be sure to attach the Bolts to the exact center of your wheels (they should snap to position when close) to ensure smooth motion. Add some sponge grips to the ends of the plank to give your sack person something to grab onto, and help start a desired motion.

MOTORIZED VEHICLES

If you want to generate a form of transportation that relies on more than gravity and the strength of your sack person for power, try swapping out one of the standard Bolts for a Motor Bolt on the basic vehicle you just created. Once attached, your vehicle is ready to roll gallantly off into the awaiting level. To give your sack person control of the motion, stamp a Switch onto the plank and connect it to the Motor Bolt. Any Switch works for one-way travel, but if you would like your sack person to be able to go forward and backward, the best option is using a 3-way Switch with its behavior set to Direction. Once all is set, adjust the Motor Bolt's speed setting until your new transport moves just the way you want.

ROCKET POWER

If these conventional vehicles are still just too slow to suit your needs, consider drawing on Rocket power. Create a small sponge rectangle for riding. Attach a Rocket to one end and set its boost to the appropriate level for your desired effect. The Castor Wheel, found in the My Objects window of your Goodies Bag, works nicely for smaller vehicles like this. Glue two to the base of your sponge. Be sure to add a Grab Switch, and attach its Connector Tab to the Rocket before leaving your Popit. Once all is set, you should have a vehicle with quite a bit of get-up-and-go.

Travel in Style

These simple vehicles are only a base for your creativity. By combining some imaginative design elements and Decorations, you can create anything from the Gardens' Wooden Steed to the Canyons' Mine Carts, from the cool Cars of the Metropolis to the Air Ship of the Islands.

9 ADVANCED OBSTACLES

Using everything you have learned throughout your time in *LittleBigPlanet*, try to build some advanced level elements that bring wonder and amazement to any sack person who happens upon them.

On the Grid

There are pros and cons to using any of the Small, Medium, or Big Grids found at the top of your Start Menu. When building complex items that need to line up and be level, it is essential to turn the grid options On and Off at different stages of construction. Try to practice building with it On and then Off to see when and how a grid is most beneficial. The following two tutorials utilize the grid options a good deal, and can help you learn how best to use them.

Let's Get Crafty!!!

PUZZLING PLATFORMS

Adding a puzzle element to moving platforms can be a tricky way to increase the amount of skill needed to complete your level. To create a basic puzzle platform, start by selecting the Medium Grid from your Popit Settings. Build a center column, four quadrants wide and one plane thick, ascending to the height you would like your platform to be. Place your column on the third plane back. Decrease the width of your material to two quadrants while increasing its depth to two planes. Run this thinner section of material down the center of the top quarter of your column. Next, construct a beam on the center plane roughly one quadrant high by 20 wide. Place your plank level to the floor with just enough room for your sack person to fit under the outcropping you created earlier. Place another column outcropping directly below the plank. Now, add a short overhanging lip to your beam on either side, and connect it to the lower column outcropping with a Piston. Open the Piston's Tweak Menu and set its motion to reflect the distance you would like it to carry your sack person (try not to extend past the center column). Set the Piston to Stiff, and exit the Tweak Menu. Finally, add a few blocks into your plank short enough to fit under the upper outcropping. Your sack person must now navigate through this obstacle with well-timed jumps. If you want to increase the challenge, try adding more moving parts to block the path. Remember to be careful: the more moving elements you use, the more the Set Movement Phase option becomes necessary.

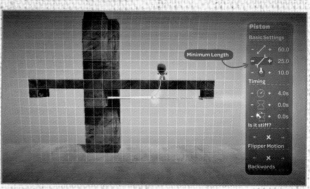

CONVEYER BELT

Conveyer Belts are very difficult to construct, but building one can solidify everything you have learned by forcing you to make several elements work together flawlessly. So why not give it a try? Start by selecting the Big Grid out of your Popit Settings. Build a long stretch of material two quadrants high, twenty quadrants wide, and one plane thick. Place this structure on the farthest plane back. Now, swap to the Small Grid and create a thin rubber cylinder one quadrant in both height and width and one plane deep. Attach a Motor Bolt to its center and adjust the Bolt's Tightness to 10.0, its Speed to 4.5, and its direction to Counter-Clockwise. Once set, select the cylinder and use [13] to copy it. Create 19 copies for a total of 20 cylinders. Attach each cylinder via its Bolt to the metal structure you constructed. Use the grid to guide each cylinder. Once completed, you should have created a level surface out of the now spinning cylinders. Extend the depth of your metal structure to enclose the spinning wheels on each side, and then place an emitter on the new wall on the right side. Using Dissolve, construct a plank one quadrant high, two quadrants wide, and one plain deep. Place a Magnetic Key Switch at its left tip, and attach the Connector Tab to the Dissolve. Decrease your Switch's Trigger Radius, and deactivate visibility. Set the corresponding magnetic key on the left wall of your metal structure, ensuring that when the Dissolve plank reaches the end of the rubber wheels, its Switch is within range. This plank is going to function as the belt of your conveyer. Decorate it as you see fit. Once the plank looks the way you want, use the Capture Object tool to copy the plank into your My Objects window. Open

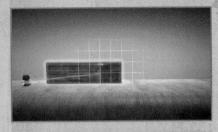

the Tweak Menu for the emitter you placed earlier and select your plank as the emitted object, placing it atop the right end of the rubber wheels. Set both Item Settings to 0. Now, Toggle Frequency to 1.0, set both Life Time and Max Emitted to ∞, and Max Emitted At Once to 10. Once you leave the emitter's Tweak Menu, you should be left with a fully functioning Conveyer Belt. It does take a few moments for the belt to fill with planks and begin functioning properly. If, for aesthetic reasons, you would like to cover your work, simply glue a panel over the beginning and end of the Conveyor Belt.

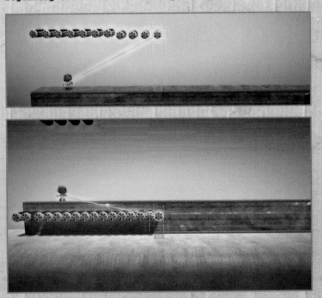

Give It Time to Get Going

Items like Conveyer Belts take a few moments to reach optimum performance. As such, it is a good idea not to place them at the beginning of your levels where a sack person might happen upon one of your brilliant constructions before it is ready to be seen.

Creation

Creating:
Building a Level

- -

It's time at last to put all the building knowledge you've attained into practice and create an actual level. Choose a good-looking seal on My Moon, pull out your Popit, and prepare to get crafty.

Objectives

Meet Your Maker

1

Setting a Spooky Tone

2

Bridging Sections

3

A Gaseous Grave Site

4

The Bat Brothers and a Tide of Skeletons

5

Arachnophobia

6

A Rocky Ascent

7

Epic Crossing

8

Approaching the Mausoleum

9

A Level's End

10

Creepy Crafting

Each level has a story and a personality all its own. This particular crafty construction is a step in the spooky direction. The blank canvas your sack person finds itself in now is about to be transformed into Lenard the Pumpkin's Haunted Graveyard.

Adding Music

The addition of music to your levels is a matter of personal preference. As you progress through the construction of this level, try to feel out areas you think would be best served by the addition of music.

CHECK AND PLAY

BY PURCHASING THIS GUIDE, YOU HAVE GAINED ACCESS TO SEVERAL ADDITIONAL LEVELS PROVIDED BY BRADY. THIS SECTION PROVIDES DETAILED INSTRUCTIONS ON THE CONSTRUCTION OF THE FIRST OF THESE EXCLUSIVE INSTALLMENTS: 'THE HAUNTED GRAVEYARD' BY LENARD THE PUMPKIN. IF YOU EXPERIENCE ANY DIFFICULTY WHILE BUILDING, IT MAY HELP TO PLAY THE COMPLETED VERSION THROUGH A FEW TIMES TO SEE HOW THE ORIGINAL MECHANICS LOOK AND FUNCTION IN PLAY MODE.

① MEET YOUR MAKER

As you have likely noticed, each level within *LittleBigPlanet* has characters who want to help your sack person progress and reveal the stories behind each area. In the Haunted Graveyard, one of those characters is Lenard the Pumpkin, who also happens to be this level's Curator Creator. Open the level by building Lenard and creating a small space for him to explain what has happened to his graveyard.

Know where You Work

The level you are constructing ultimately takes place in the Wedding background. Setting the background has no direct effect on building, so it can be done at any time. There are, however, a few factors you should take into consideration when deciding what to do with your background. Once a chosen background is activated, you can preview which environmental elements are visible during different stages of your level. However, different backgrounds do affect light differently, changing the hue and quality of the native light in the level. Try working it out both ways to see which you prefer.

Lenard

To construct Lenard for the first time, enter your Goodies Bag and select some sponge Material. Select the moon shape and stamp down a single layered crescent sponge slightly taller than your sack person. Tap **R3** to reverse the shape, then overlap the tips of the crescent with those of the first sponge and stamp it down, creating an oval with divots in its center.

Use the narrow ellipse shape to plant three slim ovals in the center of structure you just made. Be sure to start with the center, and then fill either side. Cover each aspect of your construction so far with the Orange Bird Sticker from the Stickers & Decorations section of your Popit. The Sticker is for color only, and when finished, the sponge ovals should be solid orange.

Now, to the side of your fledgling pumpkin, build a small block out of Dark Brown Wood. Use the Corner Editor tool to slightly pull out one of the top corners of the block. Continue using the Corner Editor to create three small spikes emanating from the base of the block. Once completed, this shape is ready to become your pumpkin's stem. Select the modified block with your Popit Cursor and copy it with **R3**. If necessary, adjust the size, then stamp it down into the top of your pumpkin, embedding it in place. Place two Creature Eyes and a Creature Mouth onto your pumpkin to transform a glorified squash into Lenard the Curator Creator. Use the Capture Objects tool to save Lenard for use later in the level.

Build It Once

Several elements, like Lenard, are used throughout the level. To remain consistent and limit the amount of times you need to build these elements, be sure to use the Capture Object tool to save them in the My Objects window of your Goodies Bag.

A Stump to Sit on

Create a wooden rectangle out of Darkest Brown Wood. Build it one plane deep with a width slightly smaller than Lenard's base and a height roughly two times taller than your sack person. Use the triangle shape to cut a few small points out of its base. Now, use the Corner Editor in much the same way you did on Lenard's stem to create an interesting root pattern.

Use the Popit Cursor to select your stump-in-the-making and copy it with **R3**. Flatten the copy by tapping **R2** and place it in front of the original stump. Use the Corner Editor again to add a few jagged points to the top of the stump. Next, use the circle shape to cut a small hole out of the front section. Now, use the Material Changer tool to transform the flat stump section into Light Brown Wood. Glue the front of the stump to the back, and then place it next to the level's Entrance and rest Lenard on top.

TAKE A PICTURE – IT'LL LAST LONGER

ONCE YOU COMPLETE THE STUMP, USE THE TAKE A PHOTO TOOL TO GRAB A QUICK SNAPSHOT OF LENARD. THE RESULTING STICKER IS A FUN REMINDER OF THE GOOD TIMES YOU AND LENARD HAVE HAD TOGETHER.

A Pumpkin with Something to Say

Pull up the Tweak Menu for the Magic Mouth you placed on Lenard. Ensure that its Trigger Radius covers the entrance, and then select Enter a Speech to input the beginning of this level's story.

Lenard's Speech:

"Please help! The Evil Zombie has stolen my BODY and taken control of my Graveyard. Prepare for the skirmish by trying to reach the Haunted House at the end of the graveyard."

To ensure that this statement gets the appropriate response, set the Cutscene Camera to a sympathetic angle and adjust Lenard's Speech to Crying.

Making an Exit

Make sure that Create Mode is paused, then place a block of Dark Matter directly above Lenard's head high enough to be well out of camera range in Game Mode. Connect the Dark Matter to Lenard's stem with a Winch. Place a Sensor Switch at the base of the stump and attach its Connector Tab to the Winch. Open the Switch's Tweak Menu. Set its Behavior to Direction, adjust its Trigger Radius to cover the stump, plus an additional sack person's stride or two, then set Inverted to Yes and Visibility to No.

Next, open the Winch's Tweak Menu. Its maximum length is already set to Lenard's stump's resting position. Decrease its minimum length to ensure Lenard leaves the screen when the Switch is deactivated, and turn the time taken down to 3.0s. Switch to Play Mode to test your work. If all is set correctly, Lenard should drop down and issue his plea as soon as your sack person walks through the entrance. Walk to the right to make sure Lenard flies away again. Return to Build Mode to continue construction.

(2) SETTING A SPOOKY TONE

Now that the level's objective has been established, use the next section of the level to set the tone and give your sack person a few basic obstacles to overcome.

Ghostly Apparitions

The first ghoulish apparitions your sack person meets in this graveyard are a pair of ghastly ghosts. To create them, retrieve some Peach Floaty from your Materials window and stamp it down in a teardrop shape roughly two times your sack person's height. Rotate the teardrop so its tip is pointed down. Using the Corner Editor, mold the teardrop into a ghostly form. Pull out arms and add additional points to the base. Work at it until you are satisfied with the shape. Once you have achieved a suitable form, return to the Materials window and select Peach Floaty once again. Use the circle shape to carve out a mouth for your ghost by tapping ○ over an appropriate mouth-like region. Add two Creature Eyes, and then use the White Square Sticker to color your ghost. Use the Capture Object tool to save the horrible haunt and delete the original.

Taking Flight

You now have ghosts at the ready, and need only to release them into this haunted scene. Get the Wooden Planks Material from your Popit and, using the square shape, construct the beginnings of a fence next to Lenard's stump. Use the Big Grid to build the fence. Flatten the Material, than set it to the farthest plane back. Construct the fence two quadrants high by seven quadrants long. On the seventh quadrant to the right, add a small segment of fence one plane deep in front of the flat section and glue the two together. Leave eight quadrants empty, then construct a second piece of fence one plane deep, one quadrant wide, and two quadrants tall.

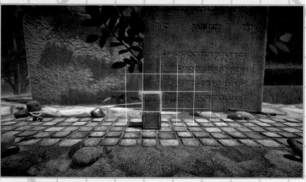

Select Dissolve from your Materials window and, on the same plane as the two fence sections you just completed, place two blocks two quadrants in from either side, leaving three empty quadrants in between. Place a metal square in the center of the Dissolve blocks and attach it to the floor. Now, connect the metal to each piece of Dissolve with a Rod. Open the Tweak Menu for the Rods, and set both to Stiff.

Get the Ghost form from your My Objects window and stamp one into each piece of Dissolve. Be sure the tips of the Ghosts do not enter the floor below. Place a Sensor Switch on both Dissolve blocks and attach its Connector Tabs to the block each is attached to (the Switches should not need to be adjusted). Next, retrieve the Monsters Sound Effect from the Audio Objects window of your Tools Bag and place one by the Sensor Switch on both squares of Dissolve. Adjust each audio element to activate upon destruction, and set its sound to Ghost.

Cover your work by placing a second flat section of fencing in front of the ghosts, leaving them to peek over the barrier at an approaching sack person.

Finishing Touches

Take a few additional moments to add decorative touches to the scene before moving on. On the right end of the fence, add a third quadrant in height to the flat section, then create a block two planes deep, one quadrant high/wide, and glue it to the new section of fence. Create a flat column three quadrants high and attach it to the front plane, forming a gateway into the rest of the level. Use the Skeleton pieces found in the Decorations window to make a scary skeleton on the side of your gate. Next, add Stickers wherever you deem appropriate. Have fun cranking up and stamping down some spooky stuff. When you're done, switch to Play Mode to see how it looks in an actual run-through.

Close — Level Post

Always remember to plant a Close — Level Post near the entrance. In this level, place your post next to the stump in front of the first section of fencing.

3 BRIDGING SECTIONS

All levels are comprised of a series of challenges placed one after the other. It is often necessary to make small bridging zones to ensure your theme continues throughout the whole level. Use this next section of the graveyard to generate a solid example of this type of transition.

A Hop and a Jump

Activate the Medium Grid. Select Check Fabric from the Materials window of your Goodies Bag, and set the triangle shape. Adjust the sponge's dimensions to three planes deep, and embed four one-quadrant triangles into the floor, four quadrants apart. Turn off the grid and place three bubbles in a pyramid shape in between the first two triangles. Glue the bubbles together then select them with the Popit Cursor. Copy the triple bubble with **L3** and place one between each triangle.

After the final sponge triangle, create a small ramp out of Darkest Brown Wood. Select the teardrop shape to use as the base of your incline. Start by increasing the wood's depth to fill the two back planes. Next, scale up its size then turn it so the point is facing left. Run the bottom of the teardrop into the floor, setting the angle to a scalable ascent. Once it looks right, stamp the ramp down. Switch to the square shape and add a level portion to the end of your ramp, leaving a 90-degree angle at its end. If you would like to further customize the shape of your ramp, use the Corner Editor to make additional adjustments. Once the ramp is the shape you are looking for, line the top with Check Fabric. Finally, place two bubbles and a Prize Bubble on the floor in front of the ramp.

④ A GASEOUS GRAVE SITE

Using the theme and flow of a specific level can help make very basic gameplay elements dynamic and interesting. By incorporating Horrible Gas and a mechanical booster into the graveyard theme, these very simple game features seem novel.

The Graves

Turn on the Big Grid and use Darkest Brown Wood to make a raised platform three planes deep, two quadrants high, and fourteen quadrants wide. This platform should be placed directly after the ramp and should require a small jump to board. Starting from the left side, remove a section two planes deep and one quadrant square from the front edge of the top of the platform in four quadrant intervals. If done correctly, two quadrants remain after the third depression.

Now, create headstones to place above each depression. Create a semi-circle, one plane deep, out of Basic Stone with the curve facing up. Stamp a square of stone into the bottom to complete the grave marker. Place the completed headstone on the third plane back, behind the first depression. Select your headstone with your Popit Cursor and copy it with **L3**. Use the copies to place a gravestone at the head of the other depressions.

Watch Your Step

Fill the holes in front of the first two graves with a Material of your choice. Then, use the Horrible Gas Tool to lethalise the holes you just filled. Place a Hazard Sign Sticker on the first two gravestones.

Rise from the Grave

Extend the hole in the third grave almost to the floor and create a small beam inside it. The beam should fit snugly, but be able to move up and down the hole easily. Attach the beam to the base of the hole with a Piston. Place a Sensor Switch on the front of the beam and attach its Connector Tab to the Piston. Next, open the Piston's Tweak Menu and adjust its maximum length to 17.5 and its minimum to 5.0. Turn the Time Taken down to 0.3s and set the Piston to Stiff. Now, open the Sensor Switch's Tweak Menu. Turn Behavior to Direction, set Inverted to Yes, and Visible to No. Once you leave your Popit Menu, the beam should lower into the hole. Have your sack person jump down to test the heights possible with your newly-built booster. Finally, place a Pink Arrow Sticker pointing down on the final gravestone.

Completing the Bone Yard

Line the top of the platform with Check Fabric, then place a Checkpoint before the first grave. Get Darkest Brown Wood from your Popit once again and, using the square shape, cover the front of the platform with a panel of wood. Leave all of the sponge and a small amount of the platform showing above the top of the panel. Next, place a few bubbles between each grave. To add even more ambiance, take the Real Bone in your Goodies Bag and place one on top of the panel in between each grave.

⑤ THE BAT BROTHERS AND A TIDE OF SKELETONS

Many obstacles throughout *LittleBigPlanet* can only be overcome with the help of kind characters or a bit of fearlessness. Luckily, this next section of the graveyard requires both.

The Gorge

Build two large Darkest Brown Wood structures next to the gaseous grave site. Using the Big Grid, make the first three planes deep, eight quadrants tall and twelve quadrants wide. The second should be three planes deep, seven quadrants high, and eight wide. Glue the two together and move them to directly border the gaseous grave site. Turn off the grid, and then create a Darkest Brown Wood right-angle triangle outcropping mid-way up the left side of the structure. Ensure that the outcropping is reachable using the booster grave. Use the Corner Editor to shape the out cropping and blind it into the gaseous grave element.

Use the wide ellipse shape to carve out a large gorge from the center of the wooden structure. When done, the depression should nearly reach to the floor. Now, take out your Corner Editor and use it to reshape the clean lines of the structure into a craggy cliff. Once you are satisfied with the shape of your structure, line the outcropping and both ledges with Check Fabric. Lastly, glue a Checkpoint on the higher left ledge.

Building the Bat Brothers

The Bat Brothers are an obliging trio who can help your sack person across this mammoth obstacle. Use Red Fabric to create a circle one plane deep. Place a square of Dark Matter well above the sponge circle and attach the two with a String.

Place a flat Basic Rubber right-angle triangle next to the sponge circle and use the Corner Editor to transform it into the basic shape of a bat wing. Pull the back end out far enough to make it easy to bolt it to the Red Fabric. Embed Blue Felt into the Basic Rubber to make the wing webbing. Trim the edges of the webbing with a circle. Once complete, copy the wing and reverse it to create a pair. Attach a Sprung Bolt to the end of both wings, and then attach them to the back of the Red Fabric circle. Adjust the Bolts so the wing's resting position is straight out from the sponge. This may take some trial and error. Be sure to leave a good amount of bounce in your Bolt.

Create a flat Basic Cardboard circle the same diameter as the Red Fabric. This circle is the base for your bat's face. Attach two cardboard triangles toward the top to function as the bat's ears. Next, glue the Cardboard to the Red Fabric. Now it's time to decorate. Use the Black Circle Sticker to color the bat black. Flip the Japanese Angry Eye Sticker upside-down to use as your bat's eyes. Use the Sakura Flower Sticker for a nose and the Scary Mouth Sticker, also upside-down, for its mouth.

Crossing the Gorge

Use the Popit Cursor to copy the hanging bat you just created and stamp down two more. Move the first so it hangs to the left of the outcropping by the gaseous graves. Replace the String with a Winch. Adjust the Winch so its highest point allows your sack person to just barely reach the upper tier of the cliff from the outcropping. Place a Grab Switch on the Red Fabric of the bat and attach its Connector Tab to the Winch. Adjust the Switch's behavior to Direction. Now, place a Magic Mouth on the bat. Open the mouth's Tweak Menu and set its Trigger Radius to cover the outcropping.

Bat's Speech:

"I'm the first Bat Brother. We're here to help. Grab hold!"

Take the remaining two bats and place them on either side of the gorge. Set them to ensure your sack person can swing from one to the next to cross the gorge. Try placing the first bat slightly higher than the one on the right. Move them back and forth until you are satisfied with the difficulty level of the crossing.

Skeleton Tide

Now that your sack person can cross the gorge, try filling it with some lethal skeletons looking to add to their numbers. Start by ensuring Create Mode is Paused, then build a thin flat strip of Dark Matter near the bottom of the gorge. Make sure it is short enough to fit through the mouth of the chasm above. Next, use the Small Grid to make a line of cardboard cubes along the length of the Dark Matter, leaving a few quadrants empty between each. Attach each block to the Dark Matter with a Wobble Bolt. Open the Tweak Menu of each Bolt and set its Movement Phase to a random number. Be sure no neighboring Bolts have the same Set Movement Phase. Working in the Decorations window of your Popit, attach a Skeleton Arm to each block, facing up. Un-Pause the game to make certain each arm moves unrestricted and seemingly of its own accord.

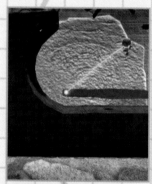

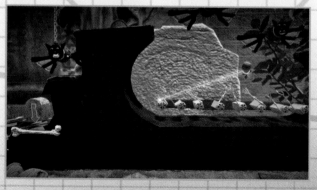

Build a structure three layers deep that fills the mouth of the gorge, then use the Horrible Gas Tool to transform the structure into a red gaseous hazard. Be sure to set the gas color before lethalising the structure; it cannot be adjusted afterward. Use your Popit Cursor to place the strip of skeleton arms into the gas. Create a flat piece of Light Brown Wood to cover your work. Once the covering is the shape you would like, stamp a piece of Dark Matter into it where it won't be seen by the game camera. If you try to glue it down, you may accidentally attach it to the Cardboard blocks, preventing the skeletons' motion.

Corrective Vision

Try swinging across the gorge. Notice that even with the covering, the Wobble Bolt strip is not entirely hidden. To completely hide the mechanics and give the section an even eerier tone, use two separate Camera Zones to control exactly how this section is perceived.

Place the first Camera Zone in the center of the wooden covering piece. Open its Tweak Menu and set the new game camera using the Adjust Target option. Pull the camera to the left and angle it up slightly, and then tilt it to the right. When set, the camera should be looking up at the swings, displaying the entire chasm mouth. Set the camera's trigger to cover the edge of the left hand cliff and the entire swinging section. Then turn Track Player down to 0.

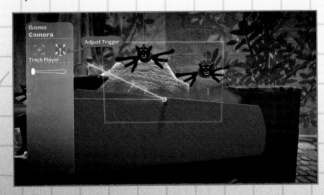

Set the second camera in the center of the Check Fabric on the cliff to right. Adjust the camera to pan to the right, angled slightly down. Set its trigger to cover the borders of the right hand cliff and a little beyond. Finally, set Player Tracking to the halfway mark.

Add a Prize Bubble to the outcropping on the left cliff and several score Bubbles to the top of both ledges. Test the swing section to ensure everything looks correct. Make any needed adjustments to the camera before moving on.

⑥ ARACHNOPHOBIA

Getting creative with decorative uses for craft materials is a great way to add additional layers of interest to a level. Proper use of these elements can help tie a theme together, or highlight customized creations. In the next section, pay attention to the way each aspect adds something to the others.

Ground to Stand on

To start this section, try building the ground it is going to take place on. Activate the Big Grid and select Darkest Brown Wood in the teardrop shape. Stamp down a three-layered teardrop, four Quadrants high. Turn the structure so the point faces the cliff to the left. Swap the teardrop for the square shape and create a long strip, three layers deep. The strip should start from the bottom edge of the teardrop and continue ten quadrants to the right. Turn off the grid, and add a second smaller teardrop on the opposite end. Point the tip to create a slope to the ground. Delete the point of the larger teardrop and use the square shape to create a right angle in the bottom left hand side of the structure. Place the structure on the floor against the cliff and fill in any remaining holes. Use the Corner Editor to further customize the shape of your ground, and then line the tops of the two hills with Check Fabric.

Use the square shape to create a short column a bit higher than an athletic jump could carry your sack person. Use the Corner Editor to transform the column into a weathered outcropping, and place it in the center of the flat surface. Now, line both the top of the column and the larger wooden base with Check Fabric.

Spider Webs

Next, use a combination of Dark Matter and String to create a spider web for the backdrop of this section. Turn on the Small Grid and make a flat Dark Matter square. Stamp down the first square to use as a center point, then place four more squares twelve quadrants out in each direction. Place another set of squares in the four equivalent diagonal points, creating eight equally-spaced points. Move in by five quadrants and create another eight points. Use String to connect each outer point to its neighbor. Do the same with the inner points. Now, attach each outer point to its corresponding inner point and each inner point to the center.

Once completed, select the entire web and move it to the back plane. Place it so that the bottommost Dark Matter square is touching the floor and the entire web is centered to the structure you just completed.

Create two large arcing structures out of Darkest Brown Wood. Set them up so that the first is emanating from behind the cliff, while the other is placed on the floor behind the right hand mound. To create these level elements, build large flat panels, then carve out the basic shape. Use the Corner Editor to fine-tune the silhouette, then place them accordingly. Once completed, these structures should surround the top of the web.

Finish the spider web by connecting each outer point to the surrounding environment.

Evil Arachnid

Next, build a scary spider to patrol the web. Start by building a thin strip of Basic Polystyrene and attach four Creature Legs to its base. Place two Creature Brains on top, and set both to follow. Pull the small spikes from your Tools Bag and glue one to the front of the Polystyrene strip and another beside it on the bottom lip.

Now, transform this basic enemy into a creepy crawly. Get some Basic Cardboard from your Goodies Bag and create a spider head out of a combination of an overlapping medium ellipse, a circle, and a square. Use the Corner Editor to adjust the shape to your liking. Switch to Tin Foil and use the teardrop to embed a fang in the spider's head. Place three Creature Eyes appropriately, then glue the head to the front of the creature's body. Ensure that the head obscures the spikes. Return to Basic Cardboard and place a teardrop over the rear of your spider's body to serve as its hindquarters. Attach the teardrop with a Wobble Bolt.

To complete this eight-legged illusion, decorate your spider with Stickers. Turn the Purple Skull Skirt sideways and use it on both the head and rear of the spider. Now, place two Cute Hair Stickers on the spider's back to form a red hourglass.

Completing the Scene

To complete this section, place a Checkpoint on the top of the first mound and glue it in place. Next, place a Prize Bubble on top of the center outcropping. Open the bubble's Tweak Menu and fill the Prize Bubble with the Sticker of Lenard you took earlier. Now, any hopeful sack person must make use of the spider to collect this priceless Prize Bubble.

{7} A ROCKY ASCENT

Transforming objects and items you have collected can be a useful way to add interesting level elements without departing from the theme of your level.

Appropriating Rocking Grass

Retrieve the Rocking Grass object you collected in The Gardens. Shrink it down to approximately half its original size, then place it on the front plane. Move to the center plane and stamp down a second Rocking Grass ramp. Before placing the second ramp, reverse its direction and increase its size to the point that only an athletic jump from the end of the first ramp allows your sack person to land on the second. Use the Material Changer Tool to transform the Green Floral Fabric into Check Fabric and the Dark Brown Wood into Darkest Brown Wood.

Higher Ground and a Flaming Tree

On the third plane back, build a large block out of Darkest Brown Wood. This block should require the use of the second Rocking Grass ramp to mount. Use a variety of shapes and the Corner Editor to add character to this higher plane. When complete, the block should be comprised of a slightly raised peak on the left side and a waving segment ending with a minor incline to its right. Line the peak and waving sections of the platform with Check Fabric.

Remove the Rainbow Tree from your Goodies Bag and place it on the final back plane. Glue its base to the platform you just completed near the right side. Use the Sticker & Decoration Edit Tool to remove the Straight Cobra Body Stickers and the White Flowers from the tree. Retrieve the Corner Editor once more, and transform the treetops into jagged spikes. Complete the metamorphosis by setting the tree ablaze with the Flame Tool.

Finishing Touches

Ensure that the section you just completed is an appropriate distance from the arachnid section. Move the entire section closer or farther based on need. Once the location is settled, place a Checkpoint in between the two areas and place several more Score Bubbles within the scene. Build a restraining wall two planes deep near the end of the costume platform, guaranteeing that a sack person must scale the three platforms to proceed.

⑧ EPIC CROSSING

Large obstacles that require several elements to work together can add impressive sections to your levels.

The Other Side of the Valley

Ensure Create Mode is paused, and then turn on the Big Grid. Use the grid to count out fifteen spaces from the base of the restricting wall you built at the end of the Rocky Ascent. Place a block of Darkest Brown Wood to mark the location, then count another eight spaces over and twelve spaces up. At this second point, create a platform ten quadrants wide and three planes deep. Use a variety of shapes and the Corner Editor to connect this platform with the marking block you left on the floor. Roughly eight quadrants up, create an outcropping just large enough for

a sack person to stand on. Above the outcropping, build a steep, slightly curved section of the cliff face that builds to a vertical ascent. Fill in any holes in the structure and ensure your wood extends deeply enough that the game camera only picks up solid matter.

Building a Level

293

Next, use Orange Wood to construct a dying tree. To Fabricate the tree, select the square shape and build a short trunk then several offshoot branches. Use the Corner Editor to slim the shape and add points and bends then add several Real Green Leaf decorations. When the tree is ready, glue it on the third plane back, mid-way up the curved incline above the ledge.

Line the ledge with Check Fabric, then create three small steps by carving the triangle Check Fabric into the cliff face. Now create a small Darkest Wood triangle. Use the triangle to create a wedge between the top of the tree trunk and the cliff face. Ensure the fit is snug, then glue the triangle in place. Now check to make sure that your sack person can use the sponge steps to climb from the ledge to the trunk of the tree. Once complete add Score Bubbles to the ledge and path above.

Adding the Obstacle

Select any Material out of your Goodies Bag and use it to make a swirling pattern, three planes thick, in the open space between the rock ascent and the cliff you have just created. When you complete the design, use the Horrible Gas Tool to transform it into lethal gray smoke. Create a warning sign by placing the Hazard Sticker on a strip of flat triangle-shaped cardboard. Add a short handle to the base of the sign and attach it to the front of the restraining wall at the end of the rocky ascent with a Wobble Bolt.

Pumpkin Lift

While Paused, place a copy of Lenard a short distance from the edge of the ledge at the end of the rocky ascent. Position him so your sack person can jump from the edge of the platform and grab his base. Once Lenard is placed appropriately, attach him to both the flaming tree and an inner branch of the dying tree with Winches. Open the Tweak Menu of the Winch attached to the dying tree and note its maximum length setting. Set its time taken to 8.0s, then exit the menu. Next, open the Tweak Menu of the Winch attached to the flaming tree. Match the maximum length to the other, then set its time taken to 8.0s as well. Remember the minimum length setting of this Winch, then return to the previous Winch's Tweak Menu and set its minimum to match. Next, attach two Grab Switches to your pumpkin and connect each to a different Winch. Set both Switches to Direction, and then invert the Switch attached to the burning tree Winch. Un-Pause to test the effect; if set correctly, Lenard should be resting in the position in which you placed him. By jumping and grabbing hold, he can transport your sack person all the way to the ledge.

Can I Offer You a Ride?

Once everything is set correctly, open the Tweak Menu on Lenard's Magic Mouth to enter his Speech.

Lenard's Speech:

"You'll never find your way through that fog. Grab hold and I'll take you as far as I can."

9 APPROACHING THE MAUSOLEUM

Transforming objects and items you have collected can be a useful way to add interesting level elements without departing from the theme of your level.

Reaching the Platform

Add a half crescent to the edge of the platform above the ledge where Lenard transports your sack person. Flatten the top to create a more suitable ridge. Run Check Fabric across the ridge and the wooden floor of the Platform slightly below. Now, add a Checkpoint on the inside of the crescent and a few Score Bubbles on top.

Place a Winched Bat Brother just above the base of the tree. Set the minimum length to allow your sack person to jump off at the top of the crescent. Be sure to add a Grab Switch set to Direction to ensure your sack person's ride up is ready and waiting.

On Hallowed Ground

Use the Small Grid to create a flat section of Bumpy Concrete five quadrants wide by eight quadrants tall. Place this sheet of concrete on the back plane and glue it to the center of the platform, leaving six quadrants visible. Construct a thin piece of concrete two planes deep and the same width as the back section, and then place it on the ground directly in front of the segment you just glued. Build a roof for your mausoleum out of a concrete octagon that's been cut in half. Match up the two straight lines with the outer perimeter of the morose mausoleum.

Construct a flat concrete cross and glue it to the roof of your developing crypt. Next, build a circle that could cover almost the entire cross. Cut a smaller circle out of the center of the first, then copy the hoop with **L3** and stamp it into the cross. Now, place a Prize Bubble into the center of the concrete crypt. Open the bubble's Tweak Menu and insert one of your most prized constructions.

Create three thin pieces of Dissolve to cover the three empty slats of the crypt. Place a Sticker Switch in the center of the forward-facing Dissolve wall and attach its Connector Tabs to the three dissolvable panels of the mausoleum. Open the Switch's Tweak Menu and set your Lenard Sticker as the trigger. Once the trigger is set, use Stickers to decorate the dissolvable walls to match the concrete. Add a border to let your sack person know where to place the Activation Sticker.

Messenger Bat

Decrease its size then place another hanging bat to the right of the Sticker-sealed crypt. Place a Magic Mouth on the bat, and add a clue to the crypt puzzle in its Speech box.

Bat Speech:

"Lenard always says, 'A picture's worth a thousand words, and a picture of me is worth two thousand — or at least a Prize Bubble!'"

Just Dropping In

Create a thin ledge out of Dissolve just below the Dark Matter supporting the messenger bat. Embed a small piece of Dark Matter into the ledge to keep it in place then set the bat on top of it. Place a Sensor Switch on the ground below the crypt and attach its Connecter Tab to the Dissolve.

⑩ A LEVEL'S END

At a certain point in each level, there is only one thing left to do: end it.

Final Transition

Use a large three-layered Darkest Brown Wood circle to build an upward sloping path away form the crypt and toward the finish. Use the square shape to build a long wooden walkway past the incline. Embed Check Fabric triangles into the curving surface, then line the entire walkway beyond in Check Fabric as well.

Look to the Future

Near the beginning of the walkway, place a proud Lenard. Because this is part of a multi-chapter story, use Lenard to introduce the next chapter.

To the right of Lenard, create a small-scale haunted house seemingly perched atop a tall hill in the distance. Start by stamping down a flat Cardboard oval roughly the size of the hill you would like your haunted house perched on. Carve a smaller oval into the right side of the first, then slid the two behind the walkway and glue them in place. Use Stickers to decorate the cardboard to make it look like mountains. Create the outline of a haunted house using triangles and squares of Darkest Brown Wood. Clean up the construction with the Corner Editor, then stamp it into the top of the taller hill. Place a few one-plane-thick half circles in the foreground to create an even greater feeling of depth, and decorate them similarly to their flat counterparts.

Finally go through this final area and place several Score Bubbles to reward any brave Sackperson who made it this far.

Lenard Speech:

"You Made It! Now you're ready to face the evil Zombie! Hurry! He's hiding in the haunted house!"

Once you set Lenard's Speech, enable the Cutscene Camera to pan up to show off the haunted panorama, while Lenard praises your sack person's level completion.

Scoreboard

Place the Level's Scoreboard a short distance past the miniature haunted house. Try decorating it with the Black Square and Green Skulls Stickers. All that's left to do is open the Board's Tweak Menu, and stock this finish line with ample rewards.

Interviews and Trophies

Interviews

Anton Kirczenow

Senior Programmer

WHAT ROLE DID YOU PLAY IN THE LBP PROJECT?

Senior Programmer. I joined near the start and coded many things like the Sackboy animations, cloth, explosions, fire, and tamed the wild SPUs to make the game go fast.

BACKGROUND?

I'm from Vancouver, Canada. I had a lot of Legos as a child.

WHAT WAS YOUR FAVORITE PART ABOUT THIS PROJECT?

Getting away with murder coding mad, risky, original things that any sane manager would strictly forbid.

WHAT WAS THE MOST DIFFICULT THING ABOUT CREATING A GAME THAT OOZES CREATIVITY AND IS SIMULTANEOUSLY INTUITIVE?

When you let people do *anything*, performance and stability become very hard to guarantee.

WHAT MAJOR TITLES HAVE YOU WORKED ON?

Black & White 2, Fable II, & Impossible Creatures

WHAT KEEPS YOU IN THE INDUSTRY?

Games are really the only platform that offers such a wide array of programming challenges to choose from. Plus, you get to laugh till it hurts by blowing stuff up and making silly jokes all day long.

DESCRIBE THE MOST CHALLENGING TASK YOU WERE FACED WITH AND HOW YOU RESOLVED IT.

Boshing out the green light version from virtually nothing on crazy new hardware in six months. With a miracle.

WHAT'S THE SINGLE BEST THING ABOUT LBP?

Sackboy, of course!

WHAT WOULD THE IDEAL REVIEW OF THE GAME SAY?

They'd just not be able to stop playing long enough to write anything.

DO YOU HAVE ANY SUGGESTIONS TO SOMEONE GETTING STARTED IN THE GAMING INDUSTRY?

Pay attention in math class.

WHERE DO YOU SEE GAME CODING HEADING IN THE FUTURE?

Ever more luscious, dynamic and interactive.

What's your:

Favorite thing about LBP?

That I can make stuff in popit I could only dream about in Lego.

Favorite emote?

Tongue slobberingly happy

Favorite costume item?

Borat swimsuit

Favorite level?

Skulldozer

Favorite book?

The Silmarillion, by J. R. R. Tolkien

Favorite movie?

Mulholland Drive

Favorite all-time game?

Duke Nukem

Favorite gaming snack food?

Cookies!

Current gaming obsession?

Guitar Hero 3

Current non-gaming obsession?

My kids

Biggest hobby?

Electric guitar

Favorite quote?

"If I wanted to like, read stuff, I would go to school or something."

Secret?

Buckets of coffee

Best level factoid?

The Mines has 6931 physics convexes in it!

Dave Smith

Co-Lead Designer

WHAT ROLE DID YOU PLAY IN THE LBP PROJECT?

Co-lead Designer and Gameplay/Physics Programmer. I sometimes helped fill the dishwasher as well.

BACKGROUND?

A long history of tinkering with programming and making games. The first big title I worked on was *Fable* where I mostly wrote AI for the villagers. More recently I started up Media Molecule with a few friends.

WHAT WAS YOUR FAVORITE PART ABOUT THIS PROJECT?

Seeing the game evolve as we were making it. So many details of the design were constantly in flux until late in the process. We have screen shots and videos of the game at various points in its development. When I look back at them, I'm always surprised at how much things have changed and improved. While there are several aspects of the game that are very different to how I initially imagined them, the core of the game is a pretty accurate incarnation of our initial ambitions.

WHAT WAS THE MOST DIFFICULT THING ABOUT CREATING A GAME THAT OOZES CREATIVITY AND IS SIMULTANEOUSLY INTUITIVE?

Endless iteration. We were making our levels at the same time as the tools. As we changed the tools, the sort of levels we were making changed. And as we changed the levels, it changed what we needed to make the tools do. In some ways, the creative tools and the levels are two sides of the same coin. It was a very creative process, but had many design problems and technical difficulties along the way.

WHAT MAJOR TITLES HAVE YOU WORKED ON?

Fable was a pretty big title, but *LittleBigPlanet* is the most ambitious project I've worked on.

WHAT KEEPS YOU IN THE INDUSTRY?

The miracle of being able to make money out of doing something that I love.

DESCRIBE THE MOST CHALLENGING TASK YOU WERE FACED WITH AND HOW YOU RESOLVED IT.

My most challenging task was to help start a new studio at the same time as making a high profile game in a somewhat new genre. I resolved it by hiring a bunch of intelligent people to do all the hard work for me.

WHAT'S THE SINGLE BEST THING ABOUT LBP?

Hmm. The combination of play, create, and share. Is that one thing? You sort of need all three of these to make the experience fully work. You need to create something in order to have something to share. You need to share something in order for it to be played. You need to play so that you can be inspired by other people to create.

WHAT WOULD THE IDEAL REVIEW OF THE GAME SAY?

LittleBigPlanet tried something new and succeeded

DO YOU HAVE ANY SUGGESTIONS TO SOMEONE GETTING STARTED IN THE GAMING INDUSTRY?

If you want to make games, you learn by making games. Don't expect the industry to train you in the basics. If you have the passion, then teach yourself. If you can't be bothered, this probably isn't the industry for you.

WHERE DO YOU SEE GAME DESIGN HEADING IN THE FUTURE?

I see the beginning of a new growth of inventiveness in design. The industry has stagnated a little with too much emphasis on technical trickery. Making games prettier or sound better is by no means bad thing, it will continue to improve, but I think the consumers are growing a little weary of this technical trickery and are looking for truly new experiences and new ways to interact with other people. For this reason, the increasing prevalence of high speed internet connections and new peripherals are perhaps more exciting than simply increasing raw power.

What's your:

Favorite thing about LBP?

Being constantly surprised by players inventions

Favorite emote?

Happy! While waving my arms to make an air guitar gesture.

Favorite costume item?

The secret costume which turns you into the precursor to Sackboy. A 2d purple rectangle with a yellow square for a head. It's a difficult costume to find but once you've got it you really don't need any of the others.

Favorite level?

Meerkat Kingdom

Favorite book?

Catch 22, by Joseph Heller

Favorite movie?

Spirited Away

Favorite all-time game?

Yoshi's Island

Favorite gaming snack food?

Crisps

Current gaming obsession?

Taiko Drum Master

Current non-gaming obsession?

Sleeping. Sometimes a little juggling.

Biggest hobby?

Reading

Favorite quote?

Sorry but I can't remember! It was very clever and witty. You'd probably have been very impressed.

Secret?

I have no secrets

Best level factoid?

Try completing the final level without losing any lives.

Jim Unwin

Interface Designer

WHAT ROLE DID YOU PLAY IN THE LBP PROJECT?

I look after big things like Popit and the Craft Earth as well as minutiae like fonts and icons. When
we were figuring out the interface, we started from the player putting the disc in the machine and
designed the experience from there.

BACKGROUND?

I've been in and out of the games industry for ten years. I've also done a lot of graphic design,
illustration, and I've even worked as a chef.

WHAT WAS YOUR FAVORITE PART ABOUT THIS PROJECT?

That A-Team moment when the plan came together, when you could invite a bunch of friends to play a level you'd just created and it all worked.

*WHAT WAS THE MOST DIFFICULT THING ABOUT CREATING A GAME THAT OOZES CREATIVITY AND IS SIMULTANEOUSLY
INTUITIVE?*

One of the many design principals we stick to is that the game *should just work*. The player doesn't need to know about polygon counts or physics
meshes or any of the math that happens behind the scenes. Making these complex things easy and fun for new players while retaining the depth for
advanced players was a difficult balance. That is where the idea of tweaking came from, of giving players more options as they need them.

WHAT MAJOR TITLES HAVE YOU WORKED ON?

Tomb Raider, *The Movies*, *Home* and a bunch of eyetoy stuff.

WHAT KEEPS YOU IN THE INDUSTRY?

It is whole heap more fun than web design.

DESCRIBE THE MOST CHALLENGING TASK YOU WERE FACED WITH AND HOW YOU RESOLVED IT.

The most difficult decisions have all been about what features we want to keep and which we have to cut. In a studio like Media Molecule, which is full
of good ideas, keeping the player's experience focused has been a constant struggle. For every good idea in the game we have ten waiting in the wings.
Hopefully the best of these will reappear in the future as downloadable content.

WHAT'S THE SINGLE BEST THING ABOUT LBP?

Having no idea what people will make with it. I'm excited to see what happens next.

WHAT WOULD THE IDEAL REVIEW OF THE GAME SAY?

It is great now, but wait until you see what the community creates!

DO YOU HAVE ANY SUGGESTIONS TO SOMEONE GETTING STARTED IN THE GAMING INDUSTRY?

Work hard. And get a portfolio! A bunch of mods or flash games will be much more impressive than a piece of paper with a qualification on it.

If you are going to study, then choose a more general subject that isn't specifically games related. Learning how to use Ubersoft 8.1 means your
knowledge will be out of date in a couple of years. Learning how colour theory or composition work will be useful forever.

WHERE DO YOU SEE GAME DESIGN HEADING IN THE FUTURE?

As computers become more powerful and the industry expands then hopefully the tools will improve. Currently it feels like we're all stuck in the 1950s
making Hollywood epics. The games industry is still waiting for its digital video camera, for the cheap, off-the-shelf tool that allows one or two people
to take an idea and quickly make a game on their own.

What's your:

Favorite thing about LBP?

Creating!

Favorite emote?

Happy #2

Favorite costume item?

The plaid material

Favorite level?

Wobble Poles...I challenge anyone to beat my high score!

Favorite book?

It changes on a monthly basis, but currently *Gravity's Rainbow* by Thomas Pynchon.

Favorite movie?

The Princess Bride. Easy!

Favorite all-time game?

Advance Wars: Black Hole Rising

Favorite gaming snack food?

I really like sour candy.

Current gaming obsession?

I'm currently recreating all my favourite games with *LittleBigPlanet.* I guess at some point I'm going to pick up and get addicted to *Team Fortress 2* again.

Current non-gaming obsession?

Rock climbing.

Biggest hobby?

Drawing

Favorite quote?

There is a Murakami quote about how by writing something down you change its meaning. I can't find my copy of the book though. I wonder who I lent it to?

Secret?

I don't keep secrets and it is constantly getting me into trouble.

Mags

Company Accountant

BACKGROUND?

I ran my own business for many years.

WHAT WAS YOUR FAVORITE PART ABOUT THIS PROJECT?

Watching a bunch of massively talented people coming together and knowing that they would produce something amazing.

WHAT WAS THE MOST DIFFICULT THING ABOUT CREATING A GAME THAT OOZES CREATIVITY AND IS SIMULTANEOUSLY INTUITIVE?

I have no idea, but I did see some furrowed brows around the office!

WHAT MAJOR TITLES HAVE YOU WORKED ON?

This is my first.

WHAT KEEPS YOU IN THE INDUSTRY?

My employment contract.

DESCRIBE THE MOST CHALLENGING TASK YOU WERE FACED WITH AND HOW YOU RESOLVED IT.

Getting highly creative people to understand my need for little bits of paper with figures on them.

WHAT'S THE SINGLE BEST THING ABOUT LBP?

The people that made it.

WHAT WOULD THE IDEAL REVIEW OF THE GAME SAY?

Buy this now!

DO YOU HAVE ANY SUGGESTIONS TO SOMEONE GETTING STARTED IN THE GAMING INDUSTRY?

Recruit wisely.

What's your:

Favorite thing about LBP?

Sackgirl

Favorite emote?

Happiness

Favorite costume item?

The bunny ears

Favorite level?

Mags the Mechanic's levels obviously!!

Favorite book?

Love in the time of Cholera by Gabriel García Márquez

Favorite movie?

Lord of the Rings Trilogy

Favorite all-time game?

Tiddly-winks

Favorite gaming snack food?

Chocolate

Current gaming obsession?

None

Current non-gaming obsession?

Building a shed in my garden

Biggest hobby?

Gardening

Favorite quote?

The darkest hour is just before the dawn

Secret?

Never tell anyone your secrets!

Best level factoid?

The bluebells in the English garden are true English bluebells and not Spanish ones.

Marcos

Co-Lead Designer

WHAT ROLE DID YOU PLAY IN THE LBP PROJECT?

My main role was design and coming up with ideas, but as I've worked in the industry as an artist for many years, I did a lot of modeling early on, and tried to set the technical standards/methods we use for the materials, meshes, etc. Mostly, I just get really moody when things aren't how I want them, until people give in.

BACKGROUND?

I started as a coder/artist on the C64 (way back), moved to concentrate on art (less of a headache), did this for many years, working on many 8-bit/16-bit games, worked for Bullfrog and Lionhead, then decided to dabble in coding again, so taught myself C++ and made *Rag Doll Kung Fu*, then decided to start Media Molecule with some people that helped me with *Rag Doll Kung Fu*.

WHAT WAS YOUR FAVORITE PART ABOUT THIS PROJECT?

It's the first game I've worked on that I'm looking forward to playing once it's released. I have many ideas for things I want to make with it.

WHAT WAS THE MOST DIFFICULT THING ABOUT CREATING A GAME THAT OOZES CREATIVITY AND IS SIMULTANEOUSLY INTUITIVE?

Everyone that works at Media Molecule is very talented, and has great ideas, many of which are in the finished product. For me it was hard taming it all, and making sure that it all stayed focused.

WHAT MAJOR TITLES HAVE YOU WORKED ON?

Much old 8-bit stuff (the one most worth mentioning there is *Paint and Create* – a package aimed at kids – there are some seeds of ideas in there that are similar to *LittleBigPlanet*!). *Theme Park, Magic Carpet, Dungeon Keeper, Black and White, Fable, Rag Doll Kung Fu…*

WHAT KEEPS YOU IN THE INDUSTRY?

My mortgage. But in or out of the industry, making computer games is my hobby, so I'd be doing that anyway.

DESCRIBE THE MOST CHALLENGING TASK YOU WERE FACED WITH AND HOW YOU RESOLVED IT.

Convincing other people on the team about some of my ideas. I would usually resolve it by making a video that would show it in action, either that or just be really, really miserable and angry.

WHAT'S THE SINGLE BEST THING ABOUT LBP?

It really does feel like a great team effort, and we don't yet know what it is capable of. I'm very proud to have been a part of it.

WHAT WOULD THE IDEAL REVIEW OF THE GAME SAY?

Sorry, I don't have time to write a review of *LittleBigPlanet*. I'm too busy making something awesome that the world needs to see.

DO YOU HAVE ANY SUGGESTIONS TO SOMEONE GETTING STARTED IN THE GAMING INDUSTRY?

If you want to go to university to learn something, choose a subject that isn't exclusive to the gaming industry. (ie. programming, art/animation, music, etc.) When you get in it, you might find you don't like it. Some larger companies don't treat people very well; they rely on the fact that young people are willing to work whatever.

WHERE DO YOU SEE GAMING ART, DESIGN, AND SOUND HEADING IN THE FUTURE?

Each of these in isolation will continue to take advantage of whatever technology allows them to do, but as a whole, I think the future holds much more immersive experiences. I have this dream of something that turns your whole room into a kind of 3d projector screen, so you'll be there, amongst dinosaurs, or futuristic cities, floating around on your sofa.

What's your:

Favorite thing about LBP?

The flexibility of the create tools. I can let my imagination go wild.

Favorite emote?

Angry

Favorite costume item?

Devil horns

Favorite level?

The final boss fight—it's a genius use of switches.

Favorite book?

All the books by Carlos Castaneda

Favorite movie?

Apocalypse Now

Favorite all-time game?

Mario 64

Favorite gaming snack food?

Nice fruit juice and empanadas.

Current gaming obsession?

Making things in *LittleBigPlanet*

Current non-gaming obsession?

Getting ready to have my first baby

Biggest hobby?

Making games. I've been messing around on my old Commodore 64 again recently.

Favorite quote?

"It's unlucky to be superstitious." Graham Plumbly

Secret?

I have a few. But they're secret.

Best level factoid?

The English Garden Background is based on my back garden at home.

Mark Stephenson

Game Designer

BACKGROUND?

I studied Graphic Design at college and then got into gaming through testing games at SCEA.

WHAT WAS YOUR FAVORITE PART ABOUT THIS PROJECT?

Working with really genius people who weren't afraid to break rules and go against convention.

WHAT WAS THE MOST DIFFICULT THING ABOUT CREATING A GAME THAT OOZES CREATIVITY AND IS SIMULTANEOUSLY INTUITIVE?

There wasn't anything difficult apart from the usual development process (iterations on gameplay, etc.)
and keeping up with them. If you are a creative person with many ideas, there will be nothing difficult to do in LBP.

WHAT MAJOR TITLES HAVE YOU WORKED ON?

Croc 2 for PlayStation 1, *Red Dog* for Dreamcast, *SWAT: GST* for PlayStation2, *GhostRider* for PlayStation2 and various other unreleased/unannounced games.

WHAT KEEPS YOU IN THE INDUSTRY?

Seeing new gameplay ideas and (having played games for so long) seeing how gaming evolves is constantly interesting.

DESCRIBE THE MOST CHALLENGING TASK YOU WERE FACED WITH AND HOW YOU RESOLVED IT.

The main challenge is to continually be creative. I constantly read books, watch films, and buy art books to remain inspired. I also keep a notebook close at all times to note down any ideas I might have.

WHAT'S THE SINGLE BEST THING ABOUT LBP?

Obviously, the main game is great to play, on your own or with others; but for me, the Create aspect is the most exciting. The thought of thousands of people expressing their creativity through LBP is mind boggling.

WHAT WOULD THE IDEAL REVIEW OF THE GAME SAY?

The ideal review would not generalize LBP as a 'platformer' and instead focus on the fact that LBP allows players to create their own worlds.

DO YOU HAVE ANY SUGGESTIONS TO SOMEONE GETTING STARTED IN THE GAMING INDUSTRY?

Play lots of games and understand how they work. LBP is a great starting point for budding designers to make gameplay, good and bad, and then learn basic game mechanics that can apply to many different types of games.

WHERE DO YOU SEE GAME DESIGN HEADING IN THE FUTURE?

Online gaming is going to be huge. As will 'Web 2.0' type gaming. What do I mean by that? I mean that games will become more intelligent, more intuitive, more friendly (casual you could say), and generally more social and open.

What's your:

Favorite thing about LBP?

Posing. I love being the first over a tricky bit and then posing at the top to taunt the other players.

Favorite emote?

The 'I've lost my contacts' pose is always funny. Tilt the controller to look at the floor and then hold both L1+R1 to put your hands out to touch the floor.

Favorite costume item?

I like the patchwork with the glowing eyes. And sometimes the white cotton skin with the chicken bits (beak, wings, etc). I like flapping the wings :)

Favorite level?

Hmm, hard one. It's either Zen Garden 1 or Magicians Palace.

Favorite book?

I rarely read a book more than once but I've read *The Hobbit* by J. R. R. Tolkien a few times. I mostly like non-fiction though, especially travel diaries.

Favorite movie?

Impossible to answer, too many to mention.

Favorite all-time game?

Apart from Mario/Zelda games? Hmm, *Ico* I think; that game is beautiful in both

design and art. I also like the *Tomb Raider* series; I like adventuring.

Favorite gaming snack food?

Waitrose Almond biscuits or Japanese Coconut Sable biscuits

Current gaming obsession?

Catching up on games that I've missed and playing *Survival Kids* Wii in Japanese (I'm learning Hiragana)

Current non-gaming obsession?

My wife, Aya :)

Biggest hobby?

Er, gaming?. I like to travel too.

Favorite quote?

Less is more.

Secret?

I have no secrets; it's best to be open and honest.

Best level factoid?

I think Boom Town contains the most collectibles. 75ish I think.

Paul Davis

IT Manager

WHAT ROLE DID YOU PLAY IN THE LBP PROJECT?

Generally keeping everything working and stopping the developers from hitting the equipment with hammers, or anything close to hand.

BACKGROUND?

IT. I used to work in Schools and the Finance industry before coming here.

WHAT WAS YOUR FAVORITE PART ABOUT THIS PROJECT?

The first time playing with other people. Nothing beats slapping or sticking a giant ear on someone's other sackperson just as they finish their awesome costume

WHAT WAS THE MOST DIFFICULT THING ABOUT CREATING A GAME THAT OOZES CREATIVITY AND IS SIMULTANEOUSLY INTUITIVE?

I think it's trying to put yourself in someone elses shoes and figuring out what that person needs to create things.

WHAT MAJOR TITLES HAVE YOU WORKED ON?

Only LBP—so far

WHAT KEEPS YOU IN THE INDUSTRY?

The people. You can't beat the people here at MM; they're all intelligent but not one has a big ego and we're all good friends.

DESCRIBE THE MOST CHALLENGING TASK YOU WERE FACED WITH AND HOW YOU RESOLVED IT.

When I first got here, their systems were in a bit of a mess so I changed the whole core of MM. I had to do that without forcing down time on anyone else, so worked nights for a week and no one noticed anything except things got more reliable and worked faster. ☺

WHAT'S THE SINGLE BEST THING ABOUT LBP?

Playing with others. You can spend a good half hour in the pod before even starting a level having a laugh. I think it's brought the fun back into games.

WHAT WOULD THE IDEAL REVIEW OF THE GAME SAY?

10/10 100% Finally, something different and new on the market.

DO YOU HAVE ANY SUGGESTIONS TO SOMEONE GETTING STARTED IN THE GAMING INDUSTRY?

Start at the bottom and show initiative. Get hired in a role, *any role*, and make sure you do it, but don't be afraid to try other things too. For example, get hired as a tester, create some cool levels and they'll promote you to level designer.

WHERE DO YOU SEE GAMING HEADING IN THE FUTURE?

I saw for the first time a working headset that allows you to control things like movement and firing with no movement at all—just a thought.

What's your:

Favorite thing about LBP?

Playing with others

Favorite emote?

Anger, it's cute

Favorite costume item?

Frying pan

Favorite level?

The Dancer's Court, love the mechanics in it

Favorite book?

The Wheel of Time series, by Robert Jordan

Favorite movie?

Boondock Saints

Favorite all-time game?

Syndicate

Favorite gaming snack food?

Pizza

Current gaming obsession?

Nothing has grabbed me for ages and I'm waiting for *Warhammer 40k Online*

Current non-gaming obsession?

Cars

Biggest hobby?

Cars

Favorite quote?

Assumption is the mother of all mess ups

Secret?

On rollers you can do a grab jump to fling yourself farther

Best level factoid?

Not really a level thing, but if you run from side to side in the pod, you can make it swing. I just think it's cool. ☺

LittleBigTrophies

We realize what you're thinking...

EVEN MORE STUFF TO COLLECT?! Fantastic! And you'd be right! These trophies are awarded to players that experience all aspects of the game: Single-Player, Story Mode, Creation, Sharing, Tagging, Crazy Feats, and even some Odd Deeds. Here's a list of everything you need to know to get them all!

Bronze Trophies

1 THE GARDENS

Complete the 3 main levels in *The Gardens*

POINTS 15

2 THE SAVANNAH

Complete the 3 main levels in *The Savannah*

POINTS 15

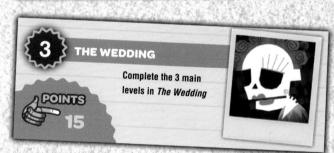

3 THE WEDDING

Complete the 3 main levels in *The Wedding*

POINTS 15

4 THE CANYONS

Complete the 3 main levels in *The Canyon*

POINTS 15

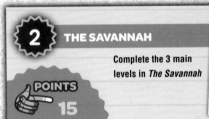

5 THE METROPOLIS

Complete the 3 main levels in *The Metropolis*

POINTS 15

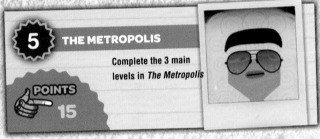

6 THE ISLANDS

Complete the 3 main levels in *The Islands*

POINTS 15

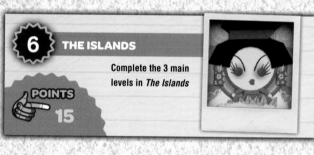

7 THE TEMPLES

Complete the 3 main levels in *The Temples*

POINTS 15

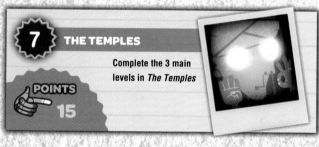

8 EXPERT CREATOR

Complete all levels in the *Tutorials*

POINTS 15

9 **ARTIST**

Place a sticker

POINTS 15

15 **TREASURE HUNTER**

Collect 75% of prizes on story levels

POINTS 15

75%

10 **HOMEMAKER**

Customize Pod

POINTS 15

16 **2X MULTIPLIER**

Get a 2X multiplier on any level

POINTS 15

x2

11 **FASHION SENSE**

Choose a costume

POINTS 15

17 **8X MULTIPLIER**

Get an 8X multiplier on any level

POINTS 15

x8

12 **TREND SETTER**

Customize another character with Stickers or Decorations

POINTS 15

18 **CRANIUM COLLECTOR**

Kill 100 enemies total

POINTS 15

100

13 **FORAGER**

Collect 25% of prizes on story levels

POINTS 15

25%

19 **SECRET STICKERIST**

Sticker a Shoe in *First Steps*

POINTS 15

14 **STICKY FINGERS**

Collect 50% of prizes on story levels

POINTS 15

50%

20 **INCREDIBLE SPEED**

Travel at incredible speed

POINTS 15

21 INCREDIBLE HEIGHT

Travel to incredible height

POINTS 15

22 SACKBIRD

Spend 8 seconds or more in the air

POINTS 15

23 FRIENDLY

Complete a level cooperatively (with two or more players, online or offline)

POINTS 15

24 PARTY PERSON

Complete a level online with 3 friends

POINTS 15

25 SOCIALITE

Complete a level online with 3 non-friends

POINTS 15

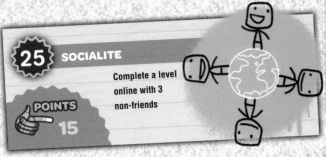

26 TOP OF THE CLASS

Win a 4-player game

POINTS 15

27 TRAVELER

Complete a community level

POINTS 15

28 FIRST!

Be among the first 10 people to complete a community level

POINTS 15

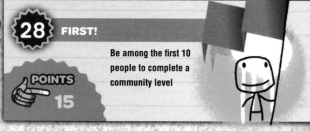

29 OPINIONATED

Tag a community level

POINTS 15

30 NEIGHBOURHOOD WATCH

Heart 5 community levels

POINTS 15

31 NETWORKING

Heart 3 authors

POINTS 15

32 TALKATIVE

Post a comment on a community level

POINTS 15

33 CREATOR

POINTS 15

Build and save a level with a certain amount of stuff in it (measured with thermometer)

34 TEAM CREATOR

POINTS 15

Build a level cooperatively with a certain amount of stuff in it (measured with the thermometer)

35 PUBLISHER

POINTS 15

Publish a level

36 LOOK WHAT I MADE

POINTS 15

A level you published was played by 5 or more people

Silver Trophies

1 **JUST BEGINNING**

Complete all the
main path story
levels

POINTS

30

2 **20X MULTIPLIER**

20X multiplier

POINTS

30

x20

3 HI SCORE

POINTS 30

Collect 1,000,000 points total on any levels, including community levels and your own

4 BOOTY MASTER

POINTS 30

Collect all items on story levels - Get 100% on each (Includes mini games/levels)

5 DR FRANKENSTEIN

POINTS 30

Create a living creature

6 CROWD PLEASER

POINTS 30

A level you published was played by 50 or more people

7 FEEL THE LOVE

POINTS 30

A level you published was hearted by 10 or more people

8 CELEBRITY

POINTS 30

You were hearted by 5 or more people as a player

Gold Trophies

1 PLAY

POINTS 90

Ace all story levels, including mini-levels— but not the mini-games where you have to die to complete them

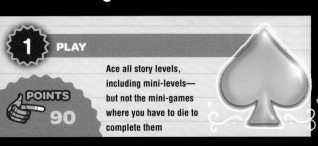

2 CREATE

POINTS 90

Get your levels hearted 50 times and get hearted 30 times as a player

3 SHARE

POINTS 90

Play 150 community levels, tag 50 levels, and heart 10 levels

Platinum Trophies

1 PLATINUM TROPHY

Awarded for collecting all other trophies.

LittleBIGPlanet™
OFFICIAL STRATEGY GUIDE

WRITTEN BY GREG OFF, STACY DALE, AND JAMES MANION

ISBN: 0-7440-1044-6

Printing Code: The rightmost double-digit number is the year of the book's printing; the rightmost single-digit number is the number of the book's printing. For example, 08-1 shows that the first printing of the book occurred in 2008.

11 10 09 08   4 3 2 1

Manufactured in the United States of America.

BradyGAMES Staff

Publisher	**Marketing Director**
David Waybright	Debby Neubauer
Editor-In-Chief	**International Translations**
H. Leigh Davis	Brian Saliba
Licensing Director	
Mike Degler	

Credits

Sr. Development Editor	**Lead Designer**
Christian Sumner	Keith Lowe
Screenshot Editor	**Production Designer**
Michael Owen	Tracy Wehmeyer

A Special Thank You from the Editor

I've been lucky during my tenure as a strategy guide editor to work with some amazingly talented individuals across all fields. This project showed me just how special some of those people could be when I was introduced to Media Molecule and *LittleBigPlanet*. How can you conceptualize "fun?" How does someone wake up, go to work, and have conversations that redefine the incorporation of creativity into a game? I'll honestly never know how *LittleBigPlanet* was made, but I consider myself lucky that it was. There are always going to be those few, cherished games that call to you over the years and force you to relive them. Those games that make you a better person because they left inside you a kernel of happiness that won't ever be discarded. *LittleBigPlanet* has joined those ranks for me. So, this "thank you" isn't to an individual, or a couple people, it's to anyone who had a hand in bringing such a wonder to my doorstep.

BradyGames Acknowledgements

Thanks to everyone at Sony Computer Entertainment who jumped in and made this little treasure of a guide possible. Leo Cubbin, Richard Daniels, Eric Fong, James Riordan, Kyle Shubel, Pete Smith, & Mark Valedor. Special thanks to both Chuck Lacson and Ken Chan for making sure this thing made it into your hands on time.

Working with Media Molecule was an incredible experience. It's odd how they can make even the most horribly stressful days fun. Thanks to Paul Davis, Shaun Elstob, Kareem Ettouney, Alex Evans, Mags Hardwick, Mark Healey, Anton Kirczenow, Daniel Leaver, Francis Pang, Siobhan Reddy, Dave Smith, Mark Stephenson, & Jim Unwin.

Martin Lynagh suffered through the entire process with a smile on his face and a laugh in his voice. For that, and for a million other reasons, he has our heartfelt thanks.

Lastly, we'd like to thank everyone at OH Bans Productions for writing this amazing guide, and the two incredible guide designers who brought the words to life. Thanks Greg, Stacy, James, Tracy, and